DETERRITORIALISATIONS... REVISIONING
LANDSCAPES AND POLITICS

Edited by Mark Dorrian and Gillian Rose

Contents

Black Dog Publishing Limited
London and New York

DETERRITORIALISATIONS... REVISIONING
LANDSCAPES AND POLITICS

Edited by Mark Dorrian and Gillian Rose

©2003 Black Dog Publishing Limited,
and the authors

Designed by Gavin Ambrose

Printed in India

**Architecture Art Design
Fashion History
Photography Theory
and Things**

Black Dog Publishing Limited

5 Ravenscroft Street
London
E2 7SH
UK

T 44 020 7613 1922
F 44 020 7613 1944
E info@bdp.demon.co.uk

PO Box 20035
Greeley Square Station
New York NY 10001-0001
USA

T 212 684 2140
F 212 684 3583

www.bdpworld.com

All opinions expressed within this publication
are those of the authors and not necessarily
those of the publisher.

British Library Cataloguing-in-Publication
Data.

A catalogue record for this book is available
from the British Library.

ISBN: 1 901033 93 7

Landscapes and Theatricality

Landscapes and Bodies

Photo Essay

Contested Landscapes

Acknowledgments

This book has developed from a conference entitled Landscapes and Politics which was held at the University of Edinburgh between 23 and 25 March 2001. Its publication has been made possible by a grant from the Graham Foundation for Advanced Studies in the Fine Arts. Funding has also been received at various stages from the Geography discipline of The Open University and the Architecture discipline in the School of Arts, Culture and Environment, University of Edinburgh.

Many people contributed to the development, organisation and running of the conference. Bob Morris and Charles Withers supported the project at the start, and a grant from the University of Edinburgh's Moray Endowment Fund provided seed funding which enabled us to appoint James Howe to act as the conference secretary in the early stages. The advisory committee – Denis Cosgrove, Elizabeth Ermath, John Dixon Hunt, Elizabeth Lebas, Patricia Macdonald, Doreen Massey, and Kate Soper – scrupulously read the abstracts, provided recommendations, and were a source of great encouragement. Barbara Bender was also very supportive of the project. Mike Shaw designed the impressive conference posters, and Caitlin DeSilvey, who joined us shortly before the event, provided good humour and organisational efficiency. We're indebted to our colleagues who read papers for absent speakers and/or chaired sessions – Richard Coyne, Matthew Gandy, Adrian Hawker, John Lowrey, Angus Macdonald, Susanne Seymour, Joe Smith, Dagmar Weston and Dorian Wiszniewski – and to the students who helped out in various ways before and during the conference – Bruce Currey, Mohamed Eid, Miriam Kelly, Vasiliki Kynourgiopoulou, Ming-Kang Liang, Hsiao-Wei Lin, Sian Loftus, Luciana Flores Martin, Linda Wati Njoman, Calvin Ruyssen, Mike Shaw, and Greg Wilson. We are, in particular, grateful to Isabel Roberts who provided constant help throughout the development of the conference, and who was largely responsible for its smooth running.

Stephen Bann, Denis Cosgrove, and Iain Boyd Whyte supported the project during its development into a book, and Duncan McCorquodale of Black Dog Publishing provided perceptive responses to the papers submitted. Thanks also to Catherine Grant of Black Dog, and to Gavin Ambrose for his excellent design for the book.

Finally, we are grateful to the authors for their forbearance during what has been a lengthy editorial process, and to all those who attended the original conference. We hope they feel this volume has captured something of the range and spirit of the event.

Introduction

**Mark Dorrian
and
Gillian Rose**

1.

The mobility and equivocality of the term 'landscape' has often been emphasised by scholars. "Why is it," J B Jackson began the first essay of his *Discovering the Vernacular Landscape,* 1984, "that we have trouble agreeing on the meaning of *landscape*? The word is simple enough, and it refers to something which we think we understand; and yet to each of us it seems to mean something different."[1] However, notwithstanding the polysemy that Jackson discerned in its 'everyday' useage, discussions of the term – including his own – have tended to locate its meanings as being in operation around two clearly distinguishable, yet at times strategically interconnected, poles. On one hand there is a referral to the eye, whereby 'landscape' is understood as the outcome of a pictorial, representational practice which ideologically stages its referent (nature, land, an estate, etc.) in relation to a viewing subject, thereby inculcating a 'way of seeing' that comes to extend beyond the immediate relations with the artwork itself. And on the other, there is 'landscape' as used in a more general way to describe the socio-cultural moulding of the physical environment by collectivities and individuals. Here it usually implies something like organisation or system and tends to be used in a para-aesthetic sense. When considering the word in this way, scholars have drawn upon the pre-modern etymologies of its constituent units in the Germanic languages, and Jackson's essay is in this regard characteristic. The new definition of 'landscape' that he develops in it – "a composition of man-made or man-modified spaces to serve as infrastructure or background for our collective existence" – was an attempt to dispense with the optical bias which he found in 'official' renderings – a "portion of land which the eye can comprehend at a glance" – while, at the same time, maintaining connotations of visuality (composition, background).[2]

This polarity continues to be helpful in understanding aspects of the development of landscape studies over the last 25 years. Important work, developing out of the Marxian tradition but informed by iconographic and structuralist modes of analysis, and increasingly feminist and post-structuralist approaches and concerns, have focused on the historical emergence and constitution of landscape, as an idea and a practice, in the early modern period. But on the other hand, there have been claims that this is overly exclusive and has encouraged an unduly restricted interpretation of the term; and so it has been confronted by work which, while it shares a number of the critical approaches outlined above, has tended to be more anthropologically informed and less, in terms of its preoccupations, euro- and oculo-centric (this last point being connected to the phenomenological affiliations frequently displayed by authors in this 'second strand' of contemporary landscape studies).[3] If the emphasis in the first instance tends to be on landscape 'from above' (the proprietorial view), that in the latter tends to be 'from below' (the 'everyday' lived and experienced landscapes of social groups, Jackson's "vernacular landscape", etc.).

The persuasiveness and acumen of the 'ocular' accounts of landscape have led to a strong identification of the term with a thematics of power. The argument, to paraphrase the by now classic account by the cultural geographer Denis Cosgrove, runs as follows. 'Landscape' is an ideological concept: "It represents a way in which certain classes of people have signified themselves and their world through their imagined relationship to nature, and through which they have underlined and communicated their own social role and that of others with respect to nature."[4] Landscape emerges as a practice during the period of the transformation to capitalism, one important aspect of which was the commodification of land. Under this new situation, the human relationship to land is characterised by estrangement (which, at the same time, turns out to be the condition of possibility for the appreciation of a landscape as an aesthetic object).[5] The pre-modern, immanent, 'insider' has been replaced, at least among the landholding classes, by someone who stands outwith the scene and, in so doing, exercises a previously unavailable degree of control. For this reason, Cosgrove argues, the concept of 'place', which is a more enveloping notion and which does not carry the implication of control, is antithetical to the "landscape idea".[6] Landscape appears at the historical moment (sixteenth century Italy) which also saw the development of the theory of linear perspective, this being the technical correlate of the estranged view: both conventions (landscape/perspective) "reinforce ideas of individualism, subjective control of an objective environment, and the separation of personal experience from the flux of collective historical experience".[7] On this account, the arts of landscape, in their conditions of emergence acted as handmaidens to the new dispensation: they naturalised it, and representationally effaced the contingencies of the new commodity relation with land under the reassuring artifice of the pastoral.[8] Thus, landscape is a mode of representing land and nature that reproduces the gendered and racialised particularity of the landowning class. It is a view from above, both literally and socially, that hides those who work on the land and who cannot own it while, at the same time, erasing its own specificity.

Even if it begs some questions (about, for example, the instability of representational forms which problematises their operation as instruments of power), this is a very convincing account that analyses the idea and practice of landscape as embedded within a system of power relations and suggests that it is exercised as a form of cultural power.[9] But at this point a question might come to mind, namely: what would it be to think of 'landscape' as an oppositional term? Clearly some idea of landscape, thought in a generalised way, often intersects with senses of community, group belonging, and identity, and so in concrete political situations may be drawn upon in the face of specific external threats. But, the question remains as to whether there are other possibilities available within the tradition of thought which approaches landscape in terms of the critique of ideology.

Here it might be useful to look at two texts which are particularly suggestive in this regard. The first of these is a short essay by Jean-François Lyotard entitled "Scapeland". In this, Lyotard accepts and adopts the relationship between landscape and estrangement, but he follows through the connection in an unusual way and, by so doing, radicalises its implications. Immanuel Kant, in his discussion of *Vesania*, or "systematic madness" in *Anthropology from a Pragmatic Point of View*, deployed a landscape trope to illustrate the condition: "The soul is transferred to a quite different standpoint, so to speak, and from it sees all objects differently. It is displaced from the *Sensorio communi* that is required for the unity of (animal) *life*, to a point removed from it – just as a mountainous landscape sketched from an aerial perspective calls forth a quite different judgement about the region when viewed from the plain."[10] Taking Kant's illustrative conjunction of landscape and madness, the perception of landscape as a kind of madness, Lyotard observes that this arises through a condition of estrangement whereby "the mind is transported from one sensible matter to another, but retains the sensorial organisation appropriate to the first".[11] The "sensible matter" is unassimiliable by the mind in its new position, and it is in this condition, Lyotard argues, that we encounter landscape. The 'ocular' argument sketched out above both associates the traditional painterly landscape view, and more generally the "landscape idea", with the exercise of control and power over what comes within its purview, and draws an opposition between it and 'place'. Lyotard's response is that firstly, to the contrary, the landscape view, in its relationship to the subject, is all about 'place' and 'placing'; and that secondly, to the contrary, it has nothing to do with landscape, at least insofar as landscape is thought as estrangement, for this is precisely the moment at which power over the object would falter. In the familiar spectator-landscape relationship, what is pictured is tamed and domesticated. Its raw state is brought into form and made consumable (through perspectival technique, etc.).[12] It addresses the viewer and confirms his subjectivity, accommodating itself to him while at the same time placing him in relationship to it. All is secure, settled, placed. The scene is narrativised, is verbally articulable, and thus has what Lyotard calls a "destiny". 'Landscape', in the sense that Lyotard develops, is the disruption and dissolution of this. To have a "feel for landscape you have to lose your feeling of place": it is without destiny, something that resists the compositional powers of eye and mind.[13] Consequently landscapes are temporal and fleeting and when they arise before us we are dumbstruck, "lost travellers" as he puts it.[14]

It may be complained that Lyotard is simply displacing terms while leaving the edifice intact. But it seems to us that he is probing an experience (his text is full of concrete examples) which in 'everyday' speech is often called 'landscape' – the use of that word being testament to the non-availability of any other – and which claims, which can claim, no epistemological authority over what is encountered.[15] Lyotard's text is interesting, not least because it displaces the relationship between landscape and the eye, and resituates the term *vis-à-vis* the question of subjectivity. There are aspects of his formulation which seem close to the Lacanian Real: "landscape... should be thought... as the erasure of a support. If anything remains, it is an absence which stands as a sign of a horrifying presence in which the mind fails and misses its aim."[16] But Lyotard's text also bears some suggestive similarities (not least in the allusion to the "lost traveller") to Ernst Bloch's remarkable geologico-philosophical essay of 1932, "Berlin as Viewed from the Landscape". Bloch's text is less focused on sense and experience than Lyotard's, but hinges equally around the theme of estrangement: the key here is the estrangement of the city from the earth due to the uncanny, groundless ground upon which Berlin is built: "the landscape itself does not appear to be quite right; and to this extent, it resembles the exciting, unreal city".[17] Settlement in this mobile, fluid landscape, never develops in terms of depth, and the relationship with the ground remains strangely abstract. "The unformed landscape", Bloch writes, "strongly hindered the settlers.... from ever adapting to it, from praying to the mountains or sheltering in the caves".[18] Compared to the landscapes of southern Germany there is none of the rich immanence of "Goethean nature" here. It is clear that the shadow of Heidegger is hanging over Bloch's argument. "Munich and the Bavarian region are only more obvious in demonstrating how they are bound up with the landscape... Even now, the old magic of hearth, field, and mountain here mythologically plays along with a reactionary or, at best, static form of consciousness."[19] Against this, the apparent poverty of the Berlin landscape, and the estrangement and abstraction it induces, holds a promise. The city's condition of perpetual estrangement is one in which ideology too finds it difficult to establish roots. "The Berlin of tempo and natural sparsity is likewise the one characterised by the most advanced contradiction in relation to emptiness, the most naked collapse of that which once existed, the most treacherous montage of fragments for a later time. It lies exposed in an experimental epoch, not deceptively warm amid the mountains and cultural regions of an already developed space".[20] Bloch's premonition is of Berlin as a city whose estrangement – conferred by its already deterritorialised ground – lends it a radical, and politically radical, futurity. And whatever the differences may be, we may find we catch something of the landscape glimpsed by Lyotard's "lost traveller" in Bloch's closing image of the city as no longer a place of perpetual departure, but a "new coast".

2.

One of the things that we hoped the conference from which this book derives and the book itself would be, is an invitation to re-imagine or re-vision the term 'landscape' and in so doing open expanded possibilities for its deployment and new implications for landscape research. The degree to which this has been successful is of course an open question and can be judged from the following pages; but we have tried to focus on the possible utility of the term, on what it might do. And this has entailed a refusal to accord any particular privilege to etymology. While the diachronic adventures of a word are always informative, we want to resist any tendency to establish a single meaning, by etymological means or otherwise, which would then provide a supposedly transhistorical key to the term. It seemed to us that one of the burdens of thinking about landscape was to acknowledge it in its full complexity as a zone of transaction between multiple interests, and this meant not purifying the field in advance. The problem to us appeared not so much to be the 'problem of definition' as the 'problem of the problem of definition'. Attaching an exhaustive signified to the the term seemed in danger of replaying in another arena the process of naturalisation which the definition was mobilised to expose in the first instance.

If anything, we were more interested in complicating the term, and promoting work which examined its performativity: and hence the use of Gilles Deleuze and Félix Guattari's concept of 'deterritorialisation' in the title of this collection. This refers to the possibility of deterritorialising the term, of uprooting it from its location within fixed webs of signification and transporting it, trailing a set of potentialities which can produce effects in new domains. This is certainly not an argument for evacuating, even if it was possible, the 'content' of the term, for turning it into a kind of floating signifier: on the contrary, the argument relies upon a prior 'content' which confers imminence and underpins the performative effects. Neither do we have in mind a straightforward metaphoric useage, as least as normally understood, where one term is transported to another which remains stable, and understood through it. Rather we are thinking more of a mutual interaction, which leaves neither untouched.

All this is part of a conviction that 'landscape' is a word which is 'good to think', and that this needs to be understood in terms of what it does. We need to be receptive to the richness of its substance and to the possibilities of its diversities. In particular, we want at this point to highlight four of the tensions that seem to us to structure its productivities:

The first of these is the tension between the material and the subjective. The operation of landscape can be seen in terms of a screen between a material potentiality and a subject making meaning, feeling and fantasy from it. It may be identified with the screen or, in the radicalised sense of landscape as developed by Lyotard, its dissolution.

The second tension is that between inside and outside. It is often evident that landscape works to produce or reiterate a clear distinction between inside and outside. Usually, what is contained within the limits of a landscape is 'inside', and the observer of that landscape is placed as separate from it, 'outside'. The horizon of a view, the frame of a painting, the boundaries of a garden, all mark the limit of a landscape's interior, and the existence of its exterior: but of course the inside and the outside are interdependent and mutually constitutive. In landscapes structured by the proprietorial gaze, the viewer is as much part of the landscape as that to which his gaze is directed. The eye of the viewer is the pivot point of perspective, and the lines of that geometry produce a viewing point as much as the viewer calibrates the lines. And so we can continue: horizons move depending upon where the viewer looks, and frames demand a look as much as a look desires a landscape. Inside and outside then are held in tension together through a landscape, and the effects of a particular relation between them may also be called political. Who or what can see a landscape? What or who is permitted entry into it or excluded from it? These are issues articulated through power relations.

Landscapes can also often hold together a past and a present, a present and a future, or all three together. They are often understood as repositories of the past, holding history in their contours and textures. W G Hoskins likened landscapes to palimpsests, traces upon layers of lines and marks, each left at a particular moment and still resonant, awaiting decoding.[21] Indeed, looking at landscapes as evidence of past processes and events seems a strong temptation, much stronger than seeing landscapes as offering possibilities for the future. But the meanings of landscape, whether historical or for the future, are never simply there, inherent and voluble. Instead, they are made to speak, invited to show themselves, and that invitation is the process of practising landscape which always places landscape in a present moment. This presentism is a crucial one and a political one, for it disrupts accounts of landscape which seek to ground certain claims and identities in a self-evident earth. Landscapes are always perceived in a particular way at a particular time. They are mobilised, and in that mobilisation may become productive: productive in relation to a past or to a future, but that relation is always drawn with regard to a present.

Finally, and most elusively, landscape can also mediate between the representable and the non-representable. We have already suggested as such, in our rendering of landscape as a screen in between matter and subjectivity. Landscape (in its non-Lyotardian sense) is what brings elements of matter into meaning, signification, perception and so on. But other elements of the material remain without, and haunt some landscapes with their refusal to be rendered. Similarly, other landscapes induce a certain loss in relation to the subject who is also part of that landscape. Not all landscapes invite order, pattern, system, with the effect of cohering their subject. Some, instead, issue such invitations only to rescind them.

3.

There is no doubt that landscape has become a subject of concern for an increasing array of disciplines to the extent that strong claims can now be made for it as one of the key sites, and also arbiters, of scholarly attention and debate.[22] As far as we know, there have not been attempts to account for this, but a genealogy would certainly have to reckon with a broad constellation of influences within the humanities and social sciences – which would include, in no particular order, historical materialism, hermeneutics, structuralism, post-structuralism, and feminist approaches – whose generally anti-essentialist commitments foregrounded the culturally constructed aspects of the environment, our responses to it, and representations of it and raised the concomitant question of the political operation and effects of those constructions. Also, the rise of interest in landscape is surely linked to the recent adventures of global capitalism insofar as it touches upon issues of migration and displacement, post-colonial contexts and conditions, environmental destruction, the acceleration of developments in bio-technologies, and the prospective militarisation, not just of the earth's surface, but of space itself. Thus, while the intersection of landscapes and politics is by no means the only way in which landscape as a cross-disciplinary field of study might be approached, it is certainly an important one.

The advisory panel for the Edinburgh conference reviewed over 200 papers, just under half of which were then selected for presentation. Scholars from 20 different countries attended, representing a broad range of disciplinary locations: anthropology, archaeology, architecture, art history, cultural studies, English, American and Russian literature, film studies, geography, history, landscape architecture, philosophy, political science, and religious studies. The range was wide, but given the breadth of the field one could not help but be aware of things that were missing: political-economic approaches were not well represented, for example, and there were few presentations on issues such as land rights, the exploitation of wilderness areas by mining industries and the like. And then there is the question of the strange new 'extensions' of landscape, for it is clear that developments in contemporary technologies have exploded its familiar 'frame'. Although the historical landscape view was constituted through framing devices, it at the same time implied a continuity which extended beyond the limits of the representational screen. The development of the panorama, after Robert Barker's view from Calton Hill, Edinburgh, first exhibited in 1787, can be theorised in terms of this tension between the frame and what lies 'out of field'. Today, however, the most arresting continuities are not what is on either side of the frame, but what it contains, in terms of scalar progressions, within. Perhaps surprisingly it was Kenneth Clark, usually pilloried for his conservatism, who presciently recognised this when he discussed the implications of tele- and microscopy: "We know that by our new standards of measurement the most extensive landscape is practically the same as the hole through which the burrowing ant escapes our sight. We know that every form we perceive is made up of smaller and yet smaller forms, each with a character foreign to our experience."[23] Some of the crucial new landscapes of technological and hence political intervention are at the scales demanded by genetic manipulation or nanotechnology and this is surely one of the issues with which the expanded field of landscape studies must reckon.

Yet whatever omissions there may be, the papers in this book represent an extremely wide-ranging and cross-disciplinary set of studies. Perhaps one of the most prominent aspects of the collection is the extended reflection on landscape and forms of visuality that runs through the book. The papers which deal with this are often examining much more complex forms of visual relationship than is common in landscape studies: the "fractured reciprocity" that appears in Jane Avner's paper, for example; or the "circulating look" in Adrian Ivakhiv's. This visual thematic, and in particular the complications that are explored within it, raises other questions, which are also touched on at various points in the collection, to do with what happens when the visual imperative is conceptually unhitched from landscape. What is the relationship, for example, between blindness, tactility and landscape? How might landscape be thought in terms of blindness? This perhaps returns us to some of the themes raised in Lyotard's "Scapeland": its anti-ocularity and its emphasis on the other senses.

We hope that the papers contained in this book, in terms of their content *and* the way in which they have been situated in relationship to one another, will prove interesting and provocative for those with an interest in landscapes and politics. As we conclude, in the build-up to what now inevitably looks like the first of the wars to be prosecuted under the new post-9/11 global political configuration, it seems that the question of the conjunction of landscapes and politics will not lose its importance but, to the contrary, will be one of the key future testing grounds of the political efficacies of scholarship itself.

1   Jackson, J B, "The Word Itself", *Discovering the Vernacular Landscape*, New Haven: Yale University Press, 1984, p. 3.

2   Jackson, J B, "The Word Itself", p. 8.

3   So, for example, Barbara Bender writes: "There are still those who would like to reserve the word 'landscape' for a particular, elitist way of seeing, an imposing/imposed 'viewpoint' that emerged alongside, and as part of, the development of mercantile capital in Western Europe.... If, instead of this narrow definition, we broaden the idea of landscape and understand it to be the way in which people – all people – understand and engage with the material world around them, and if we recognise that people's being-in-the-world is always historically and spatially contingent, it becomes clear that landscapes are always in process, potentially conflicted, untidy and uneasy." Bender, Barbara, "Introduction", *Contested Landscapes: Movement, Exile and Place*, Bender, Barbara and Winer, Margot, eds., Oxford and New York: Berg, 2001, p. 3.

4   Cosgrove, Denis, *Social Formation and Symbolic Landscape*, London and Sydney: Croon Helm, 1984, p. 15.

5   On the question of estrangement and aesthetic response see Soper, Kate, "Privileged Gazes and Ordinary Affections: Reflections on the Politics of Landscape and the Scope of the Nature Aesthetic", this volume.

6   Cosgrove, *Social Formation and Symbolic Landscape*, p. 19.

7   Cosgrove, *Social Formation and Symbolic Landscape*, p. 27.

8   Cosgrove, *Social Formation and Symbolic Landscape*, p. 64.

9   Well explored by the papers in Mitchell, W J T, ed., *Landscapes and Power*, Chicago: University of Chicago Press, 2002. This, the second edition, includes additional papers.

10 Kant, Immanuel, *Anthropology from a Pragmatic Point of View*, Gregor, Mary J, trans., The Hague: Martinus Nijhoff, 1974, p. 86, §52, 4.

11 Lyotard, Jean-François, "Scapeland", *The Lyotard Reader*, Benjamin, Andrew, ed., Oxford: Blackwell, 1989, p. 212.

12 Lyotard, "Scapeland", p. 214.

13 Lyotard, "Scapeland", pp. 215-216.

14 Lyotard, "Scapeland", p. 219.

15 The fact that it was a landscape that suggested to Roland Barthes the "vivid idea" of a text seems relevant here. See the discussion in Duncan, James S and Duncan, Nancy G, "Ideology and Bliss: Roland Barthes and the Secret Histories of Landscape", *Writing Worlds: Discourse, Text and Metaphor in the Representation of Landscape*, Barnes, Trevor J and Duncan, James S, eds., London and New York: Routledge, 1992, p. 27.

16 Lyotard, "Scapeland", p. 217. This is entailed by Lyotard's refusal of landscape as a symbolic code. For a different formulation which reads space/place/landscape in terms of the Lacanian triad symbolic/real/imaginary see the discussion by W J T Mitchell in the preface to the second edition of *Landscape and Power*. Mitchell, W J T, ed., *Landscapes and Power*, pp. x-xi.

17 Bloch, Ernst, "Berlin, as Viewed from the Landscape", *Literary Essays*, Joron, Andrew and others, ed., Stanford: Stanford University Press, p. 361. Bloch comments on "the swamp in which Berlin is immersed" and "the sand upon which it is built".

18 Bloch, "Berlin, as Viewed from the Landscape", p. 364.

19 Bloch, "Berlin, as Viewed from the Landscape", p. 370.

20 Bloch, "Berlin, as Viewed from the Landscape", p. 371.

21 Hoskins, W G, *The Making of the English Landscape*, London: Hodder and Stoughton, 1955.

22 See Hunt, John Dixon, "Taking Place: Some Preoccupations and Politics of Landscape Study", this volume.

23 Clark, Kenneth, *Landscape into Art*, Harmondsworth: Penguin, 1956, p. 150.

Fluid and Viscous Landscapes

Fluid and Viscous Landscapes
Mark Dorrian

Fluidity within a landscape is often, if in truth only rhetorically, confined to certain clearly identifiable elements within it: to rivers, waterfalls, lakes, seas, or to the reflecting pools, channels, and fountains of designed landscapes such as the extraordinary hydraulic garden of the Villa d'Este outside Rome, or the courtyards of the Alhambra palace. On other occasions, however, the conduits of fluidity within a landscape are less clearly defined, and the aqueous substance expands to constitute a landscape that is in itself watery. This may result in a viscous condition in which the distinction between 'water' and 'ground' is cancelled, their admixture complete, or at least so complex, that it requires a special kind of knowledge or cunning, the kind that a guide must have, to find one's way across the marsh, quagmire, quicksands or swamp. Equally, those interstitial landscapes moulded by the sequential advance and recession of water are of relevance here, whether nutrient rich river floodplains, or the ecologically complex littoral zones between tides. These are areas in which the landscape is literally mobile, and where representation fails to bind it in the face of both staggering morphological intricacy and temporal instability. The estuarine landscapes adjacent to major cities such as London were classic sites of anxiety for the nineteenth century urban imagination and figure in novels of the time as strange, indeterminate, shadowy spaces where the physical flotsam and jetsam of industrial capitalism is washed up with its human counterparts: the vagabonds, criminals, and vagrants for whom these uncertain and unworldly terrains, sites of encounter and transformation, provided good concealment.

Rivers, to the contrary, characteristically play a much more 'official' role. Frequently deployed as emblems of nations, they permit internal navigation, and are longstanding ciphers of the productive 'health' of the land itself. Luke Gernon's phallocentric colonial epistle of 1620, which imagined Ireland as a recumbant woman, pictured the country's rivers as "blew vaynes trayling through every part of her like ryvoletts".[1] However, whether seen as navigable channels upon the surface or blood-vessels within the country's body, rivers, compared with the ambiguous watery landscapes already discussed, tend to be 'above board'. Indubitable markers on the land, they become cemented, as boundaries, into the organisation of political territories, and their crossing, such as that of the Rubicon, stands as a mark of intent. Passage across them is often difficult and emblematic: in myth it is won at a price, or through some trial in which the hero is often pitted against a personification of the river itself. In today's 'globalised' world, in which radical material inequalities are answered by paranoia, militarism and a hardening of national border controls, this confrontation continues to be played out daily, although now between migrant and policeman.

Even the river, however, whose topographic clarity has allowed it to stand as a marker of the difference between life and death, may become duplicitous. One thinks here of those moments where it 'goes underground', of the swallow-holes, and of the multiple waterways and caves that it hollows out when it meets a soluble ground; or of the unravelling at its delta where it establishes tentative and less appropriable conditions.

In this section three essays are collected together: the first two deal with representations of rivers, the third with the swamp. Each of the papers carefully contextualises the production of the representations in question, and examines their symbolic valencies and cultural and political operations.

Tim Barringer's study of nineteenth century images of the Hudson and the Thames demonstrates how the courses of these rivers were narrativised in paintings and prints. Looking closely at the Hudson River paintings of Thomas Cole, and those of the Thames by his English namesake, George Vicat Cole, Barringer shows the ways in which the sequential narrative of each river's journey could come to stand as an allegory of the historical vicissitudes of its nation. While the journey from source to sea might be read as a story of progress, Barringer suggests an altogether more pessimistic interpretation which he links to the respective political orientations of the two painters, orientations which were then being challenged by developments in the contemporary metropolitan political and commercial cultures.

Questions of narrativisation are also at issue, albeit in a very different way, in Noa Steimatsky's paper. Her starting point is the article, "For a Film on the River Po", published by Michelangelo Antonioni in 1939. Antonioni's text was accompanied by a sequence of nine photographic stills terminated by an aerial image. Locating the latter within the complex of ideas revolving around aviation and aerial photography in Italy in the wake of Futurism and Mussolini's Ethiopian campaign, she reads the sequence as articulating a set of tensions (between an emergent Neorealism and a modernist representational programme, etc.), which turn upon the collapse of the landscape as an auratic presence, a collapse epitomised by the alienation-effects of the aerial view. Steimatsky sees a correspondence between the cancelling of connotation and narrative possibility effected by this closing image and the fragmentary footage that remains of the film that Antonioni went on to shoot between 1942 and 1943, *Gente del Po*, in which the flickerings of narrative are incessantly blocked. In the paintings analysed by Tim Barringer in the previous paper the river is a semiotic and narrative vehicle; but with Antonioni's cinematic modernism, it is opaque and resistant, its linear movement no longer accommodated to narrative sequence but descriptive only of its own progressive evacuation.

Finally, Jia-Rui Chong examines how the swamp has been figured in Afro-American literature. Arguing that Afro-American cultural production is more topophilic than is usually acknowledged, she raises the possibility of a 'pastoral' response to landscape which is thought in terms of protest and resistance and not, as is usual, in terms of the naturalisation of class, gender and race relations. Her focus is on writing whose narratives draw upon the swamps of the American South, the areas lying beyond the margins of the cultivated plantation lands which had been reclaimed by slave labour. It was in these dangerous and densely vegetated areas that a runaway could find cover and a difficult, and perhaps, temporary, liberation. Chong points to Zora Neale Hurston's novel, *Their Eyes Were Watching God*, 1937, as an important re-writing of the normally phobic swamp narrative: here the protagonist, in this space of resistance and difference, at last finds a subtle identification with place. The swamp, with its ambiguous, mixed viscosity, its "grey indeterminacy", as Chong describes it, suggests an anti-essentialism which stands as a counterpoint to the black and white discourse on race.

1   Gernon, Luke, "A Discourse on Ireland, Anno 1620", *Illustrations of Irish History and Topography, Mainly of the Seventeenth Century*, Falkiner, C Litton, ed., London: Longmans Greene and Co, 1904, p. 349.

"Our English Thames" and "America's River": Landscape Painting and Narratives of National Identity
Tim Barringer

The course of a great river can bear a multitude of interpretations, in each of which physical, social and symbolic geographies intersect.[1] The river's journey from source to sea implies a narrative, just as the trip inland and upstream by river demands a sequential retelling: both can carry a heavy metaphorical freight. The flow of a river from source to sea offers obvious parallels with other linear events, the course of human life or the rise and fall of a nation or an empire. Each location along the river's banks is understood in relation to the others, upstream and downstream, so that every view on the river's banks must take its place in an assumed series. To juxtapose representations of these landscapes, in an exhibition or series of paintings or a bound volume of prints, is to restage the river's narrative, a complex and multi-layered story. This essay explores these themes in relation to nineteenth century representations of two great rivers, the Hudson and the Thames, which hold a special place in the imaginative life of their respective nations. Each emerges from an obscure source deep in the rural heart of the nation; each becomes a great industrial artery; and each passes through an imperial city to the sea, ocean and trading empire beyond. The narrative of the river's course can, both in the case of the Hudson and of the Thames, be read as a progressive loss of innocence, moving from country to city, from protected heartland to the dangers of the open seas; but it can also be read as a narrative of national progress, a move from past to present. Close contextual interpretations of sample images will reveal the complexities and ambivalences which were an inherent part of river narratives in the nineteenth century.

For the whole course of the nineteenth century, rivers were far more significant as national economic arteries than they are today; in terms of freight and passenger transportation, traffic on large rivers enjoyed a brief heyday between the development of steam powered watercraft and arrival of the railroad's hegemony in the mid-nineteenth century and declined, at least in relative terms, after that. The nineteenth century was characterised by the coming to maturity of the processes of industrialisation, urbanisation and modernity in Britain and the USA. The modernity of the navigable river was paradigmatic in the age of canal transportation, its image heroic and progressive. Indeed, rivers and canals played a decisive role during the transitional period between from what E A Wrigley has called the "advanced organic economy" of the canal age and the "mineral based energy economy" in the age of steam, a transformation including the shift from waterborne to rail transportation, the rise to dominance of machine-powered industry, and the move from a rural to a predominantly urban culture.[2] These are profound cultural and environmental as well as economic shifts, and landscape painting was the art form best fitted to encapsulate and interrogate them. The transition from one historical moment to another can be immediately discerned by comparing John Constable's *Scene on a Navigable River*, 1817, and Turner's *Rain, Steam and Speed*, 1844.

Figure 1
Thomas Cole,
The Oxbow, 1836,
New York,
Metropolitan
Museum of Art.
Gift of Mrs
Russell Sage,
1908. (08.228)

Constable knew the value of the navigable river, which allowed grain to be brought to his father's mills and sacks of flour to reach the lucrative city markets. Turner was swept away by sheer physical excitement, as he witnessed a locomotive crossing the Thames at Maidenhead on Brunel's great bridge, from which its antiquated predecessor, the ancient road bridge, was only dimly visible in the distance. In *Rain, Steam and Speed* the change from river to rail, from horsepower to steam power, is viscerally apparent.

The historical development of the United States has been understood as a confrontation between mankind and the environment, an epic of transformation, though this model neglects to take account of the experience of native Americans. Inevitably, the interaction – sometimes violent collision – of nature and a European form of culture is the major preoccupation of American landscape painting. The meeting of modern American civilisation with the wilderness is dramatised in Thomas Cole's *View from Mount Holyoke, Northampton, Massachusetts after a Thunderstorm (The Oxbow)*, 1836. (figure 1) The left of the composition preserves the storm-shattered landscape of the untouched wilderness, the pure creation of God; on the right, around the nurturing bend of the Connecticut River, is cultivated farmland, an idyll of agrarian plenty and social harmony. The tide of history is, it seems, moving inexorably from right to left, from East to West: the forest is destined to be swept away and the land brought under control. The sublime will yield to the beautiful, chaos to order. Cole, however, held ambivalent views about the onward march of progress, and portrays himself, a tiny figure in a tall hat, perched amid the boulders. *The Oxbow* reveals the paradoxes underlying nineteenth century American landscape painting, which celebrated the beauty of the wilderness at the moment of its historical transformation. Even if we are not prepared to go as far as one interpretation of this painting, which sees in the bend of the river a great question mark over the future of America, it is significant that Cole chose a navigable waterway with which to articulate his main theme.[3] Indeed, in his *Essay on Landscape Scenery*, Cole provided a narrative account of the river's course:

Its sources are amid the wild mountains of New Hampshire; but it soon breaks into a luxuriant valley, and flows for more than a hundred miles, sometimes beneath the shadow of wooded hills, and sometimes glancing through the green expanse of elm-besprinkled meadows... the imagination can scarcely conceive Arcadian vales more lovely or peaceful than the valley of the Connecticut....[4]

This is a journey from primeval wildness (still visible to the left of Cole's composition) to a perfected New World reconstitution of European civilisation. On the valley floor can be seen a Jeffersonian idyll of small landholders safely united for the common good but mainly free from outside interference, deriving a wholesome living from bountiful but cultivated nature, of which the river is the most visible symbol.

Like the Connecticut River in *The Oxbow*, the Hudson and the Thames each occupy a mediating position between nature and culture, between past and present: each has played a central, iconic role in the imaginary and the economic life of the nation. Landscape painting and printmaking provided a nexus of symbolic representation allowing the image of the river to articulate celebratory narratives of national development and destiny; yet, as in *The Oxbow*, they also reveal deeply-held cultural anxieties about industrialisation and modernity. And unlike the Connecticut River, the Hudson and the Thames move beyond "Arcadian vales" peopled by a contented yeomanry and flow into major commercial and industrial cities, a more challenging environment at the very heart of modernity. Rivers, for New York and London, were the very lifeblood of economic survival, bringing in food from the provinces and allowing trade to flow inland and out to sea via the metropolitan docks. This final stage in the river's journey, from past to present and future brings with it a confrontation with energy, power and wealth, but also with pollution, corruption and decadence. Powerful narratives of national history and identity are articulated by such images – the journey down the Hudson followed America's progress from wilderness to civilisation through the action of providence. Charting the course of the Thames one glides from the medieval to the modern, from feudalism to democracy. From Windsor and Runnymede one passes to Westminster, as if traversing history through the process of peaceful reform, echoing the Whig narrative of Macaulay's *History of England*.[5] The paintings and aquatints I have chosen for this exploratory essay are picked somewhat serendipitously from the vast available archive. By staging a comparison between the Hudson and the Thames, however, I hope to draw attention to the common visual language employed in two bodies of work usually considered in isolation, but also to contrast the very different social, economic histories and cultural and imaginative geographies which each river traverses.

The dialogue between the Hudson and the Thames can be staged very clearly through a comparison of Turner's *England: Richmond Hill, on the Prince Regent's Birthday*, 1819, and Jasper Francis Cropsey's *Autumn on the Hudson River*, 1860. Both Turner and Cropsey aimed to epitomise their respective nations in these grandiose oil paintings, Turner even claiming to do so in his title, and each does indeed enshrine cherished conceptions of national identity. Yet differences of iconography immediately force themselves upon the viewer. Turner's keynote is tradition, from the courtiers in the foreground, to the cricketers and royal barge in the middle ground, and the rolling woodlands beyond. A quotation from James Thomson's *Seasons* of 1727 accompanied the title, reaching back into the Augustan, pre-industrial past. Cropsey's painting, like Turner's, was completed in London, during a period in which the American painter was engaged in an unsuccessful bid to capture British patronage; Cropsey also painted English scenery, including a version of *Richmond Hill*. Although he based the work on sketches made on the spot, Cropsey's work may indeed have been influenced by the grand, Claudean vista of Turner to which he had ready access in London. However compelling the formal links, Cropsey's painting represents a Hudson far broader than the Thames, and it is a couple of bourgeois tourists, not an aristocratic party, who enjoy the view. An idealised settlement can be seen, modern, but blessed not only with Puritan church towers but also touched by a divine ray of light which bisects the composition. The timeless social stratification (despite various genre details) suggested and seemingly endorsed by Turner is replaced by a bourgeois idyll. Shipping plies the river which, no wilderness, is fully incorporated into a mercantile economy. Turner's burnished colours blend the Thames valley with recollections of Claude, while Cropsey's vibrant reds and yellows inject a new world vivacity into an ancient compositional formula. If Turner was courting royal patronage and lamenting the lost world of courtier-artists like Watteau, Cropsey only glanced over his shoulder at a past golden age, welcoming instead the winds of social and economic change.[6] American associations, as Cole wrote in 1835, are of the present and the future, a commercial and industrial future which beckons visibly to the viewer of *Autumn on the Hudson River*.[7]

An Island Stream

The Thames Valley was richly endowed with historical and picturesque associations. The royal river had been extensively painted and drawn in the eighteenth and early nineteenth centuries. From Roman times, the Thames had played a major role as a navigable river, a supremacy as a commercial artery which was challenged for the first time by the extensive rail network of the mid-nineteenth century. There is no better introduction to its importance for the nineteenth century imaginary than the letterpress to William Westall's bound volume of aquatints, *Picturesque Tour of the Thames* published by Ackermann in 1828:

> THE THAMES, as an island stream, is surpassed in magnitude and in the length of its course by many of the rivers of continental countries. It is equally true that, in the point of boldness, grandeur, sublimity and variety, the scenery along its banks cannot be placed with that which can be found in more mountainous regions. If however, its climate is not blessed with the charms of perennial spring – if its atmosphere is not embalmed with the fragrance of orange groves or forests of spice... – if its current is not broken by picturesque masses of rock, or diversified by foaming cataracts; – its shores at least display all the softer graces and all the attractive loveliness of Nature in her sweetest mood, heightened by the taste, skill and ingenuity of man: – they are decorated by the venerable monuments of antiquity, and by the prodigies of modern art: – they abound in historical recollections and interesting associations; and the ample bosom of this noble river bears... the riches of every region of the globe; which place their merchants on a level with Princes and their traders with the great of the earth.[8]

Although it spins out a line of negatives so long as to challenge syntactical coherence, this passage ends up by asserting the Thames' unique characteristic: the elegance of the past and the dynamism of the present are held in a stable historical symbiosis by the flowing waters of the river. The success of British mercantile capitalism has brought wealth "from every region of the globe" allowing the peaceful marriage of the "noble" river and its new overlords, "merchants on a level with Princes". Languages of class mingle with those of empire. The text is a paean to gentlemanly capitalism.[9] The title page bears a disarmingly honest vignette of the source of the Thames by Samuel Owen, with the small spring in the middle distance dwarfed by the central motif, an ingenious if dirty steam pump which maintained the water supply for an industrial navigation on the site. But with

Figure 2
R G Reeve after
William Westall,
*Park Place near
Henley on
Thames, Seat of
Fuller Maitland
Esq*, aquatint,
from William
Westall and
Samuel Owen,
*Picturesque Tour
of the River
Thames*, London:
R Ackermann,
1828, New
Haven, Yale
Center for
British Art

the pages of Ackermann's book the river progresses through scenes of tranquil agriculture and past grand country houses and more modest piles of the gentry such as *Park Place near Henley on Thames, Seat of Fuller Maitland Esq*, set in Reptonian parkland. (figure 2) In Westall's idealised view, genteel picnickers and fishermen turn the well-ordered banks of the Thames into an Augustan garden of pleasure. Later in the series, Oxford's familiar skyline was distanced from the viewer not only by a pastoral scene with cattle in the middle ground, but also by the river itself (with a commercial barge, horse and bargee on the towpath, carefully depicted). Modernity had begun to affect even the ancient university town. Windsor provided a well-known vista, richly overlaid with historical associations, and beyond the Palladian villas of Richmond we reach London, where the newly opened Waterloo Bridge symbolises the perfectible enlightenment city. The dynamic energy of Georgian imperial capitalism can be seen afloat in the Pool of London, in Samuel Owen's celebration of *The Custom House*. (figure 3) This plate encapsulates commerce as the source of a quiet social revolution, for unlike the traditional social order of aristocracy, yeomanry and peasantry glimpsed on the banks of the upper Thames, in modern London 'traders' rival 'the great of the earth'. Beyond the capital, Greenwich provides a reminder of British naval prowess. At Gravesend, the great river meets a choppy Turnerian sea, allowing shipping from the Port of London access to a global trading empire. Every one of these images could sustain detailed analysis, but my point here is to explore their cumulative meaning as a narrative sequence. Despite multiple appeals to historical tradition, the Thames in Westall and Owen's plates provides a heroic, cumulative narrative of national growth and development, finding a climax in the commercial and civic energies of the present.

There is a vast body of imagery representing the River Thames created during the mid-nineteenth century, much of it worthy of detailed analysis, and some, such as Turner's *Rain, Steam and Speed*, canonised by a substantial literature.[10] But it is a more obscure, yet more extensive, treatment of Thames subjects to which I shall now turn in a little more detail. By 1880, the upper reaches of the Thames had become the favourite place of escape for affluent Londoners, who travelled by train to

the picturesque and (at least until the arrival of such tourists) largely unspoiled villages and market towns. It was perhaps with this audience in mind that the leading dealer of the day, William Agnew commissioned the Royal Academy's leading landscape painter, George Vicat Cole, 1833-1893, to create a series of 25 large paintings following "The Thames from its source to the sea".[11] It was intended to publish a volume of engravings of the entire series, which never materialised, but the third volume of Robert Chignell's grandiloquent *Life and Paintings of Vicat Cole, RA* contains photomechanical reproductions of most of the series. Never a painter of great originality, Cole had nonetheless transformed the unspectacular countryside of the home counties into academy paintings of considerable force and grandeur. The Thames series, begun in 1880, was conceived from the first as "a work of national importance" and Agnew planned to publish the series as a volume of engravings, an updated version of Westall's picturesque tour.[12] In *The Source of the Thames*, exhibited in 1882 (figure 4), Cole alighted on a more tranquil spot than Westall 50 years earlier, choosing the Seven Springs near Cheltenham and excluding the human presence entirely. This is the pre-history of the river, a vision of unsullied innocence seen at spring time, with indigenous flora and fauna such as primroses and collared doves. The Thames wells up from deep underground just as British civilisation is rooted in its native soil. As the series proceeds, the many modern and Georgian Thames-side houses and any hint of industry were scrupulously avoided in a sequence of images presenting the upper Thames as a timeless arcadia. Cole found in the historic vistas of Oxford, ripe with associations, no hint of modernity, though to achieve this effect he had to retreat to Iffley, while Westall and, earlier still, Turner, had employed closer vantage points. Cole's biographer, an Oxonian barrister and the artist's brother-in-law, insists that Oxford "touched [Cole's] national feeling; its old buildings had a strange charm for the painter's eye and the memories which they call up of past generations of scholars, poets and statesmen, appealed to his imagination".[13] Yet the reality of contemporary Oxford, so easily accessible from London by train, by no means conformed to Cole's needs at this stage of the unfolding national narrative. While earlier picturesque accounts like Westall's emphasise the specific associational qualities of Oxford, retelling and alluding visually to the historical dramas

Figure 4
George Vicat
Cole, *The Source
of the Thames*,
1882, untraced.
Photogravure
from Robert
Chignell, *The
Life and
Paintings of
Vicat Cole, RA*,
three vols.,
London: Cassell,
1898,
frontispiece
to vol. III

played out there, for Cole only humbly archaic scenes of reaping with obsolescent scythes and osier trees by the banks of the brimming river could serve to signify the necessary distance from the modern and the metropolitan. By reducing the dreaming spires to the very distance the historic university could preserve its mythical power, a trope and viewpoint exploited by Thomas Hardy a decade later in *Jude the Obscure*, 1895.

Cole's project was not only a topographical one; it was also a manifesto for an embattled tradition of English landscape painting from the perspective of the senior academician in the discipline. And indeed the choice of a self-consciously national project paralleled the attempt to buttress the critical standing of a 'National School' (English landscape painting) under attack from across the Channel. His colleague, and fellow enthusiast for Thames boating, the painter of historical genre George Dunlop Leslie, noted that Cole was "a thorough Englishman, and his landscapes are... enhanced by the fact that he never gave way to the prevailing fashion, as so many English painters are prone to do, of portraying English landscape in the French style".[14] While the recent "morbid development" in French landscape, according to H Schütz Wilson in the *Magazine of Art* in 1878, "technically termed that of the 'impressionists'" placed "a very small *Ego* in the place of nature", Cole, and his followers, by contrast were "content to render through beauty that which he really sees in nature".[15] Cole paid homage to one of his models among earlier English landscape painters in *Iffley Mill*, 1884, which clearly acknowledges the work of Constable through the technique of flecked lead white paint to suggest movement in the poplar trees. By the mid-nineteenth century, through texts such as the Redgraves' *A Century of British Painters*, Constable had come to be synonymous with the timeless representation of untamed nature and for a loathing of the 'monster city', rather than the bracing inscription of modernity which his own contemporaries had sensed in his work.[16] Beyond Oxford, *Wargrave*, 1881, is a nostalgic reprise of Constable's *Stratford Mill*, 1820; the prominent white carthorse surely a nod in the direction of the famous *White Horse*, 1819; Cole's horse, however, is an anachronism in the age of steam-driven transportation, a symbol of a lamented past rather than the productive vigour of the present.

Moving downstream, the Victorian painter endowed *Pangbourne* with a sense of quiet decay, bathing in evening light places which were actually struggling agricultural market towns, often with dirty industries, such as tanning, which seriously polluted the river. The paradoxes implicit in Cole's attempts to stave off modernity's impact were multiple: not the least of them was his own practice of using a large steam launch as a mobile studio. It was essential, however, to expunge all hints of the modern from the upper river, in order to allow the Thames to stand as a paradigm for the course of English history, moving from a scene of pure nature through a medieval idyll. Cole deliberately sought out atypical, picturesque costumes and archaic agrarian practices in his upper river subjects. He had to dodge the Great Western railway viaduct in his view of *Windsor Castle*, 1883, following the compositional precedent of Turner in preference to facing the modern reality of his subject. His biographer insisted that Cole "boldly effaces the monstrous structure and restores, in all its grandeur, a view which none of the present generation has been happy enough to see".[17] After a recapitulation of Turner's view of Richmond, with middle class ladies replacing the Prince Regent's party, we reach the ideological heart of the series, a celebration of *Westminster*, which the *Art Journal* saw as "an epitome of the life of the English nation".[18] Here the Tory Romanticism of Pugin and Barry's building provided a centrepiece for a work that summarised "the three chief factors of its greatness – England's faith, England's commerce, England's government".[19] The symbolic import of this journey was not lost on Sir Frederic (soon to be Lord) Leighton, an astute rhetorician, who as President offered a tribute to Cole at the Royal Academy banquet shortly after his death in 1893:

A type of England were the scenes on which
He loved to dwell – the coppices, the glades,
The rolling pastures fading from the green,
To distant blue, the summer slumbering
On brown-tipped corn. But most of all, our English Thames
Had won his heart and occupied his hands,
Its stream he followed down with faithful brush
Throughout its length from where, within the grass,
Its gurgle first is heard, to where, far off,
Sullied and salt, it rocks on turbid tides
The carriers of the commerce of the world.[20]

As Leighton's topographical narrative suggests, industry finally emerged in the ambiguous ten-foot canvas *The Pool of London*, 1888 (figure 5), purchased by the Chantrey bequest and now in the Tate, an essay in the industrial sublime in which a central shaft of dramatic light is almost consumed by billowing clouds of smoke and pollution. The Pool was the nexus of international commodities, central to the financial dealings of the city, and one of the key nodes mediating between the British mainland and empire, between the commodity production and the financial sectors of the economy. No less a figure than Gladstone commended this work for representing "a scene of commercial activity so as to impress upon it... the idea and character of *grandeur*".[21] Vicat Cole's series, then, could be read as a Whiggish progress from a primitive past to a present marked by a Liberal economic and political triumph; incremental reform, rather than revolution, has left intact such historical markers as the Tower of London, the Monument and St Paul's, but has surrounded them with surging economic activity. In this view, the scene is a passionate marriage of market capitalism and British traditions. Yet a darker reading of the series is possible; moving from the pristine world of nature through the glory days of English history, we arrive finally in a hell's brew of polluted industrial chaos. The sequence could represent a Ruskinian fall from grace, a dystopian corollary to William

Figure 5
George Vicat Cole, *The Pool of London*, 1888. London, Tate. The painting is reproduced here from a photograph made in c. 1896 because it is at present in poor condition, severely marred by surface dirt.

Morris' *News From Nowhere* of 1891, in which a journey begun among the fogs of industrial Battersea leads back up the river across time and place to a medieval idyll in the Cotswolds.[22] There are reasons to suppose that Vicat Cole would have supported a Ruskinian radical-Tory critique rather than Gladstone's classical liberal interpretation of the politics of the Thames landscape. The artist named Thomas Carlyle as his favourite prose author, and perhaps found in *Past and Present*, 1843, a text whose critique of modernity he could endorse.[23] In allowing both of these contrasting readings, however, Cole's series perfectly encapsulates the ambivalent implications of the Thames for the late-nineteenth century British imagination.

"An Unbounded Capacity for Improvement by Art"

If the Thames emphasised the longevity of English traditions, while questioning their trajectory in the present, the journey between New York City from the upper reaches of the Hudson raised fundamental questions about the identity of the young American nation.[24] The river passes through some spectacular mountain and wilderness scenery, and along its banks are cliffs, rolling hillsides, agricultural pastures and a great range of natural scenery. At the beginning of the nineteenth century it balanced elements of the sublime and of the picturesque: it belonged partly to the cherished American wilderness, partly to a neo-feudal arcadia marked out by long-established colonial agricultural settlements of Dutch and English origin. Having seen the Thames, the Rhine and the Tiber on a European tour between 1829 and 1832, Thomas Cole gave serious thought to the status of the Hudson in relation to the major rivers of the old world. "The river scenery of the United States", he wrote,

> is a rich and boundless theme. The Hudson for natural magnificence is unsurpassed. What can be more beautiful than the lake-like expanses of the Tapaan and Haverstraw as seen from the rich orchards and surrounding hills? Hills that have a legend, which has been so sweetly and admirably told that it shall not perish but with the language of the land. What can be more imposing than the precipitous Highlands, whose dark foundations have been rent to make a passage for the deep-flowing river? And ascending still, where can be found scenes more enchanting? The lofty Catskills stand afar off – the green hills gently rising from the flood, recede like steps, by which we may ascend to a great temple, whose pillars are those everlasting hills, and whose dome is the blue and boundless vault of heaven.

By asserting not only its natural majesty, but also its growing literary and cultural traditions (in the works of Washington Irving and James Fenimore Cooper) Cole was concerned to stake the claims of the Hudson against those of the great European rivers. Far outstripping the Thames for natural beauty, it could not yet compete in terms of historical associations, which were as yet unformed. The Rhine, he acknowledged, "has its castled crags, its vine-clad hills, and ancient villages"; but the Hudson, by contrast, "has its wooded mountains, its rugged precipices, its green, undulating shores – a natural majesty, and an unbounded capacity for improvement by art".[25] Here an ambivalence enters Cole's texts, for the art which will transform the Hudson is not that of the landscape gardener, but of industrial capitalism. The future, rather than the past, marked out the Hudson's uniqueness.

Change was, indeed, underway. The opening of the Erie Canal in 1825, an event widely celebrated by popular lithographers and engravers, inaugurated a half century when the Hudson River, thus linked to the Great Lakes, provided one of America's most important routes for the transportation of iron, timber and stone from the north to New York and beyond. It also opened a passage for massive immigration into the mid-Western plains and prairies. A watercolour of the canal, made by John William Hill in 1829, celebrates the taming of the wilderness into a landscape of productive industrial geometry, lock-gates and warehouses dominating the foreground, and enclosed fields covering the distant hillsides.[26] Only a single wispy repoussoir tree survives from the picturesque mode. An appreciation of landscape generally emerges in cultures undergoing rapid industrialisation of this kind, and the United States was no exception.

The spectacular journey from New York City up "America's River" raised fundamental questions about the relationship of nature and culture in the United States.[27] The Erie Canal and the Hudson offered both the spectacle of American economic development and a new ease of access to areas of wilderness which spawned a burgeoning tourist trade among the industrial and commercial bourgeoisie. By 1824 there were several steamers a day from Manhattan to Albany, a 12 hour journey, carrying tourists as well as commercial passengers.[28] An uneasy set of negotiations between the industrial and the picturesque can be discerned in the series of almost two-dozen coloured engravings which make up William Guy Wall's *Hudson River Portfolio*, published between 1821 and 1825.

During the next half century, the Hudson River valley, and especially the surrounding mountains and lakes, emerged in the essentially touristic art of Cole, Durand, Cropsey, Gifford and Church as perhaps the most resonant of all national scenery of the period. An entire generation of painters, based in New York City, came retrospectively to be known as the Hudson River School through their enthusiasm for the apparently virgin wilderness of the upland regions of New York state traversed by the river.[29] Thomas Cole's journey up the Hudson in 1825 in search of subject matter, the pivotal moment in his career, has been enshrined in art history as the founding moment of American landscape painting.[30] Cole's biographer, Louis Legrand Noble, seems to suggest that the artist's imagination raced up the river faster than his physical body could manage – "From the moment when his eye first caught the rural beauties clustering round the cliffs of Wehawken, and glanced up the distance of the Palisades, Cole's heart had been wandering in the Highlands and nesting in the bosom of the Catskills."[31] The Hudson offered a transition from the world of materiality into a spiritual realm. "Friends of my heart" began a poem he wrote about the same time,

> Lovers of nature's works
> Let me transport you to those wild, blue mountains
> That rear their summits near Hudson's wave.
> Though not the loftiest that begirt the land,
> They yet sublimely rise....[32]

Cole responded to the journey upstream from New York with the vivid drama of works such as *View of the Round-Top in the Catskill Mountains*, 1827. (figure 6) In this remarkable work, the viewer's gaze passes, in a gambit typical of Cole's distinctive version of the sublime, from a mountainous foreground, conducive to a Burkean effect of terror, through a mysterious and ill-defined middle ground to a harmonious distance, in which the Hudson, dotted with shipping, provides both the symbolic and actual transport to safety and homecoming.[33]

From 1836 Cole made a deeper investment in the Hudson scenery by moving to Catskill, overlooking the river: the very fact that a celebrity artist was prepared to reside in this area signified a change in its fortunes. His works depicting the area were prominently exhibited in New York, the most prestigious element in the growing visual culture of the Hudson Valley. Both before and after his death in 1848 Cole's studio became a place of pilgrimage for younger artists, critics and patrons. Cole's only pupil and his successor, Frederic Edwin Church, painted surprisingly few major works in the Hudson River Valley, but after purchasing a plot of land across the river from Cole's former home, in 1860, and extending it in 1867, he created, in dialogue with the architects Richard Morris Hunt and Calvert Vaux (architect, with F L Olmsted, of Central Park in New York City), the spectacular Moorish villa *Olana*, which was built between 1870 and 1872. It was from the upper windows and lawns of *Olana* that Church painted a series of supremely fluid and spontaneous oil sketches of the Hudson river. Church privileged nature over culture, minimising the Hudson's busy tourist and industrial traffic and concentrating instead on the fleeting effects of light and atmosphere. His main competitor, Albert Bierstadt, famed for his Western landscapes, erected in 1865-1866 *Malkasten*, an impressive pile also commanding Hudson views. And not to be outdone by his rivals, in 1867 Jasper Francis Cropsey built *Aladdin*, also overlooking the Hudson, at Warwick, New York, but was forced to move in 1885 to the smaller *Ever Rest* at Hastings-on-Hudson. The domestication of the wilderness continued apace as the commuter rail network allowed swift access to New York City from ever more distant locations up the Hudson valley. All these artists produced tranquil Hudson sketches but few wished to portray it as a massive commercial artery.

Figure 6
Thomas Cole,
View of the Round-Top in the Catskill Mountains,
1827
Oil on panel,
47.31 x 64.45cm
Museum of Fine Arts, Boston.
Gift of Martha C Karolik for the M and M Karolik Collection of American Paintings, 1815-1865.
(47.1200)

Just as tourists passed up the Hudson on steamers and yachts to escape into a rural idyll, the passage from upstate downriver to New York City offered a journey towards a modern, urban American sublime, a narrative of national progress. Something of the wonder of the new metropolis, seen across the mouth of the Hudson River, can be found in *Lower Manhattan from Communipaw*, 1880, by Thomas Moran, a painter associated principally with the grandeur of Western landscapes; his brother Edward Moran produced a series of images of New York harbour, after 1886 proudly including the Statue of Liberty. *Lower Manhattan*, a curious combination of breathless fantasy and directly observed realism, was described in 1879 as "a silver dazzle of sugarbaking palaces rising among the mists and exhalations of a universal thaw"; the glistening, fantastical cityscape of New York seems too daunting to approach across the icy expanse of the Hudson.[34]

What, then, are we to make of the Hudson's symbolism in the nineteenth century? A heroic industrial journey downstream which signifies the conquering of the wilderness? Or an escapist return upstream to an Edenic and uncorrupted world such as Thomas Cole wished to lead us to? The answer of course is that both these readings of the river derive from the condition of modernity and the development of industrialisation. Implicit in the genre of landscape painting is the tendency to abandon topography in favour of grander themes; to aspire to the condition of history painting. The spectacle of the Hudson tempted Asher Brown Durand to fantasise a sunlit capitalist utopia on its banks in his allegorical landscape, *Progress (The Advance of Civilisation)*, 1853. Industrial modernity to the right complete with a glistening industrial city, telegraph poles and steamships, contrasts with the melancholy and leafy darkness of the American Eden, and its native inhabitants, in the left foreground. The *Knickerbocker* described this optimistic visual fable as "purely American. It tells an American story out of American facts, portrayed with true American feeling...."[35] It is an inversion of the potentially melancholy story told by Thomas Cole's *Oxbow*, and once again it is a river – this time seemingly the Hudson itself – which carries the message of American triumphalism. The Hudson, then, like the Thames, bore ambivalent and contradictory interpretations deeply intertwined with conflicting political accounts of the course and identity of the nation.

River Landscapes and The Course of Empire

Thomas Cole, more than anyone, saw that rivers were not merely topographical or economic features, but rather the bearers above all of allegorical meaning, and sought in 'a higher style' of landscape painting the visual means to address these grander themes.[36] In one of his more blatant allegories, Cole saw the *Voyage of Life*, 1840, as taking place in a craft passing down a broad river flowing from calm, beatific origins of childhood through the troubled rapids of manhood and merging with the ocean at the point of death. More closely allied to the Hudson and the Thames is a possible reading of Thomas Cole's great cycle of five canvases, *The Course of Empire*, 1836, which follows an imaginary city from its origins in the *Savage State*, through a classical moment in the *Arcadian, or Pastoral State*. The cycle moves through time and is more or less static in place – the same distinctive and fictional mountain appears in every scene. After the vainglorious imperial spectacle of *Consummation* (figure 7) comes the inevitable *Destruction* and a final empty vista of *Desolation*.[37] There is a broad consensus in the recent literature that, although not strictly an American subject, the sequence offered a parable of American history and Alan Wallach convincingly identifies Cole's programme as being one of opposition to the expansionist, utilitarian and democratic platform of Andrew Jackson against the gentrified, agrarian Federalism of Cole and his patrons.[38] The great river upon which the empire city stands is, in this reading, a mythic version of the Hudson in the past, present and potential future. Seen at the point of its intersection with the ocean, the river carries a terrible

Figure 7
Thomas Cole, *The Course of Empire: Consummation of Empire*, 1836. New York Historical Society. Gift of the New York Gallery of Fine Arts. (1858)

warning for the New York modernisers, against whom Cole's animus is extensively documented. The river in *Consummation*, decked out with barges like the Hudson on the day of the opening of the Erie Canal, has not yet run its course, just as American history is still in the making.[39] Following Byron and well-worn conventions reaching back through Gibbon to the classical world, Cole proposes an inevitable cyclical decline in which every empire's hubris must meet its nemesis, just as every river must inevitably run its course. In Cole's final canvases it is the river which allows the marauding barbarians to enter the city and invade, in a John Martin-like scene of waterborne violence; and the empty river dominated the composition of *Desolation*, in which the wilderness reasserts its primacy, framed by the ruins of civilisation.

While such a local reading of the *Course of Empire* is entirely convincing, it is not the only possible interpretation of the cycle; indeed I want to suggest here that Thomas Cole, born in Bolton in England, was also alluding to the overweening ambitions of the empire at whose heart he grew up, and whose crisis and ultimate military victory in the Napoleonic Wars he experienced during his adolescence. The British Empire had, it seemed in 1776, run its course: the United States would grow from the wreckage of British imperialism. Cole's canvases made explicit reference to British topography: the first stirrings of civilisation, in the *Pastoral or Arcadian*, are represented by a recognisably English structure, Stonehenge, a mainstay of Romantic landscape painting thought at the time to have been a Druid temple. *Consummation of Empire* (figure 7) could easily be read not only as a commentary on imperial London, with commercial and government buildings astride a fantastic depiction of the River Thames in the decadent, but opulent, regency and personal reign of George IV. There are close parallels with Constable's likewise panoramic view of the *Opening of Waterloo Bridge by the Prince Regent in 1817*, completed in 1832; stone bridges were a feature of the London landscape but not that of New York. Cole's description alludes to "a conqueror robed in purple", a role that George IV much enjoyed on the back of Wellington's military victories. The creamy fantasy architecture of *Consummation of Empire* has as much in common with imperial

London, where Cole had been a visitor from 1829-1831, as with Trajan's Rome. In particular, Cole's classical pediments seem to recall the theatrical stucco of John Nash's Cumberland Terrace, 1826, in Regent's Park.

The *Course of Empire* also parallels the narrative course of the Thames as a metaphor for British history as articulated by Westall in his journey down the Thames, following a path from savagery, or at least from nature, through an Augustan classical age to a consummation of empire through commerce and neo-classical metropolitan splendour. But it is the late-Victorian vision of George Vicat Cole (no relation to Thomas) which resonates most closely with the Romantic pessimism of the American artist's vision of half a century earlier. The Thames passes through an idyllic classical moment between Oxford and Windsor, and reaches a religious and constitutional consummation at Westminster before plunging onward into the capitalist anarchy of the Pool, a kind of destruction of the picturesque ideal. A hint of desolation could even be identified in a final study of the 'Nore' lightship, in the Thames estuary, the proposed subject for the final canvas of the Thames, but with the timing of a character in a Victorian novel, Vicat Cole died while working on this valedictory image. The high Tory pessimism of the English Cole parallels the apocalyptic Federalism of his older American namesake; landscape and politics are inextricably bound together in their works.

Thomas Cole's allegorical city astride a great river is, of course, sufficiently multivalent and flexible an allegorical figure to encompass both American and British history; the great river is both the Hudson and the Thames, and its expansive allegorical frame could just as well embrace both the Rhine or the Nile. The Tiber, which had seen the rise and fall of Rome, was clearly a common point of reference. Nineteenth century artists in both Britain and America traversed these great waterways, I believe, with the same quest for an underlying narrative as Cole sought to illustrate in his cycle, and found in the topography of rivers sufficient metaphoric power to articulate grand schemes of national history and destiny.

1   This essay derives from my work on an exhibition, *American Sublime*, Tate Britain, 2002. For fuller readings of many of the images described here see my essay "The Course of Empires: Landscape and Identity in America and Britain, 1820-1880" and catalogue entries in Wilton, Andrew and Barringer, Tim, *American Sublime: Landscape Painting in the United States, 1820-1880*, London: Tate, 2002, pp. 38-65. I am grateful to the editors of the present volume for their helpful comments.
2   Wrigley, E A, *Continuity Chance and Change: the Character of the Industrial Revolution in England*, Cambridge: Cambridge University Press, 1988, chapters 2-3.
3   See Baigell, Matthew and Kaufman, Allen, "Thomas Cole's *The Oxbow*: a Critique of American Civilisation", *Arts*, 55, January 1981, pp. 136-139.
4   Cole, Thomas, "Essay on American Scenery" [1835], reprinted in McCoubrey, J W, ed., *American Art 1700-1960: Sources and Documents*, Upper Saddle River, NJ: Pentrice Hall, 1965, pp 98-109; 106.
5   See Babington Macaulay, Thomas, *History of England since the Reign of James II*, London : Longman & Co., 1849; Butterfield, Herbert, *The Whig Interpretation of History*, London: G Bell and Sons, 1931.
6   Gage, John, *J M W Turner: a Wonderful Range of Mind*, New Haven and London: Yale University Press, 1987, p. 178.

7   Cole, "Essay on American Scenery", p. 108.
8   Westall, William and Owen, Samuel, *Picturesque Tour of the River Thames*, London: R Ackermann, 1828.
9   See Cain, P J and Hopkins, A G, *British Imperialism: Innovation and Expansion, 1688-1914*, London: Longman, 1993, esp. pp. 53-101.
10 On *Rain, Steam and Speed* see for example, Gage, John, *Turner: Rain, Steam and Speed*, New York: Viking Books, 1972; Daniels, Stephen, "Turner and the Circulation of State", *Fields of Vision: Landscape Imagery and National Identity in England and the United States*, Cambridge: Polity Press, 1993, pp. 112-145.
11 See my *The Cole Family: Painters of the English Landscape, 1838-1975*, Portsmouth: Portsmouth City Museums, 1988, pp. 94-110 and Chignell, Robert, *The Life and Paintings of Vicat Cole, RA*, London: Cassell, 1898, vol. III. Except where otherwise stated, the location of Vicat Cole's paintings cited in the text is untraced.
12 *The World*, 6 May 1885.
13 Chignell, *The Life and Paintings of Vicat Cole*, vol. III, p. 22.
14 Leslie, G D, to Chignell, Robert, nd.c. 1894, quoted Chignell, *The Life and Paintings of Vicat Cole*, vol. III, pp. 142-3.
15 Schütz Wilson, H, "Our Living Artists: Vicat Cole, ARA", Cassell's *Magazine of Art*, vol. I, 1878, p. 150.

16 Daniels, Stephen, "John Constable and the Making of Constable Country", *Fields of Vision*, pp. 200-242, especially pp. 207-209. See also Redgrave, Samuel and Richard, *A Century of Painters of the English School*, London: Smith, Elder & Co., 1866, esp. vol. II, p. 387.

17 Chignell, *The Life and Paintings of Vicat Cole*, vol. III, p. 108.

18 *Art Journal*, 1892, quoted Chignell, *The Life and Paintings of Vicat Cole*, vol. III, p. 123.

19 *Art Journal*, 1892, quoted Chignell, *The Life and Paintings of Vicat Cole*, vol. III, p. 123.

20 Leighton's speech was given in prose, but was evidently translated into blank verse by a correspondent of the *St James's Gazette*, the only form in which it survives. Barringer, *The Cole Family*, p. 95.

21 Barringer, *American Sublime*, p. 98.

22 Morris, William, *News from Nowhere, or An Epoch of Rest*, first serialised in *The Commonweal*, 1890, and published in book form in 1891. See *News from Nowhere and other Writings*, with an introduction by Wilmer, Clive, Harmondsworth: Penguin, 1993.

23 Chignell, *The Life and Paintings of Vicat Cole*, vol. I, p. 15.

24 The physical geography of the lower Hudson Valley is the subject of an excellent study by O'Brien, Raymond J, *American Sublime: Landscape and Scenery of the Lower Hudson Valley*, New York: Columbia University Press, 1981.

25 Cole, "Essay on American Scenery", p. 106.

26 See Voorsanger, Catherine Hoover and Howat, John K, eds., *Art and the Empire City: New York, 1825-1861*, New York: Metropolitan Museum of Art, 2000, p. 444, cat. 106.

27 O'Brien, *American Sublime*, p. 5.

28 See Robertson, Bruce, "The Picturesque Tourist in America", *Views and Visions: American Landscapes before 1830*, Nygren, Edward, ed., Washington DC: Corcoran Gallery of Art, 1986, pp. 199-204; Kenneth Myers, *The Catskills: Painters, Writers and Tourists in the Mountains, 1820-1895*, Yonkers, NY: The Hudson River Museum, 1987, pp. 31-32.

29 Avery, Kevin J, "The Historiography of the Hudson River School", *American Paradise: The World of the Hudson River School*, Howat, John K, ed., New York: Metropolitan Museum of Art, 1987, pp. 3-20. Kevin Avery demonstrates that the phrase was intended to be disparaging, and was coined only in the late 1870s when the work of these artists had come to seem dated. It is now used in a celebratory fashion, though its parameters remain somewhat indistinct.

30 See Wallach, Alan, "Thomas Cole: Landscape and the Course of American Empire", *Thomas Cole: Landscape into History*, Truettner, William and Wallach, Alan, eds., New Haven and London: Yale University Press, 1994, pp. 23-113, esp. pp. 28-31.

31 Legrand Noble, Louis. *The Life and Works of Thomas Cole* (1853), Vessell, Elliot S, ed., Hensonville: New York, 1997, p. 34.

32 Cole, Thomas, "The Wild", quoted Howat, John K, *The Hudson River and its Painters*, New York: Viking Press, 1972, p. 36.

33 See Wolf, Bryan Jay, *Romantic Re-vision: Culture and Consciousness in Nineteenth-Century American Painting and Literature*, Chicago: University of Chicago Press, 1982, p. 177.

34 Quoted Nancy Anderson et al, *Thomas Moran*, Washington DC: National Gallery of Art, 1997.

35 Quoted Roqué, Oswald Rodriguez, "The Exaltation of American Landscape Painting", in Howat, *American Paradise*, p. 40.

36 Quoted Kelly, Franklin, *Thomas Cole's Paintings of Eden*, Fort Worth, Texas: Amon Carter Museum, 1994, p. 17.

37 For a full analysis of *The Course of Empire*, see Barringer, Tim, "The Course of Empire" in Wilton and Barringer, *American Sublime*, pp. 95-110.

38 See Wallach, Alan, "Landscape and the Course of American Empire", *Thomas Cole: Landscape into History*, Truettner, W and Wallach, A, eds., pp. 23-111, and Miller, Angela, *The Empire of the Eye: Landscape Representations and American Cultural Politics, 1825-1875*, Ithaca and London: Cornell University Press, 1993.

39 See for example Anthony Imbert after Archibald Robertson, *Grand Canal Celebration*, lithograph from Cadwallader Colden *Memoir... at the Celebration of the Completion of the Grand Canal*, 1825. See Voorsanger, Catherine Hoover and Howat, John K, eds., *Art and the Empire City: New York 1825-1861*, p. 450.

Regionalism to Modernism: Antonioni, 1939
Noa Steimatsky

For Paolo, and his Po

On 25 April 1939 – designated also as the year XVII, the seventeenth year of the Italian Fascist regime – Michelangelo Antonioni, film critic, publishes in the magazine *Cinema* an article, accompanied by photographic illustrations: "For a Film on the River Po".[1] Although he had previously written for the local *Corriere Padano* published in his native Ferrara, Antonioni's article in the prestigious Roman film magazine with national circulation can be seen to constitute a first statement of intent regarding filmmaking. *Cinema*, an officially sponsored "Publication of the National Fascist Federation of the Performing Arts", was an important arena for filmmakers and writers who were beginning, in the late 1930s, to articulate the aspirations of Neorealism. Umberto Barbaro, Giuseppe de Santis, and Luchino Visconti – all names identified with Neorealist culture in the years to come – were among the contributors to this bi-weekly, under the directorship (1938-1943) of Vittorio Mussolini, the Duce's son, military pilot, and promoter of Italian film culture. Under the auspices of one so intimately identified with the establishment, the *Cinema* group could enjoy considerable protection.[2]

Did they need protection? Within the limits of *Cinema*'s ephemeral newsprint, surrounded with period Deco graphics, advertisements for airline services to Addis Ababa, for Kodak film, Coty face powder, perfume, and toothpaste, one could find in the late 1930s articles attending to the marginal, anti-monumental, un-heroic vision of Italy.[3] Yet these proto-Neorealist elements were most likely read in light of regionalist trends such as *strapaese* – the glorification of rural life in keeping with Fascist folk mythology in the 1930s.[4] Regionalism, like other modes and styles of the period, could exhibit the 'correct' affinities in the face of the regime, but it could also be channelled to anti-Fascist ones in Post War culture. *Cinema* in this way evidenced, up to a point, Fascism's assimilative cultural policy: not a properly 'pluralistic' outlook, but rather one that could transform – if necessary by repressive measures – any discourse into a self-serving cultural asset under the guise of apparent tolerance. Such was the insidious cultural make-up of Italian Fascism. Seen in this light, it is not surprising that so few artists and intellectuals had to leave when they could continue working under its auspices with relative freedom at home.[5]

While lending itself to association with early writings on Neorealism, "For a Film on the River Po" binds its regionalist-documentary pretext with a modernist thrust. For modernist movements such as Art Deco, Rationalism, a second Futurism, and several currents of abstraction persisted and circulated under Fascism. Neorealism would seek to avoid the tainted connotations of such modernisms, turning instead to realist narrative fiction in its attention to the regional, the quotidian, the marginal. Already sensing the realist fallacies and sentimental pitfalls of a Neorealist agenda in its infancy – not yet sufficiently distinct, perhaps, from a heroic, mythologising, Fascist regionalism – Antonioni can be seen at this early moment to search for a distinct mode of articulating his own Neorealist bent in modernist terms. I will suggest that Antonioni was willing to risk the linking of pre- and Post War Italian modernism, putting it to new practice, initially in documentary filmmaking, *vis-à-vis* a changing, discordant environment. Already the 1939 article situates Antonioni in an oblique relation to the aspirations of his colleagues, betraying the ambivalence of a formative moment when diverse, indeed contradictory, trends in late-Fascist Italian culture converged.

While apparently focused on limited subject matter – the cinematic rendering of a particular regional landscape – "For a Film on the River Po" evokes larger questions about the ways in which location shooting complicates the relation of documentary to fiction, the relation of profilmic actuality to rhetoric and poetic functions, the figuration of place in the national imagination, the binding of landscape in history. All of this may not have been apparent in 1939, but even anthologised as it is today the text may not suffice to clarify the article's larger implications. Its searching, meandering style evolves in a series of negations: Antonioni dwells on what filmmaking should *not* be, and only begins to envision in this way what it might become. Yet surrounding this convoluted text, the photographic illustrations – not reproduced in subsequent reprints and translations – will make salient a modernist consciousness seeking clarification *vis-à-vis* diverse modes of landscape representation.

Even as he is cautious about projecting a subjective mood upon the landscape, Antonioni maintains throughout his essay a notion of *genius loci* – a spirit of place that would figure the "destiny" of the region as a whole. Yet Antonioni goes on to describe this destiny via the material, economic, and social terms dictated by the river, which thus lends itself to culture, and to art. The yearly floods punctuating the life of the river dramatise the continued confrontation of the forces and rhythms of nature *vis-à-vis* human endeavour and its modern sense of temporality and change. For

> ... the years did not pass in vain [not for people and] not even for things. There came also for the Po the time to awaken. And then there came iron bridges on which long trains clanged day and night, there came six-story buildings spotted with enormous windows vomiting dust and noise, there came steam boats, docks, factories, fuming chimneys, even more canals with cemented levees; this was, in short, an altogether modern, mechanical, industrialised world that came to turn upside down the harmony of the old one. And yet in the midst of this dissolution of their world, the population had no regrets.[6]

The revolution of modernity is, then, no cause for nostalgia. Antonioni's concern will be how to adjust the culture's imagination to these material changes. What emerges here is the conviction that recurs in Antonioni's later writings, namely, that cinema is instrumental in this process of adjustment – and that it is especially suited, as a medium, to a mediating role between the modern environment and human perception and imagination in transition. "All this" – he goes on to say – "can seem to be but is not literature. It is, or wants to be cinema. It remains to be seen how it can be translated into practice. First of all there arises a question: documentary or fiction film?" In questioning the adequacy of the medium by which to articulate a landscape in transition; in going on to complicate the notion of documenting as well as narrating the landscape, Antonioni in effect problematises that which many of his *Cinema* colleagues will take for granted. For Neorealism will go on to claim a privileged status exceeding generic classifications, unproblematically colliding a 'correct' aesthetic and ideology that is guaranteed – so Neorealism implied – by shooting on location in hitherto neglected (and thereby realist) sites.

Figures 1-4
"For a Film on the River Po". Antonioni's entire essay as first published in *Cinema*, no. 68, April 25 1939, pp. 254-257

Ma nemmeno per le cose gli anni passano invano. Venne anche per il Po il tempo del risveglio. E allora furono ponti in ferro su cui lunghi treni sferragliano giorno e notte, furono edifici a sei piani chiazzati di enormi finestre vomitanti polvere e rumore, furono battelli a vapore, darsene, stabilimenti, ciminiere fumose, perfino altri canali dagli argini in cemento; fu insomma tutto un mondo moderno, meccanico, industrializzato che venne a mettere a soqquadro l'armonia di quello antico.

Eppure, in mezzo a questo scempio del loro mondo, le popolazioni non hanno sentito rimpianti. Lo avrebbero voluto, forse, ché la loro natura scontrosa e contemplativa non si adattava ancora al nuovo stato di cose, ma non ci son riuscite. La evoluzione, a un certo punto, non soltanto non le disturbava ma in certo modo le accontentava. Cominciavano a considerare il fiume nel suo valore funzionale; sentivano che si era valorizzato e ne erano orgogliose; capivano ch'era diventato prezioso e la loro ambizione era soddisfatta.

* * *

Tutto ciò può sembrare, ma non è, letteratura. È, o vuol essere, cinematografo; resta a vedere come può tradursi in atto.

Prima di tutto s'impone una domanda: documentario o film a soggetto?

La prima forma è senza dubbio allettante. Materiale ricco, suggestivo, che va dai larghissimi tratti di fiume, vasti come laghi e talvolta interrotti da isolotti, alle stretture dove il Po, scortato com'è da selvagge piante, assume aspetti di paesaggio africano; dalle casupole malandate addossate agli argini, con l'eterna pozzanghera nel cortiletto davanti all'uscio, alle villette novecento con lo *chalet* a fior d'acqua, che si anima certe sere di lievi musiche sincopate; dagli argini a picco alle graziose spiagge pretenziosamente mondane; dai molini natanti alle imponenti fabbriche; dalle barche ai motoscafi, agl'idroscivolanti della Pavia-Venezia; e via dicendo.

Materiale abbondante ma pericoloso, perchè si presta a facili inclinazioni rettoriche. Per cui, se ci alletta il ricordo di un magnifico documentario americano sul Mississippi: THE RIVER, ci lascia perplessi la trita formula del «com'era e com'è», del «prima e dopo la cura». Nè ci tranquillizzerebbe l'intrusione di un esile filo narrativo. Diffidiamo degli ibridismi in genere, e di quelli dello schermo in particolare, dove non sarà mai troppo celebrata la forma che detta indirizzi precisi e non consente incertezze. O da una parte o dall'altra: l'essenziale è sapere esattamente quello che si vuole. Abbastanza recente è l'esempio offertoci da Flaherty, che pure è autore degno della massima stima. Nella sua DANZA DEGLI ELEFANTI, infatti, a causa del dissidio fra documento e racconto, il motivo lirico del lavoro, quella specie di religione panica della giungla, trova la sua più genuina espressione nelle sequenze documentarie, dov'è solo il tormento della scoperta poetica, altrove disturbata dalla narrazione.

* * *

Dovremo dunque accogliere l'idea di un film a soggetto? Detto tra noi, abbiamo molta simpatia per questo *documento* senza etichetta, ma non bisogna precipitare. Anche qui, naturalmente, non mancano gli ostacoli, primo fra tutti quello d'ideare una trama che risponda appieno ai motivi più sopra ventilati. Già gli americani,

Barche e vapori alla riva di Pontelagoscuro

Veduta aerea di Pontelagoscuro e del ponte ferroviario per Padova

ai quali nessun tema sfugge, ci si son provati. Due loro pellicole — vecchissima l'una: IL FIUME, di qualche anno fa l'altra: LA CANZONE DEL FIUME — ebbero buon successo, specie la prima, dal punto di vista contenutistico la migliore. Però ambedue erano molto lontane dal nostro pensiero e dalla nostra sensibilità.

Ma non vogliamo, qui, dar consigli a chicchessia e tanto meno suggerire trame. Ci basti dire che vorremmo una pellicola avente a protagonista il Po e nella quale non il folclore, cioè un'accozzaglia d'elementi esteriori e decorativi, destasse l'interesse, ma lo spirito, cioè un insieme di elementi morali e psicologici; nella quale non le esigenze commerciali prevalessero, bensì l'intelligenza.

MICHELANGELO ANTONIONI

257

A documentary that would develop via picturesque anecdote of rural culture past and present, Antonioni fears, might lend itself to *cliché*. While praising Pare Lorentz's 1937 film of the Mississippi, Antonioni is wary of "the trite formulas of 'as it was vs. as it is', 'before and after the cure'", and "the eternal river". The American example suggests to him, perhaps, an abbreviated, uninterrogated passage from nature to modernity. Celebratory, overdetermined narratives of progress, set in mythified landscapes, were certainly a reigning principle of Italian documentaries, not only fiction films, of the period. In the essay's closing phrases he begins to describe a film that approaches an identification of the spirit of place with a purer cinematic vision.

> It suffices to say that we would like a film having as protagonist the Po, and in which not folklore
> – that is, a heap of extraneous and decorative elements – will draw attention, but the spirit....
> A film in which not the commercial need prevails, but the intelligence.[7]

Although he advocates precision and clarity as cinematic virtues, Antonioni's writing here is often obscure. His implicit critique of the pitfalls of Fascist production – some of which elements survived in Neorealism – remains generalised, resorting to vague notions of unmediated, a-rhetorical, idealist 'essence', and not yet formulated as a positive, material aesthetic. In practice, Antonioni's Post War documentaries and, most eminently, his fiction film work launched in 1950 went on to explore imaginative resolutions to such problematic terms. But at this early stage, more coherently than the written text, the photographic illustrations surrounding it, taking up more than double its space, step in where language fails to confront that which "is not literature" but "is or wants to be cinema". And it is this visual essay, running alongside the verbal one, that will also make salient those aspects of contemporary Italian culture that inform the inception of Antonioni's thought.[8]

Organised in groups, the first eight of the nine stills are in horizontal format approximating filmic aspect ratio. The first pair (figure 1) jointly titled *Nets for fishing in the Po waters* presents different angles on the same subject, comparable to separate frames in a single cinematic shot. With the shift from first to second still the fishing net screens a larger portion of the river, flattening the landscape, thus sliced in quasi-geometric sections, against the photographic surface. The intersection of the principal lines of the net and the distant riverbank heighten this geometry, which further disrupts figure and ground dichotomy. The implication of movement in the course of re-framing *between* the two images, as a product of shifting figure and ground relations, is repeated in the essay's other photographic groupings.

The three stills on the facing page where the text begins, jointly titled *The banks of the Po*, (figure 2) depict the perpendicular shapes of trees and vegetation against the lighter background. In the top photograph the branches constitute the foreground, in the second the middle ground, and in the third image the river fills the foreground while a slim row of trees is synonymous with the horizon line. In sequence, these images describe a movement of distancing of figures against the alternately stacked water – bank – sky elements, combined with the suggestion of lateral motion along the river. Following this exercise in figure and ground relations, the next page is divided between a pair of photographs titled *Day and Night on the Po* (figure 3) and contains the only human figures in the entire sequence, silhouetted and puny under the high horizon. Both stills are dominated by large expanses of water, effecting an interplay of surface and depth, reflection and opacity. The water surface, approaching the frame in magnitude, becomes comparable to the surface of the photograph itself.

As the top photograph's caption on the last page (figure 4) indicates, this is the bank of Pontelagoscuro, the small town on the south bank of the Po that will serve years later as the first stop in the protagonist's unhappy voyage in *Il Grido*, 1957. This is familiar landscape to Antonioni. Ferrara, his native city, is just a few miles from here. And as we are on the outskirts of an urban centre, the built riverbank with its railroad bridge exhibits the first marks of industrial modernity in relation to what were thus far pure rural landscapes lacking clear contemporary orientation. Directly below this photograph, in the only vertical format of the series, is the last still – but it is one that, in fact, could be rotated and viewed at any angle. This *Aerial View of Pontelagoscuro and of the Railway Bridge to Padua* is centred on the same site but frames a much wider landscape, complete with factory buildings evidenced by massive chimney smoke, and a network of what appear to be warehouses, canals, roads. Whatever marks of modernity we already noted are now heightened, for the camera work involved here is itself more emphatically part of this modernity. And whatever human scale and viewpoint may have marked the previous stills it is now radically altered as we identify this photograph as part of a photogrammetric or military project whose aim is objective, instrumental cartography or reconnaissance.[9]

Here Antonioni's essay concludes. With the striking terms of the last image it is no longer only a formal correspondence, discerned in the first eight stills, that marks the consciousness emerging in these pages. For the aerial photograph also suggests that the correspondence between the landscape and its mode of representation, between modernity and modernism, is historically and politically placed and it begs a question: how can the Italian landscape, propelled into modernity during Fascism, fulfill a modernist programme *while* accommodating an emerging Neorealism? For the aerial photograph makes salient a modernist desire – suited, we shall see, to Fascism's inclinations in the late 1930s – for a controlling, unifying perception, crystallising reality as an aesthetic object. But Antonioni's documentarist's conscience is also drawn by the lesson of photographic contingency, amplified by the sense of movement and temporality that the *sequence* brings forth: the always specific, indexical image that testifies to the ephemeral, the changing. How might documentary cinema respond to the tensions between traditional auratic fullness and its modern depletion in the regional landscape, between the persistent and the changing, between an earlier modernist moment and its necessary revision in light of what has come to pass?

The aerial photograph emblematises spatial perception in modernity. More radically so than photography as such had already intimated, the human figure now disappears from the position of both viewer and viewed: it is no longer the measure of things; at most it may register as a minute graphic mark, a dot, in the aerial photograph. The aerial views of Nadar, who turned his lens on 1856 Paris from a balloon, foreshadowed developments in aeronautic and short-exposure photography during the First World War.[10] The scientific applications of these distant, compressed topographies, to be deciphered by specialised reading appealed, as well, to a range of modernist and avant-garde sensibilities.[11] For Le Corbusier the airplane is itself a supreme example of the selective achievement of functional comprehensive form, while the aerial view affords a modern perception *par excellence* – one which unmasks the no longer viable traditional forms of landscape representation and urban planning. The camera's automatic, instrumental claim is amplified by the apparatus that bears it, the airplane, promoting the photograph's indexical, evidentiary function. Yet the anti-illusionistic effect of the aerial photograph – departing from ordinary perceptual notions of resemblance that rely on upright and thereby anthropomorphic parameters, the sense of scale and dimension, concave and convex, figure and ground relations – has lent itself not only to 'scientific' but also spiritualistic conceptions of abstract art. Hitherto imperceptible forms, abstract patterns emerging to perception

Figure 5
Gerardo Dottori,
Umbria, oil,
1934. Yale Photo
Collection

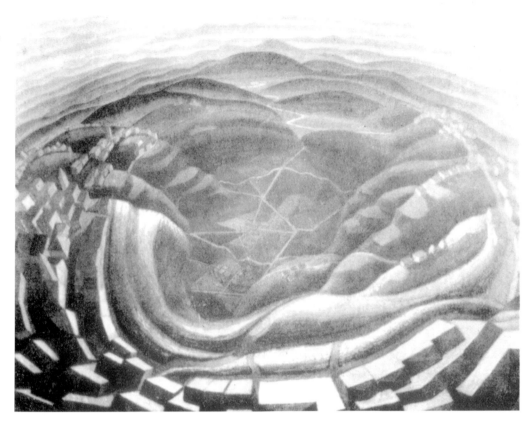

Figure 6
Filippo Masoero,
*From the
Airplane*, aerial
photograph,
1935. Yale Photo
Collection

for the first time, now suggested the possibility of a hidden reality that awaited this lofty view of the whole, as if pertaining to some grander plan, grasped by the photograph's surface optics. This was one way to conceive of abstraction as already inherent in the environment, and to reconcile the difficulty of non-representational art with the realist, testimonial value of photography. For as the landscape is vacated in the aerial view, it becomes alien to itself.[12] The ideological ambivalence underlying this condition, and the aesthetic to which it gives rise, registered on numerous cultural fronts in Italy of the 1930s.

Italy's early and most influential avant-garde, Futurism, was revived with the school of *aeropittura* – aerial painting – propelled in a 1929 manifesto and an exhibition of 41 *aeropittori* in Milan in 1931.[13] Perhaps capitalising on the imaginative force of the figure of Gabriele D'Annunzio as militant pilot-artist, *aeropittura* extended Futurism's original engagement with the dynamism of modern life, focusing on the beauty of flying machines that transfigure the human environment, or else destroy it – also cause for Futurist celebration. Italy's imperialist aviational exploits in East Africa themselves re-invigorated the aerial imagination of F T Marinetti and his retinue. The posters, murals, set and pavilion designs, architecture, sculpture, painting, and photography identified under the larger umbrella of *aeropittura* celebrate the conquering of space and the liberation of perception from the forces of gravity and from a limited human viewpoint. *Aeropittura* could stress a spiritualistic sublimation of its potentially aggressive connotations in notions of mystic power, the intoxicating embrace of a Fascist sublime. Gerardo Dottori's aerial landscapes perhaps epitomise this trend: their circular forms, inspired by the whirling experience of flight itself, are matched by the rounded horizons that evoke the shape of the earth in a cosmic dimension. (figure 5) Diverse perspectives and scales simultaneously dynamise the image in good Futurist form interlaced, however, with regionalist materials: Dottori's recognisable Umbrian landscapes, the roofs and bell towers of Perugia, or the gulf of La Spezia, reach towards the bluish distance where entire towns, rivers, and gleaming lakes float upward on the surface of the canvas. In these and numerous other examples we witness the confluence, through the aerial point of view, of regionalist impulses, nationalist/imperialist sentiments, and a universalist modernist engagement with the conditions of perception and representation at large. Critics have suggested that it is precisely due to this confluence that *aeropittura* served to disseminate modernist culture in 1930s Italy while cultivating de-centred, heterogeneous, "local avant-gardes".[14]

Aeropittura aspires to capture the regional landscape from outside itself, from a dynamic technological viewpoint that ultimately identifies the airplane with the camera. The Futurist photography manifesto of 1930 promotes aerial vision as supplanting traditional humanist pictorial depictions of the landscape.[15] *Aerofotografia* offers, instead, vast terrains captured from above, emphasising vertiginous height, the sensation of soaring or plunging at great velocity, shifts of scale and perspective that dynamise space, bringing a new consciousness even to familiar urban monuments or regional features.[16] Landscape in near abstract optical tracing, achieved by long or repeated exposure in acrobatic flight as performed by Filippo Masoero over the centre of Milan, lent itself to avant-garde sensibilities. (figure 6) Masoero was in fact a fiercely patriotic fighter pilot who had associated with D'Annunzio and Marinetti and, devoted to photography and cinema, was appointed in 1930 director of the Istituto LUCE (L'Unione per la Cinematografia Educativa) in Rome, and then volunteered for aerial reconnaissance missions on the Ethiopian front. Artistic explorations of innovative image technology, and the encompassing, inspiring beauty of the aerial view appear inseparable from militarist associations in that historical moment, epitomised in Masoero's career.[17] We might say that in aerial culture a utopian Futurist universe made local, and a modernist vision of

Italy made universal, lent themselves to Fascism's containment of oppositions, its desire to command space in all of its dimensions. For such images inspire first by their exertion of power in the superior possession of vision and knowledge that aerial reconnaissance affords, but also by way of preparing for an actual – not formal or metaphorical – controlling and levelling of the terrain by aerial bombardment. In Italy of the late 1930s, fresh from its colonial exploits and the declaration of empire, the aerial view thus came to embody the perfect aestheticisation of Fascist aggression.

All this could not have been far from view in Antonioni's immediate *milieu* on the board of the magazine *Cinema*, where a glaring exemplification of the cultural intersections that concern us here may be located in the person of Vittorio Mussolini. The Duce's son had just moved from aviation on the African colonial front to the forefront of Italian film culture, becoming involved in film production and, in 1938, becoming chief editor of *Cinema*. Just prior to this, capitalising on the general excitement over the war in Abyssinia, he published in 1937 a popular account of his exploits there, illustrated by aerial photographs with such captions as *A pretty burst of bombs*. These are matched by descriptions such as this:

> I still remember the effect I produced on a small group of Galla tribesmen massed around a man in black clothes. I dropped an aerial torpedo right in the center, and the group opened up just like a flowering rose. It was most entertaining.[18]

Back in Italy and into the movies, Mussolini the younger contributed to the production of the vastly successful fiction film, Goffredo Alessandrini's *Luciano Serra pilota*, 1938. Based on a semi-autobiographical account of Filippo Masoero's experience, the film celebrates Italian aviation, wedding the persistence of Italian patriotism, heroic-paternal values, and nostalgia for one's native region, to the ambition to expand the horizon through flight, itself synonymous here with imperialist expansion. Heightened melodrama alternates with impressive location work involving masses of extras and the expertise of aerial cinematography. But the conflation of these elements is subjugated to a propagandistic imperative that sentimentalises the technology, positing imperialist warfare, epitomised by the aerial exploits, as an emotionalised force of nature. The film was allegedly titled by the Duce while, puzzlingly, Vittorio himself was credited as *auteur* in two raving reviews by Michelangelo Antonioni.[19] The passion for aviation and for cinema was continuous for the young Mussolini. His applying of the heroics of one to the other held a fascination, even for the discerning film critic.

Vittorio Mussolini would have had the access to such images as the aerial photograph of Pontelagoscuro, perhaps from military manoeuvres in the Po Valley. At least he may have raised or inspired the idea of the aerial photograph that concludes Antonioni's vision of a film devoted to a regional landscape with such a departure from traditional imagery. My suggestion of shared 'authorship' here bears, I believe, some metonymic potency; even figuratively it is at least as suggestive as Antonioni's ascribing of *Luciano Sera pilota* to his senior editor. What matter are the connotations and contexts made salient by these professional and personal ties. It takes a full-fledged Fascist sensibility like that of Vittorio Mussolini, or like Marinetti's, to explicitly glorify – always from a distance, or from the air – the experience of war. But attenuated and, incredibly, still optimistic versions of this aesthetic were evidently still prevalent in the late 1930s, despite the exposure of Fascism's worst faces in the colonial misadventure in Africa and the racism developed in its wake, culminating in the pact with Hitler. Now, Antonioni's meandering text and its illustrations certainly do not prescribe such Fascist visions, but they are not neutral either.

Figures 7-10
Michelangelo
Antonioni's *Gente
del Po*, 1942-
1947: frame
enlargements

The rejection of nostalgic regional lore and decorative anecdotes of progress may be seen to offer some resistance to folk mythologising and heroic melodramatic aggrandisement, Fascist or otherwise. One might say that, hesitant as it is, the article does confront in the aerial image the tensions of a modernist consciousness brought to the regional subject matter at a particular historical moment; that in the shift to an altered perspective it discloses the problematic connotations of a unifying, universalising, possessive vision under late Fascism. The suggestion of movement and temporality inscribed, we have seen, in the sequence begins to suggest an oscillating, contingent perception that will rise to the fore when Antonioni turns to film practice some years later.[20]

There is a way in which Antonioni's photographic sequence constitutes a lesson on the possibility of a Neorealist documentary in open form, by which to sort out what remains of cinematic modernism after the war. Yet while Antonioni's filmic images of the Po will on some level be strikingly reminiscent of the 1939 photographic illustrations, their new cinematic syntax, their editing and temporality offer important departures from that early *exposé*. In the winter of 1942-1943 on the riverbank across from where Visconti was working on *Ossessione*, far from centres of power, from the monumental and mythic connotations of Rome and the south, and from the softer contours of Tuscany that make up the ideal image of Italy in the touristic imagination, Antonioni shot his *Gente del Po* (*People of the Po*). About half of the footage, whose negatives were stored in Venice during the particularly violent period following its shooting, was lost. In 1947 – a year after Roberto Rossellini explored this same landscape in the final episode of his *Paisà* – Antonioni assembled what remained in some ten minutes of stirring filmmaking.[21] The difficult conditions and interrupted history of the production, the violent shifts in political climate and prolonged struggle in the north of Italy from 1943 through the end of the war have all left their scars on Antonioni's first film. Perhaps the loss both of footage and of pre-war illusions that marks this production was *itself* important. These marks of loss and fragmentation seem to have foregrounded a principle of contingency, inflecting tensions of identification and alienation, referentiality and abstraction, realism and modernism in ways that inform the issues I have been discussing.[22]

Between quotidian detail and a movement of emptying-out of the landscape fragments of river life, unpursued plot clues traverse, as it were, the documentary body of *Gente del Po*. Though the voice-over points out potential Neorealist story elements – "a man, a woman, a child" – these are allowed no development or resolution, their dramatic or sentimental potential is blocked by the image of the river itself in stark, inert compositions. A bicycle rider crosses the frame. The commentary summons him from the background of the riverside town, as from the documentary order of the film. For the duration of a single startling shot he pulses with narrative possibility, a figure sharply drawn only to be withdrawn again as the ground will re-emerge to the fore. A girl is sitting on the bank, her back to the camera in medium shot; the bicycle enters the frame between girl and camera. Several planes – river, bank, girl, bike – all compete for space in this dense and suddenly dramatic framing as the rider now settles down, partly concealing the girl as she turns to cast upon him an unfathomable look. His sports-shirt with the logo "DEI" – a contemporary, solid make of bicycles – looms large on the screen, its modern graphics a striking intrusion upon what one has envisioned as a romantic moment in the timeless embrace of the river. Then the camera pans away to the empty expanse of bank, river, opaque sky beyond – suspended landscape elements, signifying nothing in particular, emptying out the little narrative all in the duration of a single shot. (figures 7-8) This emerging principle of abstraction, of dissolution, inflects the film at every level. From narrative promise to the sports-shirt that blocks preceding connotations, and from the intrusive pause over its upright graphics to the opaque landscape that refuses even the consolation of a receding distance, we witness what is surely the earliest and paradigmatic instance of Antonioni's cinematic modernism.

In its look upon the regional, Neorealist subject matter, *Gente del Po* maps a space of oscillating, fractured textuality and visuality that approaches a modernist perception of all things private and public. The grey expanse of the river – "flat as asphalt", the voice-over observes – fills the frame repeatedly, opaquely; the graphic division of light and shade on a wall; the Metaphysical premonition of the empty provincial piazza bordered by arcades whose perspectival suggestion is blotted by the bright light and sharp contrasts; the high angle shots of the barge effaced by smoke in the course of a camera movement (figures 9-10): all these turn attention to a rendering of the landscape *as* cinematic space in process of being drained. These are not Neorealism's consoling, reconstructive gestures. The aerial photograph that concluded Antonioni's early essay emptied the landscape of traditional connotations and narrative anecdote: so too, following the linear movement of the river, in the film's closing images the landscape is vacated, as is the film itself. Yet the view is not subjugated here to an encompassing figure except under the sign of mutability, change: the tentative voice of a modernist consciousness exploring the spaces that open up in between realist codes and the contingency of the everyday, of the ephemeral, the profilmic.

In describing this particular position we might now recall that of all the major filmmakers to emerge in this period leading to the great flowering of Italy's Post War film culture, Antonioni is the only one to dwell so rigorously on the documentary. But rather than simply appealing to its means of articulation (actual locations, non-professional actors, etc.) in the service of Neorealist narrative or historical reconstruction, we see him preoccupied with distilling cinematic form from the profilmic subject at hand. It may be that a documentary consciousness sharpened his sense of taking nothing for granted, nothing as settled and coded, realist or otherwise, in the face of Post War contingency,

Figures 11-12
Michelangelo
Antonioni's *Noto
Mandorli
Vulcano
Stromboli
Carnevale*, 1992:
frame
enlargements

so much amplified by the sharp shifts in power and ideology, the disappearance of people, the transformation of the landscape itself over the course of the war. The uncertain terrain that he had begun to explore so early could not be quite accommodated, perhaps, in a film culture that identified its project of Post War commemoration and reconstruction with narrative consolation, and could not always afford to be interrogatory or reflective. Thus, at the height of Neorealism and through the end of the 1940s, Antonioni remained occupied with documentary production on the margins of Neorealist practices. While his choices invite some comparisons with the work of Visconti and Rossellini, Antonioni's concerns, bound up with a pre-war modernist promise that could not be taken to its conclusion during Fascism, had to wait before they re-surfaced in radical form in 1950, in feature film production.

Antonioni's grasp of the landscape as a distanced, alienated terrain recurs as a critical, transformative principle much wider in its potential than the aerial view we have located as a paradigm. The view from the iron bridge in *Cronaca di un amore*, 1950, and from the tower of *Il grido*, 1957, were already striking instances, *L'avventura*'s island views, in 1960, came to be the most celebrated, and the finale of *L'eclisse*, 1962, is perhaps the most radical of Antonioni's elaborations on this mode of seeing. The island where a character has disappeared without a trace, the deserted towns and vacant hotel corridors, the crossroads in the EUR Roman suburb to which the camera, but not the protagonists, returns – these achieve an "intelligence" of place stripped of "extraneous and decorative elements" as of coded rhetorical devices that would mediate human presence, and pastness. Antonioni's discovery of abstraction at the heart of the figure and of the figurative potential of the void is propelled by a documentarist's sense of the unfolding of the profilmic in the duration of a shot, the unravelling of relationships in time and space consciously differentiated from the suggestion of cause and effect, the persistence of narrative and expository remnants. His crystallising of a spirit of place – a regional specificity that still carries realist values – is thus

bound up with its apparent opposite: the withdrawal of definite figuration, a modernist dissection of the conditions of representation. Antonioni's work was, from the start, thus based in a fracturing of the figure so as to test the ground and see how ground emerges *as* figure, capturing the movement by which one evolves into the other.

It takes astonishing form in one of his latest works. Produced by ENEL (Italy's national electric company) in 70mm colour stock for the Italian pavilion at the Seville Expo, the eight-minute short *Noto Mandorli Vulcano Stromboli Carnevale*, 1992, incorporates extensive aerial cinematography of extraordinary resolution in the last three of its five Sicilian landscape vignettes. Antonioni returns here to *L'avventura*'s locations in Noto's elevated bell tower, going on to invoke such late Neorealist locations as Rossellini's *Stromboli, terra di Dio*, 1951, and even Fellini's crowded piazzas in the closing images of 'Carnevale'. The aerial views still have the power to transform our sense of orientation, dimension, depth: precipices and folds of earth that appear in one instance as small dunes in tight framing are revealed in the next as voluminous mountainous expanses. (figure 11) Iridescent sulphuric cracks, vast or minuscule (it is often unclear which) emit fumes that at times envelope the frame entirely. (figure 12) The terrain, surveyed by smooth gliding motions heightened by the synthesised music, seems presented from a radically exteriorised outlook, through the eyes of one separated from the earth, perhaps the survivor of an unseen but yet sensed cataclysm. As moving image, the fuming earth seems to heave and pulsate like a corporeal presence, an immanence waiting to unfold. The empty and the full, the deserted and the populated views, the primeval and the devastated become strangely alike in this short film: they are thus raised to a new figural order. In the wake of the Cold War, on the margins of Europe, do these images speak of an exhaustion of resources at the end of history, or some new-age transformation of consciousness *vis-à-vis* a still living, breathing earth?

In the half century that separates Antonioni's 1939 photographic essay and first documentary from these Sicilian landscapes the re-casting of the relation between modernity, or late-modernity, and its conditions of representation in motion pictures has not been resolved, but its attendant anxieties perhaps augmented by a still altering environment, as well as by the progress of image technologies – the transfiguration of the very notion of reference and reproduction, photographic and actual. A fundamental ambivalence about this relationship is still at work in the most eloquent instances of fiction and documentary, in cinematographic, digital, and virtual spaces. Antonioni located his first arena for such an interrogation in his native landscape, bringing into play there the profound tensions of Italian culture between the world wars. But it was following the camera's recording of hitherto unseen atrocities, following the panorama of European and other landscapes levelled by more than just a camera's vertical outlook, that one came to realise how altered must be the look upon the terrain, brought in all its devastation to its surviving beholders.

This essay draws on an original longer version, with additional materials and emphases, titled "From the Air: the Genealogy of Antonioni's Modernism" in Allen, R, and Turvey, M, eds., *Camera Obscura, Camera Lucida: Essays in Honor of Annette Michelson*, Amsterdam: Amsterdam University Press, 2002.

1   Antonioni, M, "Per un film sul fiume Po", *Cinema*, no. 68, 25 April 1939, pp. 254-257. Though I offer in what follows my own translations from this text I have often consulted "Concerning a Film about the River Po", in Overbey, D, ed. and trans., *Springtime in Italy: a Reader on Neo-Realism*, Hamden, CT: Archon Books, 1979, pp. 79-82. Page references for all quotations are to the original Italian version.

2   See Gian Piero Brunetta's account of the *Cinema* group in his *Storia del cinema italiano*, vol. 2: *Il cinema del regime 1929-1945*, Rome: Editori Riuniti, rev. ed., 1993, pp. 220-230.

3   E.g., Flaiano, E, "Le ispirazioni sbagliate", *Cinema*, no. 61, 10 January 1939, pp. 10-11; Purificato, D, "L'obiettivo nomade", *Cinema*, no.78, 25 September 1939, pp. 196. The introduction to my dissertation, "The Earth Figured: An Exploration of Landscapes in Italian Cinema", New York: New York University, 1995, dwells on these and other texts devoted to the promotion of location shooting in that period.

4   *Strapaese* ('ultra-country') and *stracittà* ('ultra-city') coexisted as Fascist themes. The former's regionalist cult posited itself as the pure Italian alternative to urban, internationalist modern culture, which it understood as un-Italian and thereby un-Fascist. James Hay describes the documentary and fiction films of the 1930s devoted to these themes in *Popular Film Culture in Fascist Italy: the Passing of the Rex*, Bloomington: Indiana University Press, 1987.

5   See Ruth Ben-Ghiat's lucid summary of this strategy in her *Fascist Modernities: Italy, 1922-1945*, Berkeley: University of California Press, 2001, pp. 1-15.

6   Antonioni, M, "Per un film sul fiume Po", p. 255.

7   Implicit here is Antonioni's identification of an intrinsic "intelligence" of place with an "intelligence" proper to film as such.

8   One is tempted to ascribe the Po river photographs to Antonioni himself: though uncredited, they are close to his taste and his eye as we come to know it from his subsequent work. They were, at the very least, surely selected and approved by him. I dwell on the provenance of the last photograph below.

9   Photogrammetry is that branch of aerial photography that serves cartography. The term "instrumental" I borrow from Allan Sekula who uses it to discuss the aesthetic-ideological bind between the realist/scientific/military applications of aerial photography, its aesthetic appreciators, and its progeny; see "The Instrumental Image: Steichen at War", *Artforum*, December 1975, pp. 26-35.

10 See *Vues d'en haut: La photographie aérienne pendant la guerre de 1914-1918*, Paris: Musée de l'Armée; Nanterre: Musée d'Histoire Contemporaine, 1988.

11 Among numerous examples it may suffice to cite Robert Delaunay's 1922 painting of the Eiffel Tower modeled on a 1909 balloon photograph, which Le Corbusier used for the cover of his book *The Decorative Art of Today* (1925). See Newhall B, *Airborne Camera: The World from the Air and Outer Space*, New York: Hastings House, 1969, pp. 104-105. In the Soviet Union Alexander Rodchenko, El Lissitzky, and Kasimir Malevich pursued new spatial explorations in painting, sculpture, and photography explicitly informed by the airborne camera. Aaron Scharf summarises these trends in *Art and Photography*, 1968; London: Penguin, 1986, pp. 294-297. The vertical city views taken from Berlin's radio tower by László Moholy-Nagy suggest the continuity between the conditions of aerial photography and the modernist possibilities of extreme high angle composition generally.

12 In his *Theory of Film: The Redemption of Physical Reality*, New York: Oxford University Press, 1960, pp. 13-18, Siegfried Kracauer sees amplified in the aerial view a "precarious balance" between the "realist" and the "formative" affinities of the photograph. In the photography essay of 1927 Kracauer implied, however, that the formal possibilities of the photograph, emblematised in the aerial view's "reduction" or abstraction of its objects, is inseparable from its privileged access to modern reality. The ambivalence of the photograph enables the tensions of surface and depth, abstraction and documentary referentiality to inform modern consciousness regarding the material basis of phenomena. See Kracauer S, "Photography", in Levin, T Y, ed. and trans., *The Mass Ornament: Weimar Essays*, Cambridge, MA: Harvard University Press, 1995, pp. 61-63.

13 See Crispolti, E, *Il mito della macchina e altri temi del futurismo*, Roma: Celebes, 1969; Crispolti, E, *Aeropittura futurista aeropittori*, Modena: Galleria Fonte D'Abisso Edizioni, 1985; Crispolti, E, "Second Futurism", in Braun, E, ed., *Italian Art in the 20th Century: Painting and Sculpture 1900-1988*, Munich: Prestel Verlag, 1989, pp. 165-171; Passoni, F, *Aeropittura futurista*, Milano: Collezione "Le presenze" della Galleria Blu, 1970.

14 Cristpolti, E, "Second Futurism", pp. 168-169, cites Marinetti's claim of "five hundred Italian *aeropittori*" in his 1934 presentation at the Venice Biennale. Among them Crispolti counts the Ligurian ceramist Tullio D'Albisola, who trained Lucio Fontana and, at the other end of Italy, the Sicilian Futurist Pippo Rizzo who was an influence on the young Renato Guttuso.

15 The manifesto, dated 11 April 1930, was published on the first page of a special issue of *Il Futurismo*, 11 January 1931. It was signed by Marinetti and the *aero*-painter and photographer Tato, pseudonym of Guglielmo Sansoni.

16 See Lista, G, *Photographie Futuriste Italienne 1911-1939*, Paris: Musée d'Art Moderne de la Ville de Paris, 1981, pp. 74-75.

17 Lista, G, *Futurism & Photography*, London: Merrell, 2001, p. 145.

18 Originally in Mussolini, V, *Voli sulle Ambe*, Florence: Sansoni, 1937. English translation of this excerpt is in Barker, A J, *The Civilizing Mission: a History of the Italo-Ethiopian War of 1935-36*, New York: Dial Press, 1968, p. 234. Sekula quotes this passage in association with Walter Benjamin's citation from Marinetti's 1936 manifesto that celebrates "the fiery orchids of machine guns" in war's aesthetic forging of a "new architecture, like that of the big tanks, the geometrical formation flights, the smoke spirals from burning villages." See the "Epilogue" and last footnote to "The Work of Art in the Age of Mechanical Reproduction", *Illuminations*, Zohn, H, trans., New York: Schocken, 1969, pp. 241 and 251.

19 This was still on the pages of *Corriere padano*, October 26, 1938 and December 10, 1938. Sam Rohdie translates segments from these reviews in his *Antonioni*, London: BFI, 1990, p. 30.

20 One finds little in film production of the period that correlates to such an oscillating perception as Antonioni's article suggests. Many films narrativised, like *Luciano Serra Pilota*, a romanticised incorporation of modernity and regionalist, or proto-Neorealist values: consider Alessandro Blasetti's *Terra madre* (1931) and *Vecchia guardia* (1935), or Roberto Rossellini's *La nave bianca* (1941) and *Un Pilota ritorna* (1942). Documentary cinema was engaged in the raising of modernity to consciousness, yet again in heroic/poetic forms that left little room for interrogation of historical conditions: e.g. the work of Raffaello Matarazzo and Francesco Pasinetti. Curiously, among journals produced by Istituto LUCE to inform about Fascism's accomplishments in the spaces of daily life, in rural, industrial, urban, or colonial landscapes in transition, one finds scattered instances wherein an engagement with modernity is grafted on an open chronicle form that allows for the contingent, the dissonant trace to persist against the gripping embrace of Fascist instrumental filmmaking. For detailed discussion see the full version of my essay cited above.

21 Geoffrey Nowell-Smith dwells on this return to the Po valley by those who will become the most significant Post War Italian filmmakers in "Away from the Po Valley Blues", *PIX*, 1, Winter 1993/4, pp. 24-30.

22 My use of of the term "contingency" is influenced by T J Clark's discussion in *Farewell to an Idea: Episodes from a History of Modernism*, New Haven, Connecticut: Yale University Press, 1999, pp. 7-11. Clark suggests that Fascism's appeal lay in the promise of immanence and certainty it offered as a solution to the difficulty of modernity's contingency.

Remapping the Muck: Place and Pastoral in Afro-American Studies
Jia-Rui Chong

The most famous slave narrative, *The Narrative of the Life of Frederick Douglass*, 1845, begins with spatial coordinates: "I was born in Tuckahoe, near Hillsborough, and about twelve miles from Easton, in Talbot county, Maryland." Douglass, whose autobiography is a foundational text for Afro-American Studies, did not know much about who his father was or when he was born, but he did know one thing: where he was coming from. Such precision of place reminds us that the slave experience was very much defined by geography.[1] After all, boundaries between freedom and bondage, relative danger and relative safety, could be mapped according to the Mason-Dixon Line and the Ohio River. By a simple spatial displacement, the move from Tuckahoe (the agricultural South) to New York (the urban North), Douglass could transform himself from 'slave' to 'man'. Even if the trope of correspondence between moving North and achieving liberty did not necessarily hold true in fact, geography has been a concern in Afro-American literature since its beginnings. In this paper, I will begin by sketching out the place of 'place' in Afro-American Studies, discuss the different lenses that can be used to view place, especially the pastoral lens, and then choose one case study, the swamp, to test what I see as distinctive Afro-American attitudes to place.[2]

That the Afro-American experience can be seen generally in terms of dislocations makes the sense of place very important. The Middle Passage of 1526-1808, the Great Migration of 1910-1930, segregation, the concentration of blacks in urban housing projects, and more recently the departure of middle class blacks from cities into suburbs and from northern cities back to the South mark different eras in black American history. We can see the mid-twentieth century Civil Rights movement as a struggle for place: a place on a bus, a place in the classroom. Although Houston A Baker argues that Afro-American cultural production is 'atopic' – that is, placeless – I will argue that Afro-American cultural production is actually quite 'topophilic'.[3]

In evaluating attitudes to place, we can specify two extremes of responses to the environment: hostile and celebratory. In the Afro-American cultural production that is hostile to the environment – in the work of Richard Wright, for example – hostility is often used to register discontent with mainstream American politics and society. It is not surprising, then, that such writing takes place in the city, since rural idylls have typically reinforced the status quo in America and glorified the South, a place that historically figures as a site of horror for blacks.[4] Billie Holiday's "Strange Fruit", 1939, is an example of taking the southern idyll head on: the song does not contradict the idea of a fertile Southern landscape, but shows how that fertility yields too much death and torture.[5] But compare "Strange Fruit" to Alice Walker's *In Search of Our Mother's Gardens*, 1982, where the landscape "of silent bitterness and hate" can be turned into creative potential for the black artist, because the South is also full of "neighborly kindness and sustaining love".[6] This is a kind of response to the landscape I will call 'pastoral'.

Because of its tangled history, "pastoral" is a term that is difficult to use precisely. But I follow William Empson and Raymond Williams when I use it as a "structure of feeling" that idealises non-urban landscapes – especially gardens – where 'simple' folk live contentedly in communal harmony without the contamination of crude lucre. Critics of the genre have pointed out that pastoral, which works on implicit comparisons (e.g., 'nature' versus 'city', 'rural' versus 'urban'), has tended to idealise feudal values against encroaching capitalist agriculture, efface labour from the landscape, and "imply a beautiful relation between rich and poor" through artifice.[7] It has hardly been a genre of protest, encouraging complacency rather than revolution.

Leo Marx argues for a distinctively "American" pastoral, forged in the 1840s, in which a "counterforce" introduces the pressure of time and change upon the "idyllic" so a "middle landscape" can be established. The symbolic representation of this design is the machine in the garden.[8] However, Marx's work, one of the core books in American Studies, confines itself to the canonical white, male, heterosexual writers. Although he uses the term "American" unqualified, his study of American pastoral overlooks a wide range of American writers, including those who are women, Native American, black and/or queer.

Scholars such as Annette Kolodny have tried to complicate Marx's formulation with respect to gender, but so far there have been few studies of an "Afro-American pastoral".[9] There are several good books that examine place in Afro-American culture, including Melvin Dixon's *Ride Out the Wilderness*, 1987, and Farah Jasmine Griffin's *Who Set You Flowin'?*, 1995.[10] Dixon studies the motifs of the wilderness, the underground and the mountain-top, showing how they compose a moral geography of social and political progress. But his landscapes are allegorical, and he seems less interested in particular, non-universal places. Griffin reads place more sensitively, appraising images of the rural South through the lens of northern migration narratives. For her, the urban is primary, which only reminds us that space should also be read from the non-urban perspective.

Few critics have tried to describe an Afro-American pastoral or black American pastoral as such. Robert Bone, in *Down Home*, 1975, deals with pastoral and anti-pastoral traditions in short fiction. Clearly extending his sympathies to the latter, Bone is more concerned with condemning the way "jungle-bunny" writers used the pastoral mode than with describing their pastoral landscapes.[11] Maria K Mootry, however, does try to describe "black pastoral" in her doctoral dissertation, *Studies in Black Pastoral*, 1974, and in an essay, "Love and Death in the Black Pastoral", 1977. In her dissertation, she does not draw any comprehensive conclusions about what Afro-American writing might have to say to the pastoral genre or assert the existence of a distinctive mode, choosing instead to describe Empsonian versions of idealised rural life. In the later article however, she does specify a "black pastoral": one that expresses "simultaneously the artist's commitment to an American Dream and his awareness of forces that impinge on that dream". Her usage puns on the word "black", such that the term means Afro-American but also suggests how a pastoral ideal is "juxtaposed with some sort of macabre death".[12] These works are a start, but more ecosensitive readings of Afro-American literature, especially pastorals, are necessary to complicate the existing body of writing about the American environment and to fill in the gaps of Afro-American criticism.

To narrow the study, I will focus on the South because it is a particularly contested terrain with respect to race, gender, and class. This area along the south-eastern coast is important because it is where the idea of 'America' began and where white America most explicitly inscribed its pastoral fantasy. Indeed, the first European colonists saw the Southern plantation as a potentially paradisiacal refuge and centre of cultivation.[13] For Thomas Jefferson, it was the blueprint for an ideal agrarian republic. But for black people, who first appeared upon the shores of Virginia as things-to-be-owned rather than as a people-who-could-own, the Southern plantation was more problematic.

The primary ecological feature of this area is wetland, defined by ecologists as a place that has shallow water or saturated soil, accumulates organic plant materials that decompose slowly, and supports a variety of plants adapted to saturated conditions.[14] "If drained", notes the *Dictionary of Environmental Science*, a wetland is "often highly fertile".[15] "Swamp", a kind of wetland, has become a catch-all term for the meeting of land and water and has become identified with the Old South. Although colonists in New England also encountered wetlands, the fetid, mosquito-ridden conditions in the South proved more troublesome and more prevalent.

For the most part, mainstream white American culture has seen the swamp as a problem: an inhospitable, diseased, disorderly, feminised and hellish place in need of reclamation. Most recently we can see the negative connotations in the way the botched presidential election in 2000 in the United States was characterised as a "swamp" or a "morass".[16] But swamps have had a long history of ill repute. The nineteenth century guardian of morals, Harriet Beecher Stowe, did not even attempt to veil her disdain: she described Southern swamps as "regions of helpless disorder, where the abundant growth and vegetation of nature, sucking up its forces from the humid soil, seem to rejoice in a savage exuberance, and bid defiance to all human efforts to penetrate and subdue".[17] It certainly helped the moral condemnation that the kinds of animals in swamps, especially the cursed Satan snake of Genesis, matched the iconography of Judeo-Christian Hell. The response of European colonists to such evil, then, was to 'reclaim' the land: that is, to use gangs of black slaves to dredge and drain the land to ready it for cotton, rice and sugar fields, as well as the spacious Big House. Such 'improvements', however, did not entirely obliterate the swamp's threats: many white families still felt besieged from all sides by sticky heat and noxious infection, seeking 'healthful' vacations on higher, drier land.[18] Moreover, there was an obsessive fear of swamps as strongholds of black resistance. Ever since the flight of Nat Turner and his band to the Great Dismal Swamp in 1831, whites were fascinated by slaves' ability to survive in wetlands and also worried that the fugitive gangs would lure away obedient slaves.[19]

The swamp, metonymic of the South, persists as a *topos* throughout Afro-American cultural production as well, and provides a litmus test for differing, highly-charged responses to the American environment. I will trace the historical arc of Afro-American responses to the swamp, with particular attention to Zora Neale Hurston's novel *Their Eyes Were Watching God*, 1937, and go on to discuss why such a study matters.

At the beginning of the Afro-American experience, blacks' primary interaction with the swamp involved dredging it for plantations and living on a 'reclaimed' parcel of land surrounded by it. The swamp could provide a short respite from harsh plantation life, a passageway to freedom, or even a new site of settlement. According to Eugene Genovese, the amount of time a slave spent in a swamp depended on how much he or she depended on others – slaves on his or her own plantation, slaves on other plantations or friendly whites – for supplies.[20] Once slaves scrabbled over the fence into the wetlands fringing the plantation, starvation was a very real fear. It was tiring, difficult work to catch rabbits or the occasional possum, as Solomon Northup explains in the self-authored *Twelve Years a Slave*, 1853. Moreover, bad weather, disease-carrying mosquitoes, snakes and alligators often foiled the best-laid plans. In the swamp, nature existed in its most brutal form, full of 'wild beasts' and thick plant growth that obscured clear lines of vision.[21] Only some slaves considered it a final destination, for these wetlands were uncertain places that had the potential for escape and survival, but also death.[22] Moreover, when plantation owners discovered that a slave had tried to escape, they sent in armed hunters with bloodhounds. Because bloodhounds easily overtook running men, and could pick up scent trails even after prey crossed a river, slave narratives dwell on their particular ferocity and killer instinct. The dogs, more than the hunters, struck terror in the hearts of slaves.[23]

But slaves made more than 8,400 escape attempts between 1790 and 1860.[24] Though fear of the muddy wilderness led many slaves to pray for God's protection in the swamp or recall stories of Biblical deliverance, it was certainly not a God-forsaken place. The swamp regularly hosted meetings or conversion experiences for evangelical Christians, set the scene for transplanted Yoruba, Ashanti and Dahomey practices that required trees and water, and often served as the home of the plantation conjurer.[25]

For slaves, this ability to relocate themselves was empowering, especially in a world where movement was regulated by the slavemaster. In literary history, narratives about slave life were also about escape, showing how the popular nineteenth century white travel narrative "mask[ed] another [narrative] of confinement and immobility".[26] Slave narratives were compelling because they drew attention to blacks' geographical restriction in an age in which the popular imagination saw itself moving freely about. Lisa Brawley argues that because fugitive slave narratives were produced "precisely during the period in which tourism was being codified as a pedagogy and paradigm of normative American personhood", the fugitive slave became a "fugitive tourist" whose story mimed the conditions of national mobility and marked its limits.[27] Although a sojourn in the swamp was hardly armed revolt, it was a defiant act against a system of racialised circumscription.

What happened to attitudes towards the swamp when slaves could become more than tourists in the landscape? With Reconstruction, when slaves could (ostensibly) own property, African Americans found that they had a new potential for mastering the land. W E B DuBois considers the freed person's relationship to the swamp in the didactic *The Quest of the Silver Fleece*, 1911, set at the turn of the century. DuBois' swamp can be a beautiful place, full of "great shadowy oaks and limpid pools, lone, naked trees and sweet flowers; the whispering and flitting of wild things, and the winging of furtive birds", but pleasant descriptions such as this are fragile and rare. More often, the swamp is depicted as "sinister and sullen" territory, a gothic hell where "devils" and "witches" work evil deeds amid deep-rooted thorns, "long gnarled fingers of the tough little trees", "oozing mud and fetid vapors".[28] While in DuBois' narrative all that is white and sanitised is not necessarily ideal, he does not present the swamp *qua* swamp as a desirable landscape. It is too full of evil: drinking, exploitative interracial sex, and Elspeth (DuBois' swamp monster who practices witchcraft and encourages all of the aforementioned sins in her cabin). The swamp in *Quest* opposes cultivation of all kinds (the agricultural cultivation of the Southern plantation and the intellectual cultivation of a cosmopolitan education) and the built Big House.

It is only when the main character Zora returns to the swamp with a sophisticated education and the intent to cultivate the land for the black people of Toombs County, Alabama that the swamp nears an ideal landscape. Racial salvation, the problem DuBois is trying to work through in this novel, can only occur in "the transformed swamp – now a swamp in name only", not the place of exuberant undergrowth and mysticism described at the beginning of the novel.[29] Even if this Jeffersonian agrarian 'garden' is more racially egalitarian and does not efface labour from the landscape,

DuBois' novel still reproduces much of the European colonists' prejudice against wetlands. It is still preoccupied with 'improving' the swamp.

Zora Neale Hurston's novel *Their Eyes Were Watching God*, however, enjoys the swamp *as it is*, alligators, big cypresses and all. In Hurston's rewriting of the swamp story, it is a place of pleasure where Janie chooses to go and leaves unwillingly. Although some critics classify *Quest* as pastoral, it is not until *Their Eyes* that the structure of feeling towards the swamp takes on a pastoral quality.[30] Even though Hurston's first description of the swamp – Nanny's story – recalls the fearsome terrain of the slave narratives, Janie does not passively accept received knowledge.[31] Preferring to find things out for herself, she asserts, "Ah done lived Grandma's way, now Ah means tuh live mine", and goes happily and hopefully to "de muck".[32] Her journey remaps the values laid on the territory by the mainstream American and also the Afro-American imagination.

In one sense, Nature – especially the unfettered "big beans, big cane, big weeds, big everything" kind found in the Everglades – is the heroine of this novel. Very early on, Hurston identifies Janie with that kind of vibrant fecundity: more specifically, the sexy pear tree in bloom. Her voluptuousness is the same voluptuousness as the growth on the muck: "Ground so rich that everything went wild."[33] This land of abundance does not resemble the place where starvation threatened runaway slaves. Nor is it the place mainstream attitudes associate with debauched (especially female) sexuality. Here, Janie's sex drive is seen as healthy and *natural*. (Thus only Vergible Woods – whose name sounds like Veritable Woods [True Nature] – is the right man for her.) Only in the Everglades can Janie's "soul crawl... out from its hiding place" and enjoy itself.[34] It is a place of "dancing, fighting, singing, crying, laughing, winning and losing love every hour. Work all day for money, fight all night for love. The rich black earth clinging to bodies and biting the skin like ants."[35] Although money is a reason for going to the swamp, it is not an end in itself. Tea Cake and Janie manage to create their own "fun and foolishness" despite their lack of cash, scorning those like Jodie Sparks whose happiness depends on the money that props up social position.[36]

What terrorised previous swamp visitors does not scare Janie. She enjoys the dangerous game of night-time alligator-hunting and is not crippled by a fear of snakes. Moreover, going deeper into the Southern jungle does not inspire old slave fears of being 'sold down the river'. Rather, Janie's southerly travels bring a growing contentment and subjectivity instead of more suffering and 'stuckness'. The only slave-and-swamp-associated fear that still has any teeth is the bloodhound. Tea Cake gets the better of a weird dog-cow monster which makes a cameo at the end of the novel, but he does not escape unscathed. Because the dog has rabies, the bite dooms Tea Cake, scars Janie (when Tea Cake bites her in the arm), and forces her to kill the man she loves. Indeed, Hurston's Everglades are not all sweetness and light: although it is in the muck that Janie can be herself, people work and suffer here as well as play. The danger of disease and death is real; her relationship with the muck is not carefree tourism. Indeed, there is always the awesome power of the natural world to reclaim the swamp from human settlement. The storm, described in Biblically-inflected language that conflates God and Nature, reduces the swamp-dwellers to the humble position of Noah (i.e., watching God), destroys homes and leaves piles of dead bodies.[37] Yet the hurricane also sanctifies the swamp as a location for divine revelation. So even though mainstream convention sees the swamp as a God-forsaken place, Hurston, like many Afro-American artists, invests this landscape with positive spiritual significance, a place to witness God's work. For Janie, memories of the muck mingle both love and terror. When she is back in Eatonville at the end of the novel, she must cope with Tea Cake's painful death. But the final image is a *rapprochement* with the landscape that caused her lover's death: Janie pulls "in her horizon like a great fish-net" and drapes it over her shoulder.[38] This last image of healing rounds out an Empsonian pastoral harmony among people themselves and between people and the environment. At ease with herself and the world, Janie has arrived home.

After *Their Eyes*, swamps continue to appear in Afro-American cultural production. Toni Morrison's novel *Tar Baby*, 1981, shows an excellent awareness of the history of swamp representation, naming this place of jelly-like rot and entrapping hags "seins des vieilles" (witch's tit) and using it to embody disorder, uncleanness, the irrational, the magical, and ancient, jealous female sexuality.[39] But even if the swamp is scary, the characters in the novel come to respect its power. The recent film *Eve's Bayou*, 1997, also plays up the gothic characteristics of swamps with lingering camera shots of eerie tendrils and reflecting water in the Louisiana Bayou.[40] But the uncertain, the feminine, and the weird are all good traits. Eve's maturation requires learning respect for the mysterious and learning to negotiate the muck.

So why does a study of the swamp matter really? First, it matters in American literary history, showing us the diversity within 'American' pastoral. It provides a cautionary tale against lumping Afro-American spatial perception with an unhyphenated 'American' one, since it took until the late twentieth century for mainstream America to value swamps as places – to call them 'wetlands' with a positive connotation.[41] It also provides a cautionary tale against homogenising all Afro-American spatial perception without considering gender since stories of female empowerment are often situated in the swamp. Second, it reminds us that studies of the Afro-American experience should include studies of the 'country' as well as the 'city' (so far as the 'city' can be distinguished from the 'country'). Most studies of place in the Afro-American experience have concentrated on the urban experience: the Harlem Renaissance, Richard Wright's Chicago, the Black Arts Movement, etc.. Of course, this is not surprising considering that most blacks lived in urban centres in the twentieth century and cities are sites of great literary production and dissemination.[42] It is only more recently that black artists and critics have set about reclaiming the South as a site of black creative production.

But most importantly, an examination of swamp representation in Afro-American writing can make us reconsider the usual dismissal of pastoral as a mode that encourages complacence. Richard Wright condemned Hurston's novel for "swing[ing] like a pendulum eternally in that safe and narrow orbit in which America likes to see the Negro live". He cared little for *Their Eyes* because, in depicting contented characters, it did not hold the South responsible for terror against blacks or dramatise any significant confrontation of blacks against whites; it only reinscribed the happy darky stereotype.[43] Wright's complaint is the same complaint levelled at more traditional pastoral: that pastoral falsely assumes a happy relation between landlord and tenant. Wright certainly had cause for suspicion, since, in 1930s America, pastoral implied conservative politics. Apologists for slavery had long praised the sympathetic connection between black people and the land and thought that divorcing them was misguided. Groups such as the "Fugitive" writers argued that such a divorce was unhealthy for black people and for the nation as a whole.[44] So affirming the connection between black people and the land could downplay the history of suffering and provide a reason *not* to improve black peoples' situation. But while it is true that Hurston's personal, particular story does not support any (Marxist) model of progress, Wright is unfair. His criticism does not allow for conflicting interpretations of black people's location in America and overlooks the possibility that descriptions of landscape can protest. Hurston's vision of the undrained swamp as a beautiful place regardless of its agricultural worth is subversive: if slavery was awful because it put a monetary value on human life in a capitalist economy, reappraising swamps could bring into question how any thing – or person – is valued.

Because the swamp is a 'border ecosystem' and 'ecotone' where dualist notions of strict land and strict water cannot function, it provides a particularly apt objective correlative to concerns of race. In the black-and-white discourse of race relations in America, swamps embody grey indeterminacy. "We cannot essentialize wetlands", William Howarth points out, "because they are hybrid and multivalent."[45] The difficulties that ecology confronts when it tries to define wetlands have their analogy in the 'social science' of racial definition. Wetland scientists William J Mitsch and James G Gosselink note that "because fluctuating water levels can vary from season to season and year to year in the same wetland type, the boundaries of wetlands cannot always be determined by the presence of water at any one time'.[46] If we substitute in 'race' or 'blackness" for wetlands and 'black blood' for water, we see that the statement could very well offer a critique of the arbitrary one-fourth or one-eighth rules of race that existed for so long in America.

Thus a study of Afro-American responses to the swamp can open larger political questions. Landscape vocabulary has so permeated the Afro-American imagination that the concepts are adapted for discourses outside that of just agriculture or geography. Consider, for instance, Martin Luther King, Jr's paraphrase of Isaiah in his famous 1963 speech: "I have a dream that one day every valley shall be exalted, every hill and mountain shall be made low, the rough places shall be made plain, and the crooked places shall be made straight and the glory of the Lord will be revealed and all flesh shall see it together."[47] In choosing this specific passage, he emphasises the analogous position of devalued places and devalued African Americans. An ecosensitive text can thus become one more alternative code of protest and self-definition for a people whose modes of communication have been historically policed. As the narrator of Ralph Ellison's *Invisible Man*, 1952 says, "If you don't know where you are, you probably don't know who you are."[48]

So we must bring politics, economics, history, race and gender into the garden. This is what Jamaica Kincaid said she did at a recent Garden Conservancy celebration. "Why must people insist that the garden is a place of rest and repose, a place to forget the care of the world, a place in which to distance yourself from the painful responsibility that comes with being a human being?" she asks. Although the audience thought her question "unforgivable", she reminds us that we should not ignore the labour of slaves in creating plantation gardens or the modern-day people who create our own gardens.[49] Though Kincaid might further investigate her own privileged position as erstwhile planter, she does prompt us to consider, in our appreciation of gardens, who plants the flowers we so admire, what work was involved in that planting, what might have existed there before, what exists around it now and why. We started with Frederick Douglass, who put place into politics; we end now by putting politics into place.

1 Douglass, F, "Narrative of the Life of Frederick Douglass", *Norton Anthology of American Literature*, Baym, Nina, et al, eds., 4th ed, vol. 1, New York: Norton, 1994, p. 1939. The specification of a place of, but not a date of birth, continued as a slave narrative convention. See Olney, J, "'I Was Born': Slave Narratives, Their Status as Autobiography, and as Literature", *The Slave's Narrative*, Davis, C and Gates, H L, Jr, eds., New York: Oxford University Press, 1985, pp. 152-153.

2 I use 'place' as Lawrence Buell uses it: a space to which meaning has been ascribed and which has been assigned distinctness and value. Any location has the potential to be a place. Its 'thereness' is indispensable to the vision of the place whether virtually or immediately perceived. This 'thereness', of course, is elastic since places evolve, degrade and ameliorate. See Buell, L, "The Placeness of Place", *Writing for an Endangered World*, Cambridge, MA: Harvard University Press, 2001, chapter 2.

3 Baker, H, *Blues, Ideology, and Afro-American Literature: A Vernacular Theory*, London: University of Chicago Press, 1984, p. 5. 'Topophilia' is geographer Yi-Fu Tuan's word for a perception of place that broadly includes "all of the human being's affective ties with the material environment". See Tuan, Y-F, *Topophilia*, New York: Columbia University Press, 1974, p. 93.

4 By 'the South' and 'Old South' I mean the states along the south-eastern Atlantic coast that did not give up black slavery until the Civil War.

5 The lyrics were written by Lewis Allan, a pseudonym for Abel Meeropol, but the song has become identified with Holiday's interpretation.

6 Walker, A, *In Search of Our Mother's Gardens*, London: Harcourt Brace Jovanovich, 1983, p. 21.

7 For various definitions of 'pastoral', see Preminger, A and Brogan, T V F, eds., *The New Princeton Encyclopedia of Poetry and Poetics*, Princeton: Princeton University Press, 1993; Empson, W, *Some Versions of Pastoral*, London: Chatto and Windus, 1968; and Williams, R, *The Country and the City*, London: Hogarth, 1973.

8 Marx, L, *The Machine in the Garden*, Oxford: Oxford University Press, 1964, pp. 24-32, 226.

9 Kolodny, A, *The Lay of the Land*, Chapel Hill: University of North Carolina Press, 1975, p. 7.

10 Dixon, M, *Ride Out the Wilderness: Geography and Identity in Afro-American Literature*, Urbana: University of Illinois Press, 1987. Griffin, F J, *"Who Set You Flowin"": the African-American Migration Narrative*, Oxford: Oxford University Press, 1995.

11 Bone, R, *Down Home*, New York: Putnam, 1975, pp. xvi, 124-138.

12 Mootry, M, "Studies in Black Pastoral: Five Afro-American Writers," diss. Northwestern University, 1974; and Mootry, M, "Love and Death in the Black Pastoral", *Obsidian*, vol. 3, Summer 1977, pp. 5-11.

13 See Cash, W, *Mind of the South*, New York: Knopf, 1941; Harrison, *Female Pastoral*, and Singal, D, *The War Within*, Chapel Hill: University of North Carolina Press, 1982.

14 Mitsch, W J and Gosselink, J G, *Wetlands*, 2nd ed., New York: Van Nostrand Reinhold, 1993, pp. 22, 32.

15 *Dictionary of Environmental Science*, Glasgow: Collins, 1990, p. 420.

16 See Berke, R, "Contesting the Vote: The Florida Governor", *New York Times*, 8 Dec 2000, p. 1, and Brownstein, R, "The Presidential Transition", *Los Angeles Times*, 17 Dec 2000, p. 1.

17 Stowe, H B, *Dred*, Boston: Phillips, Sampson, 1856, p. 189.

18 See Aiken, C, *The Cotton Plantation South Since the Civil War*, London: Johns Hopkins University Press, 1998, for more on nucleated settlement patterns.

19 Miller, D, *Dark Eden*, Cambridge: Cambridge University Press, 1989, pp. 90-94. Cowan, T, "The Slave in the Swamp", *Keep Your Head to the Sky*, Gundaker, G, ed., Charlottesville: Virginia University Press, 1998. pp. 193-207.

20 Genovese, E, *Roll, Jordan, Roll: the World the Slaves Made*, New York: Vintage, 1974, pp. 648-651.

21 Of the slave narratives I have read, Northup, S, *Twelve Years a Slave, Puttin' on Ole Massa*, Osofsky, G, ed., New York: Harper and Row, 1969, is the most descriptive of the swamp environment.

22 See Cowan, "The Slave in the Swamp", p. 197.

23 See Northup, *Twelve Years*, p. 297 and Genovese, *Roll*, p. 651.

24 This number comes from the number of newspaper advertisements for runaway slaves in five states between 1790 and 1860 in Franklin, J H and Schweninger, L, *Runaway Slaves: Rebels on the Plantation*, Oxford: Oxford University Press, 1999, p. 328. Genovese gives the figure 1,011 as the number of slaves that lit out in one year – in this case, 1850 (648).

25 Dixon, *Ride Out*, p. 3 and Cowan, "The Slave in the Swamp", p. 205.

26 Hardack, R, "Water Pollution and Motion Sickness: Rites of Passage in Nineteenth Century Slave and Travel Narratives", *Emerson Society Quarterly*, vol. 41 no. 1, 1995, p. 1.

27 Brawley, L, "Fugitive Nation: Slavery, Travel and Technologies of American Identity, 1830-1860", diss. University of Chicago, 1995, pp. 7-10.

28 DuBois, W E B, *The Quest of the Silver Fleece*, New York: AMS Press, 1972, pp. 13, 45, 90, 153.

29 DuBois, *The Quest*, p. 426.

30 See Mootry, "Studies".

31 Hurston, *Their Eyes*, pp. 17-18.

32 Hurston, *Their Eye*, p. 108.

33 Hurston, *Their Eyes*, p. 123.

34 Hurston, *Their Eyes*, p. 122.

35 Hurston, *Their Eyes*, p. 125.

36 Hurston, *Their Eyes*, p. 122.

37 Compare the passage to Genesis 6:1-8:12.

38 Hurston, *Their Eyes*, p. 184.

39 Morrison, T, *Tar Baby*, New York: Signet, 1981, p. 8.

40 Lemmons, K, (dir.), *Eve's Bayou*, Trimark, 1997.

41 Although Miller says the turning point came in the 1850s, and William Howarth the 1700s, according to Buell and Mitsch and Gosselink the general populace was still repulsed by swamps until the 1970s. See Miller, *Dark Eden*, pp. 8-17; Howarth, W, "Imagined Territory", *New Literary History*, vol. 30, Summer 1999, pp. 509-540; Buell, *Writing*, chapter 6; Mitsch and Gosselink, *Wetlands*, pp. 565-567.

42 See Andrews, A and Fonseca, J, *The Atlas of American Society*, New York: New York University Press, 1995, pp. 68-69.

43 Wright, R, "Two Negro Novels", *New Masses*, 5 October 1937, p. 25.

44 See Rubin, L, ed., *I'll Take My Stand*, London: Louisiana State University Press, 1977, pp. 260-261.

45 Howarth, "Imagined Territory", p. 520.

46 Mitsch and Gosselink, *Wetlands*, p. 23.

47 King, M L K, Jr "I Have a Dream", in Gates, H L, Jr and McKay, N, eds., *Norton Anthology of African American Literature*, New York: Norton, 1997, p. 82.

48 Ellison, R, *Invisible Man,* New York: Random House, 1992, p. 569.

49 Kincaid, J, "Sowers and Reapers", *New Yorker*, 22 January 2001, pp. 41-45.

Emergent Landscapes
Patricia Macdonald

in collaboration with Angus Macdonald

From series:
This is not a natural wilderness: and it is not a picture of a natural wilderness either:
9 frames from 360-degree aerial, almost treeless, panorama above the Doire Daraich (a remnant old-growth woodland), from Rannoch Moor in the northeast to Ben Nevis in the northwest, Central Highlands, Scotland, 1993/2001, and details, Fujichrome prints

These images show an ecologically 'devastated terrain' which once supported much greater biodiversity, and a much larger human population than it does now. The most significant indicator of this loss is the lack of natural tree-cover. A mosaic of different kinds of native woodland, heath and wetland, with its associated varied wildlife, once occupied 50-75% of the land area. This has now been reduced, mainly by felling, burning and continued over-grazing, principally by domesticated sheep and deer populations maintained high for hunting as a sport, along with historical climate change, to a figure of 2-4%. The result is a 'wet desert' which is very far from being a 'natural wilderness'. It has been estimated that a sustainable maximum red-deer population for Scotland, one which did not seriously damage the land, might be around 50,000; the present red-deer population, due to lack of appropriate management over wide areas of the Highlands, is in the region of 400,000.

From series:
*This is not a
natural
wilderness,
and it is not
a picture of
a natural
wilderness,
either:*
Detail: Treeless
landscape, deer
tracks and
wooded island,
Rannoch Moor,
Scotland, 1993,
Fujichrome print

On a physical level, these images describe ice-sheets melting in spring. In the first image, the cracking process looks violent; in the third image, it appears more 'joyous'; the central image is a place of stasis or potentiality.

At a metaphorical level they explore psychological meanings of 'freezing' and 'thawing': the thawing of the heart, the softening of harsh attitudes; the process of opening up, of accepting incoming energy into frozen areas of the mind.

Change of state series, no. 1: Melting ice, Loch Moraig and Loch Mathair-Eite, Rannoch Moor and Forest of Atholl, Scotland (triptych), 1990. Fujichrome prints

This piece relates to Rilke's eponymous poem-cycle. It conveys the idea of loss, but also those of sensuous delight in the things of the world, of acceptance and of resolution, which Rilke profoundly explores. It may also be read as a kind of ecological parable.

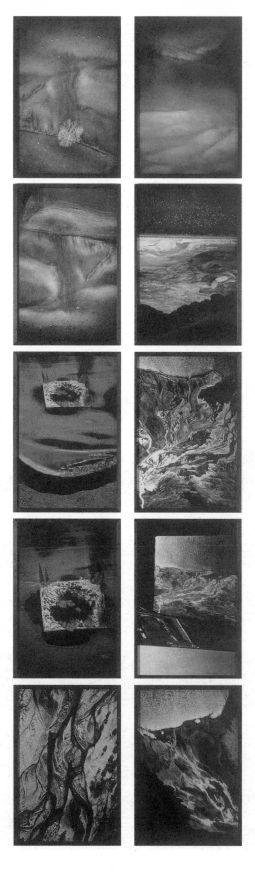

The Sonnets to Orpheus (10-part work), 1995, and detail (no. 4), Ilfochrome prints

Patricia Macdonald in collaboration with Angus Macdonald

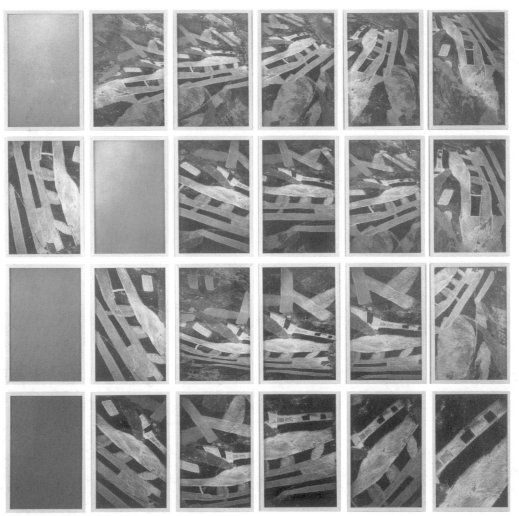

This piece shows a grouse-moor – a deadly board-game – seen simultaneously in various spatial ways and from various points of view, including that of the hunted grouse. The piece considers ideas of freedom and constraint, of hunting and being hunted, and different systems of perception.

It contrasts two superimposed versions (actual and conceptual) of the linear grid of mechanist modernism with the non-linear, circling feedback-loops of the 'strange attractor', one of the mathematical 'signatures' of the emerging holistic, 'organicist' world-view.

Patricia Macdonald in collaboration with Angus Macdonald

Landscape, Identity and Estrangement

Landscape, Identity, and Estrangement
Gillian Rose

For Jean-François Lyotard, estrangement is landscape's essential quality. In his essay "Scapeland", it is the unknowability of its material qualities that estrange the subject from the landscape, a landscape that is "so many untamable states of matter".[1] In this essay, the sense of an outsider relation to landscape is most tangible, and all the chapters in this section also explore the geometry of an outside inextricably bound into the interiority of a landscape.

Ursula Seibold-Bultmann in her paper addresses the estrangement that may follow the difference between the perception of land and its representation. Her discussion of some recent land art suggests that it marks the limit of language's ability to describe the land. The other contributors, however, address estrangement as a quality of the power relations articulated through particular visions of landscape. In these landscapes, identity is paramount: who you are, who you are seen to be, how you see and are seen. These dynamics are structured by social power. Classed, gendered, racialised and nationalised positions are produced through these landscapes, which enable some subjects to produce claims over others. Michelle Sipe explores a certain kind of nineteenth century middle class English and Scottish femininity as it deployed a particular vision of landscape to assert its own identity in bourgeois households of the time. But that femininity also looked out beyond its landscaped gardens and saw other people as in need of landscaping; landscape both empowered some women and made others the subjects of and for improvement.

The papers by Deborah Sutton, Sandra Scham and Robert Grant also all engage with efforts to remake the landscapes of others, and in so doing to make various estrangements. Sutton looks at the British Empire in India and its persistent efforts to aestheticise the Toda of the Niligri Hills in southern India, which misrecognised many of their practices. Scham takes the contemporary case of Palestine, exploring the ways in which archaeology is appropriated by a politics of precedence. Robert Grant looks at the publicity material produced to persuade people to leave Britain and settle in various colonies, again in the nineteenth century. He too notes those whom this material left estranged in its production of frontier landscapes: indigenous populations of many kinds.

This section suggests then that estrangement may be an innate quality of landscape, an effect of its bringing together of inside and outside, or representation and material matter. But it is also very often an effect of power: the ability of some notions of landscape to displace others and hence, as Grant suggests, to both depend on and reproduce certain 'social architectures'.

1   Lyotard, Jean-François, "Scapeland", *The Lyotard Reader*, Benjamin, Andrew, ed., Oxford: Blackwell, 1989, p. 215.

"From the River Unto the Land of the Philistines": the 'Memory' of Iron Age Landscapes in Modern Visions of Palestine
Sandra Arnold Scham

The Battle of the Archaeologists

In the summer of 2000, before the Middle East erupted in what has now become a grinding daily cycle of violence and retribution, *The Jerusalem Report* published an article on Iron Age Palestine, an interesting departure for this journal. Although archaeology is a matter of great interest in Israel it is not a subject that regularly finds its way into news magazines. The story was featured on the cover and illustrated by a photograph of Michelangelo's *David* accompanied by a rather lurid headline, "Demolishing David", appearing in dangerously close proximity to the uncircumcised genitals of the famous statue.[1] The article purported to describe, among other things, the real story of how some Israeli archaeologists are collaborating with Palestinians to destroy the Bible.

Israeli scholars who question or reject the paradigms of the past, have always been vulnerable to accusations of providing aid and comfort to the enemy. In few places in the world is the distant past given such immediacy as in the region that was once known as Ancient Palestine.[2] The fact that the founding of the State of Israel in 1948 was partially predicated on the Biblical history of the region during the Iron Age has made this period a subject of deeply patriotic sentiments which have prompted numerous public and private efforts to make the past 'come alive' for people living and visiting there. Israel is the land of the ubiquitous ancient history diorama, where models and simulations of Ancient Israelite buildings appear in the most unlikely places. A new Israeli museum, opened during the current *intifada,* shows a virtual Jewish Temple rising above the actual ruins of an Islamic palace.[3] The *Jerusalem Time Elevator*, an exhibit designed to frighten small children into an appreciation of their heritage by showing, in three-dimensional living colour, virtually every conflagration that has affected Jerusalem since its founding, is in the city's international press building.

Palestinian claims of an historical occupation dating from the Bronze and Iron Ages have less apparent physical manifestations but are steadily growing in popularity. Some Palestinian scholars disavow the Bible and its relevance to archaeology, but others suggest that the Biblical narratives support Palestinian views of the past. Yasser Arafat is known to have lectured Palestinian school children on the importance of remembering their Jebusite (Canaanite) ancestors in Jerusalem. This surprisingly iconoclastic attempt by a Muslim to establish cultural roots in the *Jahiliah* (the dark ages before Islam) has, as a clear sub-text, the contention that Palestinians had a pre-Israelite presence in the land.[4] The more commonly acknowledged association of Palestinians and Philistines, similarly, has been used both to establish an ancient foothold in the land and to counter the Zionist beliefs about historic resettlement. One of those beliefs is that the ancient Land of Israel, the "Greater Land of Israel", extended from the "Euphrates to the Sea." The phrase contained in the title to this paper is a more frequent one in the Bible, "from the river unto the Land of the Philistines", and more accurately reflects what most Biblical scholars believe about the ancient geography of Palestine. The coast, which contains most of Israel's population centres today, was Philistine in Biblical times and never Israelite.

The interest of Palestinian Arabs in the landscape of the Iron Age may have arisen partly in recognition of the fact that tradition is a less compelling basis for hegemony, to Western minds, than history. However, something more fundamental is being articulated by the refusal, on the Jewish side, to admit to the multi-cultural character of Iron Age Palestine and the insistence, on the Palestinian side, that Ancient Israel was either insignificant or non-existent. The feeling is strong in Israel, regardless of political affiliations, that post-modern multi-cultural visions of the past will eradicate the Jewish nature of the State. Palestinians, conversely, fear that recognition of the past presence of Jews, like recognition of Israel itself, establishes "facts on the ground" leading to an appropriation of land.

Cultural 'Memories' of the Iron Age

The varying ethnic characterisations of Iron Age Palestine have grown out of a bond between land and culture that is enduring and rather unique to this part of the world. Beyond the barren fact that this is a contested landscape divided between two peoples, one that in recent times was conquered by the other, are the cultural perceptions of this landscape forged by the collective remembrances of its inhabitants. Simply viewing the region as one for which two ethnic groups are struggling implies a certain equality of status for the two peoples which is clearly not present in this situation. Both groups may have seen themselves at different points in their history as displaced. One of these groups, however, has now established a powerful nation state founded, in part, upon the belief in and attachment to its ancient narrative of displacement. The narrative of displacement for the other group followed on the heels of this very same event. Thus, while one group commemorates its Independence Day, the other commemorates its *Al-Naqba* (catastrophe). We in the West, living in a post-colonial world, are apt to label such instances – those in which a largely Western culture is seen as oppressing a non-Western one – as a case of coloniser and colonised.

It does not serve our understanding of the landscape of Palestine to characterise it in terms of simplistic historical dualities, however, and I think that it is necessary to approach the terms with more precision. While there is no doubt, today, about which is the dominant culture, the modern presence of Jews there is not, strictly speaking, based upon concepts such as exporting superior culture to a backward people or exploiting a colony for the benefit of a mother country. Thus, for all that its impact upon the indigenous population of Palestinians has been no less disastrous, the ideology behind the Jewish settlement is not an imperialist one.

Cultural memory is a major part of that ideology and, though it is neither a realistic memory nor, certainly, a recent one, Jews *do* recall the landscape of Palestine. It is a recollection that is inextricably bound up with religion and what can best be described as an apotheosis of loss. The commemoration of disasters some two thousand years and more in the past is a salient characteristic of Jewish religion. The smashing of a glass at weddings is a recognition of the destruction of the

Temples in Jerusalem. The Psalm that begins "By the rivers of Babylon" and ends with "If I forget thee O Jerusalem" is repeated at every Jewish wedding and many other celebrations.

Zion and Zionism in Jewish consciousness find their origins in Iron Age Palestine, most particularly, in the reigns of Kings David and Solomon.[5] Nonetheless, though Jerusalem and the place of the Temple were not forgotten, the State of Israel for almost 20 years managed to exist without them because there were other memories and other landscapes to consider. Feelings about these pre-1967 landscapes is summed up by Meron Bienvenisti in *Sacred Landscape:* "Brimming with a burning faith in the right of the Jewish People to return to its homeland, the Zionists strove to anchor this right in the landscapes of the Bible."[6]

The cultural memory of Palestinians in the territories is not that of a 'colonised' people. Palestinians in the territories, as opposed to Arabs living within the internationally recognised borders of Israel, have not been substantially 're-educated' to accept an alien culture and language. Nonetheless, the familiar topography of Palestine has assumed an alien and pervasive new presence. Unlike a colonised people, many Palestinians, regardless of where they live, feel irrevocably cut off from the land because its familiar topography has assumed that new presence.[7] Loss, here too, permeates views of the landscape but the loss is decidedly more recent and has a modern reality. The Philistine-Palestinian association grew out of that feeling of loss. It *was* the coast, with its vital Islamic and Ottoman centres of Haifa, Acre and Jaffa, that until fairly recently constituted the focus for Palestinian yearning for the landscapes of the past.[8]

Jerusalem is now the site upon which the hopes and fears of Palestinians and Israelis rest. For Jews, Jerusalem represents the quintessential Jewish religious dichotomies of joy and sorrow and exile and redemption. Here, Israelis have recognised a far greater connection with the ancient past than they did on the Mediterranean coast; and here, Palestinians have found that their past and present have come together to form a deep link unlike that which they experienced with other parts of the landscape. Jews talk about the "Temple Mount" as if the Temple still existed even as religious Jews face this area three times a day during prayers and express the hope for the rebuilding of the Temple there. Though the re-establishment of a Temple in Jerusalem is not even a thought in the minds of most Jewish inhabitants of the country, most Jews, even secular ones, will support the significance of Jerusalem to all of Israel by quoting its prominence in the Bible.[9]

For Palestinians, the *Haram al-Sharif* represents the remnant of their culture and their own hopes for a real redemption of their land and place in the region.[10] In overly simplistic terms, we can see that embedded in the 'memory' of one culture, regardless of political or religious outlooks, Jerusalem represents an incomplete return to Zion. Embedded in the 'memory' of the other culture is the reflection that Jerusalem establishes a vital connection between a people and its co-religionists elsewhere in the Middle East. Vital because, today, its most frequent, and most debilitating, contacts are with the alien Jewish culture. As Edward Said has written: "Perhaps the greatest battle Palestinians have waged as a people has been over the right to a remembered presence, and with that presence, the right to possess and reclaim a collective historical reality, at least since the Zionist movement began its encroachments on the land."[11]

While Palestinians are, now, the "people without a land" in the Middle East, the old Zionist view that Palestine was a "land without a people", or at least without much of a people, is still alive in the minds of many Israelis who entertain the hope that the Arabs of the region can be safely ignored one day.[12] Said speaks of the unpopulated archeological sites of colonialist antiquarians and this forced separation of people and 'important' places lives on in Israel. The Israeli urban renewal of the old city of Jaffa is a good example of this. The planners saw the removal of a large percentage of the resident population, mostly Arab, as the only way to achieve their goals of making the old city a tourist attraction. Consequently, Jaffa is today about as authentic and representative of the cultures of the Middle East as an Aladdin ride at Disneyland.[13]

The Evidence – What do we know about the Lifeworld of Iron Age Palestine?

Habermas has given us the concept of 'lifeworld' which, in an archeological context encompasses the total environment – artifactual, natural and human – as people live it and live in it.[14] The lifeworld of Ancient Palestine was, by all accounts a complex one. It was the land of one of the oldest, if not the oldest, agricultural traditions in the world and home to a very early development of animal husbandry and the use of animal 'secondary products' (milk, wool, traction, etc.), as well as the domestication of fruit trees (olives, grapes, dates, figs, etc.).[15]

Nevertheless, despite the antiquity of some of these events in the Near East, in the minds of the peoples of Ancient Palestine it seems clear that they recognised that sedentary agriculture was not a prerequisite for human subsistence and that there was, in fact, life before farming. Jeremiah like other writers of the Bible saw the desert, or wilderness, which is more accurately characterised as grazing lands for sheep and goats, as a metaphor for a heroic and nomadic, tent-dwelling past, although it is not clear that such a past ever truly existed in Palestine.[16] Early economies in this part of the world were fluid and it is supposed that cycles of 'nomadisation' and 'sedentarisation' were common in ancient times. These terms usually refer to the responses of agro-pastoralists to environmental or other changes, following which they may emphasise either mobile herding or, alternatively, sedentary agriculture.[17]

One of the key debates now preoccupying archaeologists who work on Iron Age Palestine has to do with ethnicity of peoples in the Iron Age, in particular the ethnicity of Early Israelites.[18] Biblical archaeologists and historians have been bandying this term about for some years now with little consideration for the immense difficulties presented by attempting to identify the ethnicity of peoples in the distant past.[19] As subjectively determined entities, ethnicity and cultural identity are often impossible to locate in the archeological record.[20] Obviously, the not-so-hidden agenda of this great search for cultural identity is the establishment of a connection between Iron Age Palestine and modern Jews in Israel. Commonly held assumptions in Israel are that the origins of today's Jewish religion can be found at Iron Age 'Israelite' sites.[21] For their part, Palestinian explorations of ethnicity have much to do with the argument – that they believe is well demonstrated at continuously occupied sites – that there is a great affinity between the cultures of modern Palestinians and those of the distant past.[22] In the absence of concrete evidence in the archeological record, including recognisable similarities between ancient and modern social and cultural traits and ancient and modern symbols, both of these assumptions are conjectural.

The second debate has to do with the 'settlement of the central hill country' during the Early Iron Age and more importantly the settlement of the Israelites in the land. Surveys of the hill country of Palestine do indicate that the region was more settled in the Iron Age than the Late Bronze Age.[23] Most of these sites, however, were small hamlets at relatively high elevations and in the northern hill country. In addition, a number of important Late Bronze Age sites seem to have continued into the early Iron Age. The base for northern hill country sites was clearly sedentary agriculture. Cisterns, terraces, olive oil installations and a number of other agriculturally related artefacts testify to this. To the extent that new settlements represented a different cultural group, and this is by no means clear, it is likely that the population of most of the sites was mixed. Proximity to older larger sites and to the major routes in the region, seem to have been primary factors influencing the location of new settlements.[24]

The southern hill country, which is the traditional territory of Israel's first monarchs, was actually sparsely settled in both the Bronze and Iron Ages, with the exception of Jerusalem. At the same time, the rural people of the south were closer to the urbanised peoples of the coast and the Transjordan, supposed 'alien' cultures, than they were to their alleged co-religionists in the north. Their subsistence strategy seems to have emphasised animal husbandry over sedentary agriculture although limited cereal cultivation seems to have been practised. Flocks of sheep and goats appear to have been more sizeable at these southern sites than at the northern sites. Sheep and goat products, we suspect, would have been popular trade items with their urban neighbours.[25]

The early Iron Age in Palestine thus represents a period in which the north and south hill country, the setting of the 'unified' tribes of the Bible, were quite separated by economy, topography and the characteristics of the cultures in their immediate proximity. The northern settlements were closest to Canaanite and Phoenician cities and the southern closest to Philistine sites. Given these factors, any real 'unity' between the sites of the north and those of the south seems unlikely.[26] If there was an eventual cultural affinity much later in the Iron Age, during the period for which we have some contemporaneous records, it could have been a religious one created through inter-marriages between the tribal chiefdoms of the north and south. Perhaps an economic alliance of hill country peoples against the tribes of the Transjordan and the urbanites of the coast was possible. In any event, the region clearly retained its multi-cultural and multi-religious character throughout the period.

Who Owned the Garden of Eden?

A recent exhibition at the Israel Museum, entitled *Landscapes of the Bible*, was a rich sampling of borrowed paintings by European masters showing the Palestine of their imaginations – Palestine as it never could have been. These conceptions of a green and forested land, however, are not so very far from the ways in which Israelis at the beginning of their nationhood fantasised about the landscapes of the past. They came to "make the desert bloom" but they also posited that it was Arab agriculture that had turned the land into a deforested wilderness.[27] The Arabs came, so the ancient history has been taught until recently in Israel, into a land once fertile and forested, into *our* land, and depleted its soils and destroyed its trees.

There is no discussion as to whether the modern Arab population had forebears in the mythical 'Israelite' Iron Age. From our perspective in the West, it is difficult to determine when modern Palestinians began to lay claim to the Iron Age Philistine culture or to the Canaanite and Jebusite cultures. The Philistine connection has linguistic support in that, at least since the 5th century BC, the Greek term *Palestine* has been known and was used to refer to the land of the Philistines or, as some scholars believe, to the whole land of Israel.

All of the assertions about the 'true heirs' to Iron Age cultures in Palestine raise the question of whether these are completely invented traditions and, as such, unworthy of note by serious scholars. It is perhaps not too radical a statement to say that neither Jews nor Arabs can be seen as having a more valid claim on the cultures of the Iron Age than anyone else in the region. In spite of this, both cultures have been too quick to dismiss the 'memories' of the Iron Age posited by the other. A review of articles on both sides of the main debate on the cultural character of Iron Age Palestine provides examples of this. A Palestinian scholar, who characterises Zionists as "romancers and dreamers", states that, for Jews, "[T]he temple, and the conviction that al-Aqsa is built on its ruins has been the source of exaggerated sentiments..." and concludes that, "Palestine is neither the land of knighthood nor the promise of return."[28] A more recent article by an archaeologist whose views support Jewish connections to Iron Age Palestine states,

> Still more disturbing is the fact that in the last few months Palestinian activists, some of them archaeologists connected with the new Palestinian Authority... have written a history of Palestine for school textbooks... that all but eliminates any reference to Israel.... Their 'Palestine' is Judenfrei. The Zionists... have no place in this Palestine, no historical claim to it.[29]

Neither of these statements offers any surprises to those who are familiar with this scene. The first is atypically mild for Palestinian opinions about Israel, which have become increasingly more strident, but the implications of both are clear. Israelis are neo-Crusaders and the Palestinians are neo-Nazis. It is a tragic irony of the current perceptions that Israelis and Palestinians have of each other that their worst accusations are, ultimately, couched in terms of their most painful struggles with different enemies and at different times. So it seems that Israeli and Palestinian memories of the past are hostages to a history of disastrous contacts with European cultures. In the Palestinian case, those contacts took place in the land itself. For Jews, they were elsewhere.

Jewish claims are supported by the putative continuity of language and religion and Palestinian claims are supported by the putative continuity of geography and culture. Exiled Palestinian poet Mahmoud Darwish speaks of the land of his birth as: "... the color of face, and the warmth of body, The light of heart and eye, The salt of bread and earth... the Motherland".[30] His landscape is an embodied one, a vital physical reminder of his identity, past, present and future. To Israeli poet Yehuda Amichai that same landscape is one that is inhabited by: "All the generations before me... " who "... Donated me, bit by bit, so that I'd be, Erected all at once, Here in Jerusalem, like a house of prayer....".[31] This is the Landscape (capitalisation intentional) of Western history – a nationalist one that calls to mind the sacrifice of generations, the longing for nationhood and the miracle of renewal and rebuilding in the land of ancient forebears.[32] It is not to wonder that the preeminent Jewish vision of the Landscape of the past is an immutable two-dimensional map of an ancient monarchic hegemony that resulted from victorious struggles with others. For Palestinians, that map has become an ever-shifting cultural mosaic from the Late Bronze Age forward, and it is the land itself that is immutable. Though embattled, divided and perpetually invaded by foreigners they believe that, in the end, the land will remain with those who have been loyal to it, who tilled its soil and planted its olive trees.

1   Gross, N, "Demolishing David", *Jerusalem Report*, 11 September 2000, pp. 1-8.

2   Although 'Palestine' is today used most often in a political sense it has a long history as a geographic designation and I refuse to relinquish what is, to me, a more lyrical term for the region in favour of dissonant phrases like 'Israel and the West Bank' or 'Israel and the Palestinian National Authority'.

3   Scham, S, "A Fight Over Sacred Turf – Who Controls Jerusalem's Holiest Shrine", *Archaeology*, vol. 55 no. 1, 2001, p. 62.

4   Scham, S, "The Archaeology of the Disenfranchised", *Journal of Archeological Method and Theory*, vol. 8 no. 2, 2001, pp. 183-213.

5   Shapira, A, "Introduction", *Essential Papers on Zionism*, Reinharz, J and Shapira, A, eds., New York and London: New York University Press, 1996, pp. 1-32.

6   Benvenisti, M, *Sacred Landscape*, Berkeley and Los Angeles: University of California Press, 2000, p. 46.

7   Said, E, "Palestine: Memory, Invention and Space", *The Landscape of Palestine: Equivocal Poetry*, Abu-Lughod, I, Heacock, R and Nashef, K, eds., Birzeit-Palestine: Birzeit University Publications, 1999, pp. 3-30.

8   Khalidi, R, *Palestinian Identity: The Construction of Modern National Consciousness*, New York: Columbia University Press, 1997, pp. 16-17.

9   Scham, "A Fight Over Sacred Turf", pp. 62-67, 72-74.

10   Khalidi, *Palestinian Identity*, pp. 30-33.

11   Said, "Palestine: Memory, Invention and Space", p. 4.

12   Silberstein, L, *The Postzionism Debates: Knowledge and Power in Israeli Culture*, New York and London: Routledge, 1999.

13   Bowman, G, "The exilic imagination", *The Landscape of Palestine*, Abu-Lughod et al., pp. 53-78.

14   Hodder, I, Shanks, M, Alexandri, A, Buchli, V, Carman, J, Last, J, and Lucas, G, eds., *Interpreting Archaeology: Finding Meaning in the Past*, London and New York: Routledge, 1995, pp. 239 and 241.

15   McCorriston, J, and Hole, F, "The Ecology of Seasonal Stress and the Origin of Agriculture in the Near East", *American Anthropologist*, vol. 93 no. 2, 1991, pp. 46-69. Sherratt, A, "Plough and Pastoralism: Aspects of the Secondary Products Revolution", *Patterns of the Past: Studies in Honour of David Clarke*, Hodder, I, Isaac, G and Hammond, N, eds., Cambridge: Cambridge University Press, 1981, pp. 261-305 and Grigson, C, "Plough and Pasture in the Early Economy of the Southern Levant", *The Archaeology of Society in the Holy Land*, Levy, T, ed., New York: Facts on File, 1995, pp. 245-268.

16   Feliks, Y, *Nature and Man in the Bible*, London, Jerusalem and New York: Soncino Press, 1981.

17   LaBianca, O, Hesban, I, *Sedentarization and Nomadization*, Berrien Springs, Michigan: Andrews University Press, 1990.

18   See Brett, M, ed., *Ethnicity and the Bible, Biblical Interpretation Series 19*, Leiden: Brill, 1996; Dever, W, "Archaeology, Ideology and the Quest for an Ancient or Biblical Israel", *Near Eastern Archaeology*, vol. 61 no. 1, 1998, pp. 39-52; Dever, W, "Ceramics, Ethnicity and the Question of Israel's Origins", *Biblical Archaeologist*, vol. 58 no. 4, 1995, pp. 200-213; and Sparks, K L, *Ethnicity and Identity in Ancient Israel*, Winona Lake, Indiana: Eisenbrauns, 1998.

19   Scham, S, "The Days of the Judges: When Men and Women Were Animals and Trees Were Kings", *Journal for the Study of the Old Testament*, 97, 2002, pp. 4-5.

20   See Barth, R, ed., *Ethnic Groups and Boundaries: The Social Organisation of Cultural Difference*, Boston: Little, Brown and Co, 1969; Despres, F, ed., *Ethnicity and Resource Competition in Plural Societies*, The Hague: Mouton, 1975; and Jones, S, *Archaeology and Ethnicity: Constructing Identities in the Past and the Present*, London and New York: Routledge, 1997.

21   Avigad, N, *Discovering Jerusalem*, Jerusalem: Israel Exploration Society, 1980, and Barkay, G, "The Iron Age II-III", *The archaeology of Ancient Israel*, Ben-Tor, A, ed., New Haven: Yale University Press, 1992, pp. 302-373.

22   Nashef, K, "Khirbet Birzeit." *Journal of Palestinian Archaeology*, vol. 1 no. 1, 2000, pp. 1-32.

23   Scham, "The Days of the Judges", pp. 27-29.

24   Finkelstein, I, *The Archaeology of the Israelite Settlement*, Jerusalem: Israel Exploration Society, 1988.

25   Bloch-Smith, E and Nakai, B, "A Landscape Comes to Life", *Near Eastern Archaeology*, vol. 62 no. 2, 1999, pp. 3-93.

26   Finkelstein, I, "Ethnicity and the Origin of Iron I Settlers in the Highlands of Canaan: Will the the Real Israel Stand Up?", *Biblical Archaeologist*, vol. 59 no. 4, 1996, pp. 198-212.

27   Feliks, *Nature and Man in the Bible*, pp. 112-113.

28   Shaheen, M, "Palestine: A Case of Romance in Western Eyes", *Proceedings of the Third International Conference on Bilad al-Sham-Palestine*, Amman: University of Jordan Press, 1980, p. 183.

29   Dever, W, "Archaeology, Ideology and the Quest for an Ancient or Biblical Israel", *Near Eastern Archaeology*, vol. 61 no. 1, 1998, p. 50.

30   Darwish, M, "A Lover from Palestine", *Splinters of Bone*, Bannani, B M, trans., Greenfield Center, New York: Greenfield Review Press, 1974, p. 23.

31   Amichai, Y, "All the generations before me", Schimmel, H, trans., *Poems of Jerusalem,* New York: Harper and Row, 1988, p. 3.

32   Scham, "The Archaeology of the Disenfranchised", pp. 183-184.

"In this the Land of the Todas": Imaginary Landscapes and Colonial Policy in Nineteenth Century Southern India
Deborah Sutton

> The object of Government, ever since I have known the Nilgiris, has been to protect the Todas against themselves.[1]

This paper explores the ways in which questions of land and landscape are imbricated within the above statement, a statement which, for all its paternal and judgmental authoritarianism, continues to inform popular sentiment and legislative practice aimed towards peoples and communities variously classified as 'primitive' or 'indigenous'. The argument I will put forward uses the aperture of land and revenue policy to highlight the reliance of oppressive and restrictive legislation upon the rhetoric of protection and the sentiments of landscape.

This exploration focuses upon the transformation of a place into a view on the Nilgiri hills of South India in the nineteenth century, a view which became emblematic of the colonial encounter and which acted as a space of compensation for less scrutinised parts of the colonised landscape, where government tried and failed to assert its surveillance and authority.

This paper also takes an opportunity to problematise the relative disregard by contemporary land rights forums of the significance of the nineteenth and twentieth century colonial interventions. Much contemporary literature regards colonialism as a layer which can be peeled away from a context leaving a pristine and authentic 'indigenous voice' about land.[2] Forms of colonial authority introduced new landscapes of signifiers and measurements of entitlement and control over resources, furnished by maps, signatures, leases, deeds and registries. As this chapter will demonstrate, the implementation of official cognisance over land remained far from meeting its own criteria of efficacy. But a new grammar was created through which land rights were expressed, contested and proven. Without engaging with histories of the colonial genealogies of land legislation, rights and disputes, I would argue that contemporary advocacy risks reducing itself to fetishism and platitude.

Colonised Land and Colonial Policy on the Nilgiris

The Nilgiri mountains are located at the southern end of the Western ghats, a chain of mountains that runs down the western side of peninsular India. The cool plateau of the Nilgiris was subject to colonisation by fragmented waves of settlers from the second decade of the nineteenth century onwards. The hills offered a proximate and relatively sparsely populated environment for the recuperation of European health made fragile by the heat of the plains. The building of hospitals, sanatoria and prisons was quickly supplemented by the establishment of private and government plantations of coffee, and later tea, eucalyptus, acacia and chinchona (from which quinine was extracted). From the 1820s onward, the Madras government entertained a series of plans to establish settler colonisation on the hills and initiated programmes of land grants and sales to retired soldiers, to gentlemen administrators and enterprising speculators. The place of the Nilgiris as the principal hill station of South India was cemented in 1881 when Ootacamund, the largest settlement, became the summer seat of government for the Madras Presidency.[3]

In 1843, the Court of Directors in London, who exercised ultimate executive authority over the ast India Company, ordered that the land-rights of all the hill communities on the Nilgiri mountains be limited henceforth to usufruct.[4] The hill communities were separated and enumerated according to a categorisation of subsistence and habitat into five groups: the cultivating Badagas, the pastoralist Todas, the artisan Kotas and the forest dwelling Kurumbas and Irulas. This ethno-agrarian schematic has, until fairly recently, provided the divisions upon which all further ethnographic elaborations were based.

The Court's decree followed a series of contentious and acrimonious land disputes on the hills between settlers, hill communities and government centred on the rights of settlers to buy or be granted land, questions of compensation due to existing occupiers and the rights of government in regulating land appropriation.

Despite the dramatic, and often traumatic, transformations effected upon agrarian society in South Asia by British colonial intervention, colonial rule rarely explicitly aimed at the alteration of the existing social organisation of productivity. Improvement and reform were, in principle at least, to be beholden to existing social forms. The exceptionalism of the Nilgiris and other hill areas like it never escaped this policy, despite the sustained lobbying of settlers in the second half of the century who yearned for the privileges enjoyed by white settlers elsewhere in the British Empire. The occupation of the Nilgiris produced two conflicting, though often interwoven, approaches to colonisation. The Madras government sporadically took pains to point out in clear terms that the violation of indigenous occupation on the hills was unacceptable whilst simultaneously entertaining grandiose plans for settlement which made the physical displacement of the hill communities and the disruption of their economy inevitable.

Settlement legislation attempted to reconcile the tensions of settler colonialisation by creating two distinct landscapes of authoritarian cognisance: one of indigenous occupation, the other of colonial settlements and plantations. Occupants of these two landscapes would pay differential assessments, even on adjacent lands; their rights would be recorded in separate registers and governed by different principles of revenue policy. The landscape of rights on the hills was defined in a land document called the *patta*. The *patta* identified the land by name, sometimes by its relative position to other holdings, rivers and woods, and specified the amount of annual revenue payable by the holder, or *pattadar,* to government. Until the 1860s, *pattas* were largely held collectively and did not represent a record of individual private land rights. Shifting cultivation was widely practised on the hills and in many cases *pattas* had never referred to a specific plot of land, and certainly not one identifiable through the imperfect topographical knowledge of the revenue officers. The government relied on village officers to collect rents and to distil the information held within the *patta*. The latter service they performed selectively.[5] For the incoming settlers, the revenue authorities created elaborate and, in the settlers' view restrictive and expensive, land sale rules that prevented settlers purchasing land rights directly from indigenous communities. Fundamentally, these rules asserted government's position as proprietor of all unoccupied lands and ultimate landlord over all occupation; settlers and indigenous communities could acquire rights to occupy, cultivate or graze only on the payment of an annual rent. However, not only did government lack anything approaching the necessary topographic knowledge to enforce such a system of land rights, for the first 30 years of colonisation neither hill communities nor settlers saw any advantage in the involvement of government revenue officers in the process of buying or selling land rights. The revenue authorities struggled to know and control the course of colonisation, battling against headstrong settlers who resented government's involvement and against members of indigenous communities who routinely bamboozled settlers and government by 'selling' land for which they held no recognised claim or right.

Legally and politically, the revenue authorities could not refuse to recognise sales between settlers and hill communities so long as purchasers could produce a *patta*. In order to maintain a stake in the land market, government could do little aside from adjudicate in disputes on the few occasions when either side desired the participation of the revenue officers, and to register purchases against the names of planters at the Collectorate, the one service that settlers were keen to secure from the district officials.

The Court's order of 1843 failed to restrict sales between hill communities and settlers, but it did mark a key episode in the exceptional discourse which evolved around the land-rights of the Toda communities. Only in the case of the Todas was the decreed usufruct given a topographical specification. Within an area of three bullahs (about eleven and a half acres) of their villages, or *munds*, their usufruct rights were declared to be 'absolute' and protected from alienation.[6] The Court outlawed "the grant of any lands in the vicinity of their places of residence in the hope that these may be hereafter cultivated by the Todas themselves when they shall be induced to engage in cultivation".[7] This protection afforded by the grant, therefore, was to be transitional; to last only as long as it took the Todas to begin to cultivate.

A second formal allocation of land to the Toda communities was made in 1863. Representatives of the Toda community asked that an additional nine bullahs (slightly over 34 acres) under grazing *patta* be made over to them. At their suggestion, the nine bullahs of land was made over to each *mund* on the 'understanding' that the land was not to be sold.[8]

After 1863, when asked for the total extent of Toda land holding on the Nilgiris, the revenue officers would simply multiply the 46 acre allowance by the total number of known *mund* sites.[9] The precision of the official figure for Toda lands belied the haziness of the knowledge government actually possessed and the ability of government's surveyors to impose any order over the agrarian landscape through official allowances and demarcations. Neither the 1843 nor the 1863 allocations had ever been surveyed as the Court of Directors and the Madras Government had ordered. The local authorities admitted that the land allocations were of "rather indefinite location" and that the Todas continued to graze their herds of buffalo over the "whole of the plateau".[10] When attempts were made to demarcate allocated land, official knowledge was easily sabotaged. "Todas", complained an Assistant Collector, "with a view no doubt to create confusion and throw difficulty in the way of the sale of wastelands are in the habit of putting up similar marks [to those of the official survey] as suits their convenience".[11]

The topography of *mund* cognisance created foot-holds in an increasingly confused and complex agrarian landscape. The reservation of "land adjoining Toda munds" became a general rule guiding land allocation in a still barely mapped landscape.[12] In 1859, a settler's three year old purchase was annulled by the Madras Government on finding that the land he had bought at auction was in the "immediate vicinity of a Mund appropriated by the Todas to religious rites, and that its occupation by Mr. Rohde is a great inconvenience to them".[13] The complaints of other communities were deconstructed and eventually dismissed by generally unsympathetic revenue officers. The existence of shifting cultivation, which was regarded by colonial revenue authorities throughout British India as backward, environmentally detrimental and even criminal, only encouraged revenue officers to dismiss the appeals made by cultivating communities that their land had been wrongfully appropriated by settlers. While shifting cultivation allowed hill communities to prosper from land hungry settlers without damaging their own holdings, as colonisation accelerated the lack of spatial specification on their land documents left the indigenous communities without the ability to fend off settlers who encroached, uninvited, on their lands. The Toda *munds*, meanwhile, became a landmark in land sale arbitration; and their protection a beacon of government's righteous maintenance of 'indigenous rights' against the more pervasive tide of colonisation and displacement.

During the 1850s and 1860s, however, nothing was done either in practice or in principle to prevent the Toda communities from selling their lands. The District Collector stated that the Todas were "at liberty to sell the lands allowed to them by Government on a reduced rate... adjacent to their munds" and *pattas* obtained from Todas along with "sale deeds", which were nothing more than an acceptance of the sale signed by the purported *pattadar*, were routinely registered at the Collectorate.[14]

"In this the land of the Todas": the Iconography of the Mund[15]

A discourse, and legislative praxis, accumulated around the Todas which regarded them as fundamentally different from the other communities on the hills and implicitly different from other pastoralist communities of British India.[16] Administrative correspondence stressed the need to protect "the character of this singular and interesting race" and warned that "unless prompt means are taken to ameliorate it, they will soon sink into the level of their neighbours".[17] These neighbours were not the settlers who displaced them, but the cultivating Badaga communities. While the Badagas, who represented the most numerous competition to colonisation, could be dismissed as "Native Settlers" and compared to the superstitious and wasteful peasant producers of the plains, the far smaller Toda communities, who posed little threat to incoming settlements, were celebrated as manly, aboriginal, "hardy, fearless, superior in stature".[18]

In 1869, the *Madras Mail* carried an advertisement for a firm of photographers: "We would especially mention a view of the Toda Mund near Sylk's, Kandalmund, which is *essentially characteristic* of the Neilgherries, and a large vignette of a Toda, which would give a very perfect idea to the 'old folks at home' of the original inhabitants of *the land we live in*."[19] Photography transformed the image of the *mund* into an internationally recognised signifier of the Nilgiris and more specifically, the Nilgiris colonised by Europeans.[20] "Prosthetic memories" were created which fixed the idea of the Todas in the colonised landscape and conferred recognition of the settler's place on the mountains.[21] A European hunter related an, undoubtedly apocryphal, tale to the local paper of how, on accidentally losing his clothing in a brook, his cry "was answered promptly by a Lord of the Soil [a Toda]... who covered the bold sportsman with his toga, and enabled him to proceed with the chase".[22]

Figure 1
Illustrated title
page from
Baikie, R, *The
Neilgherries
Including an
Account of their
Topography,
Climate, Soil and
Productions; and
of the Effects of
the Climate on
the European
Constitution*,
1857. Courtesy
National Library
of Scotland

This associative geography between the settlers and the Todas and between the Todas and the Nilgiris, relied upon the (dis)placement of the Todas into separate space, a space made physically and discursively distinct from the tensions and antagonisms intrinsic to the indigenous/settler encounter. The frame of that space, I argue, was the tableau of the *mund*.

In visual representations, the image of the *mund* became the key medium by which the significance of and investments made in the Todas were understood. The surrounding wall which was a feature of most *munds* was excluded from these early travellers' portraits, dating from the 1820s and 1830s respectively, to give a sense of openness and visibility. The distinct backdrop of the half-barrel Toda dwellings, the indigenous forest, or shola, and the absence of production became the signifying characteristics of the *mund*, and by extension, of the Todas themselves. (figure 1) Later photographs produced as part of 'scientific' ethnographies, borrowed the form of earlier lithographs and sketches and mirror almost exactly the composite elements of the earlier representations. (figure 2)

Other communities were photographed 'on site' in ethnographic studies though none as habitually as the Todas. Images of other communities tended to be used as illustrative props to the exhibition of 'representative' assemblages of material culture.[23] The *mund* was more than a fragment of the history of ethnography or archaeology. It was constructed as an idealised space within settler cosmologies, acting as a linkage between settlers and the hills. Guidebooks to the Nilgiris recommended a visit to a *mund* and supplied directions.[24] A genre of narratives evolved around the image of the *mund* characterised, like other narratives of place created in settler societies, by an implicit emphasis on unobstructed passage and access.[25] In these narratives, access to *mund* sites is absolute though the *mund* is not deliberately visited but rather 'happened upon':

> A sabbath evening I happened to walk in the woods not far away from my house... I scarcely knew how long I was walking when I suddenly found myself in the midst of a stone enclosure... The merry sound of voices heard from all sides showed that I was not alone and on looking before me I saw a queer, pleasant sight – five little huts, most curiously and ingeniously built rose before me....[26]

Figure 2
"A Toda Mand":
Plate 1 in
Marshall, W E,
*Phrenologist
Amongst the
Todas, or The
Study of a
Primitive Tribe
in South India
History,
Character,
Customs,
Religion,
Infanticide,
Polyandry,
Language*,
1873. Courtesy
National Library
of Scotland

Descriptions of visits to the *munds* created a strong aesthetic of an open landscape of which the settlements were a seamless part:

> At length, descending to a valley round a wooded shoulder, we came on one of the loveliest spots one could picture; a sort of wide hollow, sheltered by some hill-tops, clothed with the richest sward, and having some fine trees and shola about, in which the evening sunlight was glinting exquisitely. But what at once arrested our attention was that on the sward, surrounded by all this beauty, stood three or four erections, the queerest and quaintest you could conceive. It was hard to believe that they were human habitations, though some human figures sat in front, quite as strange looking as the dwellings. They sat on the grass, basking in the sun, completely wrapped in their blankets, nothing being visible above but their heads, covered with a bush of thick, coarse black hair...." You have wished to see a Toda-mund exclaimed our friend; there is one!"[27]

The idealised space of the *mund* became a theatre in which visitors learned, rested and refreshed themselves in the beauty of primitive nature. These accounts are sensory, written to emphasise the tangibility of the experience, and dwell on the first hand, physical experiences: "The doorway is so small that to get inside one has to go down on all fours, and even then some wriggling is required."[28] This quote emphasises the unquestioned assumption of access onto the lands of the Todas, to their settlements and even into their homes.

The benevolent, sentimental fascination communicated by these encounter narratives was not replicated in non-literary encounters. Settlers were capable of lying to and bullying Toda communities where they stood in the way of a land appropriation. Complaints made against the Todas by settlers in the course of colonisation were as common as against any other community whose land rights or simple proximity were resented by settlers as a threat, nuisance or inconvenience.[29] In the 1850s, a group of European residents clubbed together and offered the Todas of a *mund* nearby their homes Rs500 for only one cawny (approximately 1.32 acres) of land, "simply to get rid of them".[30] Yet images could, and did, suggest a quiet and desirable proximity between colonisers and the *munds*. An image of a *mund* with a bungalow immediately behind it was exhibited at the Paris International Exhibition in 1867. This was the public face of the settler/Toda encounter, not the threats and bribery which actually furnished the proceedings of many land appropriations. The *mund* sight became a space of consumption and of compensation, where a virtue could be made of non-colonisation. It was a space into which colonial anxieties could be displaced and soothed.

Within this theatre, the inhabitants of the *munds* were assigned a mechanistic relationship with the environment that so impressed the visitor.[31] Their agency was detached from the shape of the sholas, created by the firing of pasture; the shape of their huts became derived from the genius of the natural landscape, not from their design and labour.

Enumeration and Ethnic Topographies

The first attempt to address the disparity between the official land allocations and the landscape as the Todas lived within it was made in 1871 by District Commissioner J W Breeks, himself an amateur ethnologist.[32] Breeks attempted to 'call in' all Toda *pattas* in order to more firmly secure the 66 *pattas* which had been issued to members of Toda communities: less than half were produced at the Collectorate; the others, the *pattadars* claimed, had been "lost or destroyed".[33] Breeks, on the orders of government, issued fresh *pattas* for all the Todas' grazing grounds assigned in 1863, and entered on the back of them in red ink: "... the Puttadar has no right either to sell the land or fell the shola or fell the shola and sell the wood".[34] An announcement was placed in the *District Gazette*, and sporadically repeated over the next two decades, cautioning the public against the purchase of Toda lands and stating that no Toda, including those in whose names the *pattas* were issued, had the right to sell.[35]

In response to these restrictions Todas who wished to alienate land entered into long term lease agreements as a means of circumventing the restrictions of the *pattas*.[36] To government officials, these leases represented a devious and profiteering manipulation of official restrictions, restrictions only set in place for the good of the community who now undermined them. The lease alienations were received as further proof that the Todas were unfit to manage their own lands. In 1879, the Commissioner ordered that the Todas should be warned that any long leases given would be "constituted as an absolute transfer" by government and would result in the permanent loss of the lands.[37] This threat was only likely to encourage planters to endeavour to obtain Toda land by lease in the hope that they would derive permanent rights to the land in the course of government's punishment of the Toda *pattadars*. Another disciplinary measure recommended was the cancellation of the *patta*; the land leased would be re-appropriated by government, though only after the lease on which it has been temporarily alienated had expired.[38] Both of these measures were directed solely against the Toda vendor. Neither measure would upset the rights guaranteed by a private land market to those who were deemed fit to participated in it fully. In the 1880s these measures were supplemented by penal assessments imposed on alienated Toda land in an attempt to deter buyers.[39] On detecting fraudulent purchases, however, government was disinclined to enrage settlers, and enter into a legal minefield by attempting to impose punishment after decades of unencumbered practice.[40] Liability for infringements of the restrictions imposed by inalienable *patta* bore down exclusively upon the Toda community.

The dubious legal status of land inalienability required the investment of an ethnic topography in Toda lands which only government could be trusted to protect and, if necessary, enforce.[41] Accordingly, the Madras government now charted its own policy toward the Todas as one of accommodation and generosity: as having been persistently directed towards ensuring the existence of the tribe by constantly increasing the areas of the reserves set apart for its exclusive use, and by constantly imposing fresh restrictions on the application of its land to any other purpose than that of grazing.[43]

The Madras government now declared that the lands of the Todas, as defined in total by the allocations of 1843 and 1863, "had ever been inalienable".[43] The understanding of 1863, volunteered by the Todas and never enforced by the revenue authorities, had become in retrospect a condition imposed by the authorities at the time of the grant.[44] With this, inalienability developed its own internal dynamic detached from the conditions from which it had emerged. The protection of lands near *munds* was now deemed essential for preservation of the "integrity of the Toda race", a preservation which the Toda communities themselves were deemed unable to ensure.[45] The land assigned to the Todas, claimed the revenue authorities, "has but little value for them, and the temptation to part with it for ready-money is irresistible".[46]

During the Revenue Settlement, the Madras revenue authorities had ordered that "No puttas for Toda reserves should be issued in *individual* names".[47] Such an exceptional restriction of land-rights could only be legal if it was not a removal but simply a continuation of existing policy. Accordingly, the revenue authorities now claimed that government had "never recognised or contemplated recognising, any *individual* rights in Todas to particular areas of land. The privileges reserved to the Todas were intended solely for the tribe, and are incapable of alienation to individuals."[48] The Madras revenue authorities ordered that Toda lands were to be specified by place-name only. Toda land holders, however, refused to accept leases without any specification of ownership and the Revenue Department grudgingly agreed that one, or at most two, names would be entered on the *pattas*, not as individual *pattadars*, but "as representing for the time a [given] Mund".[49] No rights, thought the revenue authorities, would be created by this admission and it would avoid any untoward and potentially embarrassing probing of the government's position.

By the 1880s, revenue surveys of the hills had resulted in unprecedented levels of government knowledge about the agrarian landscape and revealed the extent of the discrepancy between official and private perceptions of the extent and exercise of land rights. The Toda communities held an aggregate of slightly more than 5,000 acres, almost double the official allowance.[50] This figure, although dramatic, was no different from the general trend on the hills. The survey had consistently found claims to cultivated lands and estates to be far in excess of officially registered holdings. Landholders, both settlers and hill communities, were generally given the opportunity to maintain their extended limits by paying revenues upon them and initially the revenue surveyors followed the same course with Toda claims. In the case of the Todas, however, the inclusion, and therefore legitimisation, of excess lands by surveyors enraged the Madras government who condemned the inclusion as "absolutely destitute of authority" and demanded an explanation.[51] The Madras government ordered that the Todas were to be confirmed in possession of only that area produced by a multiplication of the number of *munds* by the allowance.[52]

Despite the renewed certainty in the minds of the revenue authorities of the size, function and constituent parts of a *mund* site in practice, the official account of Toda lands was wildly uneven; varying from over 100 to less than three acres.[53] What mattered to government, however, was the creation of an aggregate 'fit' between *mund* allocation and *pattas* by the revenue survey.

By the 1880s, the idea of a complete transfer of the management of Toda land rights to government was gaining currency.[54] It was through the exceptional authority of the Forest Department, one of the world's first 'environmental agencies', that the proprietary rights of the Toda community were finally and completely undermined. Every Toda *patta* contained forest, a rapidly depleting resource on the hills and one to which colonial government throughout India claimed exclusive and absolute rights. The Forest Acts legislated a programme of official reservation of the forests of British India, allowing government to assert a extraordinary degree of control over the forests and the communities that depended upon them. The intensity of forest reservation was exceptional on the Nilgiris mountains; the forest authorities showed an enthusiasm for official reservation that settlers, and less bluntly, local revenue officers, ridiculed as 'mania'.[55] By 1887, 66% of all land, including 96% of all unoccupied land on the hills, was reserved or scheduled for reservation.[56] The Madras Presidency Forest Act of 1882 claimed to offer exceptional, and protectionist, rights to the Toda communities. Unlike every other community on the hills, and almost every other community in British India, the Todas were exempt from paying fees in reserved forests open for grazing, neither were they subject to charges for the collection of forest materials for their own use.[57] This apparent latitude, though much resented by forest officers who regarded the presence of any local community's usufruct in forests as a damaging encroachment on the interests of scientific forestry, was in practice a fairly seamless part of a conservation agenda which imposed unprecedented restrictions on access to everyday and essential resources. A petition written by, or more likely for, a group of Todas in 1884 elaborates the reality of the latitude supposedly allowed to them:

> a Toda who wants to cut down a tree in a reserved shola has to get a certificate from the Deputy Tahsildar [a local revenue officer] that he is a person who has the right to do so, he then has to find a forester and obtain as order for a Forest Guard to accompany him to the shola and mark a tree which he may be permitted to take.[58]

The apparent entitlement afforded to the Toda communities, therefore, was tightly restricted to 'provable' ethnicity and subject to (physical) invigilation by forest officers. This 'allowance', which in everyday practice translated into restriction and inevitable illegality on the part of the subject community, throws into sharp relief the nature of authoritarian measures of protection exercised across real social and economic spaces.

The Forest Department continued, however, to bemoan the obstacle which Toda land rights presented to the reservation of forests. In 1892, the reserve notification of a substantial forest on the hills was abandoned after it was found to consist almost entirely of Toda *patta* lands. In response, the Forest Department increasingly urged that the Forest Rules be extended to Toda *patta* lands.[59]

In 1894, the principle of 'joint interest' between government, through the agency of the Imperial Forest Department, and Toda *pattadars* was designed without any consultation with the Toda communities. This measure allowed the notification of *all* Toda *patta* lands under a revised Madras Forest Act.[60] 'Joint interest' management gave the Forest Department unprecedented control. Reserved forest restrictions now applied to *all* Toda *patta* land, whether grazing, cultivatable or *mund* land: the Forest Department was now responsible for mediating all Toda land rights, whether grazing, firing or cultivation.

The decades after the normalisation of the inalienability of Toda *patta* lands saw a gradual attrition of the lands held by the community.[61] The transfer of the management of the *mund* lands to the Forest Department resulted in widespread appropriation for commercial eucalyptus plantations. This official appropriation led to the permanent loss of land to the Toda communities and substantial and irreversible damage to the ecology of the hills wrought by the exotic plantations.

The Image of the *Mund*

At the beginning of the 1890s a group of Todas petitioned the District Collector for permission to cultivate their grazing lands; a request that finally satisfied the rationale of the allocation of land to the Toda communities originally made half a century before. Their request met with an initial refusal followed by a grudging permission under a host of conditions. These terms included one remarkable restriction. The Collector stated categorically that the cultivation should not "result in the deterioration of their land in the vicinity of their munds from a pastoral or from an artistic point of view".[62] Government confirmed this restriction stating that "no green sward or shola immediately adjoining...[a] mund... is [to be] dug up or destroyed". Cultivation, when permission was granted, was to be placed well away from the *mund*.[63] Two *munds* located within Ootacamund settlement were not permitted to cultivate under any circumstances. These hamlets were Kandalmund and Manjakalmund; the first was located behind Sylk's Hotel, one of Ootacamund's premier hotels, and the second was, and remains, within the government botanical gardens.[64]

By the end of the nineteenth century the inalienability of Toda lands was a legislative institution and the *mund* and its image an aesthetic, and ethical, resource. Where *munds* were located in convenient proximity to the colonising settlements, they were maintained – forcibly if necessary – to accord with spectatorial expectations derived from written accounts. For the revenue authorities, responsible for regulating the productive landscape, the tangibility of these urban *munds* fleshed out the tabular life of the rapidly depleting inalienable *mund* land allocation in the hinterland of the settlements. These two imaginary encounters were mediated by two very different signifiers, the iconography of the *mund* and the *patta*. Both representations served, within separate but intersecting realms, to assuage and accommodate the anxieties of the colonial intervention.

The story of the *munds* of the Nilgiri hills is a fable in the development of authoritarian protectionism, and one which exhibits a strong similarity to contemporary 'image heavy' ethnographic and environmentalist narratives. The land rights of the Todas, and groups like them throughout India, continue to occupy a subordinate position within conservationist or productive government property regimes. Ironically, colonial land registers are currently being resuscitated by community advocates to make claims to land under threat.[65] While colonial land records provide an important tool in subaltern assertion of land and resource rights, there is a danger that without a critical examination of the processes and social relations in which their creation was embedded, they will be used as a definitive archive of community entitlement. More insidiously, their deployment risks an implicit affirmation of the conditions of subordination, and of the ethnic and environmental topographies, which informed their constitution.

1   Campbell Walker, Colonel I, Conservator of Forests, Southern Circle to C F MacCartie, Acting Collector of the Nilgiris, 22 June 1891, Proceedings of the Madras Revenue Department, (henceforth PMRD) 26 October 1891, no. 1008, p. 725-727, Udhagamandalam District Records (henceforth UDR).

2   Battiste, M, ed., *Reclaiming Indigenous Voice and Vision*, University of British Columbia: Vancouver, 2000.

3   For a general history of hill stations in British India, see Kennedy, Dane, *Magic Mountains: Hill Stations and the British Raj*, Berkeley, California & London: University of California Press, 1996.

4   "Usufruct: the legal right of temporary possession, use or enjoyment of the advantages of property belonging to another, so far as may be had without causing damage or prejudice to it": Oxford English Dictionary. By declaring that the rights of hill communities were limited to rented use, as opposed to absolute property, the Company was principally concerned with denying the proprietary claims made by early settler entrepreneurs to lands they had purchased from indigenous land holders. Henceforth all land and rights were to be rented, on various terms, from the Government.

5   By the mid 1880s, the Madras government had succeeded in systematising the appointment of village officers on the hills and had largely replaced the indigenous officers with low country Brahmans.

6   The word mund is derived from the Badaga word mandu. The Toda word is mod. From Walker, A, "The Western Romance with the Toda". Quote from Roupell, N A, Acting Commissioner to Madras Board of Revenue, 14 November 1881, PMBR 6 January 1882, no. 23, p. 24, TNSA.

7   Dispatch of the Court of Directors, 21 June 1843, PMBR, 14 December 1843, pp. 19191-19206, TNSA.

8   Roupell, N A, Acting Commissioner to Madras Board of Revenue, 14 November 1881, PMBR 6 January 1882, no. 23, p. 24, TNSA.

9   Breeks, J W, Draft Administration Report, Miscellaneous Coimbatore Collector's Sent Letterbook, 1869, UDR.

10 J C Harrington to P Grant, 20 April 1866, Coimbatore Collector's Received Letterbook January-June 1866, UDR.

11 J C Harrington to P Grant, January-June 1866.

12 J C Harrington, Special Assistant Collector to P Grant, Collector, 15 July 1865, Coimbatore Collector's Received Letterbook, July-December 1865, UDR; PMBR 13 April 1849, no. 3, 4, pp. 2123-2155, TNSA; P Grant to Claude Vincent, 14 January 1863 and 28 January 1863, Coimbatore Collector's Sent Letterbook, 14 January 1863-28 September 1863, UDR.

13 PMRD 12 April 1859, no. 5-6, p. 115, Oriental and India Office Collection, British Library (henceforth OIOC).

14 P Grant, Collector of Coimbatore to J C Harrington, Special Assistant Collector, 28 March 1866, Coimbatore Collector's Sent Letterbook, 25 November 1865-16 June 1867, UDR.

15 Editorial, *South of India Observer* 29 March 1887, p. 2, col. 6.

16 For excellent work on other pastoralist communities in India which highlight less sympathetic portrayals, see: Bhattacharya, N, "Pastoralists in a colonial world", in Guha, R and Arnold, D, eds., *Nature, Culture and Imperialism: Essays on the Environmental History of South Asia*, New Delhi: Oxford University Press, 1995, pp. 49-85; Sabarval, V, *Pastoral Politics : Shepherds, Bureaucrats, and Conservation in the Western Himalaya*, New Delhi: Oxford University Press, 1999.

17 Minute by John Sullivan, PMBR 20 August 1835, no. 2, p. 8745, Tamil Nadu State Archives (henceforth TNSA).

18 J Ouchterlony to Deputy Surveyor General of India, 24 September 1844, Proceedings of the Madras Board of Revenue (henceforth PMBR) 14 October 1844, no. 62, pp. 13515-13529, TNSA. Minute by John Sullivan, PMBR 20 August 1835, no. 2, p. 8745, TNSA.

19 *The Madras Mail*, 22 February 1869, p. 3, col. 3 (my emphasis).

20 The prominence of the mund in descriptions of the Nilgiris and the Todas became so embedded within the colonial archive that even Baden-Powell's sober account of land tenure and revenue systems described the "curious enclosed, domed huts" of the "mand". Baden-Powell, B H, *The Land-Systems of British India: Being a Manual of the Land-Tenures and of the Systems of Land-Revenue Administration Prevalent in the Several Provinces*, Oxford: Clarendon Press, 1892, footnote, p. 185.

21 A phrase borrowed from Pierre Nora, *Realms of Memory: the Construction of the French Past, vol. 1: Conflicts and Divisions*, Columbia University Press: New York, 1996.

22 *South of India Observer*, 25 July 1885, p. 10, col. 3.

23 See Sutton, D, "Horrid Sights and Customary Rights: the Toda Funeral on the Colonial Nilgiris", *Indian Economic and Social History Review*, vol. 39 no. 1, 2002; pp. 45-70, for a fuller discussion of ethnography and collections of material culture in the nineteenth century.

24 Eastwick, Edward B, *Handbook of the Madras Presidency with a Notice of the Overland Route to India*, London, 1879, p. 291.

25 For discussion of this issue in South African settler poetry, see Bunn, David, "'Our Wattled Cot': Mercantile and Domestic Space in Thomas Pringle's African Landscapes", Mitchell, W J T, ed., *Landscape and Power*, Chicago: University of Chicago Press, 1994.

26 "A Visit to the Todas, from the Pen of a Native Lady", *South of India Observer*, 12 April 1884, p. 7, col. 2-3; see also Campbell, W, *The Old Forest Ranger; or Wild Sports of India on the Neilgherry Hills, in the Jungles and in the Plains*, London: Jeremiah How, 1842; Hamilton, R, *Game by Hawkeye*, Higginbothams: Madras, 1881; *South of India Observer*, 5 April 1887. p. 2, col. 5; *South of India Observer* 25 July 1885, p. 10, col. 3.

27 Murray-Mitchell, *In Southern India. A Visit to Some of the Chief Mission Stations in the Madras Presidency*, London, 1885, p. 362.

28 Haig, L S, "Nilgiri Hills, South India. The Todas", Undated Notebook, (c. 1890s), in the Maxwell Papers, Box XIII, Cambridge South Asian Papers; see also King, W. Ross, *The Aboriginal Tribes of the Nilgiri Hills*, London, 1870, p. 14; Campbell, *Old Forest Ranger*, p. 36.

29 A Mrs Frendman accused Todas of pilfering from her garden and causing a nuisance by passing her house, Mrs Frendman to E B Thomas, 11 January 1862, Coimbatore Collector's Received Letterbook, January-June 1862, UDR.

30 A R W Lascelles to Govt., 17 March 1856, PMBR 17 April 1856, no. 562, pp. 6076-6087, TNSA.

31 The phrenologist W E Marshall, whilst himself impressed by the scenic qualities of the *mund*, doubted that the scene held much value for the Todas: "He sees the grass. Ha! He sees the dew. Ha! He sees the forest. Ha! But apparently it is only so much cattle's food with water on it and fuel in the distance. Ha! The sun is shining on it, and the water will soon dry; then the cattle will grow thirsty." Marshall, *A Phrenologist Among the Todas*, Calcutta, 1873, p. 57.

32 Breeks, J W, *An Account of the Primitive Tribes and Monuments of the Nilagiris*, edited by his widow (S M Breeks), London: India Museum, 1873.

33 J W Breeks to Madras Board of Revenue, 13 March 1871, PMBR 27 April 1871, no. 1759, pp. 2877-2878, OIOC.

34 PMBR 6 January 1882, no. 23, p. 24, TNSA.

35 *Nilgiri District Gazetteer*, no. 10, vol. III, 27 May 1871; *Nilgiri District Gazetteer*, no. 15, vol. XII, 6 August 1880; *Nilgiri District Gazetteer*, no. 14, vol. XII, 5 November 1881.

36 Breeks, J W, Draft Administration Report, 1869, Miscellaneous Sent, 1869, UDR.

37 Commissioner's Memorandum on Toda Lands, 6 March 1879, Misc. Received Letterbook, UDR.

38 PMBR 10 February 1880, pp. 795-798, no. 208, TNSA; N A Roupell, Acting Commissioner, to Madras Board of Revenue, 4 February 1881, Proceedings of the Madras Board of Revenue 17 February 1881, no. 283, p. 850, TNSA.

39 F Brant, Collector of the Nilgiris, to Madras Board of Revenue 14 July 1883, PMBR 30 July 1883, no. 2182, TNSA.

40 During the Revenue Settlement in the 1870s, Ossington Estate was found to include large tracts of Toda *patta*. Although government believed that the purchasers had been aware of the restriction, no penal revenues were imposed because no proof could be offered that the *present* owners knew of illegitimacy of the sale; L R Burrows, Acting Collector to Madras Board of Revenue, 21 August 1884, PMBR 13 September 1884, no. 3208, UDR; PMBR 13 September 1884, no. 3208, UDR.

41 The dubious legal status of inalienability was challenged in a number of litigations launched at the end of the 1870s and the beginning of the 1880s. Two Badaga cultivators and an European planter brought suits against government when they were prevented from taking control of land purchased under Toda *patta*. Both actions were dubbed 'Toda Suits' and in both cases, to the audible relief of the Madras Government, the judges found against the plaintiffs.

42 R S Benson, Special Assistant Collector, in charge, Nilgiri Settlement, to MBR, 9 July 1881, PMBR, 6 January 1882, no. 23, p. 24, TNSA.

43 Benson, to MBR, 9 July 1881; PMRD 18 April 1882, no. 397, UDR.

44 In 1879, the Commissioner remarked that the land was granted in 1863, "on the clear understanding that they were not to sell the land", Commissioner's order, 6 March 1879, Miscellaneous Received, 1879, UDR.

45 N A Roupell, Acting Commissioner, to Madras Board of Revenue, 14 November 1881, PMBR 5 January 1882, no. 23, pp. 25-29, UDR.

46 PMBR 6 January 1882, no. 23, p. 24, TNSA.

47 PMBR 9 May 1882, no. 480, p. 221, OIOC.

48 PMBR 27 April 1882, no. 1164, p. 626, TNSA.

49 F Brandt, Collector of the Nilgiris, to Madras Board of Revenue 10 April 1883, PMBR 27 April 1883, no. 1189, TNSA.

50 F Brant, Collector of Nilgiris to Madras Board of Revenue, 11 August 1883, PMBR 12 September 1883, no. 2743, TNSA.

51 PMBR 9 May 1882, no. 480, p. 221, OIOC.

52 PMBR (Land Revenue) 27 March 1888, no. 309, UDR.

53 PMRD 21 March 1893, no. 249, pp. 405-411, OIOC.

54 In 1882, an editorial in the local English newspaper stated that: "It has been suggested by a paternal government to these innocent denizens of the Blue Hills [the Nilgriris] not to pay but to relinquish their lands to the state. The Todahs wont see the goak and can't pay." In response to a hasty and categorical denial from the Collectorate authorities the next edition of the paper published a full retraction. All the newspaper had done, however, was to repeat the gossip of the Ootacamund club and library rooms. The continual remissions of rent given by government and the fairly complete restrictions already placed on the terms of Toda land tenure made total governmental control, to some, a logical conclusion to the administration of Toda lands. The haste of the retraction emphasises the legal dubiousness of the course the revenue authorities were following, *South of India Observer*, 5 January 1884, p. 9, col. 4; *South of India Observer*, 12 January 1884, p. 10, col. 1.

55 *South of India Observer*, 10 May 1884, p. 7, col. 4.

56 See Sutton, D, *Other Landscapes: Hill Communities, Settlers and State on the Colonial Nilgiris, c. 1820-1900*, unpublished PhD thesis, Jawaharlal Nehru University, 2001, chapter 4, pp. 144.

57 *Nilgiri District Gazetteer*, vol. XIX, no. 1, 8 January 1887.

58 *South of India Observer* 26 July 1884, p. 9, col. 4.59) C.

59 F MacCartie, Acting Collector to Land Revenue Commissioners, PMRD 26 September 1891, no. 1008, pp. 725-727, OIOC; PMRD 21 January 1892, no. 402, misc., OIOC; PMBR (Land Revenue) 18 April 1993, Forest no. 283, UDR.

60 J D Rees, Collector, to Commissioner of Land Revenue, 15 April 1992, PMRD 21 March 1893, no. 249, pp. 405-411, OIOC.

61 In the 1883 Settlement Reports, 54.40 acres were registered in Paranganad as Todapatta, 601.4 acres in Merkanad and 2540.69 acres in Todanad, a total 3206.49 acres. Ten years later, 2948.67 acres of Toda patta were recorded, a figure which was reduced to 2795.1 acres by 1937. PMRD 21 March 1893, no. 249, pp. 405-411, OIOC; Development Department General Order 31 August 1837, reproduced in Appendix III, P K Nambiar, Census of India 1961, vol. IX, Part V-C, *The Todas*, Madras, 1965.

62 J D Rees, Collector, to Commissioner for Land Revenue, PMRD 28 April 1892, no. 421, pp. 675-676, OIOC.

63 PMRD 15 August 1892, no. 854, pp. 529-530, OIOC.

64 PMRD 15 August 1892.

65 Evam Piljain-Weiderman, a contemporary Toda representative, used the 1937 register of Toda patta lands in such a fashion in negotiating with the Forest Department, Piljain-Weiderman, 1999, pers. comm.

Landscape Aesthetics and the Inscaping of Class in Women's Nineteenth Century Literature
Michelle Sipe

The recurrent metaphor of landscape as the inscape of national identity emphasizes the quality of light, the question of social visibility, the power of the eye to naturalize the rhetoric of national affiliation and its forms of collective expression.[1]

Valuable work has already been done on landscape as an ideological and socio-political construct as well as on the position of women *vis-à-vis* landscape and spatial relations – the interdisciplinary work of scholars such as Gillian Rose, Susan Morgan, and Elizabeth Bohls has provided critical contributions to the theoretical study of women and the politics of space in British culture. Drawing from this tradition, my paper will address eighteenth and nineteenth century landscape as a network of spatialising activities that structure women's narratives, with an emphasis on the specific genre of domestic novels. In general, feminist readings of landscape politics have shown how masculine forms of landscape and land management have produced the corollary of feminine enclosure, whether symbolic, social, physical, or architectural. But, as many of these same critics have observed, enclosure does not sufficiently account for women's range of spatial movements and practices in nineteenth century British culture, their specific architectonics of social space.

In particular, I would like to introduce the concept of 'inscaping', a term that I have borrowed from Homi Bhabha and redefined for my own purposes. As a theoretical term, the active verb 'inscaping', can contribute to feminist readings of women's mediated relationship to landscape politics as a predominantly masculine nexus of ideas and practices. Bhabha's emphasis on the role of the imagination in the definition of English identity can be extended to include the often shifting, heterogeneous constructions of this 'inscape'. The larger goal of the project is to show how women novelists throughout the Victorian period appropriate (masculine) ideals of landscape husbandry, work that frames their access to spaces that either expand or exceed the confines of the domestic sphere: from the lady's parlour to the larder, to the spatial configuration of the working class household, to schools and philanthropic institutions. Through these appropriations, nineteenth century women actively shape a range of cultural, national, and institutional spaces and, perhaps most consequentially, the more spatially diverse and fluid spheres of intellectual and literary thought. These spatialising activities constitute what I am calling 'inscaping', activities that take as their condition of possibility the masculine production of landscape and its practices of feminine enclosure, particularly in their approach to and construction of middle class identity and 'the poor'. Through narratives that construct a particular kind of female subjectivity, nineteenth century women writers emphasise modes of self-discipline and the regulation of time, spaces and resources, qualities influenced by and often exhibited through the language of landscape aesthetics. After quickly reviewing the theoretical stakes, I will use the landscaping manuals and guides of John and Jane

Loudon, one of the most popular and productive publishing teams in Victorian England, to illustrate the entwined nature of landscaping and inscaping during the early and mid-nineteenth century. To conclude, I will focus on Elizabeth Hamilton's *The Cottagers of Glenburnie,* an early nineteenth century novel that exemplifies middle class women's active engagement with landscape husbandry and the spatial politics of early nineteenth century British culture. These examples will show the ambitious nature of women writers' interventions in the politics of landscape – their expansion of acceptable domains of discourse for women by claiming the garden as a domestic space requiring feminine supervision – literary movements that have been overlooked in Romantic, Victorian, and Postcolonial Studies. Whereas even feminist theory has tended to assume women's alienation from landscape aesthetics, I would like to posit that it is ultimately through feminine domestic and interior positions and contexts that they are able to claim agency and redefine masculine constructions of space.

As both Marxist and postcolonial critics alike have demonstrated, representations of the English countryside – whether in paintings, treatises, travel narratives, poems or novels – and landscape as an aesthetic category and practice, are inseparable from the construction and performance of national and class identities. Raymond Williams emphasises the nostalgic thrust of rural representations that tend to palliate or merely obscure social anxieties provoked by the enclosure acts in particular, but also by capitalism's more general reshaping of earlier understandings of rural and urban space.[2] Similarly, Anne Bermingham has pointed out the correspondence between "the aesthetics of the painted landscape and the economics of the enclosed one".[3] Detailed studies and histories of the discourse during the 1790s, the golden age of the landscape treatise and picturesque debate support these crucial insights and overwhelmingly demonstrate the masculine nature of landscape aesthetics and masculinist constructions of national and class identity. The debates over commanding prospects and how best to achieve them seem to consistently reflect masculine concerns of ownership and property management. Indeed, nearly all treatises on the picturesque and the English garden assume a masculine subject with the economic means, social position, and defining vision necessary to carry out abstract principles of landscape aesthetics, such as William Repton, Richard Payne Knight, and Uvedale Price were able to do on their own country homes and estates.

As Williams argues in *The Country and the City*, landscape is at once a practice and a product of private ownership and the establishment of imagined, material, and social forms of enclosure, including, as Addison claimed, a language that gives its owner "a kind of Property in everything he sees". Indeed what is at stake in the debates of the period is not just the question of what constitutes natural beauty, agreeable prospects, or the superior garden; for they are also passionate debates about England in general and English masculinity more specifically. Against the overtly social garden of the French, Englishmen celebrate a landscape aesthetic that ensures individual privacy while reflecting social status. Often understood as a set of external or exterior concepts and practices, a fundamental feature of landscape aesthetics is the extension of the masculine self, anchored in the country house, to surrounding spaces, enfolding those spaces and defining them within the context of social privileges afforded by land ownership. In other words, the social function of private, interior spaces (such as the gallery that displays lineage, wealth, and power) is imprinted on external spaces: from the surrounding gardens, parks, groves, hunting grounds, to the villages and fields beyond. Such extensions of private ownership were also, of course, built upon the aristocratic tradition of leisured travel. As John Dixon Hunt and Peter Willis have observed, "the country estate gave local form to the souvenirs of the Grand Tour".[4] Hence the extension of masculine constructions of landscape reach beyond national borders in the imposition of the owner's gaze, as

Addison so succinctly put it. Indeed, such visual enclosures were materialised in eighteenth century landscape inventions such as the ha-ha (the sunken fence that masked enclosure's economic and social effects), to which Horace Walpole's famous pronouncement attests when he referred to its inventor, Kent, as having "leaped the fence, and saw that all nature was a garden".[5]

These masculinist constructions of landscape aesthetics have, in turn, been extensively and productively analysed by feminist critics who have mapped out the gendered nature of these spatial activities and relationships – in which the aesthetic male subject positions women as passive objects within the landscape, often conflating them with Nature and making them the site for identity or self-making. Within this paradigm, women, the feminisation of land, and those who work the land, function as metonyms for the gentleman's rural retreat, a positioning that props up and works to reanchor male privilege as well as traditional class hierarchies. According to Elizabeth Bohls, characteristic features of eighteenth century aesthetic writings (including those by Addison, Shaftesbury, Reynolds, Gilpin, Price, and Knight) are "the display of a powerful abstracting impulse" and "the denial of the particular", characteristics that she argues, "enforce the distinction between those positioned within the masculine 'Universal', and thus granted the authority of the aesthetic subject, and those whose "particularity" excludes them".[6] Feminist criticism's focus on women's enclosure effectively links the containment of women to the gendering of space, from the seclusion of the country house, to the systematic enclosure of the commons, as well as the displacement of the rural poor and yeomanry during this period of sweeping economic and social change.

While the emphasis of traditional feminist criticism on feminine immobility and enclosure has yielded critical tools for exposing patriarchal assumptions and structures that shaped Victorian culture, this emphasis also tends to obscure women's physical, social and intellectual mobility, their productive share in Britain's shifting social geography, as well as their collusion with patterns of socio-spatial domination. Indeed, landscaping is often framed in critical studies as a masculine practice that works from the top down as a means of social control that insists, in Foucault's panoptic paradigm, on controlled visibility and the discrete separation of individuals and the spaces that define them. However, early or pre-Victorian culture also consists of modes of 'inscaping', a type of ideological work that situates the local, or small enclosed space associated with women and feminine concerns as the site for social transformation from the inside out. Homi Bhabha uses the term 'inscape' to highlight the symbolic relationship between landscape, subjectivity, and national identity, but I would like to borrow the active verb form of the term as a hybrid theoretical concept that can also be used to refine and extend current understandings of women's relationship to landscape aesthetics and the architectures of class and social identity that these ideals and practices at once shape and reflect. Like landscaping, 'inscaping' can be understood as a discourse with real social effects which women reappropriate in their use of the principles of land management and aesthetics within domestic contexts and rural settings.

Women as social inscapers inherit the ideological tools of a masculinist British tradition yet use these tools in ways that attest to both the changing world and the multiplicity of women's movements within it. While literary critics like Catherine Gallagher and Rosemarie Bodenheimer have examined the relationships between women's novels and social reform, focusing primarily on how the middle class uses signs of gender and class to navigate unknown, even hostile spaces, they have not explicitly addressed the British middle class ideological investment in landscape and domestic architecture, ideals rooted in a pre-industrial rural culture that have shaped more modern approaches to 'the poor', urban planning, housing, as well as domesticity and living practices. Thus, while eighteenth century landscaping was intended to reflect and anchor the autonomy of the male landowner, and to balance utility and beauty in the midst of enclosure and agricultural development, nineteenth century women inscapers redefine notions of the picturesque, of beauty, and social utility by turning their vision away from land itself to the working classes, their households, and domestic activities. If social control and class positioning are key aspects of masculinist landscaping, if enclosing and defining the boundaries of agricultural lands and parks, workers' cottages and semi-detached villas function to construct a rural poor contained by (the) landscape, women novelists create spatial enclosures of their own, in which their own imaginative inscapes demonstrate their roles as cultural producers rather than passive consumers of rural and domestic life.

As Gilbert and Gubar's feminist study has so powerfully demonstrated, enclosure does describe the situation of many Victorian women and their various confines, yet within these confines there is still communication to the 'outside' through social relationships with fathers, husbands, brothers and sons, as well as with household things such as books, engravings, sketches, maps and globes, everyday objects that incorporate the externalised masculine discourse of landscape and spatial relationships. The home functions, then, as the site of infiltration of external, patriarchal conceptions of space, where the management of space, resources, time, work and leisure produces the privacy and individuality crucial to middle class identity, feminine as well as masculine. Inscaping is the product of this infiltration insofar as the concepts and values of landscape are appropriated as material for an alternative feminine perception of social space identified within domestic contexts. While the joint scholarship of Leonore Davidoff and Catherine Hall and Elizabeth Langland's work have carefully studied the nuanced relationship between gender and class within the bourgeois household, here I want to think of the household as a conduit, a place where concepts of landscape enter the domestic space, reshaping it as well as the exterior world that the home is ostensibly defined against.

Although this comes from a slightly later moment in the conceptual history of landscape, the particular relationship between masculine exterior and feminine interior plays itself out in an exemplary way in the conjugal relations and corollary literary products of Mr and Mrs John Loudon. John Loudon, landscaper *extraordinaire*, did not just transform the pleasure grounds of the wealthy; his many treatises, periodicals, and encyclopedias also popularised landscape architecture and aesthetics for a hungry middle class audience. His marathon title pages attest to the exhaustive nature of Loudon's enterprise. Take, for example, one of his most successful early publications, which is entitled:

> A Treatise on Forming, Improving, and Managing Country Residences; and on the Choice of Situations Appropriate to Every Class of Purchasers. In All Which the Object in View is to unite in a better manner than has hitherto been done, a Taste Founded in Nature with Economy and Utility, in constructing and improving Mansions and other Buildings, so as to combine Architectural Fitness with Picturesque Effect; and in forming Gardens, Orchards, Farms, Parks, Pleasure-grounds, Shrubberies, all kinds of useful or decorative Seats according to the Rank, Fortune, and Expenditure of Proprietors; from the Cottage to the Palace. With an Appendix.[7]

While Jane Webb Loudon published more traditionally feminine works such as *The Country Companion, or How to Enjoy a Country Life Rationally,* 1845, and books such as *Gardening for Ladies,* 1854, as well as a range of instructive works for children on gardening and the natural sciences, her domestic advice is as extensive in ideological reach as her husband's detailed management of exterior landscape and architectural spaces. *The Companion's* narrator, represented as a mature woman experienced in household management, writes a series of letters to Annie, a young woman who has recently married and moved into her husband's country house. After instructing Annie on the best way to build and maintain a fire, the next objective is to dispel the house's gloominess, to improve the circulation of light and air by removing the trees that both bride and narrator agree crowd the house and limit its prospect. The following extract demonstrates quite beautifully the politics of inscaping, the use of land, labourers, and patriarchal relations to revise social spaces and relationships from within the home:

> You say you felt excessively pained when your husband said, that, though he did not think any circumstances could ever have induced him to order those trees to be cut down, he was delighted to have such an opportunity of pleasing you; and that, when you heard the workmen employed in cutting the trees down the following morning, you felt every blow they struck, and you thought he must hate you for wishing him to make such a sacrifice. These feelings are quite natural, but, in my opinion, the readiness with which your husband complied with your wishes will strengthen the bond of affection between you rather than weaken it, as there cannot possibly be a stronger proof of love than is shown in sacrificing our own prejudices in favour of the beloved object.[8]

As this passage suggests, the marriage itself becomes a set of relations that can be spatialised in potentially enabling ways. The woman, 'the beloved object' embowered in the country estate, is able, nevertheless, to use feminine discourses of love, sympathy, and domestic health to manage masculine spaces and traditional uses of land and resources. Thus, the husband's emotional attachment to the trees that for him symbolise the family's history gives way to the wife's legitimated desire to improve the sanitary condition of the house as well as the view. Of course, this event is framed in terms of feeling and affection, in which the wife's revision of the landscape is tempered by "every blow" she experiences with the destruction of the trees. In addition, she hears rather than oversees their removal, an emphasis on an alternate sense that displaces the masculine subject's prerogative of sight.

By stressing the need for light and air as well as prospect, Annie's interior point-of-view opens up the domestic space as the primary frame for the appreciation of landscape. The practice of inscaping, in effect, 'calls in the country', though not in the ways Pope intended. This process, at once narrative and spatial, is carried out in the very structure of the text. The initial view is an interior one, beginning with the workings of the household, the careful divisions of labour and space, from parlour to larder, that then moves progressively outwards, to the management of the gardens, the animals, the grounds, and, finally, into the surrounding village and its homes. The book's concluding section, "Country Duties", instructs Annie in the ways to successfully use her expertise to improve the lives of cottagers through the instruction of their daughters in cooking, cleaning, and sewing, as well as the establishment of schools. This section emphasizes, in particular, how to manage the delicate business of cottage visiting, especially ways to soften and elide its intrusive nature by properly managing proximity and distance. Jane Loudon's *Companion* – a wonderfully hybrid text, part epistolary novel, conduct book, and detailed manual on household management, animal husbandry, gardening, and cottage visiting – reappropriates the ideological goal of landscape aesthetics that her husband's work exemplifies: to harmonise class difference through the skillful management of spaces "from the Cottage to the Palace".

Preceding Jane Loudon's narrative by almost 40 years, Elizabeth Hamilton's Scottish novel, *The Cottagers of Glenburnie: a Tale for the Farmer's Inglenook*, 1808, is one of the earliest and most thorough examples of a woman's novel that treats class as a spatial entity that can be improved through the principles of landscape husbandry and the political economy of the estate.[9] The narrative's two-part structure provides the framework for the amalgamation of landscape ideals and middle class definitions of domestic harmony and individual improvement. The first half (related through flashback) is about the protagonist's own 'improvement' as a domestic servant in an aristocratic household, a masonry of middle class subjectivity, aided by genteel mentors such as Miss Osborne and Miss Malden, within a fractious feminine household abandoned by or neglected by its patriarchs. The other story is that of an elderly Mrs Mason, who after years of loyal service to the aristocratic Longlands family, mobilises her well-earned and carefully cultivated subjectivity to reform a recalcitrant Scottish village by combining principles of beauty and order from within the domestic sphere.

Orphaned at a very young age, Betty Mason is taken in and employed by the wealthy family after she charms the lady of the house with her honesty and industry. What appears at first to be a simple story of good works and rewards, however, becomes a grueling litany of domestic injustices and intrigues. Yet Mrs Mason's history of domestic labour and moral development in the aristocratic household, though contentious and often brutal, is also characterised by a series of female friendships and mentoring which enable her to survive and eventually prosper. Betty's most influential mentor is Miss Osborne, a genteel English woman who, despite her 'thorny' position as a female dependent, begins her own kind of philanthropic work by stewarding Betty's education.[10] As Mrs Mason recalls, "to her goodness I am indeed indebted for all I know. From her I learned not only to read with propriety, to write a tolerable hand, and to cast accounts; but what was more valuable than all these, from her I learned to think".[11] Thus, despite her required obedience and humility as a servant, "to think", or the independent critical thought that Miss Osborne cultivates becomes a portable (bourgeois) commodity that will authorize Betty Mason's later project of village reform. Eventually, her education and hard work enable her to rise to the status of governess for the Longlands children, and she impresses the family with her steady, yet gentle 'management' of the children as well as other servants.

After a lifetime of dedicated service, including the heroic rescue of the Longlands family's children from a fire that leaves her lame, Mrs Mason is left with no place to retire when the spoiled Lord Lintop inherits the estate. His first 'improvement' is to eliminate all of the cottages, including the one she has been promised for her years of loyalty. It is at this juncture that the instability of interior, domestic politics affect the landscape that frames the estate and its social relations. 'Poor management' and indulgence are attributed to the Lord's bad character, qualities reflected in the brutal levelling of the cottages for superficial aesthetic effect or selfish economic gain. Aristocratic neglect and indolence lead to the corruption of the family seat and the depopulation of the landscape. Implicit in Lord Longlands' 'improvements' is a critique of the excesses and injustice of irresponsible landscaping, the opening of 'the prospect' without regard for those whose labour have earned them a place on the estate. In contrast with the male landscapers' selfishness and greed, the middle class woman's practical knowledge and discourse of sympathy shape her relationship to the land and enable her to successfully reform individual households as well as village life.

While the country house's interior and grounds are barely sketched – it is domestic networks and rivalries as well as objects like embroidered chair covers and lace that define the social space of Hill

Castle – Mrs Mason's removal to Glenburnie is saturated with the discourse of landscape aesthetics. The narrator's use of this discourse is most pronounced when Mrs Mason travels. She insists on moving to her last living relative's village where she believes she can do the most good, rather than residing more comfortably with the Stewarts, the late Miss Osborne's widowed husband and daughters. Accompanied by her late mentor's family, Mrs Mason's view of the countryside on their approach to Glenburnie underscores her aesthetic eye and pleasure in the landscape:

> They had not proceeded many paces, until they were struck with admiration at the uncommon wildness of the scene, which now opened to their view. The rocks which seemed to guard the entrance of the Glen, were abrupt and savage, and approached so near each other, that one could suppose them to have been riven asunder, to give a passage to the clear stream which flowed between them. As they advanced, the hills receded on either side, making room for meadows, and corn fields, through which the rapid burn pursued its way, in many a fantastic maze.[12]

This description incorporates the undomesticated, wild nature of the sublime and the picturesque so beloved by tourist, landscape theorist, and landowner alike, in which the "uncommon wildness", its "savage" and "abrupt" nature stimulate the gentleman viewer's imagination and emotions. But the sublime and picturesque are quickly acknowledged and then discarded, replaced by a feminine discourse that supports a landscape moralised in terms of the human relationships it reflects:

> If the reader is a traveller, he must know, and if he is a speculator in canals he must regret, that rivers have in general a trick of running out of the straight line. But however they may in this resemble the moral conduct of man, it is but doing justice to these favourite children of nature to observe, that in all their wanderings each stream follows the strict injunctions of its parent, and never for a moment loses its original character. The meadows and corn-fields, indeed, seemed very evidently to have been encroachments made by stealth on the sylvan reign: for none had their outlines marked with the mathematical precision, in which the modern improver delights.[13]

In this passage, the physical landscape is infused with the domestic values of kinship, individual character, "moral conduct", as well as human labour, yet the narrator and protagonist maintain the leisured position of women capable of, and entitled to, interpret rural scenery. In addition, Hamilton does not miss the opportunity to skewer the speculator's opportunism as well as the modern improver's alienating abstraction, and the consequential neglect of a specific landscape's social and moral significance. Thus, Hamilton's critique of the excesses and abstractions of picturesque landscape adopts the distancing effect of the aesthetic observer in order to advocate women's domestic expertise as the means to manage class relations.

Her arrival at the village of Glenburnie affords another opportunity for a feminine revisioning of landscape. Emerging from the dream-like quality of the "beauty of the scene", Mrs Mason arrives at the top of the Glen, which gives her a bird's-eye view of the village. However, pleasing distances and contrasting colours and textures quickly dissolve into a detailed domestic realism, a very close, intimate view of dirt, decay, and neglect that was so lovely from a distance. After surveying the village, Mrs Mason is confronted with her cousin, Mrs MacClarty's cottage, which is splattered with mud and obstructed by a dunghill, and a lack of paving stones that create puddles of 'dirty water' discarded from the house.[14]

As the appearance of the cottage foreshadows, this latter section of the novel involves a new set of domestic trials for Mrs Mason, whose relatives resist her multiple attempts to improve the cottage's comfort and hygiene through orderly methods. One chapter fittingly entitled "A Peep Behind the Curtain" reflects Hamilton's appeal to a middle class audience, with a title resembling later Victorian *exposés* of working class urban conditions in industrial cities such as Manchester that both horrified and titillated its readers with the shocking details of how the 'other' half lived. As Mrs Mason "casts her exploring eye on the house and furniture", she is impressed with the stock of fine linen but distressed by the lack of fabric for general use, i.e. cleanliness and comfort.[15] Soon, however, Mrs Mason's senses are assaulted with sundry forms of dirt and "intolerable effluvia".[16] The windows are sealed shut and coated with grime, the morning rituals reveal chaos and lack of sanitation, bed bugs torment her with their fangs, hairs in the butter disgust her, and her ears are "assailed by the harsh form of discord".[17] Eventually such conditions prompt Mrs Mason to escape the cottage and its "squashy pool, and its neighbour the dunghill", and to find solace in the surrounding scenery.[18] But her appreciation of the landscape is, again, not simply or romantically aesthetic. Rather than an opportunity for solitary reverie or poetic inspiration, her encounter with nature is distinguished by 'gratitude' and a renewal of social responsibility:

> Seating herself upon a projecting rock, she contemplated the effulgent glory of the heavens, as they brightened into splendour at the approach of the lord of the day. The good woman's heart glowed with rapture: but it did not vainly glow, as does the heart or the imagination of many a pretender to superior taste; for the rapture of her heart was fraught with gratitude. What are all the works of man compared with the grandeur of such a scene?[19]

Hamilton's protagonist celebrates a woman's ability to appreciate natural scenery in terms of feminine sympathy and a belief in Christian providence and good works. As in the novel's previous descriptions of landscape, there is an implicit critique of the excesses and inaccessibility of the art of landscape gardening, of its artificial display and denial of community and social relations. The 'designs of man' are minimised, subtly displaced in favour of a female subjectivity whose focus on everyday life and habits of neatness, activity, and "timely attention" frame their vision of landscape.[20] Mrs Mason's moralised aesthetic appreciation of rural landscape and pleasure in the outdoors underwrite her gradual transformation of the village from the inside out, one cottage at a time.

After moving to a more hospitable village household, Mrs Mason begins to patiently reform the village cottages and their inhabitants, instilling principles of cleanliness, hygiene, and order, as well as infusing more tenuous values such as taste, duty, and decorum. She uses metaphors for land and its husbandry to instruct cottagers on how to raise their children, comparing unruly, disobedient sons and daughters to "fields" requiring "plowing" and "proper manure".[21] At the novel's close, Mrs Mason takes over the supervision of the village school; using an educational method Hamilton admired at the time, the heroine divides the students into classes of "landlords" and "tenants" whose educational instruments are hoes, spades, and seeds, tools intended to improve at once the aesthetic and moral value of the village.[22] The protagonist's successful renovation of the school and reform of the children have a ripple effect that spreads to the surrounding village, yielding visible improvements that are attributed to "the spirit of emulation excited by the elder school boys, for the external appearance of their respective homes", as well as to the girls who "exerted themselves with no less activity, to effect a reformation within doors".[23]

Focusing on the fluidity between outdoors and indoors, Mrs Mason's inscaping of the rural poor works to authorise middle class women's social roles as active producers and caretakers of a moralised landscape aesthetic meant to heal, or at least buffer, class tensions. Women's interventions in landscape aesthetics, as Elizabeth Bohls has concluded, are often diminished or contained within a set of social conventions in which 'ladies' were allowed to sketch picturesque scenery and to take an interest in landscape under the rubric of feminine accomplishments. However, Hamilton appropriates the popular tableau of landscape painting and picturesque tourist literature, "the farmer's inglenook", an image often associated with stasis, nostalgia, and an elite perspective, and uses it quite aggressively as a vehicle for social reform. Coded as a solidly middle class woman who is sympathetic rather than sentimental, Mrs Mason responds to the dirty trials of everyday life through Christian principles of cleanliness, hygiene and domestic order. While she claims the attention and commitment to class harmony that Price sought to promote on his estate, her's is a paternalism interiorised, yet mobile, intent on reshaping from within the household a wider social landscape through the mobilisation of a more efficient, rational, comfortable way of life.

1   Bhabha, H, "DissemiNation: Time, Narrative, and the Margins of the Modern Nation", *Nation and Narration*, Bhabha, H, ed., London and New York: Routledge, 1990, pp. 291-322.

2   Williams, R, *The Country and the City*, New York: Oxford University Press, 1973.

3   Bermingham, A, *Landscape and Ideology: the English Rustic Tradition, 1740-1860*, Berkeley and Los Angeles: University of California Press, 1989.

4   Hunt, J D and Willis, P, "Introduction," *The Genius of the Place: The English Landscape Garden 1620-1820*, Hunt, J H and Willis, P, eds., Cambridge Mass. and London: MIT Press, 1993, p. 17.

5   Walpole, H, "from The History of the Modern Taste in Gardening (1771/1780)", Hunt and Willis, eds., *The Genius of the Place: The English Landscape Garden 1620-1820*, p. 313.

6   Bohls, E, *Women Travel Writers and the Language of Aesthetics, 1716-1818*, Cambridge: Cambridge University Press, 1995, p. 13.

7   Loudon, J C, *A Treatise on Forming, Improving, and Managing Country Residences*, 2 vols., London: Longman, 1806.

8   Loudon, J W, *The Lady's Country Companion; or, How to Enjoy a Country Life Rationally*, London: Longmans, Green, Reader, and Dyer, 1867, pp. 14-15.

9   Hamilton, E, *The Cottagers of Glenburnie: a Tale for the Farmer's Ingle-nook (1808)*, New York and London: Garland Publishing, 1974.

10 Hamilton, *The Cottagers of Glenburnie*, p. 51.

11 Hamilton, *The Cottagers of Glenburnie*, p. 50.

12 Hamilton, *The Cottagers of Glenburnie*, pp. 124-125.

13 Hamilton, *The Cottagers of Glenburnie*, pp. 125-126.

14 Hamilton, *The Cottagers of Glenburnie*, p. 137.

15 Hamilton, *The Cottagers of Glenburnie*, p. 143.

16 Hamilton, *The Cottagers of Glenburnie*, p. 163.

17 Hamilton, *The Cottagers of Glenburnie*, p. 195.

18 Hamilton, *The Cottagers of Glenburnie*, p. 192.

19 Hamilton, *The Cottagers of Glenburnie*, pp. 193-194.

20 Hamilton, *The Cottagers of Glenburnie*, p. 207.

21 Hamilton, *The Cottagers of Glenburnie*, p. 185.

22 Hamilton, *The Cottagers of Glenburnie*, p. 387.

23 Hamilton, *The Cottagers of Glenburnie*, p. 397.

"Delusive Dreams of Fruitfulness and Plenty": Some Aspects of British Frontier Semiology c. 1800-1850
Robert Grant

In recent writings by Mary Louise Pratt, Stephen Aron, and Howard Lamar and Leonard Thompson, inter-racial and inter-cultural contact at colonial frontiers has been figured as dynamic and dialogic.[1] In these accounts, both coloniser and colonised are engaged in a process of exchange in a zone in which identity is produced from strategic reciprocity and negotiation.[2] In this paper, by contrast, the frontier is treated as a metropolitan construct, something that is given meaning and value by metropolitan interests and concerns. My aim is to recover how certain features of frontier landscapes were deployed in creating and maintaining networks of meaning that I argue coalesce around social practices and modes of behaviour in the different zones of frontier and metropolis. In this context, it is worth remembering that the inviting colonial prospects fashioned by countless nineteenth century travelogues, journals of exploration, pamphlets, illustrated views and newspaper reports were produced and consumed very far from the places they purported to depict. Colonial frontiers were sites located well beyond metropolitan control. They were landscapes far less regulated by social practices and modes of interaction familiar in the metropolitan world. Indeed, one of the central problems of the colonial frontier was the apparent ease with which such modes and practices were subject to renegotiation, slippage and decay and, in that context, the body of representations considered in this paper can be seen to offer important cues to the would-be emigrant of their proposed role and place within those distant landscapes.

In Judith Butler's work, the production of gender roles has been posited as the 'citation' of a set of normative behaviours that collectively produce/embody identity, and this model has been productively employed in a range of other contexts to explore the creation and mediation of ethnic and social identities.[3] Drawing on a common thematic in this work–that the re-iteration of particular modes of behaviour produces a social architecture that is normative – this paper stresses the role of promotional writers in 'making' frontier landscapes. By anchoring the terms on which social identity was produced in the characteristics of the landscape itself, these writers were able to naturalise that identity, marking out the terrain of belonging but simultaneously demarcating the terrain of 'others', such as native populations or pioneer settlers (the Dutch *voortrekers* in South Africa, or the Australian bushmen and Canadian backwoodsmen) all of whom, significantly, also had claims on that landscape. The abjection of frontier landscapes through those 'others' constituted a potent warning that was aimed at reinforcing the 'right' social relations at the frontier, helping secure them from that worrying tendency to slippage and decay. The other, Edenic side to frontier landscapes then becomes recognisable as a forcible reiteration, a constant rehearsal of what it took to 'fit in'.

We start with one such Edenic landscape, on the south-east coast of Australia in October 1803, as the British convict transporter the *Calcutta* nudges its way through the Port Philip headlands, an encounter described by First Lieutenant James Tuckey as an archetypal transition from old to new, from blighted past to a bright hopeful future. Gently carried by a fair wind, the stinking, sweating hulk, laden with the cast-off, the criminal and the simply unfortunate, seemed to float free from its soiled past into a harbour "unruffled as the bosom of unpolluted innocence". The phrase is Tuckey's, but it was one of many such nineteenth century Anglo-American narrations of encounter, of Europeans breasting horizons to find the dream of a new world, a landscape within which to build a new imperium. "Nature in the world's first spring", as Tuckey described it, a *tabula rasa* on which to inscribe what he imagined as "a second Rome" drawn in the wilderness.[4]

These metaphors of European civilisation, transplanted to bear fruit in distant landscapes, defined the new arrivals in terms of a transitive relationship with the future. Physical activity, personal industry, work, was to free them from their previous condition and provide the means of attaining the new. The torpid South Australian silence was consequently soon broken by Tuckey with "the 'busy hum' of... voices", the crack of axes and the bustle of civilisation, just as David Collins, Judge Advocate at Port Jackson in New South Wales had turned the "confusion" of woods there into "regularity" seven years earlier, and its silence into noiseful industry.[5] Struck by the contrast between nature "in her simplest, purest garb" and the "vice, profaneness and immorality" of the British convicts spilling ashore at Port Jackson, Collins had admitted that perhaps no group was more in need of a new future than those "depraved branches" of the nation's offspring.[6] "Nature in the world's first spring", nature "in her simplest, purest garb", nature just waiting for the transforming European hand: so many imagined futures were possible in those distant landscapes, it seemed, that emigration could be made a prospect for all classes, so potent its transformative power that it could be offered as the solution to almost every metropolitan ill.

During the first few decades of the nineteenth century, of course, the British landscape was also being transformed, physically, economically and socially. Mechanisation of cottage industries, changing patterns of land tenure and new methods of farming exacerbated painful economic conditions following the end of hostilities in Europe. Glutted labour markets and growing unemployment precipitated machine-breaking, rioting and incendiarism, while commentators struggled to explain the upheavals. Articles in medical journals anatomised working class living conditions, Parliamentary Committees interrogated witnesses on the results of industrialisation, and literary journals debated the impact of the Poor Law. The language of turbulence, riot, dissipation and want, however, disclosed another contemporary metropolitan anxiety, overpopulation, and the image of the British "hive" consequently evoked the industrial power of the nation with worrying uncertainty. As Robert Torrens fretted in 1817: "The hive contains more than it can support; and if it be not permitted to swarm, the excess must either perish of famine, or be destroyed by internal contests for food."[7]

A belief that "swarming" of portions of the British populace would relieve the pressures of overpopulation and ameliorate working class distress was a feature of much early nineteenth century literature promoting emigration to Canada, Australia, the Cape and New Zealand. In 1811, for example, the pardoned convict David Mann returned to Britain from New South Wales convinced that "new seats of empire" erected in remote parts of the globe might drain the old world of its superfluous population. In 1822, Robert Gourlay argued colonisation of Canada was of the highest importance when millions of British people were starving in the midst of plenty, or throwing themselves on the Parish for relief.[8] Enthusiasts for emigration were prone to calculating the cost of poor relief, and pointing out that no such burdens need apply in their favoured destination.[9] An association of emigration in the public mind with pauperism, social compromise and even criminal conviction had given it a bad odour in early nineteenth century Britain, although it was the object of a new breed of promoters of emigration and colonisation to change all that. Edward Gibbon Wakefield's 1833 treatment of the English social landscape in *England and America*, for example, made what were by then well-rehearsed observations on working class distress, but also pointed to a slow erosion of middle class social standing, declining returns on small capital, and crowded professions in which a living had to be made "by snatching the bread out of each other's mouths".[10] Other promoters of emigration like William Wentworth, John Howison and Nathaniel Ogle addressed their volumes specifically to the British middle class who, Ogle observed, were "unable to find employment adequate to their numbers, education, and habits".[11] These writers represented the condition of England as the product of islands groaning not only under the weight of over-population but also of over-extended capital, evoking a middle class version of the British 'hive' designed to give them a more than philanthropic interest in emigration. The intention was that they should have an interest as investors as well as emigrants, to see in it the prospect of their own financial and social advancement.

Accordingly, frontier landscapes were described, siren-like, seductively 'inviting' members of every class to surrender their metropolitan woes for landscapes of plenty as much as halfway round the globe. Thomas Godwin clucked that "nothing can be more inviting to the hand of the cultivator, than the beautiful plains of rich and valuable land" in Van Diemen's Land.[12] In New South Wales, Wentworth assured prospective colonists, a "country truly beautiful" awaited them, luxuriantly grassed and highly fertile.[13] In parts of Canada, according to Howison, the climate and soil were so productive that a kind of Land of Cockayne existed, with apple and pear orchards growing wild at the sides of the road, loaded with fruit and all but ignored by local settlers who need expend only the barest effort to procure the necessities of life.[14] That these kinds of idealised landscape were readily accepted is demonstrated by the evidence of British emigrants themselves, many of whom reported they had either read promotional literature before departing, or that it had actually induced them to leave. One emigrant to New Zealand recorded that prior to leaving Britain in 1842, he had read a book that told of wild pigs growing fat on peaches there, waddling about helplessly, simply asking to be killed.[15]

At their most basic, these descriptions can be seen as 'scenic' prospects, views constructed using particular framing devices and pictorial conventions. On another level, however, they were outlooks on a new life, a promise of future prosperity, what the literature generally referred to as an "independency". George Thompson suggested the field for individual enterprise was wide open at the Cape, reporting that "industry and good conduct will often elevate the most indigent individuals to a higher grade in society" there.[16] Patrick Matthew considered that even what he called the "high-spirited portion" of the aristocratic class might be useful in diffusing the "elegancies of social intercourse" in the British colonies. Provided they chose "Spartan exertion to Persian indulgence", he advised, they would commence a life of utility and gradual but sure improvement, without being indebted to either "patron or pension-list".[17] Frontier landscapes were also represented as offering healthful alternatives to the moral dissipations of the metropolis. Sidney Smith recommended a kind of prophylactic, even detumescent force in the youthful settler's relationship with the landscape, urging: "In the bush, on the prairie, at the colonial farm, if the attraction be less, the safety is the greater. The hot blood of youth sobers down in the gallop over the plain, or falls to its healthy temperature as he fells the forest king."[19]

The reality, however, was often not so agreeable. Collins matter-of-factly related the brutality of early life at Sydney Cove. His were diseased, combustible and bloody shores, haunted by hunger and insanity, and Tuckey was soon disappointed at Port Philip.[19] "The face of the country bordering on the port is beautifully picturesque", he owned,

> swelling into gentle elevations of the brightest verdure, and dotted with trees, as if planted by the hand of taste, while the ground is covered with a profusion of every colour; in short, the external appearance of the country flattered us into the most delusive dreams of fruitfulness and plenty.[20]

Delusive dreams indeed, for the soil there proved too sandy to grow grain. Water was scarce, the temperature range extreme and the *Calcutta*'s company were soon embroiled in hostilities with local Aborigines. There was little usable timber, a major impediment in such a climate, but this was compensated by an abundance of venomous snakes, mosquitoes and biting flies. In 1830, Robert Dawson warned that no country had been "so highly eulogised and so much misrepresented" as Australia. The idea that the country was universally rich and naturally productive was wrong, he pronounced. The land to the South and South West of Sydney, fine undulating country "so much talked of in England... [and] seductive bait for the attentive listeners to Australian wonders", was all but barren of fertile soil.[21] In 1838, Thomas James complained that the South Australia colony was greatly overblown by the "ridiculous and frequent panegyrics of some of its injudicious friends", while the following year, William Leigh dedicated an entire volume to the trials and tribulations of settling there.[22] George Thompson advised that new settlers at the Cape faced many privations and annoyances. "They will find among 'the orange and the almond bowers' of Southern Africa, no Elysian retreat from the every-day troubles of life", he cautioned, "and, if they ever indulged golden dreams of their realising sudden affluence, they will soon find themselves unpleasantly awakened from the absurd delusion". Personal industry, ingenuity and economy, he counselled, were necessary to succeed in the harsh frontier landscape. People from large towns or manufacturing districts would be unsuitable for the Cape Colony: "A hardy, active, and industrious class of men – accustomed to a country life, and acquainted with the management of cattle – patient of privations – persevering under difficulties – should, if possible, be fixed here."[23]

Settlers must work to get on, these writers insisted, and seize the opportunities the landscape proffered. When writers introduced strictures against "men of restless habits and unsteady dispositions", against "paupers or infirm people", they signalled that despite the often Arcadian terms in which these landscapes were pictured, idleness was no less of an abomination here than it was in the old country. Indeed, the literature was full of such references. Chapters, even entire volumes, described the "fit and unfit", "who should go", and "who would be better to stay at home", which made it clear that these were no places for the "swells" of Whitechapel and Bethnal Green or the enervated West End toff, casting the needs of the colonial frontier against metropolitan co-ordinates of class and gender. Masculinised categories of industriousness, productivity and progress were promoted as essential, while virtuous femininity was anchored by promises of a new utility and easy matrimony. In South Australia, women were most highly valued, Ogle confirmed, "their youth and finest feelings are not left to wane away in long-protracted engagements, or blighted hopes".[24] Thompson urged that whatever scheme was adopted for emigration to the Cape, a due proportion of females must be included. The evils of neglecting this proviso had been felt in more than one infant settlement, he complained, and were not unknown in the Cape, where "illicit connexions of

Europeans with females of the coloured population has but too obviously tended to the degradation of both classes". The peculiar state of frontier society, he warned, meant the British Government must take great care to avoid what he called "the enormities resulting from the deliberate creation of a state of society *repugnant to the order of Nature*".[25]

During the early decades of the nineteenth century, racial difference was still largely understood to result from causal relations between environment and racial character, an explanation originally propounded by late eighteenth century writers like Johann Blumenbach, Samuel Smith and Georges-Louis Buffon, all of whom argued for the influence of environment on race.[26] The spread of British settlers into Canada, South Africa, Australia and New Zealand, however, produced a growing need not only to register and explain racial difference but also to prioritise forms of European hegemony, and the durability of environmental explanations of racial difference is evidence of their power to provide a key to relations between race and geography in an enlarging economy of colonisation. Patrick Matthew, for example, argued there was "but a very small portion of the world where the rose-bloom is constantly domiciled on the cheek of beauty", discounting a large portion of the United States and Canada for British settlers because there, "pallor is universal". The withering effects of an arid climate were evident in the "haggard walking skeletons" of the Australian Aborigines, he continued, while the "balmy mildness and moist air" of New Zealand demonstrated an opposite effect in "the fine stately forms, smooth polished skin, and rounded beauty" of its native population. How much more then, he pondered, must this "delicious climate" benefit the British race:

> The British Fair may rely that England's Rose will not fail to blossom in New Zealand in all its native richness, giving the unmatched tinge of flower-beauty, and freshness. The danger is, that it may even throw that of the mother country into shade.[27]

Such assurances were an important element in colonial prospect-making. Their prevalence reveals how frequently forms of environmental determinism were mobilised to naturalise colonisation, providing an ethno-biological rationale for the European peopling of distant landscapes. In his two volume *Travels in New Zealand*, the naturalist Ernst Dieffenbach propounded just such a biology of settlement. In his order, humankind existed on the same terms as any other natural species and was subject to the same natural laws: "with man as with plants and animals, each kind has its natural boundaries, within which it can live, and thrive, and attain its fullest vigour and beauty".[28] If Europeans were to colonise, he believed, their success depended critically on a choice of destination properly adapted to their race. Like Matthew, Dieffenbach represented New Zealand as ideally suited to the Anglo-Saxon race, and found proof of this in the West Indies, Senegal and the Cape where, he suggested, an unsuitable climate and geography had forced European colonists into oppression and enslavement of native peoples, and rendered them "decrepit, and degenerated from the strength and vigour of the stock from which they descended".[29]

This kind of degenerationist argument was expounded by a number of mid nineteenth century writers including W Cooke Taylor, Robert Chambers and Charles Pickering, who all argued that the savage state resulted from spurning the restraints of civilised society in favour of the freedoms and pleasures of the wild, so that civilised life was progressively forgotten and eventually only ignorance and barbarity remained.[30] Most contemporary writers on Britain's colonial possessions agreed that the allure of savage life was capable of seducing the complete renunciation of civilised life. Thompson thought it an "easy and everyday process" for civilised Europeans to sink back to savagery in the Cape, while John Henderson deplored the primitive living conditions of the Australian bushman and warned that the British character was deteriorating there. He saw no reason why it should not continue to retrograde, and likewise admonished that the "descent of mankind towards a savage life is easy and rapid, while to recover a single step that may be lost, is difficult in the extreme".[31] George Craik came closest to diagnosing the problem when he cautioned against the "strong charm" of a life of adventure amongst savages. He denounced such attractions and portrayed its European adherents as social outcasts, "disinclined to systematic industry". He scoffed at the notion that savages lived in a "state of nature". Their lack of regular law and effective government was a curse, he pronounced, that led to improvidence and "perpetual discord". His description of Maori society in New Zealand, ruled by passions, where power had no restraints and incessant animosities maintained a state of constant turbulence, was intended as an object lesson to those who dismissed the institutions and laws of settled society as troublesome restraints: "Such exhibitions as this tend to make us estimate aright the blessings of civilisation."[32]

Descriptions of native populations were consequently mobilised to reinforce metropolitan conceptions of property, land ownership, and religious and social orders. Collins wrote of convict desertions to join the Australian Aborigines: "That any one who had been accustomed to the habits of civilised life should find charms in that led by the savages of this country, was unaccountable." He was particularly perplexed by women convicts who absconded to live with Aborigines, and shuddered at the thought of purchasing freedom "at so dear a price".[33] From a metropolitan perspective, these distant landscapes threatened social instability, moral degeneration, and cultural and racial hybridisation. Too far away for metropolitan controls to operate effectively, they were places where, as Howison remarked, Europeans could simply "wander out of their sphere", a complaint that foregrounded the anxious metropolitan need for some sense of boundary or 'edge' to the distant frontier.[34] In fact, it appeared as though the sheer boundlessness of the colonial landscape was responsible for dissipating social and economic energy. Return after return from the Canadian settlements in Robert Gourlay's *Statistical Account of Upper Canada* complained of the effects of crown land reserves and absentee landowners, which forced farmsteads to straggle along the frontier and enervated settler society, and Thompson ascribed what he saw as the degenerated state of Boer society in South Africa to the disadvantageous circumstances under which they existed, thinly scattered over an immense terrain, out of reach of religious instruction and free of all moral restraint.[35]

Something of the compelling force of this frontier pathology is evident in the frequency of attempts to filter the raw material of colonisation in schemes like the New Zealand Company, the Canada Company, the Australian Agricultural Company and the South Australia Association, all of which sought, in one way or another, to secure an ordered and orderly landscape of settlement. The New Zealand Company, for example, tried to balance the social mix of its settlements through the careful selection of emigrants. It offered free passage to only a very limited group of occupations it considered to fit the needs of the colony, favoured young married couples between 15 and 30 years of age, and gave preference to labourers engaged to "capitalists" who were emigrating.[36] The Company Secretary, John Ward, pointed out that the intended object of this system was to allow "the best *sort* of colonisation to proceed at the greatest possible rate", an objective to be achieved partly by allowing diligent members of the labouring classes to progress to land-ownership over time, but also by encouraging families and servants of the "well-educated classes" to settle in the country and become "instruments of diffusing the arts and manners of good English society".[37]

These prospective social geographies found visual form in the gridded plans of new settlements and the panoramic views of colonial townships frequently interleaved in the volumes, with their socially indeterminate, leisurely promenading folks, and their native presences carefully side-lined as picturesque *coulisses*. The topoi of the urban metropolitan landscape were most frequently utilised in these views, drawing on a tradition of engraved views by the likes of William Daniell, William Cooke and Clarkson Stanfield that pictured urban views, their associated rural prospects and sites of local interest.[38] The same kind of narrativisation of landscape found in Stanfield's rendering of Portsmouth, for example, can be found in Nathaniel Willis's description of Quebec with its elegant mansions in the upper town and the suburbs of Saint Roche and Saint John, the commodious and substantial public buildings and churches, the hospital, library, busy markets and warehouses.[39] The objective of these kinds of representations was to picture their favoured prospect in as alluring a light as possible and, given their common audience, it is perhaps no surprise that they employed a remarkably consistent core of devices, whether describing Portsmouth or Quebec, New Plymouth or Adelaide, Graf Reinet or Fredericton. The topographical details might change, but a singular commonality of physical, commercial and social geographies endured, all marshalled under the rubrics of 'regularity', 'progress' and 'future prosperity', and effecting their work with something approaching numbing optimism. John Stephens described Adelaide in terms of its progress and future promise, pointing out the young town's regular streets, worthy public institutions and provision for leisure, while paying special regard to the place of its governors, landowners, business and "trade".[40] John Chase's description of Graf Reinet, although brief, utilised a similar panoramic disposal of regularity and order, public institutions and commercial activity, progress and future prospects.[41] In tracing the features of Fredericton in New Brunswick, Willis wrote of a settled landscape in which comfortable, well-built dwellings confirmed the industry of its inhabitants, picking out the College, Governor's Residence, church spires and white-walled buildings, the steamers, rafts of lumber and white sails floating on the Saint John River, and outlining a surrounding landscape of rich alluvial land, dotted with cheerful settlements, open fields and comfortable farm houses.[42]

These prospects 'pictured' opportunities within the projected landscape from the orientation of the metropolitan reader, offering a rehearsal of actual possession, and translating into spatial terms the idealised new world of social relations. It is here that the images exercised power not only over a 'natural' landscape, but also over a set of class-inflected relations that derived their meaning from the social, economic and cultural concerns of the metropolitan world. The literature of colonial promotion dwelt upon a failure to resolve social tensions exacerbated by industrialisation and urbanisation but, rather than proposing solutions, it offered a vision of an alternative society, one in which the dramatisation of an idealised interaction between landscape and individual replaced troublesome social antagonisms. What emerged was a prospective future free from the horrors of urbanisation and industrialisation, of class conflict, and economic and social competition, but one simultaneously secured against the corrosive freedoms and polluting presences of the frontier.

The period from 1800 to 1850 was one of accelerating emigration from metropolitan Britain to its colonial dominions. The immense investment in emigration, the movement of hundreds of thousands of individuals across the globe, the need to manage encounters with distant landscapes and peoples, all gave the geopolitical spatialisation of metropolis and colony particular urgency. The success of colonisation was considered to depend critically on the individual emigrant's ability to conform to the moral, social and civic behaviour considered appropriate to their new circumstances. Accordingly, representations of the frontier landscape operated as framing devices within which the potentially unruly, even chaotic, aspects of frontier life could be ordered. Digging out the ideological underpinnings of nineteenth century frontier semiology exposes the conflictual spaces within which that drama of colonisation unfolded. The image of the frontier, so persistent in metropolitan renderings of colonial space was conceived, as writers like Paul Carter have noted, as a boundary continually pushed forward by heroic pioneers, but what this formulation ignores is the permeability of that boundary, the transgressive seepages across its imagined line.[43] To conceive simply of imposing a new colonial regime over the top of already inhabited spaces, landscapes with their own obdurate characteristics, oversimplifies a contingent, negotiated process. The early nineteenth century British semiology of the frontier may have attempted a decisive exclusion of all that was unfamiliar, either by incorporation or obliteration, but the very insistence of its rhetoric attests to the difficulty of containing the disruptive forces of cultural hybridisation, the erotics of miscegenation and the bewildering freedoms of its operations.

1   In this paper, 'colonial frontier' denotes those places where British emigrants arrived to people landscapes as settlers rather than where they dwelt as sojourners, engaged primarily in resource extraction. Researching material produced to promote emigration to New Zealand in mid nineteenth century Britain prompted me to consider how this related to the great volume of other contemporary material promoting competing destinations such as the Cape Colony, Canada and Australia, a comparison I see as both necessary and dangerous. Dangerous because not only can it lead to over-simplifications that mask subtly different forms of address, but also because selecting so little from such a vast field may result in choices that turn out, with hindsight, to be injudicious. But it is necessary because there are common tensions and problematics identifiable across the whole body of metropolitan representations of Britain's colonial frontier.

2   Pratt, Mary Louise, *Imperial Eyes: Travel Writing and Transculturation*, London: Routledge, 1992; Aron, Stephen, *How the West was Lost: The Transformation of Kentucky from Daniel Boone to Henry Clay*, Baltimore: John Hopkins University Press, 1996; Lamar, Howard and Thompson, Leonard, "Comparative Frontier History", Lamar, Howard and Thompson, Leonard, eds., *The Frontier in History: North America and Southern Africa Compared*, New Haven and London: Yale University Press, 1981, pp. 6-10.

3   Butler, Judith, *Bodies that Matter: On the Discursive Limits of "Sex"*, London: Routledge, 1993. See, for example, Gunew, S, "Performing Australian Ethnicity: 'Helen Demidenko'", *From a Distance: Australian Writers and Cultural Displacement*, Ommundsen, W, and Rowley, H, eds., Geelong: Deakin University, 1996; Williams, Teresa, "Race as Process: Reassessing the 'What Are You' Encounters of Bi-Racial Individuals", *The Multiracial Experience: Racial Borders as the New Frontier*, Root, Maria, ed., London: Sage, 1996; Fortier, Anne-Marie, "Re-Membering Places and the Performance of Belonging(s)", *Theory, Culture & Society*, vol. 16 no. 2, April 1990, pp. 41-64.

4   Tuckey, John, *Account of a Voyage to establish a Colony at Port Philip in Bass's Strait,... in the Years 1802-03-04*, London: Longman, Hurst, Rees, and Orme, 1805, pp. 150 and 190.

5   Tuckey, *Voyage to... Port Philip*, p. 187.

6   Collins, David, *Account of the English Colony in New South Wales*, 2 vols., London: Cadell, Jun and Davies, W, 1798 (vol. 1) and 1802 (vol. 2), vol. 1, p. 7.

7   Torrens, Robert, *Paper on the Means of Reducing the Poor Rates*, London: the author, 1817: quoted in Everett, Nigel, *The Tory View of Landscape*, New Haven and London: Yale University Press, 1994, p. 169.

8   Mann, David, *The Present Picture of New South Wales*, London: John Booth, 1811, p. 37; Gourlay, Robert, *Statistical Account of Upper Canada*, 2 vols., London: Simpkin & Marshall, 1822, vol. 1, p. 547.

9   Charles Hursthouse, a zealous promoter of British settlement in New Zealand, estimated that £5 million was spent annually maintaining hundreds of thousands in a condition of permanent poverty: Hursthouse, Charles, *Emigration: Where to Go and Who Should Go*, London: Trelawny Saunders, 1852, pp. 17-18.

10   Wakefield, Edward Gibbon, *England and America*, 2 vols., London: Richard Bentley, 1833, vol. 1, p. 95. The title was published in the United States the following year (New York: Harper & Brothers, 1834).

11   Ogle, Nathaniel, *The Colony of Western Australia*, London: James Fraser, 1839, p. v; Wentworth, William, *Statistical, Historical, and Political Description of the Colony of New South Wales*, London: G & W B Whittaker, 1819, pp. 403-404; Howison, John, *Sketches of Upper Canada*, Edinburgh: Oliver and Boyd; London: G and W B Whittaker, 1821, p. 268.

12   Godwin, James, *Godwin's Emigrants Guide to Van Diemen's Land*, London: Sherwood, Jones, and Co., 1823, p. 2.

13   Wentworth, *Description of the Colony of New South Wales*, pp. 45-48.

14   Howison, *Sketches of Upper Canada*, p. 67.

15   Quoted in Fairburn, Miles, *The Ideal Society and its Enemies*, Auckland: Auckland University Press, 1990, p. 21.

16   Thompson, George, *Travels and Adventures in Southern Africa*, 2 vols., London: Henry Colburn, 1827, vol. 2, pp. 219-222.

17   Matthew, Patrick, *Emigration Fields. North America, the Cape, Australia, and New Zealand*, Edinburgh: Adam and Charles Black; London: Longman, Orme, Brown, Green and Longmans, 1839, pp. 185-186.

18   Smith, Sydney, *The Emigrant's New Home*, quoted in Hursthouse, *Emigration*, p. 99.

19   See, for example, Collins, *The English Colony in New South Wales*, vol. 1, pp. 60, 65, 69, 72, 86, 100, 105, 111-112, 122, 132 and 139.

20   Tuckey, *Voyage to... Port Philip*, pp. 157-159, 161, 163, 164 and 166-167.

21 Dawson, Robert, *The Present State of Australia*, London: Smith, Elder and Co., 1830, pp. xi, xvi and 386.

22 James, Thomas, *Six Months in South Australia*, London: J Cross, 1838, p. 129; Leigh, William, *Voyages and Travels, with Adventures in the new Colonies of South Australia*, London: Smith, Elder and Co., 1839.

23 Thompson, *Travels and Adventures in Southern Africa*, vol. 2, pp. 189-190, 196-197 and 218-224.

24 Ogle, *The Colony of Western Australia*, pp. 108-109.

25 Thompson, *Travels and Adventures in Southern Africa*, vol. 2, pp. 226 and 227(n), original emphasis.

26 Blumenbach, Johan Friedrich, *De generis hvmani varietate nativa liber* [On the natural varieties of mankind], Goettingae: A. Vandenhoek, 1781; Smith, Samuel, *Essay on the Causes and Variety of Complexion and Figure in the Human Species*, London: John Stockdale, 1789; Buffon, George-Louis, *Natural History, General and Particular*, trans., William Smellie, new edition by Wood, William, 20 vols., London: Cadell, T & Davies, W; York: Wilson & Son, 1812.

27 Matthew, *Emigration Fields*, pp. 219-220.

28 Dieffenbach, Ernst, *Travels in New Zealand*, 2 vols., London: John Murray, 1843, vol. 1, p. 2.

29 Dieffenbach, *Travels in New Zealand*, vol. 1, pp. 2-3.

30 Taylor, Cooke, W, *The Natural History of Society in the Barbarous and Civilised State*, 2 vols., London: Longman, Orme, Brown, Green, and Longmans, 1840, particularly 'Further Evidence of Lost Civilisation', chapter 12, vol. 1, pp. 246-278; Chambers, Robert, *Vestiges of the Natural History of Creation*, London: Wiley and Putnam, 1845, pp. 210-212; Pickering, Charles, *The Races of Man; and their Geographical Distribution*, London: H G Bohn, 1850, p. 310.

31 Thompson, *Travels and Adventures in Southern Africa*, vol. 2, pp. 69-70(n); Henderson, John, *Observations on the Colonies of New South Wales and Van Diemen's Land*, Calcutta: Printed at the Baptist Mission Press, 1832, pp. 44-45.

32 Craik, George, *The New Zealanders*, London, Charles Knight, 1830, pp. 282, 313, 357 and 361.

33 Collins, *The English Colony in New South Wales*, vol. 1, p. 489, vol. 2, p. 41.

34 Howison, *Sketches of Upper Canada*, p. 164.

35 Thompson, *Travels and Adventures in Southern Africa*, vol. 2, pp. 115 and 136-138.

36 See 'Regulations for Labourers wishing to Emigrate to New Zealand', in Ward, John, *Information Relative to New Zealand, Compiled for the Use of Colonists*, London: John W Parker, 1840, pp. 158-159.

37 Ward, *Information Relative to New Zealand*, pp. 130 (original emphasis) and 131.

38 For example, Cooke, William, *The Thames; or Graphic Illustrations of the Seats, Villas, Public Buildings, and Picturesque Scenery on the Banks of that Noble River*, London: W B Cooke, 1811; Daniell, William, *A Voyage round Great Britain... With a Series of Views, Illustrative of the Character and Prominent Features of the Coast*, 8 vols., London: Longman, Hurst, Rees, Orme, and Brown, 1814-1825; Stanfield, Clarkson, *Stanfield's Coast Scenery: a Series of Views in the British Channel, from Original Drawings taken Expressly for the Work*, Smith, Elder & Co., 1836.

39 Stanfield, *Coast Scenery*, pp. 26-44; Willis, Nathaniel, *Canadian Scenery*, 2 vols., London: George Virtue, 1842, vol. 2, pp. 8-14.

40 Stephens, John, *The Land of Promise: Being an Authentic and Impartial History of the Rise and Progress of the New British Province of South Australia*, London: Smith, Elder, and Co., 1839, pp. 105-107 and 110-113. See also *South Australia: an Exposure of the Absurd, Unfounded, and Contradictory Statements in James's "Six Months in South Australia"*, London: Smith, Elder and Co., 1839, pp. 9-20 for Stephens' refutation of objections to Adelaide made by Thomas James in *Six Months in South Australia*, London: J Cross, 1838.

41 Chase, John Centlivres, *Cape of Good Hope and the Eastern Province of Algoa Bay*, London: Pelham Richardson, 1843, pp. 73-74.

42 Willis, *Canadian Scenery*, vol. 1, pp. 101-103.

43 Carter, Paul, *The Road to Botany Bay*, London: Faber and Faber, 1987, in particular "Elysiums for Gentlemen", chapter 7, pp. 202-229.

Mute Skies, Lost Letters? Language, Identity and Estrangement in Recent Landscape Art
Ursula Seibold-Bultmann

In the late 1960s, a new figure entered the landscape. He or she was the land artist, as distinct from the landscape architect. Pioneers of this movement included Walter de Maria, Robert Smithson, Michael Heizer, Dennis Oppenheim and Nancy Holt. During the past 30 years, art in the landscape has evolved in manifold ways, thanks to artists like Richard Long, Andy Goldsworthy, David Nash, Paul-Armand Gette, Herman de Vries, Maria Nordman, and many others. The issues addressed by their works range from movement to stasis, from growth to decay, from permanence to transience, from form to shapelessness.[1] Against this background, I am hoping to show how some of the most interesting recent art points towards the relationship between nature and language, thus forcing us to consider the limits of what can be said and written about the landscape.[2] I will try to demonstrate that this is true both of works in which references to language are visibly present, and of others where this is emphatically not the case. My approach is one of hermeneutical explication, rather than of deductive criticism; it aims at showing in what way the works open up fields for thought, instead of locking them into fixed positions.

Figures 1-2
©the author

Given that a thinker like Jean-Jacques Rousseau saw language as the defining trait of humankind, an interest among artists in the issue of landscape and language concerns key concepts of our cultural and personal identity.[3] Here, a crucial question must be if the languages we use today enable us to perceive the landscape adequately or if, conversely, they estrange us from it. In my exploration of these points, I will focus on two very different artists. One is James Turrell, an internationally prominent exponent of American West Coast art who addresses aspects of light and space in all his works, but nowhere more spectacularly than in his so-called skyspaces. Since building the first of these in 1975, he has developed ever new variations; one of the most recent examples (figures 1-2) opened in September 2000 at Cat Cairn in the Kielder Forest in Northumberland, England.[4] My other example (figures 4-5) is a work by the Pakistani-born British artist Sher Rajah. Its title was made up of the Egyptian hieroglyphs for the eye and for the sea, and thus read "I see". It featured in the 1995 exhibition *Art in Parks and Gardens* at Uttoxeter (UK), which was curated by the Ikon Gallery in Birmingham.

Rajah's work renders the role of language more immediately palpable than Turrell's, consisting as it did of 40 polystyrene letters taken from a range of different scripts: Egyptian hieroglyphs, Chinese pictograms, Sanskrit, Arabic, Hebrew, Greek and Cyrillic (for example, these letters included a Greek 'ψ', and a Cyrillic 'Ч'). They were randomly strewn along the banks of a small stream running through a suburban park, where the artist left them to the mercy of wind and water (to give an idea of their size, the "ψ" measured 28.5 x 29 cms).[5] They had the standard light blue colour of industrially produced extra-firm polystyrene, a material which jars with nature and thus highlighted the contrast between landscape and script. However, at the same time every letter related to nature in one of two ways: either its shape resembled features of the natural world, or else the sound it represented recalled the sounds of air, water, earth and animals (for instance, the Cyrillic 'Ч' evokes the hiss of a snake, whereas the shape of the Greek 'ψ' reminds us of a flower).[6]

The picturesqueness of the scene was counteracted by the strong stress on fragmentation, disruption and displacement: letters taken out of their accustomed contexts, rearranged in an utterly unstable situation, subject to the forces of nature, not adding up to any intelligible sequence of words. The greatest possible contrast to this situation is probably afforded by the early Christian *topos* of nature as a book in which humankind can read all about God's creation: among the relevant sources cited by Clarence Glacken in his book *Traces on the Rhodian Shore*, I want to single out Athanasius who compares the creatures of nature to letters in the book of creation, which testify to the harmony of the universe.[7] Conversely, while some letters in Rajah's work may resemble creatures it offers nothing coherent to read: instead, what the letters record is a multi-voiced stutter interrupted by one or two gasps. Here it is important to note that the scripts Rajah used represent consecutive stages in the development of writing as such. In simplified terms, the general trend was away from early pictographic systems like the Egyptian hieroglyphs to the much more flexible and economical phonetic alphabets of which the Greek variety, itself derived from its Phoenician predecessor, was the first fully perfected example (however, by including Chinese characters in his work Rajah acknowledged that pictographic systems have survived to this day).[8] Since the shapes of pictograms directly relate to visible phenomena, they are a less abstract form of writing than phonetic letters. In other words, the letters Rajah used marked different degrees of abstraction from nature as seen, while at the same time these differences recalled a historical sequence.

Seen in this light, the work suggests that nature has been increasingly distanced from us by the superimposition of script upon it. Letters help to turn the landscape into an object of theoretical reflection and discourse, and Rajah himself has stressed that he is interested in how far the cultural concepts resulting from such discourse render any direct appreciation of nature impossible. According to him, we always start from preconceived ideas born of language and especially from thoughts shaped by written texts: a fact which threatens the individual's essential freedom to engage with visible reality both emotionally and spiritually.[9] More specifically, he thus highlights the question as to what the transmission of language by writing might entail for perception and cognition. Rajah's position on this has not been an isolated one in recent years; for instance, it is seconded by the American ethnographer-cum-philosopher David Abram who argues that the discovery of the alphabet gave rise to a sense of autonomy and independence from nature, and a novel experience of fixity which arose from the perfected ability to record events and thoughts. Though philosophically unsatisfactory at various points, his book *The Spell of the Sensous,* 1996, is adduced here for the wealth of physical and psychological experience it is informed by.[10] In Abram's view, letters started to function as "mirrors reflecting the human community back upon itself" and alphabetic writing caused the human senses to sever their participation with nonhuman nature.[11] He also thinks it likely that the concepts of linear time and of homogenous space separate from time depend directly on formal systems of numerical and linguistic notation.[12] According to Abram, what got lost in the process of alphabetisation was an awareness of the world as a "living field" instead of an inert and measurable array of objects. He believes that this loss threatens our very identity as human beings: "Our bodies have formed themselves in... reciprocity with the... textures, sounds, and shapes of an animate earth... To shut ourselves off from these other voices... is to rob our own senses of their integrity, and to rob our minds of their coherence. We are human only in contact... with what is not human."[13]

In order to support his claim that humankind's estrangement from nature is to a large extent due to writing, Abram refers to Eric Havelock's classic investigation into the transition from orality to literacy in ancient Greece.[14] Unlike Abram, Havelock is more concerned with the influence of phonetic writing on patterns of thought, speech and memory than with its impact on our experience of nonhuman nature. However, that does not make his ideas less central in our context. According to him, with the visual separation of language from the person who uttered it came a sharper awareness of the individual as the source of these utterances, which in turn led to the concept of selfhood (Havelock postulates that this concept was a Socratic discovery or invention later textualised by Plato).[15] If we follow his train of thought, the perception of nature does not in itself afford a sense of the subject as a separate entity, since it is only script which causes readers and writers to distance themselves from their natural surroundings. Hence, script allows them to understand themselves as reflective subjects. Therefore, whatever upsets the alphabet must also upset that concept of selfhood. If seen in such a light, scattered letters in the landscape may be read not only as fragments of scripts and cultures, but also of individual identity as understood in terms of Greek philosophy.

To sum up Rajah's stance, he takes the view that nature is not fully commensurable to writing and reading, and by implication to language as used for the past two and a half millennia. His work suggests that the act of writing about or rather into the landscape produces a screen between us and what we see in and of nature, and that we may only be able to perceive what is behind that screen if the internal logic of writing and of thought based on the experience of reading and writing is pulverised by some event or mechanism. As the artist seems to point out, what might bring this about are the forces of nature themselves. They may scatter the individual elements fundamental to any civilisation and enforce the confrontation between and mingling of different cultures and cultural histories. But they may also clear the way for rearrangement and for the discovery of looser and less loquacious patterns of approaching the landscape than those we are used to. And if we see the question of literacy bound up with that of individual and cultural identity, then such new patterns could have a profound effect on our self-understanding. Thus in the space between Rajah's letters, suffused as it is by natural beauty, we are offered both the promise and the threat of freedom. This said, Rajah's installation, like any artistically complex work, opens up more perspectives for interpretation than can be exhausted by reference to a single intellectual position or tradition like the one summarised above. We would obviously arrive at a very different point if we investigated "I see" through the lens of, say, Jacques Derrida – not only because of the French philosopher's critique of the distinction between nature and culture, but also because of his particular understanding of the relationship between pictographic, ideographic and phonetic elements within writing and, on another level, of the relationship between writing and speech as such.[16] However, since Derrida's writings are not compatible with what Rajah says about his own intentions, this is a path which I will leave for others to explore.

James Turrell for his part shows us sky, not earth.[17] (figures 1-2) His skyspaces are structures consisting of one room, with a bench running around the interior walls and with a large opening in the ceiling whose shape corresponds to that of the ground plan. This opening frames the sky, isolating it from the rest of the landscape. Many of the skyspaces have a rectangular ground plan, but the one at Kielder is cylindrical (overall diameter: 8.60 m; diameter of opening in ceiling: 3 m; overall height of interior space: 6 m; the back of the bench, which is here made of concrete, comes up to 2.3 m). In a narrow gap behind the upper edge of the bench backs – a feature of all the skyspaces – artificial sources of light, which are invisible to the viewer, illuminate the white wall above the benches vertically. They help to modulate the visitor's experience of colour, light and space – particularly at night, dawn and dusk. Another recent skyspace by Turrell, which had an elliptical ground plan, was shown at Lower Tremenheere in Cornwall on the occasion of the solar eclipse in 1999 – hence its title, *The Elliptic Ecliptic*.[18] It consisted of a wooden structure covered on the outside with aluminium barn cladding and thus blended into its agricultural environment, whereas at Kielder a concrete core is encased with stone, so that the exterior of the skyspace resembles local sheepfolds.

In order fully to experience the skyspaces, viewers have to allow a considerable amount of time. On some days, one can sit inside a skyspace for hours without seeing anything but the grey or blue sky, gradually lightening or getting darker. At other times, clouds drift through the field of vision at different speeds and altitudes. On a summer day, occasionally seeds are carried across the opening by a breeze, or a bird flies across. (figure 2) Towards evening, the colours of the clouds dissolve, and the skyspace fills with starlight. Viewers, while offered a place to absorb the prospect, can control nothing of all this.

Human language proves an unwieldy tool when directed at the subtle gradations of colour and light, the myriad shapes of the clouds, the full range of their movements.[19] However, in various ways it does impinge on the skyspaces. To start with, once one has adjusted one's gaze to the vast vistas they provide, one realises that it is almost impossible to confront the sky without remembering just how much has been said and written about it. Which particular texts one thinks of at this moment will of course depend on one's temperament and cultural background. For instance, one could refer to Byron: "Where rose the mountains, there to him were friends / Where roll'd the ocean, thereon was his home / Where a blue sky, and glowing clime, extends / He had the passion and the power to roam / The desert, forest, cavern, breaker's foam / Were unto him companionship; they spake / A mutual language, clearer than the tome / Of his land's tongue...." And further on: "Are not the mountains, waves, and skies, a part / Of me and of my soul, as I of them? / Is not the love of these deep in my heart / With a pure passion? should I not contemn / All objects, if compared with these? and stem / A tide of suffering ...."[20] These are lines which cast a quintessentially Romantic light on the relationship between language, nature and the subject: man figures as a participant in a cosmic unity which is suffused with a mutually intelligible idiom.

However, such associations on the part of the viewer, which turn the sky into a vast projection screen, may have little to do with the artist's own intentions. Therefore, we must now ask if certain identifiable texts have played a role in Turrell's *conception* of the skyscapes – and indeed we do not have to look very far. For instance, since Turrell is familiar with the work of Antoine de Saint-Exupéry – a pilot like himself – the French writer's book *Wind, Sand and Stars*, 1939, can be regarded as one likely source for the skyspaces.[21] In a dramatic passage, Saint-Exupéry describes how one night, after an emergency landing in the desert, he has stretched out on a hill and is looking up at the stars: "With no understanding at that moment of those depths, I was seized by vertigo, for with no root to cling to, no roof or tree branch between those depths and me, I was already adrift and sinking... But I did not fall. I found myself bound to the earth, from nape to heel. I let it take my weight, and felt a kind of appeasement. Gravity seemed as sovereign as love."[22]

This emotionally resonant passage certainly brings the reader close to sky and earth. However, the most interesting texts which are directly relevant to Turrell point far beyond such narrative. Among the authors he himself names, it is Maurice Merleau-Ponty who springs to mind here.[23] On the blue sky, the philosopher writes in his *Phenomenology of Perception*, 1945:

... a sensible datum, which is on the point of being felt sets a kind of muddled problem for my body to solve. I must find the attitude which will provide it with the means of becoming determinate, of showing up as blue; I must find the reply to a question which is obscurely expressed. And yet I do so only when I am invited by it; my attitude is never sufficient to make me really see blue.... The sensible gives back to me what I lent to it, but this is only what I took from it in the first place. As I contemplate the blue of the sky... I abandon myself to it and plunge into this mystery, it <thinks itself within me>, I am the sky itself as it is drawn together and unified, and as it begins to exist for itself; my consciousness is saturated with this limitless blue...[24]

We have moved one step away from language here: Instead of verbal appropriation, seeing has become the paramount experience. For Merleau-Ponty, the perceiving subject is inseparably bound up with the world, and the unity of experience originates in a profoundly dynamic and reciprocal relationship between what can best be called the body-subject and the world.[25] So if we find we do not necessarily have to speak, or indeed, think in verbal terms in order to absorb what we see from within a skyspace, then Merleau-Ponty's explanations may help us to comprehend why this is so. Turrell himself further points in this direction when he says: "In the same way [as] we could inhabit the spaces within the sky through the instrument of flight, we can consciously inhabit this space by moving the feeling of vision out through the eyes and so move consciousness out into the space".[26]

More key texts for contemplating the limits of language from the viewpoint afforded by the skyspaces are to be found among much older literature. They concern the aesthetics of the infinite and the concept of the sublime, as first developed with frequent reference to the sky by authors like John Dennis, Lord Shaftesbury and Joseph Addison.[27] According to them, vast objects and powerful events – that is, sublime sights, which they find above all in nature – move man's soul to contemplate the glory of Deity. Turrell himself, when writing about a "presentation of the Sublime", linked the term with his upbringing as a Quaker.[28] And although this was in a context other than that of the skyspaces, we should note that he has recently designed a Quaker Meeting House in Houston which features a large rectangular opening in its ceiling, under a retractable roof (1995-2000, in collaboration with Leslie K Elkins Architecture).[29] From this perspective, we must surmise that the largely silent search for God practised by the Society of Friends has informed the skyspaces to some extent.[30] However, this point should not be overemphasised, since when personally asked about the sublime, the artist stressed that his main interest is in what he calls "pure seeing", and in the emotional impact of the sublime. Thus when he speaks about the "almost excruciating context of seeing" and the "painfully beautiful blue" of the sky, the sublime becomes a particularly powerful mode of engagement with the visible world – which makes us recall its psychologically-oriented analysis by Edmund Burke, 1757.[31]

Finally, do Turrell's skyspaces suggest aspects of the infinite to which he himself does not directly refer but which may help us to calibrate more accurately our own role as writers about the landscape? Here we need to consider what Immanuel Kant said about the subject – not, however, in his definition of the mathematical mode of the sublime as given in his *Critique of Judgment*, 1790, but in his *Universal Natural History and Theory of the Heavens*, 1755.[32] In this cosmogony, he notes that the pleasure afforded by the "spectacle of a starry heaven" can only be absorbed by "noble souls", and concludes: "In the universal quiet of nature and in the tranquillity of mind there speaks the hidden capacity for knowledge of the immortal soul in unspecifiable language and offers undeveloped concepts that can be grasped but not described."[33] So here Kant identifies an aspect of cognisance which transcends nameable languages. It is of course up to us to decide whether to trust his sublime or not. However, it seems to me that if we do, then Turrell's skyspaces can make us understand the absence of specifiable language as a spiritually productive situation.[34]

Under the impression of recent ecological crises, a number of authors have vigorously stated their belief that language and writing should play a vital role in a renewal of our relationship with nature. David Abram sees our immediate task in "taking up the written word, with all of its potency, and... carefully... writing language back into the land... Our craft is that of... freeing (our words) to respond to the speech of the things themselves."[35] Almost simultaneously, the writer Martin Dean stated that "Nature as a garden or landscape is generated by our perception.... Landscape architecture may, *much like literature*, lead to a new definition of nature by revising our awareness of it.... Society may very well be realised by nature turned aesthetic and artificial.... If I am writing,... *I am the book of nature that imparts its own text through my services.*"[36] (my italics) I hope to have shown that not all artists who work in the landscape share this confidence in redefinitions of nature through human languages, no matter if such languages are those of literature or of landscape architecture. Such artists challenge us to take into account those parts of or qualities in nature which defy the scope of our existing vocabularies and grammatical dexterity. In doing so, they stake out a field for thought where the landscape, rather than receding into muteness, opens up into generative silence. This is not to say that we should give up our role as writers about the landscape. Rather, while we keep writing we ought to reckon with those artists who warn us that we need to tread cautiously along the margins of what we can and what we cannot say about it.

For vital support, the author warmly thanks both artists and the editors; Michael Hue-Williams (London); Peter Sharpe (curator, the Kielder Partnership); Christel Fricke; Barry Venning; Christoph Bultmann; and finally Graeme and Sylvia Auld, for offering a home away from home close to Cat Cairn.

1   See Tiberghien, G, *Land Art,* Paris: Éditions Carré, 1993; Garraud, C, *L'Idée de Nature dans l'Art Contemporain,* Paris: Flammarion, 1994; Kastner, J, *Land and Environmental Art,* London: Phaidon, 1998.

2   The word 'landscape' will be used throughout to denote physical nature as shaped by the most widely varied processes of alteration brought to bear on it by human civilisation.

3   Rousseau, J-J, *Essai sur l'Origine des Langues,* Porset, C, ed., Bordeaux: G Ducros, 1970, vol. I, p. 27. For the wider picture see Taylor, C, *Human Agency and Language,* Cambridge: Cambridge University Press, 1985.

4   Ordnance Survey national grid reference: NY 613 928.

5   The stream is Picknal Brook, in Oldfields Park.

6   Author's interview with the artist, 2 March 2001. Rajah did not include Latin script because he wanted the viewer to concentrate on the shape of the letters without automatically reading them. Instead, Greek was particularly relevant to him because of the fundamental importance of Greek civilisation for Western art.

7   Glacken, C, *Traces on the Rhodian Shore. Nature and Culture in Western Thought from Ancient Times to the End of the Eighteenh Century,* Berkeley and London: University of California Press, 1967, p. 203.

8   See Diringer, D, *A History of the Alphabet,* Henley-on-Thames: Gresham, 1983.

9   Author's interview with the artist, 2 March 2001. As one among several reasons for this concern, Rajah explains how early in life he studied law and then worked as a stockbroker, during which time he acutely realised to what extent the world of letters and numbers can destroy one's physical relationship with the environment. When he subsequently became an artist, he felt intense relief at the possibility of decoupling himself from language. He insists that there is no viable substitute for the visual plane, and that language informs far too much of us and in us; the idea of letters defining a person's identity is particularly loathsome to him.

10 Abram, D, *The Spell of the Sensuous: Perception and Language in a More-than-Human World,* New York: Pantheon, 1996. To name just one philosophical problem, Abram's postulation that every human psyche becomes, as a consequence of alphabetic civilisation, an entirely isolated private 'interior' unrelated to its environment including other 'minds' (p. 257) does not bear further scrutiny. Other weak points in his argument are a neglect of the Romantics' engagement with nature, as well as of post-structuralist views on writing.

11 Abram, *The Spell,* pp. 112, 188, 196.

12 Abram, *The Spell,* pp. 188-201; quote p. 257.

13 Abram, *The Spell,* pp. 32; quote p. 22.

14 Havelock, E A, *The Muse Learns to Write: Reflections on Orality and Literacy from Antiquity to the Present,* New Haven and London: Yale University Press, 1986.

15 Havelock, *The Muse,* pp. 71, 114, 121.

16 See in particular Derrida, J, *Of Grammatology,* Baltimore and London: Johns Hopkins University Press, 1976, pp. 97-316.

17 For Turrell's skyspaces see the Hayward Gallery exhibition catalogue *Air Mass: James Turrell,* London: The South Bank Centre, 1993; Noever, P, ed., *James Turrell: the Other Horizon* (exhibition catalogue, Museum für angewandte Kunst in Vienna), Vienna and Ostfildern-Ruit: MAK and Cantz, 1998, pp. 96-101, 202-204.

18 Bright, R, *James Turrell Eclipse,* London and Ostfildern-Ruit: Michael Hue-Williams Fine Art and Hatje Cantz, 1999.

19 Turrell himself, when faced with this observation, said that for him language follows experience – a statement directly derived from Maurice Merleau-Ponty (see below; author's interview with the artist, 13 April 2000).

20 *Childe Harold's Pilgrimage,* Canto III, stanzas 13 and 75. Lord Byron, G G N, *The Complete Poetical Works,* McGann, J J, ed., vol. II, Oxford: Clarendon Press, 1980, pp. 81, 104.

21 Author's interview with the artist, 13 April 2000. See also *Air Mass,* 1993, p. 30.

22 Saint-Exupéry, A de, *Wind, Sand, and Stars*, W Rees, trans., Harmondsworth: Penguin, 1995, p. 38. In the original French: "N'ayant pas compris encore quelles étaient ces profondeurs, je fus pris de vertige, faute d'une racine à quoi me retenir, faute d'un toit, d'une branche d'arbre entre ces profondeurs et moi, déjà délié, livré à la chute comme un plongeur. Mais je ne tombai point. De la nuque aux talons, je me découvrais noué à la terre. J'éprouvais une sorte d'apaisement à lui abandonner mon poids. La gravitation m'apparaissait souveraine comme l'amour" (*Terre des Hommes*, Paris: Gallimard, 1939, p. 73).

23 Author's interview with the artist, 13 April 2000.

24 Author's interview with the artist, 13 April 2000.

25 The best introduction is Langer, M, *Merleau-Ponty's Phenomenology of Perception: a Guide and Commentary*, Basingstoke: Macmillan, 1989.

26 In *Air Mass*, 1993, p. 20. Turrell also says (p. 19): "This plumbing of visual space through the conscious act of moving, feeling out through the eyes, became analogous to a physical journey of self as a flight of the soul through the planes". While working on his skyspaces, Turrell has been striving for building something more than spaces which merely sensitise the viewer: "I wanted the spaces entered to be an expression in light of what was outside. I formed an interior space to be sensitive to that which occurred in the space outside – a sensing space", p. 25.

27 See Nicolson, M H, *Mountain Gloom and Mountain Glory: the Development of the Aesthetics of the Infinite*, Ithaca/NY: Cornell University Press, 1959; Monk, S H, *The Sublime: a Study of Critical Theories in Eighteenth Century England*, Ann Arbor: University of Michigan Press, 1960; Weiskel, T, *The Romantic Sublime: Studies in the Structure and Psychology of Transcendence*, Baltimore: Johns Hopkins University Press, 1976.

28 *Air Mass*, 1993, p. 21.

29 see Noever, *Turrell*, 1999, pp. 200 f.

30 On Quaker silence, see Hubbard, G, *Quaker by Convincement*, London: Quaker Home Service, 1974, revised reprint 1985. A different kind of meeting house by Turrell which incorporates a skyspace is the Meditation House at Niigata, Japan, 1998: see Noever, *Turrell*, p. 198. A project for a Roman Catholic chapel with several interrelated skyspaces, conceived in 1977 for Giuseppe Panza di Biumo at Varese, has not been realised (see Noever, *Turrell*, p. 198). It is instructive to compare at this point what Bachelard, G, *The Poetics of Space*, 1964, M Jolas, trans., Boston: Beacon Press, 1994, pp. 183 and 199-205, said about the correspondence between "the immensity of world space and the depth of inner space" and about immensity as a category of the poetic imagination.

31 Author's interview with the artist, 13 April 2000. For discussions of the Sublime and pain, see for instance Nicolson, *Mountain Gloom*, 1959, p. 322.

32 On the former, see Lyotard, J F, *Lessons on the Analytic of the Sublime*, E Rottenberg, trans., Stanford: Stanford University Press, 1994. See also Crowther, P, *Critical Aesthetics and Postmodernism*, Oxford: Clarendon Press, 1993; and Fricke, C, *Kants Theorie des reinen Geschmacksurteils*, Berlin: de Gruyter, 1990, pp. 141-146.

33 Kant, I, *Universal Natural History and Theory of the Heavens*, S L Jaki trans., Edinburgh: Scottish Academic Press, 1981, p. 195. In the original German: "Bei der allgemeinen Stille der Natur und der Ruhe der Sinne redet das verborgene Erkenntnisvermögen des unsterblichen Geistes eine unnennbare Sprache, und gibt unausgewickelte Begriffe, die sich wohl empfinden, aber nicht beschreiben lassen."

34 Compare Didi-Hubermann, G, "The Fable of the Place", Noever, *Turrell*, 1998, pp. 45-56, especially p. 48 f.

35 Abram, *The Spell*, 1996, p. 273.

36 Dean, M, "Nature as a Book – a Book as Nature", *Journal of Garden History*, vol. 17 no. 2, 1997, pp. 171-175 (quotes pp. 174 f.).

Landscapes and the City: Event, Knowledge, Representation

Landscapes and the City:
Event, Knowledge, Representation
Mark Dorrian

To approach the city through the question of its landscapes, or landscapes through the question of the city, is immediately to invoke multiple scales and temporalities. The deceptively simple question of what is the landscape of the contemporary Western city, for example, at once brings to the fore the global and radically dispersed character of its economic hinterland. The contemporary city is bound to distant manufacturing and productive landscapes which, although (often ideologically) 'hidden' to a greater or lesser degree, have massive relevance to it. Again, we might talk of landscapes and the city in terms of the city's own 'ground', as did, for example, Ernst Bloch in the text discussed in the main introduction to this book; or of the landscapes constituted within the city by its buildings, parks and wastelands; or of landscapes as events, momentary configurations within urban conditions which appear and then dissolve.

All the papers in this section touch on different aspects of the landscape/city relationship. The first, by John Dixon Hunt, has a slightly different character to the others in that it opens with a reflection on this book, and the conference from which it originated. Noting the range of disciplines displayed, and the variety of material covered, he suggests that landscape studies now hold a centrality within scholarship which is reminiscent of the position held by literary criticism in Britain after World War I. Yet in terms of a method and model that other disciplines might provide the expanded field of landscape studies, he feels that it is anthropology's, as practised, in particular, by Clifford Geertz, that is most productive. If there is almost nothing now that landscape studies isn't about, then it finds a paradigmatic object of investigation in Venice, "a human and ecological site *par excellence*", whose cultural and environmental transactions and intricacies issue a challenging demand to interpretation. To illustrate the symbolic capacity of just one element of this total landscape, the private gardens of the Venetian Republic, it is suggested that their structure expressed and emblematically reperformed the incremental build up and consolidation of the city itself, within its lagunar environment.

The place of urban parks is a complex and important issue in any consideration of landscapes and the city. In the conclusion to his paper, John Dixon Hunt noted the aggressive symbolism that attached to Napoleon's establishment of public parks in Venice. Now papers by Dana Arnold and Stephen Kite consider, respectively, very particular nineteenth and twentieth century discourses on parks in Dublin and London. Dana Arnold proposes an interpretation of Phoenix Park, Dublin, based on Michel Foucault's discussion of the 'heterotopia'. Here the improvements carried out in the park between 1832 and 1849 are read in terms of a specular play of identity and difference in relation to the Royal Parks in London. One of these was of course Hyde Park, and in Stephen Kite's paper on Adrian Stokes, the English writer on art and aesthetics, we find it again, albeit playing a rather different role: that of a "*topos* of negation"; a "destroyed and contaminated mother", as Stokes put it. Referring to Melanie Klein's account of child development, which deeply influenced Stokes, Kite demonstrates how this "depressive" environmental reading was grounded in a psychoanalytic narrative of the loss of the child's primal object of desire and the subsequent imperative for restoration. The paper expands to examine Stokes' responses to the humanistic urban *virtù* landscapes of fifteenth century Italy, which embodied, for Stokes, an aesthetic and politico-ethical ideal of "identity in difference".

There are many ways in which the idea of the city as landscape might be thought; but in her study of the environmental polices and practices of Bermondsey Borough Council in London after World War I, Elizabeth Lebas suggests a particularly intriguing one, arguing that the idea could operate as a kind of political imaginary. She suggests that the ideology of self-sufficiency and personal autonomy that were promoted by the Council, particularly by its Beautification Committee which was established in 1922, drew upon an old, non-urban precedent: the political economy of the landed estate.

Drawing on important studies by Louis Marin and Alain Roger, Frédéric Pousin examines the development of the concept of 'urban landscape' in architectural discourse. Relating it to the longstanding tradition of landscape representation, but also to the topographic 'city-view', he analyses its conditions of emergence in the 1950s and 60s. He argues for the importance of the journal the *Architectural Review*, in whose pages the notion of 'townscape' was evolved and disseminated. Considering a sequence of books published throughout the 60s, and terminating with *Learning from Las Vegas*, 1972, Pousin describes how new representational techniques (drawing upon trends in contemporary documentary photography and cinema) were developed, which both substantiated and communicated the concept of 'urban landscape', defined its objects, and established new tools for design.

The section is concluded by Simon Grimble's subtle essay on Ian Sinclair's "book of London reportage", *Lights Out for the Territory: 9 Excursions in the Secret History of London*. Grimble locates Sinclair within a tradition of English writing in which a reflection upon the 'condition of England' is manifested through a journey leading toward a prospect, a position which will allow the relationship between detail and totality to come into view. In this kind of writing, description is, as he puts it, "always on the way to being criticism". Sinclair is sceptical of prospects, however, his approach to them is ironic and deflationary, and this leads to a volume which, Grimble argues, should be understood more as an extraordinary casebook of the relationship between landscapes and politics in the contemporary city than as a diagnosis of it.

Taking Place: Some Preoccupations and Politics of Landscape Study
John Dixon Hunt

In his review of a landscape book, the *Atlas of the Irish Rural Landscape*, edited by F H A Aalen, the literary theorist Terry Eagleton hailed its scope as interweaving "geology, archaeology, demography, social history and a host of other disciplines, moving from tourism to the rural poor, peat to parks, vernacular rural architecture to landscape management". He went on – writing this in the *Times Literary Supplement* – that the volume "demonstrates the point that, rather like literary studies, there is almost nothing that geography isn't about; but after productions as ambitious as this, literary studies had better look to its laurels."[1]

I read these remarks after returning from the Edinburgh conference, at which I made something of the same claim for landscape study that is rehearsed in a revised form below. In my own career I had moved gradually from literary to landscape studies, perhaps with an instinct for exploring just such a larger, interwoven territory as Eagleton describes (but one that was largely unmapped), making the final break decisively in 1998 when I resigned as a Professor of English Literature at the University of East Anglia and went to Dumbarton Oaks in Washington DC as Director of Landscape Studies. Yet in my talk at Edinburgh I had somewhat resisted the comparison of landscape to literary studies, perhaps being too recently liberated from the latter's constraints to want to invoke them as a model for the former. At Edinburgh I had instead proposed the parallel with an anthropology practised and advocated by Clifford Geertz. Though I am wary both of seeing land or landscapes as 'texts', which the analogy with literary study strongly insinuates, and of surrendering the study of designed and cultural landscapes to literary specialists, who clearly have their eyes upon it as an expanded colonial field for their discipline rather than led by much concern for landscape itself, I have returned to my remarks at the Edinburgh conference with some renewed appreciation of Eagleton's appeal to the parallel between geography (or landscape) and literary studies. And it is also true, as I explore below, that Geertz himself allows a strongly discursive element into his anthropology.

Yet I also came to the Edinburgh discussions, if not with a role in professional landscape practice (I am not a trained landscape architect), at least as a professor of the history and theory of landscape in a Graduate School of Fine Arts where professionals are in training. In that role I feel concerned precisely to celebrate the wide scope of landscape studies that Eagleton hails, trying to ensure that future landscape architects can bring to their design a whole congeries of knowledge, an awareness of many fields and discourses that their careers will necessarily address, whether they do so consciously or not and whether their practice will specifically require it or not. For landscape architects at their best, performing an extraordinary range of tasks throughout society, provide the spaces, the *milieux*, the environments and the arenas in which people conduct their lives.[2] While in its references and in the conditions of its making literature does indeed imply the same range of human concerns as landscape architecture, this latter activity is responsible, along with landscapes made by less direct design intervention – that is, by the slower and less deliberate processes of cultural action upon the land – for providing the very physical places where the characters, events and actions of literature as well as life are represented as taking place.

'Taking place', indeed, is what we say without thinking: our actions in both the actual or real and the virtual world of imaginative writing take from place their being, their shape, scope and trajectory. We cannot actually follow literary work without – this is surely Eagleton's implied challenge to literary studies – fully understanding the physical conditions in which people's actions are represented, taking from places their whole being as well as their becoming. Within this perspective, landscape architects in the actual world of their practice have a role, if not in effect a responsibility, to shape landscapes in ways that will encourage and enhance the best potentials of human society. If the Irish rural landscape is – and it *is* without a doubt – the long chronicle and abstract of its people, then both landscapes that are proposed by landscape architects and built will direct (as much as they will mirror) the way we live now and in the future.

Landscape studies are today highly visible. This probably goes without saying. Bookstores and libraries increasingly devote more and more space to a range of works on landscape from coffee table volumes of great sentiment and beguiling imagery (in fact, as much a cultural phenomenon to take critically as 'serious' monographs) to scientific and professional enquiries into how land and landscape are responsible for human activities. Since 9/11 in the United States, when the American landscape was cruelly disfigured, we have been offered, for example, many articles and other publications on the geography and land of Afghanistan, presumably because it is believed that territory will somehow explain terrorism.

But beyond the sheer quantity of the attention to land and landscape, the variety of their treatment is equally remarkable. This very publication, and perhaps even more the conference from which it came, testify to the quite dizzy range of topics and approaches. The geographical range perhaps goes without saying, though the organisers are to be congratulated for seeing the necessary advantage of conducting landscape research and theorising in a variety of different topographical and cultural situations; important, too, but also obvious enough, was the variety of media in which landscape was discussed – film, writing of all sorts, painting, photography and other visual forms, land art, theatre, oral or public history, etc.. More striking was the emergence of a cluster of key issues from what, to an outsider, might have appeared simply an eclectic gathering of almost any topic that could accommodate the word 'landscape'. The list of these key issues might include: hybridity in landscape ("heterotopias" in Michel Foucault's well-known formulation), and closely related to that theme, the landscape as contested space. The topics here are many, but a few particularly emergent contestations are those between memories and current exigencies, between (if you like) mental and social infrastructures, which included the shaping of landscape and its experience for tourist or heritage purposes; that between different scales of design within a landscape continuum that stretches from 'wilderness' to 'designed spaces'; and the strategic renegotiation of established terms in landscape experience – private and public, picturesque, pastoral, sublime – for contemporary purposes.[3] There were also more familiar but no less crucial themes such as the way landscapes were used to articulate political or personal identity, especially in colonial or post-colonial situations; landscape as metaphor, and perhaps most interesting the emergence of the garden within larger and alternative landscapes as both metaphor and actuality. Not that this list is complete, but those items suggest the richness and diversity of the agenda.

Figure 1
Modern visitors
at Versailles
(photo: author)

Two other remarkable aspects of the landscape field – and its representation at Edinburgh – were, first, the relative scarcity of landscape architects or at least of the perspectives one might expect them to have, and, second, the predominance of research into the experience or reception of landscapes over the history of their design or cultural formation. These two aspects are, perhaps, interconnected. As regards the first, the diversity and richness of landscape studies suggest the hard work that practitioners will have to do to keep themselves in the loop, to situate their own professional preference for 'design' within the many contingences of both history and contemporary reception of their work. As for the second, it is clear that non-professionals are more interested in how people respond to built work than are landscape architects themselves, who are the ones, nevertheless, engaged in producing it. The commentaries and publications of the profession largely celebrate intention, even their imaginative adventures (sometimes retrospectively invented) in the run-up to formulating designs, over the impact and reception of the built work.[4] The reception of landscapes clearly involves the expectations and the resources people bring to such experiences: this could relate to the necessity for re-tooling older languages of description and aesthetics – for instance, we need revisions of our banal notions of the picturesque (as have been achieved for the sublime). But it could also, most usefully, extend to the examination of the responses of those who do not readily, if at all, feel at home with those traditional languages: how a person "takes [in] place" when s/he lacks some of the available, and largely elite, mechanisms of response. (figure 1) It has been argued that contemporary society lacks a sufficient connoisseurship of landscape architecture and that this is somehow the obligation of professional designers to instill in their public: maybe.[5] However, designers have also, perhaps, to reinvent landscapes that do not depend on, say, a knowledge of Claude Lorrain or Bruno Latour.

But this explosion of landscape studies and their range are not, arguably, half as significant as their centrality, or at least the claims that can be made for their centrality. By which I mean not just that landscape was the common denominator that brought together in Edinburgh speakers from so many different countries, disciplines and cultures, but that for many disciplines not specifically focused upon landscape its study has suddenly seemed of significance to their concerns. And beyond the centrality now perceived in landscape is the confidence implied by all this work that landscape could easily become "the privileged arbiter of social thought".[6] That is a claim made, sceptically, about the emergence of literary studies after the World War I, but it reminds us how vital and central did those new studies appear at the time; I was certainly of the generation that believed in the centrality of literary criticism, along the lines of Matthew Arnold's claims in *Culture and Anarchy* for what he had called culture. Literature was not just a visible and important study, whose "boundaries cannot be drawn", as one of its proponents, F R Leavis, claimed; it was also one that asserted its right or ability to direct our whole being in society because it sees itself able to adopt a politico-philosophical position in the world.

This parallel with the emergent discipline of literary criticism at the height of its powers and confident of its ambition is a tempting analogy by which to get a handle on the current visibility of landscape studies. And within that analogy, several more detailed parallels are discernible. The role of cultural barometer that literature and in their turn literary studies felt able to assume, along with the consequent role of cultural leadership, is shared by much landscape architecture, most obviously but not exclusively at the ecological end of its spectrum. Then again, the confident claims for wholeness or complex form in literary works, for their inclusiveness and ability to absorb and foreground tensions, and for their unique ability to critique the instrumentalist reasoning of everyday "technological-Benthamite civilisation" (F R Leavis again) – all of that has palpable reflections in the claims of some landscape critics and even some designers. Literary study argues for its own distinctiveness, its qualitative difference over other disciples; landscape studies have also been known to take up that position, both within the other design professions and more largely. In minor ways, too, there were interesting parallels between the literary focus upon form rather than content and the formalist obsessions of professional design.

On the other hand, if the mid twentieth century literary critic significantly removed the author from a place of authority in his/her works and gave that power instead to the critical reader unburdened, for example, by any knowledge of intentions, the designer still seems today to reign supreme in his/her sense of the design project at the expense of the consumer. Ironically, though, the designer's name is all but forgotten on sites and in journalistic discussions of built landscapes (the architect fares little better, with a name sometimes inscribed upon a new building's foundation stone). This ironic loss of recognition may perhaps explain designers' prime emphasis upon the process and role of design as a form of compensating for their invisibility in the public realm.

But the appeal of literary criticism as a method and model for landscape studies is not as compelling, perhaps, as that of anthropology. This is especially so given that one of the more eloquent proponents and spokesmen for anthropology, Clifford Geertz, has himself claimed in *The Interpretation of Cultures*, 1973, that his cultural enquiries were comparable to, and could learn from literary criticism. What Geertz can offer, I would argue, as a crucial example to landscape studies (whether seen as the work of designers, critics, or 'consumers') is the notion that "the culture of a people is an ensemble of texts, themselves ensembles, which the anthropologist strains to read over the shoulders of those to whom they properly belong".[7] The pull of the literary analogy is again strong – Geertz's 'texts' are not always or often linguistic or syntactical structures, but the danger is that they will nonetheless be translated into explicitly verbal formulations as if that were their

Figure 2
Stormy weather on the Venetian lagoon (photo: author)

Figure 3
Detail of Lodovico Ughi's 1729 map of Venice showing gardens on Giudecca (private collection)

Figure 4
The entrance to the Garden of Eden, Giudecca, Venice (photo: author)

Figure 5
An incidental or 'removable' garden in Venice (photo: author)

inevitable or rightful medium. This is equally true of those landscape critics who search for 'meaning'.[8] But if we think of texts as being sets or ensembles of signs, systems that are ordered in ways that declare or convey meanings, then Geertz's formulation is cogent and useful.

To start with, those texts or systems of signs do indeed "properly belong" to the world out there, a world that is beyond designers or critics (who nevertheless share and contribute to its signage). It is, further, a world in which people use those "ensembles" to make their own lives intelligible to themselves. Here again is Geertz: "Believing, with Max Weber, that man is an animal suspended in webs of significance he himself has spun, I take culture to be those webs, and the analysis of it to be therefore not an experimental science in search of law but an interpretative one is search of meaning."[9] Those meanings include a wide range of concerns, from morals to aesthetics, that can be seen to parallel the scope of the literary critical agenda at its historically most demanding; this explains both Geertz's acknowledgement of it and my own need to see it as somehow a precedent or parallel activity to landscape studies. From the perspective of the latter – practitioner, critic, 'consumer' – landscape brings into play a whole nexus of both cultural concerns and attitudes towards 'nature' within which any design will take place.

The study of gardens and other open spaces like *campi* (squares) and *cortili* (courtyards) in the city of Venice has preoccupied me intermittently for many years. While this is not the place to set out any results of that research, it can be useful, in conclusion, to exemplify here some of the issues that confront, challenge and sustain landscape studies.[10]

The lagoon landscape of Venice (figure 2) is the crucial and determining fact of its existence – from its foundation as a refuge for those fleeing hostile forces on the mainland, through its continued existence as a maritime Republic, its decline under French and Austrian auspices and eventual annexation to the Italian State, and its continuing difficulties with establishing a role and a secure

physical condition for itself in yet another century. This total *milieu* of a lagoon city has involved as complex a range of human activities as has any known human settlement, and accordingly the study of it needs to draw into play an equally extraordinary repertoire of disciplines. It is a human and natural ecological site *par excellence*, where the inter-dependencies of elements and activities are always striking. Study of this "ensemble of texts", its "web of significances", then, is ideally suited to display and challenge the full extent of landscape studies.

An enquiry into how Venetian land was transformed into landscape and how gardens came to be a privileged part of that ensemble (figures 3-4) needs to consult the conventions and ideological assumptions of map- and view-making; the literatures of visitors, inhabitants and those who graduated from the one category to the other (for strikingly different perspectives on open space); painting (where Venetian painters imply and assume a knowledge of exterior spaces for their viewers); the imperative need to secure and conserve fresh water; the hydrological records that relate to both that and to the tidal behaviour of the lagoon; botanical evidence; notarial archives (for that is where property transfers and the attendant transformations of private spaces may be plotted); and

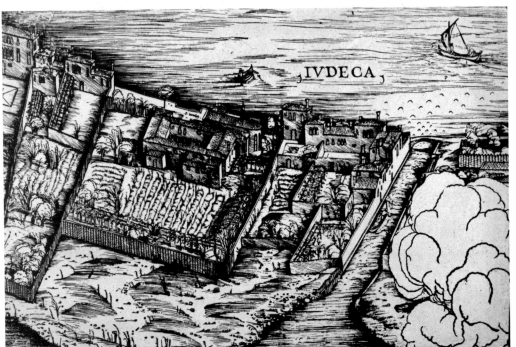

Figure 6
Detail showing gardens on the Giudecca in Jacopo de' Barbari's woodcut view of Venice, c. 1500 (private collection)

the whole range of carefully constructed myths by which the early Venetian state came to direct its history, its fortunes and above all its control and use of land that was in most cases won from the marshlands of the lagoon. It is an intriguing aspect of my work that while few specialists in any of those fields ever talk about Venetian gardens, each and every one of them actually helps me situate the history of those gardens. Needless to say, a trio of books on the gardens themselves – with one exception – fail to entertain these wider issues as part of their presentation.[11]

Habitual procedures of 'garden history' will not serve the turn of Venice, since – to take two examples – traditional narratives of formal development will not work very well, nor will any that need to rely upon the story of a succession of 'name' designers. Indeed, the usual reliance upon a design history of gardens and landscapes seems far less useful here than a narrative of their reception and use. Terminology, too, flounders in the face of different attitudes within the Venetian city (as opposed to the mainland) towards the uses of private garden spaces, which are usually established in spite of – and then protected against – an unpropitious ecology: with basic survival needs predominant, orchards and vegetable gardens, the collection of fresh water, along with salt-pans, are as much part of the total picture as flower or pleasure gardens. The establishment of what might be called 'moveable gardens' (figure 5), precious botanical specimens in pots capable of being moved when threatened by high tides of salt water, is a special extension of the term here in Venice.

When Napoleon conquered and brought down the Venetian Republic at the end of the eighteenth century, one of the means by which he cleverly imposed his will upon Venice was both by attacking church property (which had of course contained much used garden spaces) and by challenging the notion of private garden layout that had been traditional in the city since at least the fifteenth century. He did this through the establishment of public gardens; though fortunately his complete scheme for public gardens did not materialise (leaving the island of the Giudecca untouched), it was a shrewd move to turn against the special and particular forms of Venetian gardening. As I have argued elsewhere, gardens created from the very dredgings of the channels and then protected against the sea's reclaiming its materials were laid out as miniature versions of the city's gradual establishment of itself within that environment, with more and more evident control visible as the garden left the edges of the lagoon and approached the *palazzo*; in short, they were read symbolically as an emblem of Venice herself and usually displayed prominently along the bottom of all representations of the city.[12] (figure 6)

The Venetian garden is, arguably, a valuable key to understanding that rich and intriguing culture, and that historical opportunity is arguably no less relevant when it comes to seeing how the city can survive a combination of ecological blunders, economic decline and touristic invasions. Yet apart from some desultory references to green spaces – usually doubling as *campi sportivi* – the various projects that have been offered for the future of Venice since the Second World War fail to attend to the history of its gardens and open spaces. Modern planners are clearly not as shrewd or imaginative as the Emperor Napoleon; but they could, through a proper understanding of how gardens have figured in the imagination, mythology and ideology of the lagoon city, involve them once again in a new vision for that place and its still uncertain future.

1 The review was cited in publicity for the book by its publisher, Cork University Press.

2 I am particularly influenced in my insistence upon *milieux* by the writings of Augustine Berque: see especially, *Mediance: De Milieux en Paysages*, Montpellier: Reclus, 1990 and *Etre Humains sur la Terre,* Paris: Gallimard, 1997.

3 This taxonomy or scale of interventions into land has been a topic in several of my recent writings; the subject is summarised in "The Idea of a Garden and the Three Natures", *Greater Perfections. the Practice of Garden Theory*, Philadelphia and London: Thames & Hudson, 2000, chapter 3.

4 I have heard a well-established New York architect explain two of his built works by a fantastical exposition of Lewis Carroll interpreted in the light of Deleuze, but when challenged admit to the very same audience that had just listened to him that the fantasy was entirely invented after the event of the design and building. As an exercise in reception, it might, perhaps, have been fascinating, if hard pushed to explain the process by which such intricate messages came across.

5 See Riley, Robert B, "From Sacred Grove to Disney World: the Search for Garden Meaning", *Landscape Journal*, 7, 1988, p. 145.

6 Mulhearn, Francis, cited in a review, "How the critic came to be king", *Times Literary Supplement*, 8 September 2000.

7 There is no satisfactory term for those who are at the receiving end of landscape architecture: sometimes patrons, sometimes visitors, sometimes inhabitants. 'Consumers' is an unhappy term, but directs attention to the fact that landscape architecture *is* necessarily directed at people who use and enjoy it and perhaps pay for it directly (entry fees) or indirectly (taxes). Quoted by Luhrmann, T M, "The Touch of the Real", *Times Literary Supplement*, 12 January 2001. The gist of Geertz's position is set out in the famous first chapter on "Thick Description" in *The Interpretation of Cultures*, New York: Basic Books, 1973.

8 See for example: Treib, Marc, "Must Landscapes Mean? Approaches to Significance in Recent Landscape Architecture", *Landscape Journal*, vol. 14, no. 1, 1995, pp. 126-34; Olin, Laurie, "Form, Meaning, and Expression in Landscape Architecture", *Landscape Journal*, 7, 1988, pp. 149-68, and Riley, Robert (cited above, note 5).

9 Quoted Luhrmann (see note 7), from Geertz, "The Touch of the Real", *Times Literary Supplement*, 12 January 2001, p. 5.

10 For those interested there are three publications that do suggest some of the results of my work, pending the completion of a full length study: "L'Idea di un giardino nel bel mezzo del mare", (in Italian and English), *Rassegna*, 8, 1981, pp. 57-65; "The Garden in the City of Venice: Epitome of Site and State", *Studies in the History of Gardens and Designed Landscapes*, vol. 19, no. 1, 1999, pp. 46-61; and "The Garden in the City of Venice: Some Preliminary Observations" (in English and Italian), *Fondamenta Nuovissime*, M Lodola and C Occhialini, eds., Venice: Commune di Venezia, 2000, pp. 22-37.

11 These are: Gardin, Gianni Berengo, *Giardini Segreti a Venezia*, Venice: Arsenale Edizione, 1988; Albrizzi, Alessandro and Pool, Mary Jane, *The Gardens of Venice*, New York: Rizzoli, 1989; and – by far the best of them – Cunico, Mariapia, *Il Giardino Veneziano*, Venice: Albrizzi Edizione, 1989.

12 See the articles cited in note 9.

Landscapes of Negation; Landscapes of *Virtù*: Adrian Stokes and the Politico-ethical Landscapes of Hyde Park and Italy[1]

Stephen Kite

> In Hyde Park... they are burning rubbish, and peacocks with startled eyes hoot at the sinking year. London is sacked.... Character goes. The city is once again a formless continent of brick. The rumour of cold sharpens the eye to note distressing detail and endless replica.... In the mist, each brick is in travail. At this time, London, like a rough sack, holds everything.[2]

London, the unsatisfactory city, as described by Adrian Stokes in a journal entry of November 1926. Adrian Stokes (1902-1972) is numbered by many commentators, with Pater and Ruskin, among the most significant aesthetes of the nineteenth and twentieth centuries.[3] His reading of London – especially the urban landscape of Hyde Park – is (like Freud's Rome) a metaphor of the psyche, and a critique of the dystopia of machine civilisation. Against the negated *topos* of Hyde Park and its "images of dismemberment and anxious activity", Stokes posits the architectonic topographies of Italy as landscapes of *virtù*; scenes of outwardness, olive terrace and "precise contour".[4] These psychoanalytically opposed landscapes are implicitly politico-ethical, as Stokes admits in his autobiographical *Inside Out,* 1947:

> Of course it is basic human relationships... that my two landscapes describe. Hyde Park is especially a destroyed and contaminated mother, Italy the rapid attempt to restore.[5]

This essay outlines Stokes' construct of Hyde Park as seen through the lens of Kleininan psychoanalysis, then moves to Italy to examine how Stokes – in dialogue with his mentor Ezra Pound – drew on the Renaissance notion of *virtù* to envision a purposive energy that patterns the *polis*. There is a psycho-biographical sub-text; Stokes' upbringing was an Edwardian upper middle class childhood of pram journeys and walks in Hyde Park with a succession of governesses, followed by prep. school and Rugby School before going up to Magdalen College, Oxford in 1920 to read the new course of PPE: Philosophy, Politics and Economics. Then, on New Year's Eve 1921, while still an undergraduate, he travelled by train to Rapallo on the 'Italian Riviera', experiencing the passage through the Alps and the Mont Cenis tunnel into Italy, as an epiphanic re-birth into the 'counter-landscape' of the South:

> There was a revealing of things in the Mediterranean sunlight, beyond any previous experience; I had the new sensation that the air was touching things; that the space between things touched them, belonged in common; that space itself was utterly revealed.[6]

What can these contested landscapes of Hyde Park and Italy tell us about landscape, about politics, or any connections that might be made between them? Crucial to the definition of modernity is a perceived confrontation with the alienating forces of industrialisation and the portrayal of inner and outer 'waste-lands'. Contextualising Stokes with other psychoanalytical and modernist thinkers, Lyndsey Stonebridge describes "the emergence of a mythology in which writers represent themselves as coming face to face with the potential violence – historical, epistemological and psychic – of modernity in order to transcend it."[7] Adrian Stokes, she contends, "represents... one of the most important transitional moments in the history of Anglo-American modernism [a reference to his relationship with Ezra Pound] and its relation to British psychoanalysis."[8] For Stokes, landscape mirrors mind and the "hills and valleys of experience"; he writes:

> In fantasy, there are as many things inside as there are outside. It is one reason, surely, why we are often appalled by the mere immensity and confusion of the outside world, by a casual and callous aspect; why we are reassured by the beauty and order of things.[9]

I have called Stokes' Hyde Park a "*topos* of negation" for both its problematising of place, and as a theme fundamental to Stokes' criticism: the refusal of Hyde Park vectors his aesthetic.[10] Against this *topos* of negation, the humanist topographies of Italy stand as landscapes of *virtù*.

This text is veined with Freudian psychoanalysis, as developed and interpreted by the analyst Melanie Klein (1882-1960), and some outline of her theory of child development is required. The crux of Kleinian aesthetics is the notion of *reparation*. Klein, herself, said little about artistic creativity, but her followers Hanna Segal and Adrian Stokes were instrumental in shaping a coherent Kleinian aesthetic. For Klein, the infant's development is a scenario of ceaseless introjection and projection as, in the first four to five months of life, it moves from the paranoid-schizoid position, when only part-objects are recognised, to the whole-object recognition of the "depressive" phase. An 'object' in Freudian terms is the object of emotional drives. Onto the first-loved part-object, the mother's breast, the infant will project anger and frustration as well as affection. The urge to repair the world that the child feels s/he has in some way broken occurs at this later stage in infantile development, the "depressive position", when the child comes to recognise the mother and father as completely whole and 'other' persons. With this recognition comes guilt at previous inflicted aggression, as Segal explains:

> The memory of the good situation, where the infant's ego contained the whole loved object, and the realisation that it has been lost through his own attacks, gives rise to an intense feeling of loss and guilt, and to the wish to restore and re-create the lost loved object outside and within the ego. This wish to restore and re-create is the basis of later sublimation and creativity.[11]

The "experience of love from the environment" is crucial to the negotiation of the critical depressive stage as the child wins through to a well-integrated ego and a sure grasp of inner and outer reality. If the outside presents a "casual and callous aspect" a successful transition is endangered. But in successful development, Segal argues, "the experience of love from the environment slowly reassures the infant about his objects. His growing love, strength, and skill give him increasing confidence in his own capacities to restore."[12] Stokes also stresses "our emotional relationship with environment" and the fact that "landscape [is] a history of ourselves":

While it is a projection of the individual good object, our pleasure in Nature, as in art, joins us with an illimitable good object, with a fine aspect of being in general.... Love of the untouched place, of the hedgerow, the rocks, exploits the attachment to the outside whole object as well.... Here is the mother in her own ways, sufficient for the time.[13]

Stokes maintains that art's chief function is to ensure "a milieu for adults, for true adults, for heroes of a well-integrated inner world to live in... to support that inner world, to project, to re-create its image".[14] In her seminal paper on Kleinian aesthetics *A Psychoanalytical Approach to Aesthetics,* 1955, Hanna Segal takes Marcel Proust as a supreme example of "an artist compelled to create by the need to recover his lost past".[15] According to Proust, she writes, "it is only the lost past and the lost or dead object that can be made into a work of art". Proust makes the painter Elstir say: "It is only by renouncing that one can re-create." The 'broken' landscape of Hyde Park similarly represents a damaged mother-object that Stokes is driven to restore. In a late lecture, *The Future and Art*, speaking as a confessed "Londoner", he expressed life-long anxiety with its environment: "As for the Edwardian buildings in my childhood, I can truly say I experienced from them the shamelessness of pretence as if death were smug."[16] Contained within the projection of depressive anxiety is a sharp critique of the outer reality of an alienating late Imperial London that condemns the poor 'parkees' to the benches of Hyde Park and the haute bourgeoisie of the surrounding mansions to 'waiting' and convention. Here Stokes shares the trope of London as "negative oceanic feeling" with Poe, Dickens and Eliot, to which could be added the murky topodialogics of *The Secret Agent*, Stokes' favourite Conrad novel.[17] "London ever ignoble.... How few are the colonnades, how small the perpetuity of silent flank and orifice, how little by which to recognise our own ideal states."[18]

Even when presented without Ruskin's evangelism, aesthetics implicitly encodes a social agenda; Read characterises Stokes' outlook as that of the "collective individuality of liberal *humanism* in a pre-modernist setting of the Mediterranean."[19] In *Greek Culture and the Ego*, 1958, Stokes stresses those aspects of the culture that represent the integrated ego-figure and the "sublimation of unconscious phantasy", positing the "fluted Doric column and the idealised marble or bronze youth" against the "blurring states of rapture" of the Bacchic rites. In Stokes' criticism the corporeal body is constantly invoked as the mirror of the integral ego that finds its ideal embodiment in the Greek canon. While the emphasis is on art as the depressive achievement of the individual psyche, this effort is sustained within a wider acculturated landscape. Stokes writes, for instance, of the Cornish landscape of names, dolmens and mines and of the "need of the psyche to project into surroundings a history of its development, to receive from this projection an image of the psyche's architecture constructed upon firm and ancient foundations."[20] In *The Invitation in Art*, 1965, he connects the past we read in landscape to individual history via Donald Meltzer's definition of ritual. Ritual, argues Meltzer, is "the psychological equivalent of a vestigial organ whose existence, as it were, celebrates an ancient usage, while at the same time giving evidence of the individual's correct development through devoted repetition of the route created by the ancestors".[21] There are structural affinities between these wider cultural rituals, and those rituals whereby the mother and child allow spaces to grow between them; "the breast-feed becomes the good-night kiss, the play-period becomes a smile". "On a good day in a good Mediterranean place", Stokes has no difficulty in connecting individual aesthetic experience to wider "communal ritualistic meanings" and to ancestral memory: "I have the feeling that much sound, sight and act contribute to the perfecting of an Olympian figure: they reveal a sum of meaning that will not be dissipated, an eternal present into which the past has gathered."[22] Reviewing Stokes' *Greek Culture and the Ego* Richard Wollheim warns of the dangers inherent in linking the psyche's trajectory too directly to politics and culture.

Figure 1
Star Street and the clock of St Michael's Church (demolished). ©Crown Copyright. National Monuments Record

Figure 2
Gloucester Square (extensively demolished 1932). ©Crown Copyright. National Monuments Record

Wollheim mistrusts 'cultural psychoanalysis', culture has a history of its own he insists, that is modified by a thousand factors separable from the psyche, and counters Stokes' claim that "culture mirrors contrasting ego-states".[23] But Stokes is too subtle a thinker to make the parallels glib, and his praise of the Greek achievement also recognises the dark side of the *polis*: "the subjection of women... the brutal attitude to slaves and to infants [and] the ruthlessness to enemies".[24]

A late poem confirms that the Hyde Park landscape motivates Stokes' impulse to restore. Gervais stresses the "topographical musculature" of Stokes' writings, his "concern for topography, [and] his belief that to appreciate works of art we need first to steep ourselves in the natural environment from which they have been drawn":[25]

> Even though upon Hyde Park I have based
> > My life in the attempt sometimes to restore
> > To put to rights everything then feed
> > In wrong I cannot say I have succeeded
> > > Yet. The agony remains.[26]

Remembering Segal's account of Proust, Stokes' *madeleines* might be the sweets from Praed Street, the street that serves Paddington Station and marks the northern limits of his childhood landscape. In the semi-autobiographical *Smooth and Rough*, 1951, he describes the "sweet shop, the strong-lighted window glittering with mellifluous dynamite, with the exploding eroticism of the neat and sweet, sweetmeats".[27] From Praed Street it was a short walk across Sussex Gardens to home in 18 Radnor Place where "sucking secretively at night [he] reduced [the sweetmeats] to a smooth ball of stealthy ecstasy". This short journey traces the architectural spectrum of Tyburnia, the new suburb of avenues, squares and crescents, laid out on the Bishop of London's estate from the 1820s. The houses of Star Street, to the north-east of his childhood home in Radnor Place, retain the modest humanly-scaled brick terraces of the first phase of Tyburnia's development. Here Stokes found some support from the environment: "The sense of loss had to be buttoned up. I turned for reassurance very early in childhood to the clock in Star Street.... The face of the clock showed... innocence as well as some cheerful dormant power like a row of shoes in sunlight."[28] (figure 1) But there is little innocence in the looming façades of Gloucester Square immediately to the west; these stuccoed palaces reflect the later shift in style to the Victorian theatricality of Bayswater, inspired by John Nash's scenographic landscape experiments around Regent's Park. (figure 2) This is the paste-board "niggard pretension of Corinthian pilasters" that Stokes condemns in the following passage, typical of his melancholy portrayals of Bayswater:

> For myself, when I reside in Bayswater, whose soul inhabits the thudding echo of a house-maid's footfalls on a Sunday afternoon, the kitchen smells that float up between the bars of the area railings on a Sunday morning, the little pre-War confectioners that sell angelica and "cater for suppers and dances" – Wagner, Chopin – their spirit cannot even make this atmosphere forlorn, but cause the niggard pretension of the Corinthian pilasters to be still more dreary, the rain more sodden, the afternoon more unending.[29]

An odour of melancholy *does* linger in Tyburnia; a name that recalls the gallows that stood at the south-eastern corner of the district up to 1783. By the late nineteenth century the area was already becoming unfashionable, located on the 'wrong' side of Hyde Park as compared to the royally favoured Belgravia and Kensington. Like Ruskin or Wordsworth, Stokes is a writer who glories in vision, and 'blindness' is one of the most disquieting images he uses to portray the landscape of the

park. Blindness is ascribed to the "crushed-down Renault bonnets" of the cars that drone around the park, to Wren's eighteenth century alcove and to the drinking fountains. Even the fountains of the Italian Water Gardens – normally a symbol of life – are driven by the 'blind' mechanical power of oily machinery. This pervasive blindness is also politico-ethical. Stokes revolts at the poverty and control symbolised by Hyde Park, its monuments, and its restricted human and animal life; the 'parkees' – the poor, scruffy children who occupy the benches of the Wren alcove – are chained by poverty, the dogs by leads and their owners by drawing-room convention. Even the ducks and water-fowl are caged by the railings of the Serpentine. (figure 3) In Hyde Park "nature, in man and beast and flower, [is] a thing chained and divided".[30]

The sinister omphalos of Hyde Park and Victoria's Empire is The Albert Memorial (1863-1872); conceived by Gilbert Scott as a giant ciborium that enshrines Prince Albert at the apex of a world quartered into sculptural groups symbolising Asia, Europe, Africa and America. The young Stokes feared the memorial as the embodiment of paternal oppression. In Stokes' *Inside Out* the monument is discussed oedipally, in the context of the masculine monuments of the park (such as the giant Achilles statue at Hyde Park Corner and the Watts equestrian statue on Long Walk) as the epitome of male darkness and oppression. "Such figures", he writes, "were to me stern yet impotent; figures of a father, then, who both attacked and had been attacked. These statues attempted to affront the sky yet they were recipients of fog, of bird droppings and of soot: they seemed unconnected with light."[31] These landscape sculptures represent the "terrible side" of the father-image to which Donington ascribes "all the restrictive elements in tradition and spiritual authority, the dead hand of the past, the weight of law and order... the dry bones though not the living stuff of religion and philosophy, science and the arts".[32] Stokes' "suffering was... magnified by [this] Edwardian centre of Empire":

Figure 3
The Serpentine, Hyde Park. ©Crown Copyright. National Monuments record

Figure 4
Courtyard, Palace of Urbino. ©the author

The Albert Memorial was of the category, with vain groupings and pseudo-sacred steps. Here was a great fuss about solid matter; here was a thing of arrest which, unlike the prohibiting railings, protested as well as forbade. It took many years for me to discover that art was not a kind of warning.[33]

Contrast Stokes in the 'blind' landscape of a smoggy London park, to the instantaneity of his 1921-1922 vision of the Italian landscape, where past and present are collapsed into atemporal nearness:

> As the train came out of the Mont Cenis tunnel, the sun shone, the sky was a deep, deep, bold blue.... I saw... everywhere, on either side of the train, purple earth, terraces of vine and olive, bright rectangular houses free of atmosphere, of the passage of time, of impediment, of all the qualities which steep and massive roofs connote in the north. The hills belonged to man in this his moment. The two thousand years of Virgilian past that carved and habituated the hillsides, did not oppress; they were gathered in the present aspect.[34]

In the 1920s Stokes travelled widely in Italy, discovering the cities and landscapes of Venice, Rimini and Urbino. He centred his aesthetic on these places, responding to the feeling for material and space disclosed there in certain *quattrocento* works of art and architecture. At Urbino, for example, he was struck by Luciano Laurana's fifteenth century courtyard in the Ducal Palace, and the affinities between this architecture and Piero della Francesca's art. (figure 4) Laurana's "columns are brothers"[35] he writes, and Piero della Francesca's forms, "brothers and sisters at ease within the ancestral hall of space".[35] In Piero's *The Flagellation* at Urbino, the figures, in their archaic stillness, conspire to become columns and the columns are statuesque. The spaces between forms seem as measured as the forms themselves. A similar sensibility pervades the arcades of Luciano Laurana's Palace courtyard.

Stokes adopted the term *identity in difference* to describe his predilection for the non-aggressive, familial relationships epitomised in these key works of the early Renaissance, a term he took from the philosopher Francis Bradley (1846-1924) whose writings he had studied at Oxford University. In Bradley's view of reality all apparent identities are merely appearances, for their seeming existence relies on interdependent relations. At Urbino, as often in Italy, this reciprocity between part and whole (*identity in difference*) extends outwards into the landscape; the modernist architect Giancarlo de Carlo – who has spent decades working with the topologies of Urbino and its setting – sees "the pattern of the town and the pattern of the countryside [as] homologous. If you analyse a section of the cultivated countryside... you realise that nature here is man-made. If you analyse a section of the urban fabric... you see that the man-made is natural... the man-made quality of nature and the natural quality of the man-made both obey the same aesthetic laws."[36] (figure 5) These are landscapes of *virtù*. In the palace courtyard at Urbino, Stokes describes Luciano Laurana's brotherly columns as equal in their "spatial settlement" to the "new *virtù*" of Piero della Francesca's perspectival compositions.[37] Paul Smith surmises that "Stokes' [later] career might be seen as precisely an investigation into the psychological determinants of good and bad energy... into the question of where a notion of *virtù* might reside in the drives of the psyche."[38]

For a significant period in the late 20s, Stokes was inspired by Ezra Pound (first encountered in Rapallo on the Italian Riviera in 1926) in seeking an art and urban landscape that embodied *virtù*, against "the beaten, beaten thoroughfares" of industrialised Victorian-Edwardian London. There is a passage in Stokes' *Colour and Form,* 1937, that evokes the gangster movies of the period and reminds us of Baudelaire's claim that the fractured urban scenes of modernity allow no heroes save the dandy and the criminal:

Figure 8
San Zaccaria,
Venice.
From Stokes A,
*Venice, An Aspect
of Art*, 1945,
plate 37

What figure of today aesthetically best suits our streets, what figure aesthetically is best framed by our doorways? The answer is the man in a long overcoat with hand within pocket holding a revolver on which his fingers tighten. There is no gainsaying the aesthetic appropriateness of the thug in our streets and in our interiors. The idea of him [he concludes with bitter irony] saves our town from an appearance of homelessness.[39]

But recalling Wollheim's suspicion of "cultural psychoanalysis", while psychoanalysis can offer insights into our 'good' and 'bad' drives and their externalisation in art, it does not necessarily entail a wider societal framework. The notion of *virtù*, however – in reaching back to Renaissance humanism and its basis in Aristotelian communitarianism – offers a standpoint in which art and human activity is configured in the *polis*. The city state that is, for Aristotle, the "community of communities", the pre-eminent setting in which to achieve the *telos* of the good life. In writings such as *Greek Culture and the Ego*, 1958, as noted earlier, Stokes extends the notion of the restored corporeal figure to encompass the wider culture as a whole-body entity. The models are the classical world and the Renaissance wherein "the body of the city state" is co-equal with the "*seen* body of the god or goddess". Within the Renaissance, Serlio's settings for sixteenth century comedies and tragedies replicate the stages of real streets, streets which encouraged "a settled cosmogony in which man has an assigned role so that custom and ritual were rich, so that his culture itself seemed an entity, near to hand".[40] Despite Pound's virulent rejection of "Freudian tosh" in the 1920s and 1930s – a component of the split between him and Stokes – the 'good' city is a salient factor in the project of *The Cantos* to realise the *paradiso terrestre*.[41] Guy Davenport has described how Pound avoided the dark cities of Eliot to "posit the city as the one clear conquest of civilisation".[42] Among the many Renaissance cities of *The Cantos* are the *quattrocento* quarters of Venice, of Carpaccio's paintings and, above all, Sigismundo Malatesta's Rimini. Davenport maintains that the poem of *The Cantos* "rests most firmly in a deeper, stiller sense of humanity, the city and its continuity, symbolised by the goddess of field and citadel [Persephone] wearing the sanctuary of her people as a crown".[43] But there is darkness enough in Pound's politics. In *The Cantos*: "Neptunus/his mind/leaping like dolphins" is confirmed as Hitler, and Stokes expressed increasing disagreement in the 1930s with Pound's attempt to link Sigismondo Malatesta and Mussolini as exemplars of statecraft.[44] His Italian meetings had become abbreviated anyway due to his analysis with Melanie Klein. (In 1935 Mussolini invaded Abbysinia.)[45]

The early Renaissance piazza of Pienza, admired by Stokes, is a microcosmic intimation of the Aristotelian *polis*. It was shaped by Pius II between 1458 and 1464. Christine Smith argues that Pienza should not be regarded as a flawed project on the trajectory to the Platonic symmetries of the High Renaissance; in fact its diversity is purposively governed by Leon Battista Alberti's principle of *varietas*; the models are Aristotle and Ciceronian rhetoric, not Plato.[46] At Pienza, as at Urbino, we read the new Renaissance sense of the reciprocity between the city and its landscape, where "the experience of being in the urban fabric is defined and clarified by the viewer's simultaneous perception of its opposite, the countryside".[47] The buildings that frame the piazza reflect complex functions and histories; they range from the everyday brick of the carpenter's house, through the eclectically medieval-classic Communal Palace (figure 6) to the avant-garde neo-Albertian Piccolomini Palace. (figure 7) They shape figural public spaces that legitimise communal hierarchy and civic virtue, and approach Stokes' ideal of *identity in difference*. Describing Mauro Codussi's quattrocento façade of San Zaccaria in his *Venice* (figure 8), Stokes links the aesthetic of *identity in difference* to an ethical ideal of community: "Here, tier upon tier, are all the familiar forms, individual as always yet in community. From the whole façade, therefore, we obtain the impression of a vast community of individuals."[48] The varied components of Pienza's cathedral square, articulate a related impression of individual and community. While there *is* hierarchy, the architectonic setting is more inclusive than the powerful symmetries of the high Renaissance that followed; in Onian's view "the relations between spiritual and secular, institution and individual... create in the square a microcosmic unity".[49]

In conclusion we can attempt to summarise some of the politico-ethical attributes that an environment of *virtù* might embody, an environment that fosters the sense of "being at home in the world" and the sense of a "settled cosmogony" of which Stokes writes. Firstly, it will synthesise and be 'emblematic' of the energies and contributions of its patrons, artists and architects and makers.[50] It will also be 'emblematic' of the wider culture. Next, given its innate humanism, the *virtù* setting will be strongly corporeal in character and, while the outcome of both the 'good' and 'bad' drives of the psyche, will stress wholeness not fragmentation. Relations of part and whole will express the democratisation of form implied by *identity in difference*; this does not preclude hierarchy within the building, or the city and its landscape. Finally, given that *virtù* is also an attribute of substance, there will also be a stress on hapticity and material in the *virtù* landscape. Philip Bess has argued for "public spaces conducive to the common good" that foster "individual lives of learning, piety, filial affection and obligation, respect for others and the pursuit of excellence".[51]

Figure 9
Salk Institute
Photo:
© Nathaniel
Coleman.

Louis Kahn's Salk Institute, 1959-1965, (figure 9) represents an attempt within modernity to realise a *virtù* landscape. Salk famously envisioned it as a setting to unify "art and science"; a place that "Picasso could come to visit".[52] It embodies Kahn's commitment to "enduring institutions" made visible in a holistic humanist setting. *Identity in difference* is configured in the gathering of the individual study cells around the central piazza; an image of individual learning and making within wider communal obligations. Luis Barragan describes this paved court as a "façade to the sky" that draws together the heavens, the Pacific Ocean and the parched Californian landscape.

Stokes' theory of art urges holism founded on the restored corporeal figure. In our splintered urban scene his writings remind us that modernity has, at times, envisioned less fractured settings for human encounter. In *Greek Culture and the Ego* he contends:

> The basic pattern, I suggest, is once more the corporeal ego-figure. The essence of *virtù* resides in configurations that illustrate a total spirit. There is, then, kinship with preconceptions inherent in the aesthetic process. As well as greatness, the felicity of art during what might be called *virtù* periods confirms it.[53]

1   I am grateful to Ann Stokes and Adrian Stokes' literary executors Telfer Stokes and Ian Angus for kind permission to include material from Adrian Stokes' papers held in the Tate Gallery Archive.

2   Tate Gallery Archive; 8816, notebook 15.

3   See, for example Carrier, D, ed., *England and its Aesthetes: Biography and Taste: John Ruskin, Walter Pater, Adrian Stokes: Essays*, Amsterdam: G & B Arts International, 1997. This includes a critical introduction by Carrier and the republished autobiographical *Inside Out* (1947).

4   Gowing, L, ed., *The Critical Writings of Adrian Stokes, Volume I 1930-1937; Volume II 1937-1958; Volume III 1955-1967*, London: Thames and Hudson, 1978. *Volume II, Inside Out*, p. 158. Subsequent references to Gowing are given as follows: CW, II, *Inside Out*, p. 154, p. 158.

5   CW, II, *Inside Out*, p. 158.

6   CW, II, *Inside Out*, p. 157.

7   Stonebridge, L, *The Destructive Element. British Psychoanalysis and Modernism*, Basingstoke: Macmillan, 1998, p. ix.

8   Stonebridge, *The Destructive Element*, p. 19.

9   CW, II, *Inside Out*, p. 159.

10 For an analysis of the Hyde Park landscape in relation to the writings of Stokes, Conrad and Ruskin see Kite, S, "The Urban Landscape of Hyde Park: Adrian Stokes, Conrad and the *Topos* of Negation", *Art History*, vol. 23 no. 2, 2000, pp. 205-232.

11 Segal, H, "A Psychoanalytical Approach to Aesthetics", *New Directions in Psychoanalysis. The Significance of Infant Conflict in the Pattern of Adult Behaviour*, Klein, M, Heimann, P, Money-Kyrle, R E, eds., London: Tavistock Publications, 1955, pp. 384-405, p. 386.

12 Segal, H, "A Psychoanalytical Approach", p. 387.

13 Stokes, A, *A Game That Must be Lost. Collected Papers*, Cheadle, Cheshire: Carcanet Press, 1973, p. 77.

14 CW, III, *The Invitation in Art*, p. 266.

15 Segal, H, "A Psychoanalytical Approach", p. 388.

16 Stokes, A, *A Game*, p. 147.

17 See Rifkin, A, "Benjamin's Paris, Freud's Rome: whose London?", *Art History*, vol. 22 no. 4, 1999, pp. 619-632 and Kite, S, "The Urban Landscape".

18 CW, III, *Three Essays on the Painting of our Time*, p. 146.

19 Read, R, " 'Art Today': Stokes, Pound, Freud and the Word-Image Opposition", *Word & Image*, vol. 14 no. 1/2, 1998.

20 CW, III, *The Invitation in Art*, p. 295.

21 Quoted in CW, III, *The Invitation in Art*, p. 296.

22 CW, III, *The Invitation in Art*, p. 296.

23 Wollheim, R, "A Critic of Our Time" [Review of *Greek Culture and the Ego*], *Encounter*, vol. 12 no. 4, 1959, pp. 41-44.

24 CW, III, *Greek Culture and the Ego*, p. 93.

25 Gervais, D, "Adrian Stokes and the Benignity of Form: Part One", *The Cambridge Quarterly*, vol. 10, 1981, pp. 40-64.

26 Stokes, A, *With all the Views. The Collected Poems of Adrian Stokes*, Manchester: Carcanet New Press, 1981, p. 159.

27 CW, II, *Smooth and Rough*, p. 228.

28 CW, II, *Smooth and Rough*, p. 228.

29 Stokes, A, *Sunrise in the West*, New York and London: Harper and Brothers, 1927, pp. ix-x.

30 CW, II, *Inside Out*, p. 146.

31 CW, II, *Inside Out*, p. 148.

32 Donington, R, *Wagner's 'Ring' and its Symbols: the Music and the Myth*, London: Faber and Faber, 1974, p. 206.

33 CW, II, *Inside Out*, p. 148.

34 CW, II, *Inside Out*, p. 156.

35 CW, I, *The Quattro Cento*, p. 134; CW, II, *Art and Science*, p. 195.

36 Quoted in Zucchi, B, *Giancarlo De Carlo*, Oxford: Butterworth Architecture, 1992, p. 84.

37 For Stokes' description of the *cortile*, see CW, I, *The Quattro Cento*, pp. 131-37.

38 Smith, P, "Adrian Stokes and Ezra Pound", *PN Review 15*, vol. 7 no 1, 1980, pp. 51-52.

39 CW, II, *Colour and Form*, p. 13.

40 Stokes, A, *A Game*, p. 153.

41 See Ozturk, A, *Ezra Pound and Visual Art*, University of Oxford: PhD thesis, 1987, p. 438.

42 Davenport, G, *The Geography of the Imagination: Forty Essays by Guy Davenport*, London: Pan Books, 1984, p. 162.

43 Davenport, G, *The Geography*, p. 164.

44 Quoted in Tanner, T, *Venice Desired*, Oxford: Blackwell, 1992, p. 154.

45 For a wider discussion of the Pound-Stokes relationship and the notion of *virtù* see Kite, S, "Architecture as Virtù: Adrian Stokes, Ezra Pound and the Ethics of 'Patterned Energy'", *The Journal of Architecture*, vol. 6, Spring 2001, pp. 81-96. Some of the later material of this essay draws from this paper with grateful acknowledgement to *The Journal of Architecture*.

46 See Smith, C, *Architecture in the Culture of Early Humanism: Ethics, Aesthetics, and Eloquence 1400-1470*, New York and Oxford: Oxford University Press, 1992, particularly chapter 6: "*Varietas* and the Design of Pienza."

47 Smith, C, *Architecture*, p. 125.

48 CW, II, *Venice*, p. 108.

49 Onians, J, *Bearers of Meaning: the Classical Orders in Antiquity, the Middle Ages and the Renaissance*, Princeton: Princeton University Press, 1998, p. 187.

50 Stokes' notion of *emblem* and the *emblematic* approaches the aspects of *virtù* under discussion. *Emblematic* art can be perceived at a glance, yet embodies place and history. Like Eliot's poetry or Pound's *Malatesta Cantos* it orders space and memory as a "pattern of timeless moments".

51 Bess, P, "Communitarianism and Emotivism: Two Rival Views of Ethics and Architecture", *Theorising a New Agenda for Architecture: an Anthology of Architectural Theory 1965-1995*, Nesbitt, K, ed., New York: Princeton Architectural Press, 1996, pp. 370-382, p. 375.

52 Steele, J, *Salk Institute: Louis I Kahn: Architecture in Detail*, London: Phaidon, 1993, p. 12.

53 CW, III, *Greek Culture and the Ego*, p. 117.

Stephen Kite

Distorting Mirrors: Phoenix Park, Dublin, 1832-1849, and the Ambiguities of Empire
Dana Arnold

Pierre Nora's concept of a *lieu de mémoire* establishes a material, symbolic and functional site that is the product of the interrelationship between memory and history.[1] These sites embody a will to remember and record – the respective functions of memory and history. But these *lieux de mémoire* also demonstrate the ability to change their meaning and relationship to other sites. The political weighting this concept lends to sites that endure through the colonial and post-colonial era helps bring to the fore the dialectical relationship between colonial and post-colonial spaces. Zeynip Çelik's discussion of *lieux de mémoire* in Algiers relies heavily on Nora's ideas and ably demonstrates their efficacy as a mode of analysis.[2] But Çelik and, through her reading of him, Nora rely on the passage of time to fully explore the slippage between coloniser's intentions and the colonised's reception and adaption of these actions. In her identification of those moments, when the reversal takes place between the dominant and the dominated *lieux de mémoire,* Çelik uses Nora's idea of 'distorting mirrors' to summarise how the urban spaces of Algiers retained the memory trace of both colonial and pre-colonial times – narrating this history from a post-colonial perspective. I want to stay with the concept of distorting mirrors but want also to collapse the space-time dimension that is so necessary for Çelik's evocative discussion. My focus is the colonial situation in Ireland in the early nineteenth century and the attempts to create a national memory (in Nora's words) through landscape design that responded to a specific set of political and colonial circumstances. My aim is to show that in the politically charged urban landscape of Dublin, the will to create a *lieu de mémoire* brought with it a certain amount of cultural baggage that post-colonial theory allows me to unpack. But as the relationship between Ireland and Britain remains complex and has for centuries been a history of domination, appropriation and revolt, the spaces cannot provide the 'before', 'during' and 'after' that the 130 year occupation of Algiers by the French neatly supplies.

It is here that Michel Foucault's discussion of the idea of the heterotopia is useful.[3] Foucault's analysis of the spaces that act as heterotopias relies on their sustained ambiguity in relationship to other sites. A site, according to Foucault, is defined by a cluster of relations it has – in other words it is characterised by the things to which it relates rather than by its own intrinsic qualities. But certain sites have the property of being related to other sites "in such a way as to suspect, neutralize or invert the set of relationships they happen to designate, mirror, or reflect".[4] In this way places exist in society which are something like counter-sites, a kind of effectively enacted utopia in which real sites that can be found within a culture are simultaneously represented, contested and inverted. It is at this point that the analogy of the mirror used by Foucault helps to demonstrate the ambiguous relationship between utopia and heterotopia:

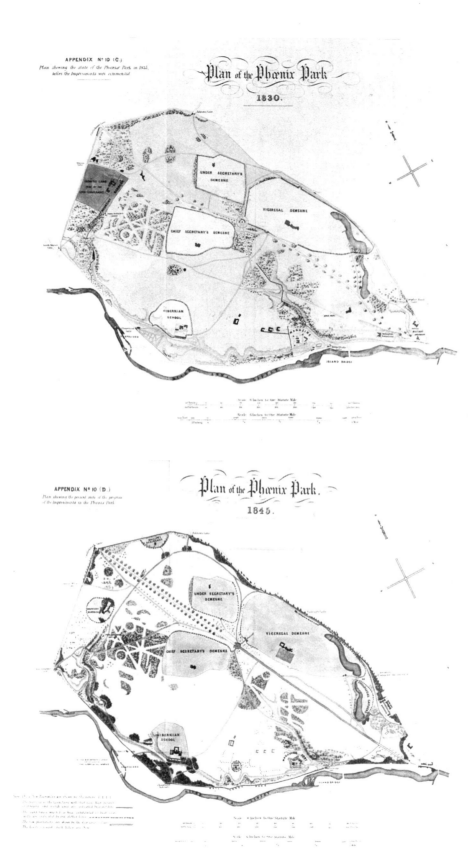

Figure 3
Watercolour of
Hyde Park Screen
and the Arch at
Constitution Hill
c1825 (private
collection)

I believe that between utopias and heterotopias there might be a sort of mixed, joint experience, which would be the mirror…. I see myself in the mirror where I am not, in an unreal, virtual space that opens up behind the surface; I am over there, where I am not… but in so far as the mirror does exist in reality… it exerts a sort of counteraction on the position that I occupy…. It makes the place that I occupy at the moment when I look at myself in the glass at once absolutely real… and absolutely unreal….[5]

The mirror analogy suggests an absence of linear temporality – a moment frozen in time rather like a snap shot, whilst also acknowledging the potential for flux and change. As a result Foucault's concept of a heterotopia can allow for the passage of time as society can make a heterotopia function in a different fashion as its history unfolds.[6] But it is the static, momentary quality that is of particular use in relation to my reading of Phoenix Park in Dublin.

Phoenix Park

Phoenix Park lies to the north-west of the centre of Dublin standing, in the nineteenth century, between the city and the countryside beyond. Prior to its improvement the park (figure 1) comprised an area with hilly aspects, boggy land, ramshackle buildings, uncontrolled grazing and was subject to frequent trespass as a result of the inadequate provision of a perimeter wall and insecure gateways. Despite these somewhat inhospitable surroundings, the colonial presence was amply represented through the Vice Regal Lodge – the official residence of the Lord Lieutenant of Ireland – and the Chief Secretary's and Under Secretary's Lodges, which were all situated in the park, each within its own private demesne concealed by overgrown planting from public view. Alongside these the Mountjoy Barracks, Hibernian Military School and the Magazine and Star Forts were all to be found. The park, however, also symbolised the city of Dublin through the Phoenix Pillar, which was both the emblem of the park and of the city itself. In this way the space of Phoenix Park operated as a kind of *lieu de mémoire* of the occupied Irish, but it was also at the same time a space in which the colonising British attempted to create a new kind of national memory in response to the changing social and political conditions in mainland Britain and to the symbolic needs of the Anglo-Irish protestant ascendancy. By the mid-nineteenth century Phoenix Park (figure 2) had been transformed

Figure 4
Early nineteenth
century
photograph of
Nelson's Column,
Dublin 1808
(destroyed 1966)
(private
collection)

into an attractive landscaped space with public areas and private, but now visible, official residences. This included a clear definition of the perimeter of the park, which was punctuated with new entrance gates and lodges. The landscape was drained, remodelled and replanted, and public pleasure grounds created. New directional axes through the park were established in the form of the Straight Avenue and other new roads, rides and walkways, and the Wellington Testamonial provided a monumental reminder of British military and imperial might.

The scale and significance of the improvement works in Phoenix Park carried out between 1832-1849 is comparable to those carried out in the Royal Parks in London earlier in the century. The Royal Parks referred to here comprise Regent's Park to the north of London and Hyde Park, St James' and Green Park, which were all situated on its western edge. Work to transform Regent's Park into an up-market development of speculatively built housing and an area of entertainment and social interaction for the urban upper and middle classes began in 1812 with work drawing to a halt some 20 years later. The parks to the west of London took on new significance with the move by King George IV to Buckingham Palace from Carlton House in the mid 1820s. As a result all three were re-landscaped and monumental entranceways into them – including the Arch at Constitution Hill, 1825, and the Hyde Park Screen, 1823 – were constructed. (figure 3) These entrances were intended to serve as monuments to the nation's military prowess through the enduring iconographic significance of the triumphal arch and their sculptural decoration which, however, was never completed.[7]

There is no doubt that the public open spaces of the urban parks in London and Dublin took on a new significance in the nineteenth century as these cities grew in size and political importance. The work in the Royal Parks in London has been shown to be one way in which the state tried to shape this urban experience and social interaction through the design of specific environments and this can also be identified as one of the motives behind the improvements to Phoenix Park.[8] Conceptualising Phoenix Park as a heterotopia brings to the fore its character as an oppositional space – both in terms of its own internal dynamics between the public and private and the symbolic and the useful, as well as its ability to reflect the Royal Parks in London – and enables us to see the significance of this urban landscape in its specific space-time location.

Figure 5
The Wellington
Testimonial
Phoenix Park,
Dublin 1814.
(photo: author)

Figure 6
Detail of bronze
relief showing
conquest of India
and names of
victories
inscribed on the
column shaft.
The Wellington
Testimonial
Phoenix Park,
Dublin 1814.
(photo: author)

The new urban landscape of London was intended to provide markers for a new national identity and the Royal Parks were the sites for many of the plans. According to a contemporary commentary from 1816 these included: "… new palaces for the sovereign and the Duke of Wellington – a national monument as memorial of our naval victories, another to the memory of general, officers and soldiers, a new custom house, Post Office and several bridges".[9] Phoenix Park had some similar associations, as it was already the site of like buildings and the remnants of the old pre-1798 system of government – most notably, the Vice Regal Lodge and the Chief Secretary's demesne. In both London and Dublin these symbols in the performance of the rituals of a patrician authority were now counter-balanced by the increasing political importance of the urban middle class whose need for some kind of aesthetic expression of identity had to be met. Here, the heterotopic function of the space of Phoenix Park is evident as the reordered park both re-presents the Royal Parks while offering a tighter, more orderly version of the same "juxtaposing in a single real place several spaces, several sites… to create a space that is other, another real space, as perfect, as meticulous, as well arranged as [its referent] is messy, ill constructed and jumbled".[10] The orderly reflection proposed by Foucault endorses the coloniser's dominance but at the same time the mirror effect reveals the uncertainties of empire whereby colonial space can reveal ambiguities in the formation of a national identity – or memory. I now want to focus on three ways in which Phoenix Park can be seen as a heterotopic reflection of London.

The National Hero – or Making a National Memory

The British military successes at Trafalgar, 1805, and Waterloo, 1815, prompted plans for monuments both to the victories and the heroic leaders – Nelson and Wellington. Commemoration of these events was a nationwide phenomenon, but few of the projects to celebrate them planned for London were successfully completed.[11] In Dublin, however, monuments were erected to both Nelson and Wellington: William Wilkins' Nelson Column had been constructed in the city centre in 1808 (figure 4) and in 1814 the Wellington Fund had been opened with the idea that there should also be a monument to the Duke in the city.[12] Not only was he already a national hero but he was born in Ireland, and was for a time the country's Chief Secretary.

The debates around the kind of monument that should be erected shed light on how national identities could be expressed. The views of J W Croker, a Member of Parliment and member of the

committee that administered the Wellington Fund, on the subject of monuments are clearly set out in his letter to the Fund's Secretary dated 7 October 1814:

> I quite agree with the committee in its predilection for a pillar. I was one of the pillarists in the Nelson case and my only wish for our column to be one of more magnificent dimensions. Great height is the cheapest way and one of the most certain of obtaining sublimity. Ten thousand pounds will bring you the highest column in the world, and will produce an astonishing effect; fifty thousand pounds would serve to erect an arch, and when it was erected you would have it dated.... Therefore, I exhort you to keep the column form. Whatever you do be at least sure to make it stupendously high; let it be of all the columns in the world the most lofty.

> Nelson's is 202, Trajan's about 150, Antonius 132 or as some have it 180, Bonaparte's in the Place Vendôme is, I think, near 200. I wish therefore that you should not fall short of 250, and I should prefer to have it exactly from the first layer to the base of crown of the statue 300.[13]

Phoenix Park was chosen as the appropriate site for the monument (whatever its final form was to be) as the Secretary of State and his chief officers lived there and, like Hyde Park in London, it was the scene of regular military exercises. (figure 5-6) In due course the Dublin Committee decided on a pillar to be designed by Robert Smirke. While there are formal and ideological similarities in placing such a monument in the Royal Parks in London and Dublin, the meaning of the Wellington column in Phoenix Park is subtly different from the London proposals. It is a statement of national pride, but one made within a colonial context and, ironically, was one of the more successful attempts to celebrate the Duke as the monuments to his victory over the French in London were dogged by controversy, apathy and ridicule.[14]

Phoenix Park as a Symbol of Colonial Rule

The works in Phoenix Park can be set in the context of the turbulent relations between Britain and its geographically closest colony during the opening years of the nineteenth century.[15] The 1798 rebellion precipitated the abolition of the Irish Parliament, or College Green Assembly, and the transfer of the government to London, although the Irish Exchequer was not amalgamated with the rest of Britain until 1816.[16] This meant that Ireland was now subsumed into British political identity. The nature of Ireland's colonial dependency changed as a metropolitan system of government was established which, although this was nominally run from Dublin, was clearly rooted in London. In the decades after the Act of Union protestant culture became an increasingly potent force in urban politics.

The governmental structure in Ireland retained some facets of pre-Union times. The Viceroy, also know as the Lord Lieutenant, and his 'court' remained in place in Dublin, despite the transfer of power to London. The Chief Secretary maintained a powerful role – often augmented by good connections with the British cabinet.[17] The two posts did not always work well together. The Chief Secretary and his Under Secretary were more politically pro-active and often used patronage of various kinds for their own political ends. Part of the development of a tighter governmental structure in Ireland in the post-Union period was state involvement with improvements in education, public health and public works.[18] Here there was more decisive and extensive intervention than in mainland Britain, which helped ensure the implementation of a metropolitan system of rule. Phoenix Park was, then, a site of both geographical and political importance in Dublin and can be seen as a focal point of the interaction between colonial rule and urban planning.

In 1829 the Act of Catholic Emancipation was passed, to which, despite much opposition, the Duke of Wellington had given his support. Charles Arbuthnot had played an important role in ensuring the necessary support of the Whig opposition, in particular Lord Duncannon and Earl de Grey. This was quickly followed by the enfranchisement of the middle classes in the 1832 Reform Act. The residency qualification of voters in this act made the protestant bourgeoisie a significant force in Irish urban politics.[19] These social, religious and political changes highlighted the requirement for a tight metropolitan government in Ireland which needed to be both effective and to have an adequate symbolic presence in the city. The protestant middle class needed to find an appropriate aesthetic expression of its national memory or identity, which was both located in and dislocated from mainland Britain. The re-design of Phoenix Park, which was so closely related to the Royal Parks in London, was one way of expressing the socio-political identity of Dublin.

Making a Colonial Space

It is against this background of social and political upheaval and re-organisation of the administration of crown lands in Ireland that a report on the state of Phoenix Park and recommendations for improvements was commissioned from the architect Decimus Burton in August 1832. The commissioners found Burton to be the obvious choice as he had previously been employed to work on the improvements in the Royal Parks in London, and had designed the new lodges as well as the Arch at Constitution Hill and the Hyde Park Screen.

Burton quickly followed up his initial report with a further survey of the state of Phoenix Park in September 1834.[20] His remarks, written after a visit to Dublin in August 1834, give a clear idea of his overall vision for the park and have a distinct resonance with his work in London. At this point it is important to remember the interconnectedness of the seemingly diverse government offices and officials, as this underscores the intentionality and complex relationships in and around the works in Phoenix Park. For instance, the Duke of Wellington was at once a celebrated war hero and the Prime Minister who prompted the reform of the Offices of Woods and Works in Britain and Ireland. His pragmatic view on the 1829 Act of Catholic Emancipation was contradicted by his strong objections to the 1832 Reform Act, yet he was concerned about rights of access to Phoenix Park by the urban middle class. Another key figure, Charles Arbuthnot, who was a close personal friend of Wellington and facilitated the 1829 Act, was also a prominent official in the Office of Woods who had done much to promote Decimus Burton as the architect in charge of the re-development of Hyde, St James' and Green Parks.[21] In this way Decimus Burton became the instrument or agent of the broader socio-political forces behind the re-design of Phoenix Park whilst ensuring continuity between it and the London parks.

The works carried out fall into three main categories: the drainage and general tidying and replanting of the park; the creation of pleasure grounds for the enjoyment of the public – especially women and children; and the re-landscaping of the area around the Vice Regal, Chief and Under Secretaries' Demesnes. Burton's scheme shows sympathy for the natural landscape of the area by creating views through to the countryside and hills beyond, and a feeling of openness and space within the park. This was to be achieved by vistas stretching across the enclosed grounds of the official residences created through the use of sunken fences rather than high walls, by the felling of tall trees and by careful planting. (figures 1-2)

One of the hallmarks of Burton's re-design of the Royal Parks in London had been the new entrances. These compact, classically-inspired lodges helped shape the character of the parks. This was also the case in Dublin and the Chapelizod Gate and lodge amply demonstrate what Burton had in mind.[22] The new lodge had no outbuildings, instead a sunken court provided storage and a small garden laid to turf replaced the plot that had been used for cultivation. Here, as in the Castleknock and Knockmaroon Gates and lodges, the creation of an ordered, public, symbolic space with which to replace a more disordered, private, useful space was of paramount importance. Chapelizod Lodge was the first to be re-sited to align with the Hibernian Military School.[23] Although the new lodge was smaller than its predecessor, it created a more impressive and secure entrance as a turnstile gate, locked each night by the Chapelizod gatekeeper, replaced the old entrance. The alignment of Chapelizod gate and the military school is important here as axiality is a recurrent feature of the plan for the park. Moreover, the amount of remodelling of the landscape required to enable the new plan is once again reminiscent of the huge undertakings in the laying-out of country house landscapes. The design of the lodge itself was typically compact and symmetrical with a temple portico front – in fact, not at all dissimilar to Cumberland Lodge, 1825, designed by Burton for Hyde Park in London.

The Straight Avenue was the essential backbone of the park giving a directional logic to the flow of traffic through it. Indeed, other avenues and roads in the park, which were also improved, met with the Straight Avenue at its virtual centre point. Here, Burton re-sited the Phoenix Pillar, the very symbol of both the park itself, and of Dublin, the capital city of Ireland and the second city of the Empire.[24] Despite its importance to the overall plan, the avenue was formed only gradually, as work in the park progressed. The Pillar was surrounded by four iron standard lamps with burners, to align with the new road – a kind of metaphorical re-enactment of the process of annexation and re-ordering experienced by the colonised at the hands of the coloniser. By 1846 the Straight Avenue was completed between the Phoenix Pillar and Dublin Gate where the unfinished Wellington monument was situated, so creating an ambiguous axis between a monument to Dublin, albeit re-sited, and a potent, but incomplete, symbol of colonial presence.[25]

As might be expected, there was a strong political motivation behind the instigation of such works. The recent works in the Royal Parks in London were intended to underline governmental authority and be of benefit to the public. Likewise, the government felt this should be extended to "the inhabitants of Dublin [who] are justified in the expectation they entertain that the favour and liberality of the Government will not be withheld of the only park attached to their capital". This "liberality" is evident in the careful use of improved landscape and increased public access. Moreover, the relationship between the London parks and Phoenix Park went beyond the uniformity of their landscaping and architectural improvements and their architect. The outfits worn by the gatekeepers, which it was decided early on in the works should be the same as those worn in St James' Park and Regent's Park, demonstrate the importance of the image of the parks and the strong connection between the works in the two cities. In this way the re-use of the design principles of the London parks can be seen as one way in which authority was exported to a colonial capital.

"o foenix culprit"

The decisions made in the remodelling of Phoenix Park offer a mirror image of those effected in London and provide us with a reading of Phoenix Park as a countersite where the socio-political co-ordinates of the reimaging of London in the opening years of the nineteenth century are re-enacted under the colonising authority of a new social élite. The newly remodelled park made the official demesnes of the protestant officers of the British government more visible; and, in turn, these residences were placed in an improved landscape setting designed for the convenience and pleasure of the public – especially the protestant bourgeoisie. The park was an important statement when seen against the backdrop of the contemporary religious and political situation in Ireland. Yet, like the Royal Parks in London, there was room for private speculative development, and the inclusion of premises for learned societies as seen in the zoological gardens, which were also laid out by Burton in both London and Dublin, tie Phoenix Park more closely to London – in particular the distinctive social environment created in Regent's Park.[26] The Commissioners were successful in their wish to encourage the use of the park causing Burton to remark "since the improvements in the appearance and police in the park have been effected the public generally are accustomed to frequent it in far greater numbers than formerly – and that the difference in this respect is more particularly observable in regard to the upper classes".[27] In this way the park was a colonising heterotopia, a meticulous space where all that was planned, but not always realised, for the London parks were mirrored in a discrete location away from the main centre of Dublin.[28] The order imposed on the space through the re-landscaping and conditions of entry and social conduct within the park, made possible through improved perimeters and boundaries, are both parts of the colonising process and of the realisation of a heterotopia. But the Phoenix Park remained a distinct urban landscape with its own identity and in later years its reversal from a dominated to dominant *lieu de mémoire* is seen in the Phoenix Park murders, 1882, and their reprise in James Joyce's *Finnegans Wake*.

1   Nora, Pierre, ed., *Realms of Memory: the Construction of the French Past: Conflicts and Divisions*, foreword by Lawrence D Kritzman, trans. Arthur Goldhammer, New York: Columbia University Press, 1998.

2   Çelik, Zeynip, "Colonial/Postcolonial Intersections: Lieux de Mémoire in Algiers", *Third Text* 49, 1999-2000, pp. 632-672.

3   See Foucault, Michel, "Des Espaces Autres", "Of Other Spaces", trans. Jay Miskowiec, *Diacritics*, Spring 1986, pp. 22-27.

4   Foucault, "Des Espaces Autres", p. 24.

5   Foucault, "Des Espaces Autres", p. 24.

6   Foucault, "Des Espaces Autres", p. 25. I discuss the history of Phoenix Park in my chapter in Arnold, D, ed., *Cultural Identities and the Aesthetics of Britishness*, Manchester: Manchester University Press, 2003.

7   For a discussion of the Royal Parks in London in the early nineteenth century see Arnold, Dana, *Representing the Metropolis: Architecture, Urban Experience and Social Life in London 1800-1840*, Aldershot: Ashgate, 2000, and Arnold, Dana, "A Family Affair: James and Decimus Burton's work in the Regent's Park", *The Georgian Villa*, in Arnold, Dana, ed., Stroud: Sutton Publishing, 1995.

8 For a discussion of the social, cultural and political significance of the Royal Parks in London in the early nineteenth century see Arnold, *Re-presenting the Metropolis*.

9 Crutwell, Richard, *Remarks on the Buildings and Improvements in London and Elsewhere*, London, 1816, pp. iii.

10 Foucault, "Des Espaces Autres", pp. 25 and 27.

11 For a discussion of the national celebration of Nelson and Wellington see Yarrington, Alison, *The Commemoration of the Hero 1800-1864: Monuments to the British Victors of the Napoleonic Wars*, New York and London: Garland, 1988.

12 Liscombe, R W, *William Wilkins,* Cambridge: Cambridge University Press, 1980, pp. 57-58.

13 Pool, B, ed., *The Croker Papers 1808-1857,* London: Batsford, 1967, pp. 21-22.

14 For a discussion of the different ways in which the Duke of Wellington was commemorated in London see my essay, "The Duke of Wellington and London", 13th Annual Wellington Lecture, University of Southampton, 2001.

15 For a detailed discussion of Anglo-Irish politics at this time see Vaughan, W E, ed., *A New History of Ireland*, vol. V, "Ireland Under the Union I 1801-1870", Oxford: Clarendon Press, 1989.

16 For a fuller discussion see Foster, R F, *Modern Ireland 1600-1972*, Penguin: Harmondsworth, 1988, p. 282 ff.

17 Foster, *Modern Ireland*, p. 289.

18 Foster, *Modern Ireland*, p. 290.

19 Recent debates have queried the relationship between the 1832 Reform Act and the rise of middle class power (see *inter alia* Wahrman, Dror, *Imagining the Middle Class: the Political Representation of Class in Britain, c1780-1840*, Cambridge: Cambridge University Press, 1995) claiming that this act facilitated the 'invention' of the ever-rising middle class rather then being precipitated by this social group. It is not my intention here to debate the merits of these revisions of historical constructions of class identities and their broader ramifications. But in this instance the case for the combined influence of the Act of Catholic and Emancipation and the Reform Act on the socio-political context of Phoenix Park is compelling, particularly within a colonial framework.

20 This report dated 27 September 1834 was printed as an appendix to the Twenty Second Report of the Commissioners of Her Majesty's Woods, Forest and Land Revenues, 1845. Henceforth Burton's 1834 Report.

21 The friendship between the Duke of Wellington, Charles Arbuthnot and his wife Harriet is well documented. The couple were known to have been confidantes of the Duke from whom he sought advice. See *inter alia* Smith, E A, *Wellington and the Arbuthnots*, Stroud: Sutton Publishing, 1994, and Bamford, Francis and Wellesley, Gerald, Duke of Wellington, eds., *The Journal of Mrs Arbuthnot, 1820-1832*, 2 vols., London: Macmillan, 1950.

22 Burton also produced designs for the Cabragh Gate and Colonel White's Gate with his report of 27th February 1839. Drawings for these submitted with Burton's report are held in the National Library of Ireland (NLI 2123, 2124, 2126 and 2127).

23 A drawing by Burton dated January 1836 showing this is held in the National Archives of Ireland, OPW 5 temporary folder HC/2/65. In 1994 a substantial amount of documentary material has become available in the National Archives of Ireland in the Office of Public Works Collection. The collection of letters, plans and designs for the works carried out in the park between 1832-1849 shed new light on the nature of the improvements and the role played by Decimus Burton and his relationship to other parties also employed in the improvements to the park. The material comprises six boxes of letters and six folders of drawings. The letters are as yet uncatalogued. A temporary reference of OPW5/Decimus Burton/Phoenix Park has been given to these. (Hereafter OPW).

24 He received permission to re-site the Pillar on 11 March 1843 in a letter from Alexander Milne (OPW). Mr Hayden provided the standard lamps and burners OPW 31 October 1843 Burton to the Commissioners of Woods. Mr John Butler was responsible for taking down the pillar and re-erecting. OPW 20 December 1843 Burton to the Commissioners of Woods.

25 OPW 15 March 1847 Burton to the Commissioners of Woods.

26 OPW 30 June 1840 Burton to the Commissioners of Woods. In an uncanny resemblance to Regent's Park in London, Burton recommended that an area between the Castleknock and Colonel White's Gates (some twelve acres) should be appropriated for villa building. See also Arnold, "A Family Affair". The Dublin Zoological Society had first approached Burton in August 1830 about a suitable layout for their gardens. Burton submitted his plan and report on 27 October 1832. A transcript of his report exists in Trinity College Library (Zoological Society Minute Book May 1830 – July 1840 10608/2/1 TCD). I am grateful to Dr F O'Dwyer for this reference and to Dr S O'Reilly for transcribing the document for me. Burton designed the Zoological Society Gardens in Regent's Park 1826-1841. The original plan is held in the Public Record Office, MPE 906 but it stands outside the concerns of this essay, which is confined to the state's intervention in the landscapes of the urban parks in both cities.

27 OPW Burton to the Commissioners of Woods 15 June 1842.

28 Foucault, "Des Espaces Autres", p. 27.

From Beautification to Sustainability: the Inner City as Political Landscape
Elizabeth Lebas

In 1934, just prior to the general elections, a poor and socialist south London municipality voiced both its achievements and dreams through a small and anonymous publication issued by the Labour Institute. Two statements, chosen from *12 Years of Labour Rule on the Bermondsey Borough Council, 1922-1934*, sum up its belief in the transforming and redemptive powers of beauty in the landscape – and much besides. How much besides cannot be contained in a single discussion. However, I shall suggest that in Britain, the political consensus forged over social reform at the turn of the last century was overlaid on an older consensus over the values and making of collective landscapes which both expressed and denied relations between town and country and between social classes. The archives and photographic collection of Bermondsey Borough Council, 1900-1965, provide us with the possibility of looking back at the environment of the inner city neither as failed or successful professional ideals, nor as legislative outcome for consumption, but as the means of a creative political engagement.[1]

These two statements reflect on the previous 12 years and anticipate the next 12. On the previous 12 years: "People who have been absent from the neighbourhood since the War [World War I] say that they hardly recognise the district, so great is the change. And Labour is responsible. It is a romantic and almost unbelievable story." And on the next 12: "The drab sordidness of Old Bermondsey will have gone forever, and the district will be illumined with touches of colour and beauty never known before. We shall have available to all the inhabitants many of the benefits of civilisation previously obtainable only by the favoured classes who can afford to live in the more desirable areas."[2]

Created in 1900 from the vestries of St John's Horsleydown, Bermondsey and Rotherhithe, the Borough of Bermondsey was to the north and east bounded by the River Thames from the Pool of London to and including Lime Reach, the entirety of its river bank lined with warehouses, docks and wharves. To the west and south it was effectively cut off from its neighbouring Boroughs of Southwark and Camberwell by the railway lines running from London Bridge. In 1931, its population had fallen to just over 113,000 people from its highest record of 190,000 in 1881. Nevertheless, its population density was estimated at 97 persons per acre, virtually the entirety living in officially overcrowded conditions. It also had the third highest rate of tuberculosis in the country. A place of hard living, of dockers, sailors and women employed in the jam, biscuit and vinegar factories. (figure 1)

Bermondsey remained an Independent Labour Party (ILP) stronghold until 1970, subsequently alternating between Labour and Liberal Democratic political allegiances. Since 1965 it has been incorporated within the Borough of Southwark, presently with a 'hung' council. Less than 30,000 people now live in the district. The Eastern Docks have vanished, generically renamed by the

Figure 1
Slum Clearance
Map, 1931

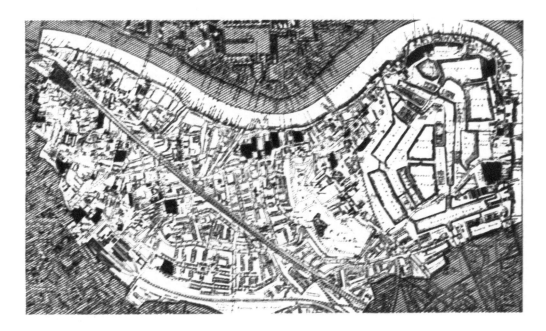

Docklands Development Corporation of the 1980s as the *Surrey Docks* – a watery land of urban farms, daffodils in bloom, malls and speculatively built neo-suburban housing units. Its warehouses have been turned into lofts; the Design Museum and the Conran Empire have taken over Butler's Wharf, itself developed over the site of the eighth century St Olaf's church, demolished in 1927 by Bermondsey Borough Council. The Jubilee Tube Line has arrived. Close to London Bridge squats the Greater London Assembly building designed by Norman Foster. Further west along the riverbank there is a Herzog and de Meuron conversion, the Tate Modern. Bermondsey is the place now of designer living, artist studios, antiques and, to give it that 'edge', that 'buzz', also the filmic location of the new romantic: the tough, male, white and racist underclass of such films as *Nil by Mouth*.[3]

Southwark Council has plans. Not for Bermondsey. Bermondsey is no more. Council policy has renamed it Bermondsey Village – but only that part of it which includes the tourism corridor from Tower Bridge via Butler's Wharf to the soon-to-be refurbished antiques market around Bermondsey Square. Until the Reformation it was the site of the largest Carthusian Abbey in Europe. By Dickens' time it was called 'Old Bermondsey' and anytime now this new pastoral idyll will become the subject of corporate and paradoxically – according to UN Agenda 21 – also the subject of sustainable development. So, is this the end of the "romantic and almost unbelievable story" promised by the Labour Institute in 1934?

This story told of the making – from the close of World War I and the beginning of universal suffrage to the coming of World War II – of a socialist arcadia in the Metropolitan Borough of Bermondsey.[4] We will return to it, but not to cast a nostalgic glance backwards to an idealised time and example of 'real' municipal power resting on a thoroughbred working class citizenry struggling to create an urban and socialist living environment in its own image. Instead, we will consider it in another way: in terms of a moment poised between nineteenth century reformism and modernist planning, a moment when the reforming impetus of the picturesque could still be felt but was being confronted by universal suffrage, State policy and the internal combustion engine. A moment when a modern life

– not the modern life of Baudelaire's boulevards or Benjamin's arcades, but rather Dickens' future imaginary of healthy children, working mothers and unionised fathers, a modern life of enfranchised citizens – had still to emerge from the confines of the nineteenth century slum. A pause in the 150 year-old history of what is now generically called 'urban regeneration'.

There is also little room here for political romanticism or nostalgia. If the Borough's identity was overwhelmingly working class, its Council was controlled by ILP notables (figure 2) and the living environment it was creating was informed as much by picturesque landscape values as by Guild Socialism. When the Independent Labour Party seized power in Bermondsey in 1922, it had taken it more than 20 years and female suffrage to wrest it from the Liberal Party's hold on the dockers. It also had to contend with ancient parish factionalism and neighbourhood rivalries. Moreover, once under ILP control, Bermondsey was effectively a fiefdom efficiently and benevolently headed by a politically ambitious 'companionate' couple, the Salters. When Mrs Ada Salter became its mayor in 1922, she was the first woman Labour mayor in Britain. She went on to become the London County Council's first woman Chair of the Parks Committee while also being Chair of Bermondsey Borough Council's Beautification Committee. Her husband, Dr Alfred Salter, himself a Council Alderman until he became Labour Member of Parliament for the constituency, one of London's three Labour MPs, ran in Bermondsey the largest General Medical Practice in the country. How this middle class Quaker couple, teetotallers and conscientious objectors, exercised power in this tough working class district is a romantic but not unbelievable story.[5] In 1939, objecting to Britain's entry into the War, they were forced to resign from office. Both died shortly afterwards.

Due to difficulties it faced, the Council's attempts to increase the number and sizes of its public open spaces and to transform the Borough into its ideal of a garden suburb was not particularly successful. Inheriting in 1922 nine public open spaces of asphalted playgrounds and semi-derelict churchyards

Figure 2
Bermondsey ILP,
1922-1925

Figure 3
Wilson Grove,
1934

constituting a total area of some eight acres, by the mid 1930s it had acquired only four more open spaces within its boundaries with a total of some 12 acres. The Borough could not compete with the food processing, warehousing, timber and leather industries for land. Furthermore, its attempted incursions into allotment lands were successfully resisted by the London County Council. It managed the development of a small garden suburb in Wilson Grove, but the Ministry of Health forbade any such further developments. (figure 3) Neighbouring boroughs complained that this local attempt at dedensification simply led to the poorest moving into their areas. Thereafter, public housing schemes took the form of balcony access flats. Southwark Park, its 80 acres laid out in 1865, was within the Borough, but for the Council it was an issue of some ambiguity. It belonged to the London County Council and so could not be claimed as a municipal provision. The Borough attempted to have the park renamed Bermondsey Park so as to be associated with it, but this was firmly resisted on the grounds that the park was named after its Parliamentary constituency.

The Council's ideal of a residential landscape was the landscape of the Garden City Movement transferred back into the inner city: a residential ideal troublingly similar and of better quality than that of the present Surrey Docks, but municipal in its provision. As for its semi-natural open spaces, their aesthetics were explicitly conventional. Gardens were laid out with virtuoso flower beds in formal nineteenth century gardenesque municipal style tempered by picturesque incidents and ruled by budgetary accountability. (figure 4) Playgrounds offered design problems which led to more innovative solutions. They either had to be integrated within the public gardens converted from churchyards, as was the playground in St James' churchyard, or they were laid out on building rubble, as in the case of Tanner Street playground, built in 1928 on the site of an old workhouse and partially funded from the sale of the land on which the demolished St Olaf's Church had stood. The Council's most modern garden lay, not within its boundaries, but at Fairby Grange in Kent, a

Figure 4
St James'
Gardens, 1920s

Figure 5
Views of Fairby
Grange, c. 1930

small estate of 20 acres given to the Council's Maternity and Child Health Committee by Dr Salter. Its Arts and Crafts style garden, its wood and paddocks, and its late Jacobean House were to play a crucial part in Bermondsey's own unique experimentation with sustainable development – 'beautification'.[6] (figure 5)

What made Bermondsey Borough Council's landscape making and management a model for other Socialist municipalities was a socially inclusive and explicit policy of improvement of personal physical and emotional well-being and the development of strategies for its representation.

The Council had two mottoes. The first, "Prevention is Better than Cure", underwrote the Council's drive – and, more specifically, that of its powerful Public Health Department established by Dr Salter – to reduce the rate of tuberculosis in the Borough. By 1939, it had declined to the London average. As important was that this campaign not only allowed the Public Health Department – with its rights to designate and purchase slum areas – to exert pressure for the replacement of private slum dwellings by public housing, but that it also provided a scientific and consensual medicalisation of its political discourse. Its companionate motto was "Fresh Air and Fun". Associated with health were leisure and pleasure and these were the purview of Mrs Salter when in 1922 she established the Beautification and Public Amenities Committee with herself as the Chair.

The remit of the Beautification Committee was far greater than maintaining the Borough's public open spaces and upgrading its physical environment. And although its public gardens did indeed become the horticultural envy of other poor urban boroughs, with over 9,000 municipal trees planted between the Wars (figure 6), its underlying objectives were more encompassing and abstract; a confluence of three mobilising ideologies.

The first of these was a reforming ideology, which aimed at the moral and cultural improvement of the working classes. This was analogous to that culminating in the foundation of the Whitechapel Gallery in Mile End, but by then it was municipal and thus perceived as emanating from within the body politic. The Beautification Committee took control of the bi-annual Fruit and Flower shows hitherto under the aegis of voluntary organisations and university missions such as the London Gardens Guild, Time and Talent and the Oxford Mission. These shows promoted competitiveness not only in the growing of plants and produce in a district once renowned for its market gardens, but also in both traditional and modern crafts. Photography was very popular. The Committee also set up the Bermondsey Popular Municipal Orchestra, a community book shop and, as arbitrator of municipal taste (and there was a municipal taste in gardening, floral decoration and ornamentation, leaning towards a pared-down Arts and Crafts style), provided floral decorations for the Council's premises.

Secondly, the Committee was explicitly mother-and-child orientated. Its open spaces were first and foremost for them and functioned as outdoor childcare facilities. The gardens and playgrounds were patrolled by a phalanx of playground attendants (including two female attendants for the small children), opening hours were extended to allow young apprentices to engage in sports after work, and every play area had not only the most up-to-date playground equipment, but also children-only supervised lavatories. (figure 7) In turn, Fairby Grange acted as a rest home for mothers. Every working mother with a child under the age of two was entitled to have, with her other younger children, an annual two-weeks' rest at the Borough's expense. Meanwhile, the Public Health Department held 'housecraft' classes for fathers.

The last and least obvious ideology promoted self-sufficiency and personal autonomy. If the Borough always balanced its books and rejected any incursions from external initiatives, and if it planted trees and decorated its council buildings with distinctive flower boxes and luxuriant front gardens, this was to visually mark its political identity. If by the late 1920s Fairby Grange provided the Borough with

all its horticultural and arboricultural requirements – and made a healthy profit from plant sales – this was a response to the difficulties of obtaining plant material after the War and a means of cheaply providing horticultural luxury. Moreover, the twin mottoes were personally and strategically intertwined. Those who took charge of themselves and wholesomely pleasured their own bodies could pay for and thus avail themselves of Borough services. Entitlement was to this extent self-defined and this was, as it were, the defining break from the past.

The municipality was, indeed, politically and financially largely self-sustaining. It was one of the largest and best employers in the district, exercising an efficient policy of direct labour which ensured jobs for the most needy and political clientelism overall. All but its most professionally qualified employees were expected to come from the Borough and all, including the most qualified, were expected to live in the Borough: and they did. By 1934 Bermondsey was a place to come from.

I would nonetheless like to suggest that this environmental and social self-sufficiency was neither entirely new nor 'modern'. What was new was borrowing from an imaginary past to make an imagined future – Guild Socialism – but this borrowing possibly also drew upon a real yet unacknowledged past where older mediations could be found between territory, responsibility and exploitation.[7] If the Borough's ideology of self-sufficiency drew upon a popular culture of individual hard work, common sense and survival, I would argue that it also drew upon another, deeper structure: that of the political economy of the landed estate. Effectively, the Beautification Department, together with the Public Health Department, the latter responsible for welfare and slum clearance, managed the Borough's social environment and landscape as would have a landed estate.

Except for hunting and animal husbandry, the Borough engaged in every activity of a landed estate; managing, extending and improving its holdings, controlling resources, allocating benefits, representing its people, looking after their physical and spiritual welfare and most importantly, place making. Fairby Grange, its 'house in the country' supplied edibles for its rest home and plants and saplings not only for its gardens and streets, but also to distinctively decorate, inside and out, its council buildings. An aesthetic and horticultural continuity between town and country and

Figure 6
Keeton Road
and trees, 1930s

Figure 7
St James'
playground,
1930s

corporate distinctiveness was thus maintained. The adapted church yard gardens retained their restorative purpose, their head stones neatly stacked against the church walls, attendance having been quietly transferred from their religious interior to their municipal exterior. Fruit and Flower Shows replaced the fairs, and the Salters showed distinguished visitors around the formal gardens. (figures 8-9)

Altogether the Council vigorously pursued strategies of self-promotion and visualisation to make for itself not only a place, but also a history from its present: essential strategies for a conceived landscape. The Beautification Department promoted private as well as public gardening, inserting flyers on gardening tips in library books. Its Superintendent of Gardens became nationally renowned as a lecturer. Between 1922 and 1953, the Public Health Department made 39 films, including a colour film of its gardens, which were shown throughout the Borough by means of a cinema van and lent to other municipalities world-wide.[8] In 1926, the Council commissioned its own bird's-eye views – aerial photographs of the Borough – and in 1927 the Beautification Department had all its gardens professionally photographed. Finally, in 1934 the Council ordered all its current schemes to be photographed before, during and after their construction, several actually being London County Council projects. The image-making of Bermondsey Council both literally and metaphorically engaged in a 'naturalisation' of its activities which, while displaying older ideals of estate 'improvements', also subversively redirected them toward new and radical political ends to produce a new and improved citizenry.[9]

Figure 8
Bermondsey
Flower Show,
1927

Figure 9
Mrs Salter with
George Lansbury
at St James'
Garden, 1930

The beginning of the end of Bermondsey Borough Council's experiment with arcadia began with the outbreak of the World War II. Over the ensuing years, two thirds of its building stock was damaged. A Ministry of Information film made by Paul Rotha in 1947 surveys the devastation and, by means of models, outlines Patrick Abercrombie's plans for its rebuilding. In the same year the National Health Service was established. By 1954 the Public Health Department and Fairby Grange had gone and, in 1965, with the creation of the Greater London Council, the Metropolitan Borough of Bermondsey vanished into the London Borough of Southwark, its landscape now managed by a 'Leisure Department'.

What does the recent political and corporate interest in Bermondsey's semi-natural landscapes, backed by consultancies, diverse voluntary groups, urban regeneration and Heritage Lottery Funding and nominally overseen by Agenda 21 mean? This is a rhetorical question, but it still needs to be asked of this and countless other inner city landscapes currently being recycled. I have tried to suggest by means of a singular and unusual example that early twentieth century municipal urban landscapes which now comprise the majority of open public spaces in the inner city were underwritten by older practices of a distinctive political economy adept at naturalising political and class relations. In the case of Bermondsey Borough Council these were appropriated to new political and constitutional ends, the most radical of which acknowledged the affirming role of beauty in an inclusive and collectively shared everyday life. There was prevention but there was also fun – and what could be more revolutionary than play?

1   My thanks to Southwark Local Studies Library for its support in allowing generous access to its archives and permission to reproduce photographs from its collection.

2   *Twelve Years of Labour Rule on the Bermondsey Borough Council*, London: The Labour Institute, 1934, pp. 2-3.

3   Directed by Gary Oldman, 1997.

4   Lebas, Elizabeth, "The Making of a Socialist Arcadia: Arboriculture and Horticulture in the London Borough of Bermondsey after the Great War", *Garden History*, vol. 27 no. 2, 1999, pp. 219-237.

5   See Brockway, Fenner, *Bermondsey Story: the Life of Dr. Alfred Salter*, London: George Allen and Unwin, 1949/1994, for a partial account of the work of the Salters in Bermondsey.

6   I have so far been quite unsuccessful in tracing the use of the term "beautification" or "beautifying" when referring to environmental improvements at the turn of the twentieth century.

7   In some ways this is a re-reading of Raymond Williams, *The Country and the City*, London: Faber and Faber, 1967, and here I am attempting to open up the idea of a notion of socialism and democracy whose basis lies elsewhere than in an urban republicanism. I am also indebted to the work of Nigel Everett and Tom Williamson.

8   See Lebas, Elizabeth, "'When Every Street Became a Cinema': the Film Work of Bermondsey Borough's Public Health Department, 1923-1953", *History Workshop Journal*, no. 35, 1995, pp. 42-65.

9   When the Eugenics Society approached the Public Health Department, it was sharply dismissed. It may be interesting to investigate whether older ideas of environmental improvement acted as substitute or alternative to that of Eugenics for transforming the urban working classes.

Visuality as Politics: the Example of Urban Landscape[1]
Frédéric Pousin

The word 'landscape' – which is derived from the ancient Greek verb *skopein*: "behold, contemplate, examine, inspect…" – has an etymological link to terms which describe modes of visual activity and experience. While scholars, drawing upon this connection, have interpreted the relationship between landscape and vision on many occasions, the role played by visuality during the historical emergence of the notion of 'urban landscape' has been less debated.[2] This paper will examine how this concept, from the outset, called for a visual description of built reality, and how such a description opened new prospects for understanding urban phenomena. By questioning the cognitive dimension of photographic images, analysing their structure and their uses, it will explore the ways in which the town and the territory were represented in the 1950s and 60s. As the debate about urban landscape arose within architecture, close attention will be paid to the question of images as professional tools for architects and townplanners.

Investigating the part played by the eye in the development of the idea of landscape, Louis Marin stressed the need to understand the bipolar relationship between the human eye and the extent of the territory before it. Even if every landscape, by definition, is meant to be looked at – nineteenth century definitions are fairly clear on this point – it does not mean that the human eye is the only condition for constituting the idea of landscape. The French dictionary, *le Robert*, in the twentieth century, gives the following: "landscape is the part of land presented to the eye by nature". Commenting on this definition, Louis Marin stressed the existence of a *Kunstwollen* assumed by the definition: a *Kunstwollen* independent of the observer, thanks to which nature can be represented.[3]

Urban landscape, by the same token, is linked to the representation of the city and to the tradition of the 'city view', an important area of investigation already mapped out by historians of geography.[4] At this point I simply want to call attention to the relationship between the 'view' and the urban landscape in order to highlight the primacy of the representation and its philosophical foundation.[5]

The idea of urban landscape is based on an aesthetic attitude as well as on an aloofness toward the city, and this is very different from the notion of urban landscape as constituted by the presence of nature in the town. In his book, *A Short Treatise on Landscape*, Alain Roger has discussed the distancing power of the artistic perception he calls 'artialisation'.[6] In this work, he shows how landscape originates in an estrangement from the land and from physical space, and that this estrangement is due to aesthetic models borrowed, in the past, from painting, and, today, from other artistic media. As photography and cinema increasingly became, in the Post War years, the main representational modes whereby the qualities of the diverse forms of the city were revealed, Roger's thesis would appear to have considerable importance for the study of urban landscapes.

When the terms 'townscape' and 'urban landscape' came into common usage in the fields of architecture and town planning, they raised questions about the representation and description of towns, which we now must consider.

The Emerging Conditions of *Townscape*

In England, just after World War II, there was a debate in *Architectural Review*, led by Nikolaus Pevsner and James Maud Richards, both well known supporters of the modern movement in architecture.[7] Their concern, at this time, was to try to rethink architectural modernity in a national context: English modernity, they postulated, might be said to originate from the native picturesque tradition. This assertion was to incite a polemic concerning the so-called 'neopicturesque'.[8] What, however, is most interesting from our point of view is that the debate was aimed at making professionals, as well as the general public, sensitive to landscape and the city, creating an awareness in which the term 'townscape' played an important role. The notion of townscape was intended to connect architecture and townplanning to visual culture; and the result was the emergence of a critical attitude toward rational and quantitative methods of townplanning.[9]

In order to appreciate the various dimensions of this venture, it is necessary to consider the links with the USA, including the exchanges and interactions between individuals. Gordon Cullen, for example, one of the major figures in the townscape movement in Great Britain, collaborated with Christopher Tunnard, a Canadian landscape architect who eventually taught city-planning at Yale University. Such connections are also clearly evident in *Architectural Review*'s interest in modern Californian architecture during the entire Post War period. In January 1949, the journal published a paper on Garett Eckbo's work, entitled "Landscape Design in the USA", and, in the following months, it carried a considerable number of other articles on townscape. In 1950 it devoted a special issue – *Man Made America* – to the American urban landscape, for which Henry Russell Hitchcock, Christopher Tunnard and Gerald Kallman were invited to investigate the American scene. This issue opened the debate about urban landscape beyond the limits of Great Britain, and argued for the necessity of developing new procedures for analysis and design.[10] Symptomatically, Las Vegas was presented as the paradigmatic anti-type – a gesture which presaged Denise Scott Brown and Robert Venturi's counter-blast, 20 years later.

A Publishing Venture

During the next ten years a number of other papers appeared in *Architectural Review* devoted to townscape and related issues: for example, new towns, road design, and urban sprawl. Dealing with a large body of visual material, the journal published studies, casebooks, proposals and counter-proposals, as well as reviews, polemics and comparisons with the American scene. Two issues on the Festival of Britain in 1951 and Brussels exhibition in 1958 proposed original interpretations of townscape, highlighting its playful quality. But, in particular, two special issues of *Architectural Review* paved the way for the debate. The first one, published in June 1955, called *Outrage*, dealt with a phenomenon dubbed 'subtopia'; and the second, published in December 1956 and called *Counter Attack*, developed foundations for visual planning. (figure 1) Both issues were based on 'casebooks', so called, that were presented as series of photographs, meant to visualise either the categories constituting the townscape (figure 2), or the characteristics of the development of the town. In the issue called *Outrage*, a route map assembled all the 'cases' along a given itinerary from the north to the south of Great Britain, with images presented as a representative section of the

territory. The 'section' was, in other words, constituted by maps and photographs. (figure 3)
The part played by photography is not surprising when seen in the light of new trends emerging
during the 50s. Several photographers such as Henri Cartier Bresson and Robert Frank aimed at
stating the facts of everyday life through its visible ordinariness. Thanks to its ability to isolate
facts from their context, photography could contribute to social criticism. The photographer's eye
had become less talkative, foreshadowing the search for the neutral position that would characterise
the New Topographics.[11]

Books Defining a Paradigm

In 1961 Gordon Cullen published *Townscape*, which synthesised a series of papers from
Architectural Review during the preceding ten years. It was one of a number of books which
appeared in the early 60s – including *God's Own Junkyard* by Peter Blake, *Motopia* by Geoffrey
Jellicoe, *Urban Landscape Design* by Garett Eckbo, and *Cities*, by Laurence Halprin – dealing with
the issue of urban landscape.[12] All developed strategies for representing architecture and the
town. But it seems to me that the key issue concerning the description and theorisation of urban
landscape that had begun in the early 50s was framed most cogently by the study of Las Vegas
carried out by Denise Scott Brown with her students in 1968, and by the subsequent book,
Learning From Las Vegas, published later by Brown, Venturi and Izenour.[13] While the phenomenology
of everyday life that had shaped artistic approaches and the concept of townscape in the Post War
period tended to be replaced by a psycho-perceptive paradigm when research into vision and the
perception of landscape was developed at the Massachusetts Institute of Technology, the approach
by Scott Brown and Venturi was closer to the phenomenological model since they argued for an
understanding of the contemporary town that was based upon the eye – an eye considered to be
totally unbiased – and upon experience. Furthermore, Venturi was convinced that readings of
the space of urban sprawl proposed by artists had to be considered.[14] (figure 4) It is therefore
necessary to contextualise Scott Brown's and Venturi's claim for the neutrality of the eye.[15] Such
a claim appears in its full significance once one takes into consideration both the phenomenological
influence and the increasingly evident trend toward minimalism in the work of American
photographers. This trend in photography led to the emergence of the topographic paradigm,
and transformed the documentary tradition once again.[16]

Learning from Las Vegas, attempted to train architects and townplanners to see the reality of the
contemporary town as it was in the late 60s. The authors' claim was that the shopping street –
the Strip in particular – demanded to be looked at positively and without preconception. Their
aim was both to develop an understanding of the contemporary town and to amass a range of
representational tools to describe the new urban environment. (figures 5-6)

While all the books mentioned above have their differences – for example, Peter Blake's *God's Own
Junkyard*, against which *Learning from Las Vegas* reacted, is a polemical work which consists of a
general survey of the pathologies of the American landscape; Cullen's *Townscape* has a more positive
tone, and attempts to introduce architects and townplanners to a new vocabulary for describing
the urban environment (figure 7); Jellicoe's *Motopia* sets out to characterise urban phenomena in
keeping with five themes that are explained through models, plans and photographs organised in an
evolutionary schema culminating in the urban utopia Jellicoe calls *motopia* – they all aim to collect
and characterise urban phenomena, assembling and presenting them through visual documents,
mainly photographs. What such images represent, above all, is a collection of data.

Frédéric Pousin

A VISUAL A.B.C.

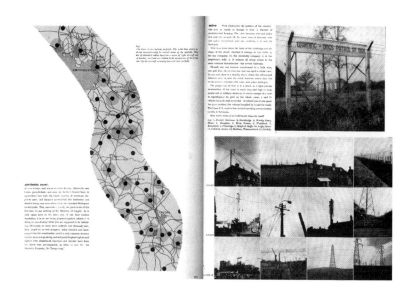

Figure 1
The Architectural Review, Counter Attack, December 1956, pp. 362-363. Categories derived from the townscape for describing the environment. Reproduced courtesy of the *Architectural Review*

Figure 2
The Architectural Review, Counter Attack, December 1956, pp. 354-355. The issue begins with the article "A visual ABC" which defines the principles of visual planning. On the left side images illustrate the failure of urbanisation. Reproduced courtesy of the *Architectural Review*

Figure 3
The Architectural Review, Outrage, June 1955, pp. 378, 379. A route map with images representing the spoilt landscape. Reproduced courtesy of the *Architectural Review*

Figure 4
Venturi, R,
Scott Brown,
D, Izenour, S,
*Learning from
Las Vegas*, 1972,
pp. 26-27. Visual
diversity
exemplified in
photographic
panoramas
inspired by Ed
Rusha's work.
©MIT Press

Figure 5
Venturi, R,
Scott Brown,
D, Izenour, S,
*Learning from
Las Vegas*, 1972,
pp. 38-39.
Visual diversity
in a frame.
©MIT Press

Figure 6
Venturi, R,
Scott Brown,
D, Izenour, S,
*Learning from
Las Vegas*, 1972,
pp. 20-21.
Unconventional
cartography
makes visible
the spatial order
of the Strip.
©MIT Press

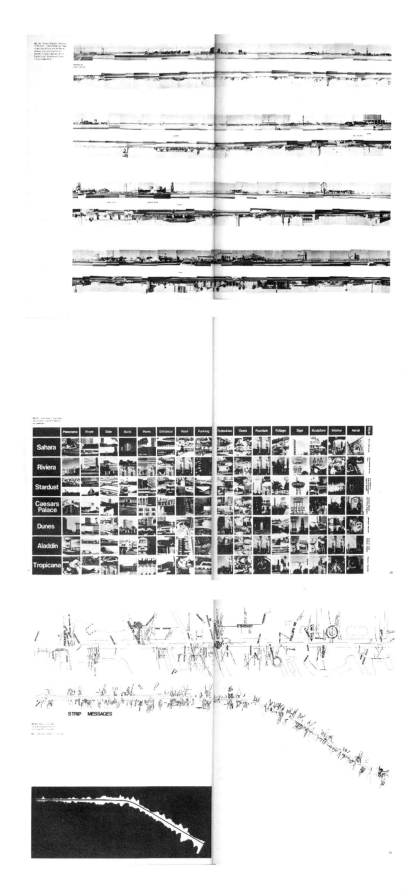

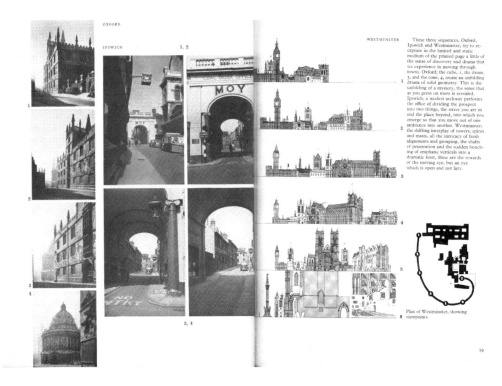

These three sequences, Oxford, Ipswich and Westminster, try to re-capture in the limited and static medium of the printed page a little of the sense of discovery and drama that we experience in moving through towns. Oxford; the cube, 1, the drum, 3, and the cone, 4, create an unfolding drama of solid geometry. This is the unfolding of a mystery, the sense that as you press on more is revealed. Ipswich; a modest archway performs the office of dividing the prospect into two things, the street you are in and the place beyond, into which you emerge so that you move out of one ambience into another. Westminster; the shifting interplay of towers, spires and masts, all the intricacy of fresh alignments and grouping, the shafts of penetration and the sudden bunching of emphatic verticals into a dramatic knot, these are the rewards of the moving eye, but an eye which is open and not lazy.

Plan of Westminster, showing viewpoints

19

Figure 7
Gordon Cullen, *Townscape*, 1961, pp. 18-19 Optics explained through the category of serial vision. Three sequences: Oxford, Ipswitch, Westminster. Reproduced courtesy of the *Architectural Review*

Figure 8
Gordon Cullen, *Townscape*, 1961, pp. 76-77. The category of *multiple use* – which is the antonym of segregation – is presented through images and words. Reproduced courtesy of the *Architectural Review*

multiple use

Or, to continue the interplay, This and That can co-exist. Ever since people got really serious about planning one of the main endeavours has been to put people into sunny, healthy homes away from dirty, smelly and noisy industry. Whilst no one will seriously quarrel with this, the principle of segregation and zoning goes marching on, with the result that we are in danger of losing the great unities of social living. The West End gets more and more offices to the exclusion of theatres and houses, vast armies of people commute, people object to having a church or a pub built in their street because of the noise. Some magistrates even say you are breaking the law if you stand still on a pavement. But true living accepts the joys of togetherness along with the setbacks. On balance it is worth it. The scene at Bankside on the Thames as it might be developed with residential development amongst the warehouses is a typical multiple use view, whilst below, the whole attitude is summed up in the French illustrations, in which the ground is regarded as belonging to all: to the players of boules and also to the train when it wants it.

foils

The last section of this casebook is devoted to the consideration that in the complex world already outlined, with its varying categories, its differing kinds of character, its buildings of diverse styles and materials, the relation of these separate entities could result in the creation of urban drama. For just as the interaction of Here and There produced a form of emotional tension, so the relationship of This and That will produce its own form of drama which will exist inside the overall spatial framework. This marriage of opposites, illustrated in the next nine pages, may be a matter of scale, distortion, tree planting or publicity, but it succeeds because This is good for That.

In Bath within the framework of the enclosure Victorian, Classical and Gothic buildings are grouped together and produce a scene as natural and comfortable as a clubroom. Below in Oxford the monumental Clarendon building shares the street with purely modest domestic buildings. We are perhaps too well used to this kind of effect in England but if you cover first one half of the scene with your hand and then the other half, something of the surprise of the situation will emerge.

77

Moreover, the books reviewed here reflect the same mutation that photographic books underwent in the 60s. Photography could no longer be considered a secondary, illustrative component of a book, nor even a document testifying to an event; rather, it came to be considered an independent medium that was capable, by exploiting the inner relationships of its images to one another and to the text, of playing a structuring role within the totality of the book. This transformation in photography encourages reflection on the social function of imagery; through their publication in book form, photographs could now reach a wide public, previously unattainable through elitist systems of distribution.[17]

Imaging the Concept of Urban Landscape

The *Architectural Review* – through its editorial programme – and the books discussed (which shared a common approach of establishing their discourse through the development of visual strategies) effectively constituted urban landscape as both a field of knowledge and a pragmatic reality. But how, precisely, were these visual strategies constructed and what part did they in turn play in constituting an epistemic field? As already noted, images enabled the authors to construct pathologies: the accumulation of *urban data* was a condition for the awareness of disorders and dysfunctions and, as a result, the identification of obsolete models and desirable new forms of order. Thus we must pay special attention to phenomena which otherwise might be viewed simply as a huge collection of images of heterogeneous facts. It is necessary to probe the meaning of the enumeration of facts, together with the organisation of images, their classification, their distribution in tables, and the correspondances established between them. Although in a book like Cullen's, the drive to categorise, and even to constitute a language, is explicit and images participate in this process, the urge to categorise is also present in the other books under discussion, a notable symptom being the use of neologisms in Peter Blake's table of contents in which terms like "townscape", "landscape", "carscape", and "skyscape" appear.

In the documents under consideration, the deployment of images furthers several objectives. Firstly, they underpin a strategy for constituting a field of knowledge as well as a pragmatic reality. The image appears as a 'mediating object' of prime importance for establishing objective orders.[18] Representative facts about the urban landscape are created by selecting and combining phenomena of urbanisation which become meaningful and manipulable by virtue of their representation. Secondly, images become key elements in a communicational strategy, creating an argument for the existence of the urban landscape, and convincing a public of professionals of its reality. And thirdly, whether photographic or graphic, the image is solicited as a pragmatic tool and appears as an instrument of design. Consequently one can identify three major functions of imagery: the creation of data and, hence, the construction of 'objectivity'; the diffusion of information and knowledge; and the creation of tools for design.

In Cullen's *Townscape*, the part entitled *Casebook* is organised according to four topics, Optics, Place, Content and Functional Tradition, which are explained through a range of categories.[19] What part does imagery play in shaping these categories? Let us, to take one example, examine the category of multiple use, which is the antonym of segregation, a key concept of functionalist zoning. (figure 8) The category of multiple use is presented through a single project drawing and two photographs, with the following commentary: "The scene at Bankside on the Thames as it might be developed with residential development amongst the warehouses is a typical multiple use view, whilst below, the whole attitude is summed up in the French illustrations,

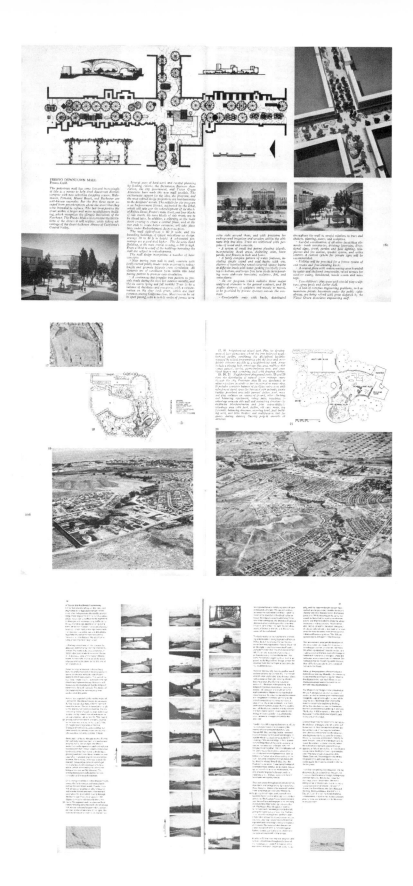

in which the ground is regarded as belonging to all: to the players of boules and also to the train when it wants it."[20]

Here, images act as typical representations or visual summaries of a category which, in turn denotes them and plays the role of a caption to them. Indeed, when Cullen explains a category, the explanation draws, in many cases, upon a description of images. Thus it is clear that imagery is of prime importance for understanding the category, and that the concept expressed through the category develops from the objects and the urban spaces which have been selected. Understanding the formulation of a concept developed from objects leads to the question of the degree to which urban spaces can be presented to the eye. In Cullen's writings, the extracts of urban space represented in images and in the categories he develops are connected by exemplification, following Nelson Goodman's definition of the term.[21] Goodman identifies four ways of signifying – or referring since, according to him, signifying is referring. Exemplification, he claims, is the form of signification principally manifested by buildings. Different from denotation, which entails connecting the symbol to the object, exemplification entails connecting the object denoted to the symbol, which reverses the relationship. Consequently, exemplification enables us to conceptualise referral in keeping with the privileged direction from object to symbol. In Cullen's writings, however, the extracts of urban space are grasped by the eye and then transformed into imagery, in a process that introduces new levels of complexity.

The second part of Garett Eckbo's book – in fact entitled "The examples" – allows us to broach the status of the example and the role played by it in another way. Here we find projects and buildings which are presented by way of graphic and photographic documents with short commentaries setting out the site data, the programme objectives and elements. Most of them come from the author's studio. They are arranged in six parts which structure the field of the urban landscape design: room and patio; building and site; building in groups; parks and playground; streets and squares, neighbourhood; community and region. (figures 9-10)

Each project constitutes a representative item of the part defined by its title and introduced by an opening essay. Such an item is constructed from a double point of view: it is made both an emblem of a set of analogical projects and an element which fits into a series that makes up each part of the book. For instance, in the part "Streets and squares", one can find gardens around office blocks, malls, the open spaces of educational buildings, the interface between a highway and its service facilities, a quay, a piazza.

Quoting Eckbo on the partitioning the field of urban landscape design:

These are categories for convenience, but their elements are real and they are useful… As used here, they demonstrate continuity in expansion of scale from individual to community spaces, and the need for richly variable sequence in this two way hierarchy of landscape space scale. From a landscape point of view, actual development projects fall naturally into these groupings, which make possible the construction of a bridge from isolated single-site design to inclusive community design. Thus they make a useful, but not the only possible framework for discussion and work.[22]

As one can see, partitioning physical continuity is necessary both for thought and action. The discourse on landscape design is established upon a partitioning of the continuity of landscape and this has to be thought out, because such partitioning of the continuity of built space is an absolute

prerequisite and a key theoretical question for the project.[23] But at the same time visual and geographical continuity is both characteristic of and necessary for landscape: the point of view taken in landscape design depends on it.

The purpose of questioning the example in a such way is to understand the tactics whereby, through the manipulation of images and representations, the field of urban landscape as a pragmatic reality widely acceptable to a public of professionals is constituted. Also at issue here is the way in which information enters circulation. On the basis of what choices are buildings or projects taken to be representative and how do they become assimilated to the medium and demands of the book?

Medium and Series

As well as questioning exemplification as a cognitive process – which enables us to analyse the link between image and the material reality connected to it – it seems of prime importance to pay attention to how images are published. In fact, the images with which we are dealing rarely appear in isolation. Usually they are organised as elements in a series which gives them both their value and signification. Whether published in journals or books, the photographic images that characterise the urban landscape are organised in discursive sequences that are meant to elicit a reaction from the reader. As already noted, the text connected to the images is sometimes polemical: as, for instance, in the reports in *Architectural Review* or the papers by Denise Scott Brown and Kenneth Frampton published in *Casabella*.[24]

Mobility

In the mid 60s, research on landscape acquired a new dimension through academic studies on the topic of road and motion. *The View from the Road*, a book by Kevin Lynch with Donald Appleyard and John R Myer, dealt with the driver's visual perception.[25] In order to express this spatial and perceptual analysis in a graphic way, Lynch created a new mode of representation. Giving up the bird's eye view as a synthetic image which could describe the expanse of the route, he borrowed techniques of representation from the cinema in order to simulate the varying points of view from an automobile: thus, visual sequences were represented through drawings or photographs taken from behind the windscreen. (figure 11)

The book, whose originality consisted in defining a new graphic language for describing visual sequences from the highway, proposed to deal with the relationship between the highway and landscape through a series of topics such as: the elements of attention, the sense of motion and space, the extension of self, orientation, sequential form, etc.. The technique constructed visual sequences by placing elements along a continuous line (as in musical notation) and this, in turn, allowed for a rapid communication and comparison between sequence alternatives. The book was directed at civil engineers as a practical tool. Thus the investigation described in its final chapters is framed by the notions and terminology just described in order to analyse the impact of an existing highway in Boston, and to illustrate how a new highway might be designed.

The experiment carried out by the English architect, Alison Smithson, between 1972 and the end of the 70s, represents a synthesis of 'townscape' intentions and the study of visual perception undertaken by Kevin Lynch and his team at the Massachusetts Institute of Technology. Smithson made a series of journeys from London to Wiltshire in a Citroën DS. Her book *AS in DS*, published in 1983, aimed at recording systematically, like a seismograph, shifts in the driver's sensibility during the period in question.[26] Over these years, which the author took as a transition between two eras, she had travelled the route many times. If systematic observation and a focus on the driver's experience of motion characterise Kevin Lynch's work, the long-term nature of her experiment (several years' duration) takes Alison Smithson's investigation out of the experimental frame of Lynch's work on perception. The originality of such an investigation lies in assuming the large cultural dimension of human perception thanks to the ingenious tactic of relating a travelling experience. Although deeply rooted in modern ideas, her investigation is nevertheless related to the English picturesque tradition. She, for example, drew inspiration from William Cobbett's travelogue, which describes the author's rides over the same part of the countryside on many occasions after 1821. Moreover, Alison Smithson focused mainly on travel through the countryside rather than through the urban landscape. Thus, receptivity to the aesthetic dimension of the landscape appears to have been as important to her project as its documentary intent. In Alison Smithson's book, its roots in the picturesque tradition (and the related interest in social and ethnographic features, common in travellers and explorers in the nineteenth century[27]), allow for beautiful sequences where the impact of impressive skies or delicate colours accompanying sudden changes of light are expressed through comparison with painting. Her writing can also express the atmosphere of night or of a sound. The travelogue model, combined with a cartography of the space that has been traversed, is not the only means Smithson used. She also exploited the photographic perceptive sequences that Lynch created (figure 12), contributing to the establishment of their canonical status. But in Alison Smithson's approach, there is no preoccupation with design methods as there is in the approaches of Lynch or Venturi. Nevertheless, she shares with them the desire to develop knowledge about the road and an awareness of the role of motion in the understanding of signs. But she does not pay particular attention to speed in her analysis of the driver's perception, because her view of the car transcends its technical aspects to consider also its comfort dimension as a room on wheels that modifies the driver's as well as passengers' sensibilities in an original way. Here, in her reading of the car, one can see an expression of an ideology of liberty and nomadism (which does not preclude her describing the effects of increasing vehicular congestion). The representation in this case includes canonical modes such as sketches, descriptive text, cartography, and serial photographs documenting perception. All of these are combined in writing that is both original and fragmented, and published together in a book shaped like the plan of a Citroën DS. (figure 13)

Canonical Images of the Urban Landscape

My focus has been upon a category of canonical images of the city: specifically, those representations that present evidence and whose structuring effect is rarely analysed.[28] Sequences of images, such as those developed by Lynch and his colleagues, may today be considered canonical images. My hypothesis is that, in relation to the development of the notion of urban landscape, new modes of representation were created which eventually influenced knowledge of the town, as well as action upon it. Some of these were based on the interpretation of canonical images; others have since, themselves, become canonical.

The notion of urban landscape was introduced to the urban planning community in the 50s and 60s in Great Britain and the USA. The challenge then was to create a field of knowledge as well as a pragmatic reality for this notion: in other words, the challenge was to create representational tools. My argument is that the new way of thinking about the city and architecture depends on producing

Figure 13
Alison Smithson,
AS in DS, 1983.
©Delft University
Press, The
Netherlands,
by courtesy

and manipulating images: photographs, drawings, and maps, as well as conventional forms of architectural representation. As epistemologists and sociologists of science have shown, such manipulation is far from a neutral or inconsequential game, but participates in – indeed constitutes – a way of thinking.[29] Organised in series, tables, opposing pairs, and leading from one to the other, images shape the ability of vision to constitute and communicate ideas. The critical discourse on the town and the means of designing it go hand in hand.

As a result of so many efforts – from Cullen to Venturi – to give consistency to the idea of urban landscape, the 'city-view' was transformed in a lasting way. It becomes far more diverse and complex than a topographic scene, skyline or elevation as conventionally purveyed in earlier historical documents.

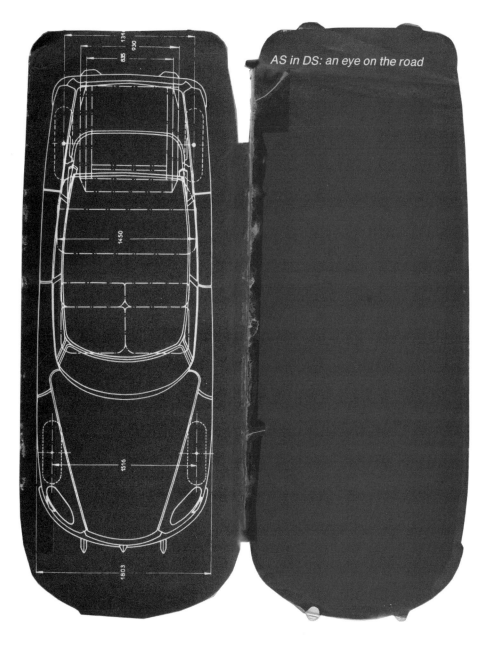

AS in DS: an eye on the road

Frédéric Pousin

1   I would like to thank Phyllis Lambert and the CCA where I developed my research on urban landscape as a visiting scholar in 2000. Many thanks as well to Cammie McAtee, Indra McEwen, Eva Maria Neumann and Mark Dorrian for their support and generous help.

2   See Cohen, Jean Louis, "Saper vedere Las Vegas", *Lotus* 93, pp. 96-108; Marchand, Bruno, "The view from the road. Le paysage de bord de route à l'âge du chaos", *Matières*, 1999, pp. 7-19.

3   Marin, Louis, "Une ville, une campagne de loin… : paysages pascaliens", *Litterature*, no. 61, fev. 1986, pp. 5-6.

4   The rhetorical function of the city view is well known. Considering this type of representation as a eulogy, for instance, makes it possible to analyse its political function. See. Besse, Jean-Marc, "Représenter la ville ou la simuler? (Reflexions autour d'une vue d'Amsterdam au XVIème siècle)", *LIGEIA 19-20*, Juin 1997, pp. 43-55; Harvey, P D A, *The History of Topographical Maps,* London: Thames and Hudson, 1980.

5   Commenting on Pascal's *Pensées* regarding town and countryside, Louis Marin investigated the relationship between landscape and heterogeneity through the notion of description. See "Une ville, une campagne de loin…: paysages pascaliens".

6   Roger, Alain, *Court traité du paysage*, Paris: Gallimard, 1997.

7   See Pevsner, Nikolaus, *Pioneers of the Modern Movement: from William Morris to Walter Gropius*, London: Faber and Faber, 1936, and Richards, James Maud, *An Introduction to Modern Architecture*, Harmondsworth: Penguin, 1940.

8   On the interpretation of picturesque by the young modern architects, see Banham, Reyner, "Revenge of the Picturesque: English Architectural Polemics, 1945-1965", *Concerning Architecture: Essays on Architectural Writers and Writing Presented to Nikolaus Pevsner*, Summerson, John, ed., London, Allen Lane, 1968, pp. 265-273. On the debts to the picturesque movement that haunt modernist theory, see Hunt, John Dixon, "The Picturesque Legacy to Modernist Landscape Architecture", *Gardens and the Picturesque*, Cambridge Massachusetts: MIT Press, 1992, pp. 285-305.

9   On radical criticism of townplanning in the 1960s, see Hughes, Jonathan and Sadler, Simon, eds., *Non-Plan, Essays on Freedom, Participation and Change in Modern Architecture and Urbanism*, Oxford: Architectural Press, 2000. On the relationships between townplanning and the picturesque, see Horton, Ian, "Pervasion of the Picturesque: English Architectural Aesthetics and Legislation, 1945-1965", pp. 66-79.

10 About the development of this debate opened by *The Architectural Review*, see Tunnard, Christopher and Pushkarev, Boris, *Man-Made America: Chaos or Control?*, New Haven and London: Yale University Press, 1963.

11 See Gunther, Thomas Michael, "La diffusion de la photographie. La commande, la publicité, l'édition", *Nouvelle histoire de la photographie*, Frizot, Michel, ed., Paris: Adam-Biro-Bordas, 1995, pp. 555-581.

12 Cullen, Gordon, *Townscape*, London: The Architectural Press, 1961; Blake, Peter, *God's Own Junkyard. The Planned Deterioration of America's Landscape*, New York, Chicago, San Francisco: Holt, Rinehart and Winston, 1964; Jellicoe, G A, *Motopia: a Study in The Evolution of Urban Landscape*, London: Studio Books Longacre Press Ltd, 1961; Eckbo, G, *Urban Landscape Design*, New York, Toronto, London: McGraw Hill, 1964; Halprin, Lawrence, *Cities*, New York: Reinhold Publishing Corporation, 1963.

13 Venturi, R, Scott Brown, D, and Izenour, S, *Learning from Las Vegas*, Cambridge, Massachusetts: MIT Press, 1972.

14 Venturi Robert and Scott Brown, Denise, "Entre imagination sociale et architecture", *L'Architecture d'Aujourd'hui*, 273, Fevrier 1991, pp. 92-95.

15 About the critical appraisal of Las Vegas' urban prospects, see Begout, Bruce, *Zeropolis*, Paris: Allia, 2001.

16 See Westerbeck Colin, "Sur la route et dans la rue. L'après-guerre aux Etats-Unis", *Nouvelle histoire de la photographie*, Frizot, Michel, ed., pp. 641-659.

17 See Gunther, Thomas Michael, "La diffusion de la photographie. La commande, la publicité, l'édition", *Nouvelle histoire de la photographie*, Frizot, Michel, ed.

18 On the concept of a 'mediating object', see Latour, Bruno and de Noblet, Jocelyn, "Les 'vues' de l'esprit", *Culture technique*, no. 14, June 1985.

19 These notions come from the *New Empiricism* and the *New Picturesque* movements, especially the notion of *functional tradition* that aims at founding on a vernacular ground the concept of *functionalism* that characterised the Modern movement in architecture.

20 Cullen, G, *Townscape*, p. 76.

21 Goodman, Nelson, *Languages of Art*, Indianapolis: Hackett, 1976.

22 Eckbo, Garret, *Urban Landscape Design*, p. 158.

23 See Boudon, Philippe, Deshayes, Philippe, Pousin, Frédéric and Schatz, Françoise, *Enseigner la conception architecturale*, Paris: Editions de la Villette, 1994/2002.

24 Scott Brown, Denise, "Learning from Pop"; "Reply to Frampton"; Frampton, Kenneth, "America 1960-1970: Notes on Urban Images and Theory", *Casabella*, no. 359-360, 1971, pp. 15-25; pp. 41-47 and pp. 25-41.

25 Appleyard, Donald, Lynch, Kevin, Myer, John R, *The View From the Road*, Cambridge, Massachusetts: MIT Press, 1964.

26 Smithson, Alison, *AS in DS, An Eye on the Road*, Delft: Delft University Press, 1983.

27 See Heilbrun, Françoise, "Le tour du monde, explorateurs, voyageurs", *Nouvelle histoire de la photographie*, Frizot, Michel, ed., pp. 149 and 167.

28 About the concept of canonical image, see the seminars "Ville-Image-Savoir" held in Paris in 2001 by the research teams "Epistémologie et Histoire de la Géographie", UMR CNRS 8504 and LADYSS, UMR 7533.

29 See Latour, Bruno, *La science en action*, Paris: La Découverte, 1989, and Lynch, Michael, Woolgar, Steve, eds., *Representation in Scientific Practice*, Cambridge, Massachusetts: MIT Press, 1990.

Somewhere To Stand: Descriptive Writing and Cultural Criticism in Iain Sinclair's *Lights Out For The Territory*
Simon Grimble

I'd like to use a line from *Cooper's Hill*, Sir John Denham's Royalist prospect poem of 1641, as an epigraph for this paper. That line is "But my fixed thoughts my wandering eye betrays."[1] My interest is in the relationship between the desire to find a prospect over a landscape which gives the observer a superior kind of authority (although that authority can be of different kinds: poetic, political, religious and scientific are some of the categories) and the fact that situating oneself in a landscape and using that as a starting point for writing gives rise to the possibility of having a 'wandering eye', and of therefore having your 'fixed thoughts' betrayed by all the things that you see. The attempt to then organise all that visual phenomena under some principle of order is therefore made very difficult, but the fact that this kind of observer is drawn to prospects as enabling some kind of epistemological authority means that that person is unlikely to give up the attempt.

When Iain Sinclair's book of London reportage, *Lights Out For The Territory: 9 Excursions in the Secret History of London*, was published in January 1997 the reception it received was generally highly enthusiastic yet slightly perplexed as to where this writing could be placed culturally and in terms of genre: an engaging difficulty in that this book about spaces, about walking around, seemed to offer an apparent enlargement of literary space by showing how much there was out there to be described by the perceptive observer.[2] Sinclair's modes of urban commentary draw on many, and international, sources, from Baudelaire's conception of the *flâneur*, through Surrealism's emphasis on the necessity of giving oneself up to chance and the unconscious in walking through the city, to the Situationist claim for the political value of the *dérive*, drifting through city streets with a purposelessness that unmasks the ideological intentionality of capitalism's 'society of the spectacle'. There are also American references: to the radical 'open field' poetics of the Black Mountain College and to Beat and Beat influenced writers such as William Burroughs and Hunter S Thompson. However, despite himself in some ways, Sinclair is also locatable in a tradition of non-fiction writing about the 'condition of England', a history that could be traced through Roy Fisher's *City*, 1961, George Orwell's *The Road to Wigan Pier*, Ford Madox Ford's *The Soul of London*, 1905, and further back, to Dickens, Cobbett and Defoe. For these writers, description is always on the way to being criticism, a means of getting between the state of what the writer is looking at and the state of the nation, and the concern of these writers about these connections is present because all have tendencies to various forms of radical patriotism. The form of this mode – resulting from its relation to reportage and to some of the most important strands in English intellectual history, tendencies towards the literary, and towards informality, empiricism, and reformism – often takes the shape of a journey to find a prospect, a view over the condition of England which will show how the part is related to the whole. Sinclair shares some of these concerns, and this essay is about the ways in which prospects over

London are conjured in *Lights Out*, but are then ironised or collapsed. The best view in the book, and its centrepiece, is that from the Thameside penthouse of the now disgraced author, businessman and Conservative politician, Jeffrey Archer, however Sinclair is certainly not able to think of this view as a prompt for political insight. But, in turn, Sinclair's scepticism about prospects (which co-exists with an attraction to them) means that there is a certain directionlessness in the book and its prose: he can't imagine a point from which the landscape will look decisively different. In the process we get a lot on the way, including an implicit alternative cultural history of Post War England, of pauperised filmmakers and whacked-out poets; so, the reader gets the England with which Sinclair identifies, as well as that which he detests. That sense of commitment and obligation means that Sinclair does not descend into pieties – or blasphemies – about forever disappearing Englishness.

For a long time, but perhaps particularly since London's mushrooming in the second half of the nineteenth century, there has been a sense that London is a difficult city to picture in a single image, that, in fact, it may stand for the difficulty of gaining a sense of the whole in modern life, of seeing things in proportion and perspective. For writers of the mid-nineteenth century who were engaged in the 'condition of England' question – which revolved around the contrast between the promise of material abundance that seemed to be inherent in 'industrialism' and the apprehension of both the material poverty of many of the working classes and the radical disruption of what was a thoroughly humanised English landscape – London presented a particular problem: as Raymond Williams noted in *The Country and the City*, London could not be said to manifest the clearly defined dimensions of class and power exhibited in the prototypical working town of the industrial north, the pre-eminent literary example of this mode being the representation of Coketown in Charles Dickens' *Hard Times*, 1854.[3] London could not be pictured by the imaginary writer/moralist as if he were standing on the Pennines looking down – from a position containing the authority of both the Old Testament prophet and the Romantic poet – on what John Ruskin called "these great and little Babylons".[4] Nor was London viewed as symbolically equivalent to Paris, its great rival as the capital of the nineteenth century, with its sense that centuries of the explicit enactment of various kinds of centralising power, of religion and of the state, had produced an environment that was inherently dramatic with the city organised as a stage around the Seine: a stage most notably populated, defined and coloured by the events of 1789-1795, 1830 and 1848. London had neither the backdrop nor the drama in the same way, and attempts to bring some grandeur to riverside proceedings – such as Charles Barry's Houses of Parliament – ended up looking inorganically related to their surroundings, and as hopelessly trying to improvise that sense by themselves, examples of a British state that did not need to articulate its power so explicitly to opponents within and without its terrain. It's notable that the Houses of Parliament, along with Tower Bridge (another piece of neo-Gothic weirdness) appear much more impressive in paintings and photographs than they do *in situ*, as if their imperial role to represent the nation to those more distant and across the seas was much more important than domestic puffery.

Another problem was London's nineteenth and twentieth century tendency to continually expand outwards, to continually throw up new ranks and types of suburbia, which were thought of – in the understanding of many – as inhabited but undiscovered. The journalist, novelist and prospective member of international literary modernism, Ford Madox Ford, wrote in *The Soul of London*, his 1905 book of sociological impressionism:

One may easily sail round England, or circumnavigate the globe. But not even the most enthusiastic geographer – one must of course qualify these generalisations with an 'as a rule' – ever memorised a map of London. Certainly no one ever walks around it. For England is a small island, the world is infinitesimal amongst planets. But London is illimitable.[5]

Whilst England and the globe can be both encompassed and pictured as single units, and can therefore be brought within the possibility of measurement and control, London stands for a epistemological failure that is, cumulatively for Ford, a sign of the sublime. We are eventually overawed by the fact that London has no one thing with which to overawe us.

One of the reasons that I am interested in the writing of Iain Sinclair in *Lights Out For The Territory* is that he appears as a variation of the "most enthusiastic geographer" described in the quotation from Ford. He is the man that attempts – in some part – to take on the insane but epic task of walking around London, a task only accepted by someone more ambivalent than the average about the choice between things and people. Enmeshed in the first chapter of *Lights Out*, Sinclair produces what would have been regarded as a manifesto if it had been put in at the beginning of the chapter rather than, in Sinclair's characteristic method, suddenly manifesting itself half-way through:

Walking is the best way to explore and exploit the city; the changes, shifts, breaks in the cloud helmet, movement of light on water. Drifting purposefully is the recommended mode, tramping asphalted earth in alert reverie, allowing the fiction of an underlying pattern to reveal itself. To the no-bullshit materialist this sounds suspiciously like fin-de-siècle decadence, a poetic of entropy – but the born-again flâneur is a stubborn creature, less interested in texture and fabric, eavesdropping on philosophical conversational pieces, than in noticing everything. Alignments of telephone kiosks, maps made from moss on the slopes of Victorian sepulchres, collections of prostitutes' cards, torn and defaced promotional bills for cancelled events at York Hall, visits to the homes of dead writers, bronze casts on war memorials, plaster dogs, beer mats, concentrations of used condoms, the crystalline patterns of glass shards surrounding an imploded BMW quarter-light window, meditations on the relationship between the brain damage suffered by the super-middleweight boxer Gerard McLellan (lights out in the Royal London Hospital, Whitechapel) and the simultaneous collapse of Barings, bankers to the Queen. Walking, moving across a retreating townscape, stitches it all together: the illicit cocktail of bodily exhaustion and a raging carbon monoxide high.[6]

I'd like to slowly explore, to use Sinclair's idiom, this passage. It's structured around a series of ambiguities, ambiguities which often take the shape of oxymora, but these apparent contradictions are defiantly stated, as if the resolve of the writer persists through the intractability of the material with which he is dealing, rather than being overwhelmed or made passive by it. The enumeration of all the things that he sees does not become limply or lamely expressed; instead, a polemical edge is maintained throughout. But these ambiguities are problematic: "walking is the best way to explore and exploit the city". Now, whilst the history of colonialism may tell us that exploration frequently leads to exploitation, it does not imply that these modes are necessarily contemporaneous. Rather, exploration implies the movement around a previously unknown space in a way that leaves that space comparatively unchanged in a material sense: if it's purposes are ultimately instrumental, then they are instrumental in an intellectual and cognitive sense and that moment is postponed in the act of exploration. The rhetoric of exploitation, on the other hand, is always about material things, about taking nature or peoples and reworking them to satisfy a set of material desires. The fact that Sinclair sees these two processes as happening at the same time in his account of how to get a perspective on London shows the closeness, for him, of the relation between seeing and writing: everything explored is very quickly on the way to being turned into literary material, into the text that the reader now has before him (and Sinclair has been extremely productive in the last ten years: every time one turns there is a new book on the shelf), and this process is a pleasure for Sinclair, a pleasure, we could say unironically, of the text. But exploitation also has other possible motivating factors: the possibility is entertained of an attitude of vengefulness towards the city, as if the writer is taking what is experienced as oppressive and then oppressing it.

However, there is an irony in the fact that Sinclair should at least partly align himself with a rhetoric of exploitation, because one of the motivating forces behind *Lights Out For The Territory* is the desire to render separate spaces (which threaten to be only known by people in their capacities as private individuals) as public spaces: to connect up the various parts of London as part of a public continuum by walking through those areas which are not those of the London's 'sights' but are, instead, the places where a wider strata of society live and work. There is an implicit opposition to a free market and Thatcherite insistence on the primacy of the private sphere, on the need for ownership and control, as if everything that was not legally possessed by the individual would have to be given up to the possibility of radical contingency. That radical contingency is – in a sense – what Sinclair is engaged in regarding in *Lights Out*: the first chapter is spent detailing a walk from Hackney to Greenwich and out to Chingford (on the way to Essex), and its focus is on all the graffiti observed along the route, including both the inscrutable hieroglyphics of the native tagger and the various statements and proclamations of London's politicised sub-cultures, of disenfranchised Kurds and Tibetans, along with more native English obscenity. Sinclair is interested in all this material because he is in some ways a conservative: only those with a highly developed sense of order are alert to all the signs of disorder which may be present in the contemporary city and think about all of the things – graffiti, refuse – which are out of place. The psychological profile has elements of the anal-retentive, of an extremely thorough-going sense of fastidiousness, but it is a fastidiousness which is being applied to the relatively uncontrollable world outside the private sphere and which therefore turns the observer into a kind of public moralist. In that mode – to return to the long quotation above – the writer often runs up against the fact that some material is much harder to use in a straightforwardly instrumental sense: "the changes, shifts, breaks in the cloud helmet, movement of light on water", which is the first material noted in that paragraph, immediately shifts to the register of the lyrical, diffuse and sometimes apocalyptic meanings of the weather. Of course, even that may be commodified in the photographs of style magazines, but the possibility is entertained that, at some level, the writer would like to be the lyricist that this soiled world is preventing him from being: the moralising comes from the distance between this lyrical sense and the world of "concentrations of used condoms" and "collections of prostitutes' cards".

Another possible reaction to this overused world is the rhetoric of escape towards new lands: in English-speaking literary culture that often means the adoption of an American idiom. Even in the quotation above, we can gain the sense that one of the reasons that the writer needs to get up and walk around is the fact that the landscape of London is perhaps thoroughly overdetermined in literary terms, but that overdetermination has been done by the past: as if London had been the centre of the most literary culture in the world but now drew on old resources, which were themselves the signs of a culture that was too concerned with the preservation of heritage. One of the things that has to be noticed and interwoven above are the "visits to the home of dead writers" as if writing itself was on the way to being marmorealised. Hence Sinclair's successful use of the non-fictional form, a form which is unclear of its boundaries and is only defined by what it is not: the strength of its claim on a readership is partly accounted for by a more general feeling that the categories of fiction, poetry and drama are suffering from diminishing marginal returns, whilst non-fiction carries much less of a sense of a pre-existent canon of texts from which a decline can be plotted. Sinclair has himself appeared on Channel 4 condemning the shortlist for the Booker Prize, and proposing his own alternatives, but if such claims were accepted then those texts would have to move to the representative centre rather than inhabiting the more authentic place of the marginalised and the repressed, a place where books are more heard about and sought after than proudly displayed in three-dimensional form.

This suspicion of the possibilities for literary and cultural complacency inherent in the overworked ground of London and England leads Sinclair to reclaim London as virgin land, a place where the individual is challenged and defined. Sinclair's title is taken from the last paragraph of Mark Twain's *The Adventures of Huckleberry Finn*, 1884:

> Tom's most well, now, and got his bullet around his neck on a watch-guard for a watch, and is always seeing what time it is, and so there ain't nothing more to write about, and I am rotten glad of it, because if I'd a knowed what a trouble it was to make a book I wouldn't a tackled it and ain't agoing to no more. But I reckon I got to light out for the Territory ahead of the rest, because Aunt Sally she's going to adopt me and sivilize me and I can't stand it. I been there before.[7]

The implication of Huck's scheme is that one – the true lover of liberty – must be always moving west to escape from a culture of regulated, commercial time, from the propriety indicated by watch-guards, and furthermore, from a culture of writing. In this rhetoric of proud independence and engagement with the materialities of nature there is an assertion of manliness, where the writing of books (and especially the feminised form of the novel) can be excused because it is a demotic account of what has happened. Sinclair is also concerned by the manly – one of the problems of literary London is that in its concern with a past literary culture it seems robbed of a present strength of mind – but he cannot claim that the land he surveys is new and unmapped: this can lead to a certain indirection and restlessness in his writing. When he is writing essayistically about the various writers and film directors that form his preferred canon of the obscure and "reforgotten" chroniclers of London then the prose can easily move along a narrative thread, but the reflections occasioned by the walks can tend to spiral off in various directions; the relation between paragraphs, and therefore the reader's desire to get between paragraphs, can become blocked and unclear. Because Sinclair does not get to the cumulative moment – the moment illustrated in the prospect poem by the point at which the poet reaches the summit and begins his act of surveying – then his writing can take on the form he discerns in Patrick Keiller's film *London*:

> Keiller stares at London with autistic steadiness. It discomforts us, we are not used to it. He freezes still lifes, arrangements of municipal flowers, swirls of brown riverwater. When some gatepost or doorway takes his fancy he gazes at it with the abstracted longing of an out-patient at a discontinued bus-stop.[8]

The alarming element in autism is that it supposes that the visual procedures of selection and focus can be suspended: everything becomes interesting but for reasons that are thoroughly unclear to the observer. He is looking for an element that he has no means of locating, and what this means is that the emphasis on manliness in Sinclair can turn into a literary version of recidivism, where the reoffender keeps returning and returning to the same scenes and the same acts, as if there were a continual attempt and failure to find an articulate version of oneself.

And yet Sinclair is suspicious of the ways in which the connection between overarching views and the fully articulate self can be made: its presumptions are implicitly mocked at various stages in *Lights Out For The Territory*. His unruly paragraphs run from being individual prose-poems and, now and again, become comic set-pieces, where irony deflates the dignity and the potential threat of the thing described, and the meaning of bathos is enacted in the most literal of ways. In his chapter, "The Dog and the Dish", Sinclair produces what is in many ways an anxious meditation on the self-protecting fashion for owning pit bull dogs of the late 80s and early 90s, a fashion which Sinclair links to the shrinking and contamination of the public sphere by the development of Rupert Murdoch's Sky satellite television. However, even in this vein, comic and satirical perspectives are glimpsed, and paragraphs become short stories:

> The stories have been around for years in the local fright sheets. 'Crazed Devil Dog Thrown Off Balcony' is one that caught my eye in the Hackney Gazette. Nkrumah Warren invited a couple of mates around to his second-floor flat for a cup of tea and a natter. His pit bull, a rare white costing £2,000, did not altogether take to the intrusion. In fact, the wretch tore the trousers from one man and tried to perform a full-frontal tonsillectomy on the other. This was taking the breed's reputation for liveliness too far. Mr Warren locked the animal in the kitchen. But the dog wasn't finished yet: he hit the door so hard with his head that he reduced it to kindling. Wanton destruction of council properties can have unforeseen consequences: Mr Warren wrestled his pet to the balcony and threw him over. The pit bull sucked air, caught a brief, privileged view of Hackney, and hit the ground, suffering a broken back. The family, who had gloried in an expensive accessory, did not give way to grief. 'I've got another,' Mr Warren remarked, 'who is absolutely fine with the baby.'[9]

This is both a critique of violence and a delighting in violence: the ravaging dog – against which Sinclair cites the need for his own "ravished inattention" – is both the element that has to be hurled to destruction and the animating presence of this piece of writing: Sinclair's own prose is energised by this canine destroyer, even as the dog is turned into contemporary Hackney's version of Alexander Pope, taking in the "brief, privileged view of Hackney" on the way to his premature demise. Finally, the possibilities for insight posed by such prospects are similarly ironised: the central chapter of the book, and the one to which the reader looks for a more synoptic account of contemporary London, circles around Sinclair's visit to the Thameside penthouse of author, politician, and man about town Jeffrey Archer, a piece entitled "Lord Archer's Prospects". And yet the visit, and the chapter, fall short. Archer does not present himself to be interviewed and pictured looking over London, standing next to his prized collection of paintings of the Thames (he owns both the view and many of the past and most famous painted versions of similar views): he does not allow himself to be seen as England's 1990s version of the *übermensch*. Instead, Sinclair finds what he characterises as an absence, a vacuum. The heat of his own political opposition to Archer is greatly cooled by the fact that the opponent seems so insubstantial:

> ... one of London's worst kept secrets... A show home for a social balloonist. Wouldn't you – if you could? If you had the bottle. If you were prepared to expose yourself to all that metropolitan magnificence: the Houses of Parliament, the Tate Gallery, the great bridges of London in perfect alignment. Nothing separating you from the heavenly dome but a few sheets of glass. You can't get more upwardly mobile without taking on oxygen.[10]

There is a sense here that it is the person with the prospect who becomes visible, that he is, in fact, transparent, and without moorings: a balloonist that is on the way to disappearing into the ether, partly because of the potential of being cowed by the greater magnificence of the things he looks outward towards. Similarly, Archer's painting collection reveals no sense of character: "Like a blindfold raid by Imelda Marcos on the Royal Academy Summer Show, the collection is driven but wildly eclectic – betraying no psychological profile, no theme, no compulsion. It is as anonymous as shop stock, an exhibition curated by a squabble of financial advisers."[11] The prospect over London is infected by this sense of vacuity: the epistemological claims built into the raised perspective over the city find, at that distance from the ground, little to begin to work with. Sinclair is relieved to get back to street-level.

As such, *Lights Out For The Territory* represents more of a casebook than a diagnosis of the relations between landscape and politics: no perspective or place is found from which things look decisively different, however much Sinclair likes to conjure with occult connections, to think about strange and devilish epiphanies. In a sense this is unsurprising: Sinclair wants to be in the middle of things, interpreting the streets and forms of radical and avant-garde culture for a wider audience, who can then follow through their interest by pursing the bibliographies that Sinclair presents for each chapter of *Lights Out* – not for him the ultimate vision of the politically or religiously transfigured London of the New Jerusalem; he is a pedagogue, a one-man literary culture, not a seer. How appropriate, then, that *Lights Out* should have been published in January 1997: it arrived, like the Labour Party's victory in May of that year, with a sense that everything could be seen differently, and yet gave no prospectus of how that different seeing would change the landscape it looked on. By November 1997 Sinclair was being referred to in the property pages of *The Guardian*: his attention to Woolwich in the final chapter of *Lights Out* was used as part of the housing market, a reason to invest in such previously neglected areas.[12] This is an irony, but not a final one, for no writer of recent years in Britain has so expanded a sense of how much there is out there, how much landscape, thick with politics.

1   Denham, J, "Cooper's Hill", *The New Oxford Book of Seventeenth Century Verse*, Fowler, A, ed., Oxford: Oxford University Press, 1992, pp. 529-530, l. 2 (p. 529).
2   Sinclair, I, *Lights Out For the Territory: 9 Excursions in the Secret History of London*, London: Granta, 1997.
3   Williams, R, *The Country and the City*, London: Hogarth Press, 1993, pp. 153-164.
4   Ruskin, J, *The Works of John Ruskin*, London: George Allen, 1903-1912, vol. 29, p. 430.
5   Ford, F M, *The Soul of London*, London: Alston Rivers, 1905, p. 16.
6   Sinclair, *Lights Out For The Territory*, p. 4.
7   Twain, M, *The Adventures of Huckleberry Finn*, London: Penguin, 1985, p. 369.
8   Sinclair, *Lights Out For The Territory*, p. 302.
9   Sinclair, *Lights Out For The Territory*, p. 57.
10 Sinclair, *Lights Out For The Territory*, p. 162.
11 Sinclair, *Lights Out For The Territory*, p. 178.
12 Jennings, Charles, "Living Quarters: Woolwich: Blank Canvas", *The Guardian*, 14 November 1997, G2, p. 39.

The Poetics of the Ordinary: Ambiance in the Moving Transitional Landscape
Krystallia Kamvasinou

What type of landscape is the transitional journey? The undesirable, ordinary, commuting journey, for instance that between city and city airports. Urbanisation, which supports new types of public spaces, produces moving landscapes. Airports, train stations, port terminals, and transport routes, have become social places of a mobile society. Transitional landscapes accompany such places. Interfaces in-between city and countryside, located on the city periphery and mostly experienced at speed, they are often disorientating: travellers, temporary inhabitants of sequential landscapes, have no clear idea where they are or where the city starts. Transitional landscapes, with their lack of identity, correspond to what Marc Augé identifies as "non-places".[1] They constitute undesirable journeys, made out of necessity and not of choice, as they do not meet any (scenic or other) expectations.

Either architectural leftovers or accommodating a permanent use of land such as industry, agriculture or residential, they are hardly ever 'designed' for temporary viewing, mobility and the elusiveness in experience that this implies. Passengers, encapsulated in high-speed means of transport, have almost no physical engagement with the route. Remoteness and detachment prevail, sensory involvement is reduced. Passengers cannot touch; they gaze. This gaze, however, is enriched through motion phenomena to a degree not often achievable otherwise; for 'ordinary' landscapes attain almost a certain charm when experienced at speed and aided by the blurred cinematic vision of the traveller. To quote De Certeau: "You shall not touch; the more you see, the less you hold – a dispossession of the hand in favor of a greater trajectory for the eye."[2]

But far from being only visual, the transitional landscape is an overlap of several layers, both physical and illusory, and so, 'ambiance' rather than place.[3]

The rhythmical movement of the vehicle; the sound of it together with other sounds or noise inside the carriage; the framed view through the window, overlapping with reflections; the sensation of speed with landscape elements such as lamp posts flashing momentarily at regular intervals keeping a sort of tempo; the feel of a breeze caused by speed penetrating the capsule; artifacts 'out there', transformed by weather and light conditions. All these contribute to a unique ambiance.

Is it possible then that a moving observer can notice the unnoticeable: things that do not exist outside of motion, situations that exist only for the duration of the passage? And could this suggest a different type of engagement?

Through subtle interventions that accentuate ambient phenomena, what is sought is an awareness of the transitional landscape experience. By this, a different type of engagement can be triggered –

not directly physical but more akin to dreaming or absorption in a performance. One could start to negotiate between things taken for granted and the hidden poetics in how we experience them.

Expectations hinder 'vision'. As Paul Virilio states quoting Alphonse Bertillon "You only see what you look at and you only look at what you want to see."[4] Poetics in the transitional landscape may thus stay invisible because no one expects it to be there. The intention of this project is to reclaim it.

1   Augé, Mark, *Non-Places: Introduction to an Anthropology of Supermodernity*, London: Verso, 1995.
2   De Certeau, Michel, *The Practice of Everyday Life*, Berkeley, CA: University of California Press, 1984, p. 112.
3   'Ambiance' is used to connote an environment composed of several overlapping layers of attention. See work on ambiance in music by Erik Satie and John Cage.
4   Alphonse Bertillon, French criminologist, quoted in Virilio, Paul, *The Vision Machine*, London: British Film Institute and Indiana University, 1995, p. 42.

Extract from
Ambient 0-3

Following pages:
Extract from
Stanstead
(December 2000)

STANSTED

transitional   temporary   undesirable   nec

poetic

beauty in the ordinary

poetics unveiled in the ordinary aided by the interference of speed and the medium

elusive **fugitive**

fictitious

journey noise object capsule signal spectacle sound captive feel of breeze cinematic vibrati ordinary

ty

non-place

terrain vague

blurred

physical

tempo

rhythm unexpected distorted

ambiance

n experience

the landscape on the move is not mute

Landscapes and Theatricality

Landscapes and Theatricality
Mark Dorrian

One of the fascinations of the landscape/theatricality juxtaposition is its potential to complicate and problematise the more familiar and straightforward models of the relationship between visuality and landscape. This is shown well in the opening and closing papers in this section. But equally intriguing is the power of theatre as a disconcerting representational domain poised between fiction and reality, a power heightened in theatrical installations occupying or creating ambiguously 'real' landscape conditions. As the first two papers here indicate, it is in this theatrical effect of the suspension of, or oscillation between, normally clear-cut distinctions that a moment of political possibility resides: the possibility that, to use Renata Tyszczuk's phrase, the "fabulous *be* actual".

Drawing upon recent theorisations of theatrical spectatorship, Jane Avner examines the entertainment staged by the Earl of Hertford for Queen Elizabeth I during her visit to his estate at Elvetham in Hampshire in 1591. Linking the event – whose scenes were played out upon a crescent-shaped lake, a reference to the courtly cult of Elizabeth as Cynthia, moon-goddess – to contemporary imperial sentiments, she describes the complex role played by the queen to whom this emblematic text was addressed. After the defeat of the British naval 'expeditionary force' in the Azores shortly before the queen's visit, the *theatrum naturae* of Elvetham becomes the occasion for the symbolic recomposition of "an imaginary and more congenial geopolitical order". In the entertainment, this was achieved through the restorative and animating power of the royal gaze. Interpreting the queen's position in terms of Barbara Freedman's characterisation of theatrical looking as structured by "fractured reciprocity", Avner describes how the entertainment strategically solicited her as both spectator and performer and hence invoked a suggestive convergence of fantasy and political reality.

Renata Tyszczuk's paper studies the remarkable gardens of the exiled Polish king, Stanislaw Leszczynski. Between 1742 and 1744, with the aid of his architect and a clockmaker, he constructed the *Rocher* – an automated village – in the grounds of the château of Lunéville. Together with the *Chartreuses*, another ideal settlement, this time inhabited by living 'villagers' who were selected from among his courtiers, the *Rocher* was a key moment in a representational strategy which produced an "exemplary 'kingdom'" that was poised between fantasy and reality. The result, as Tyszczuk describes it, was a domain "that was part theatre and part experiment", a court which provided a parodic counter-image to that at Versailles.

Finally, Ewa Kębłowska-Lawniczak examines the optical complications of Tom Stoppard's *Arcadia*. She suggests that this play, which is in important ways about landscape, can be said – in the way that it problematises and probes visual conventions and codes – to encourage what she calls "landscape viewing". By this, she means a form of spectatorship in which the clear distinctions characteristic of the theatrical scopic regime supported by the proscenium-type theatre are dissolved in favour of a more immersive, contingent, and diffused mode. The shift in landscape from the static painted screen to the mobile, temporal, and event-based forms implied in her discussion is rich in implication and seems close to many of the interests now being pursued in 'space studies' and in the arts.

The Earl of Hertford's Conceited Landscape
Jane Avner

"Whilst the Atkinsons made history, the Cricks spun yarns", the narrator in Graham Swift's widely acclaimed novel *Waterland* remarks disparagingly, as he begins the story of their combined family fortunes.[1] In recent years this seemingly self-evident distinction between making history and spinning yarns has been the focus of much critical debate. The forms and functions of narrative have been explored in a number of fields, but especially in historiography where Hayden White's work has been particularly influential in examining the ways in which history and story interpenetrate each other.[2] Though opinions differ as to exactly how and to what extent they are imbricated there seems to be general agreement concerning what the Renaissance scholar Louis Montrose has called the "historicity of texts" and the "textuality of histories".[3] Though they might not have put it in quite that way, the Elizabethans would have found nothing untoward in such a *rapprochement*. No-one who has dipped into the three large volumes recording the *Progresses of Queen Elizabeth* edited by the antiquarian John Nichols between 1788 and 1807, could be in little doubt that the Elizabethans had few qualms about spinning yarns and making history at one and the same time.[4] Both were, after all, endemic to what Mary Hill Cole in her recent study of the progresses, *The Portable Queen*, calls "the politics of ceremony"; indeed the 'cunning passages' between history and fiction are perhaps nowhere more apparent than in these records of various events in the courtly calendar – civic ceremonies, public processions, university receptions and, perhaps most strikingly of all, the Queen's visits to her more prominent subjects.[5] Particularly privileged sites for such hybrid narratives were the parks and gardens of the minor and not-so-minor nobility with whom the Queen stayed on her summer progresses. These annual peregrinations, which might well last upwards of three months, played an important, if contested role in Tudor politics, allowing the monarch to see and be seen, to speak and be spoken to by her subjects in the shires. This paper will focus on the visit she paid to Edward Seymour, the Earl of Hertford at Elvetham in Hampshire in September, 1591.[6] Despite initially inauspicious circumstances – including the estate's inadequate size and the royal disfavour in which the Earl himself had for so long languished – this was to be one of the most splendid of all Elizabethan occasions, its entertainment the only one, in my opinion, that might be compared with the Mannerist extravaganzas then being devised at princely courts on the continent. But before embarking on a discussion of the Earl's cunning landscape scenography I should like to say a word or two about the occasional art to which such scenographies belong.

As Hans Georg Gadamer has pointed out, 'occasional' art occupies a somewhat marginal place in modern aesthetics. Gadamer himself discusses portraiture and the dedicatory poem in his *magnum opus*, *Truth and Method*; but designed landscapes – such as the one I shall be discussing – are equally, even I would argue *a fortiori*, characterised by the problematics of what Gadamer calls 'occasionality', and as such are subject to similar hermeneutic constraints.[7] Though considerably more complex because of their essentially ephemeral nature and the multiple art forms involved (they were frequently dramatic, choreographic, musical, pyrotechnic, as well as landscaped events), the conditions of their creation, as with other forms of occasional art, are clearly an essential part of their meaning. Gadamer has drawn attention to this aspect and to what he refers to as the "demands" or "requirements" of the work itself which stem from it. At the risk of seeming to state the obvious I too would like to insist on the special "demands" progress texts make upon us, their belated readers, demands which centre primarily on the referential and the intentional nature of the work in question. Such texts are orientated: they seek to persuade. And while their orientation can only be understood through historical analysis, their persuasiveness falls within the more formal domain of art.

In the hybrid text I shall be looking at here, the 'artful' transformation of political reality is intimately bound up with the imaginative configuration of the land itself. The reading I offer of the Queen's visit to Elvetham will thus explore the way both history and story shape the Earl of Hertford's *theatrum naturae*. I shall argue that the ideal topographies inscribed in this, and to a lesser degree in other sixteenth century parks *mise-en-scène* for the Queen's visits, were not – as some critics have argued – simply representations of green and golden arcadias situated in a timeless world, but veritable 'occasional' texts intended to be read by their ideal reader, Elizabeth I. Elvetham's theatrical landscape could not have been designed in quite this way a month or so earlier and it could not have had quite the same impact a month or so later. But though events immediately prior to this progress visit – disastrous losses to the Spanish off the Azores the previous month – would appear to have been the subject of an ingenious and audacious rewriting in the second day's entertainment, this rewriting was, I would argue, designed to be part of a larger and distinctly more ambitious whole. The idea was hardly to dwell indulgently on the country's recent discomfiture but rather, according to the paradoxical spirit of *concordia discors*, to dramatically transform this misfortune into an imaginative image of the future – one fit for a queen. For what was most crucially at stake was the staging of Elizabeth's gaze. What occurs in this kind of *mise-en-scène*? Barbara Freedman has argued that "theatricality evokes an uncanny sense that the given to be seen has the power both to position and displace us", and such, I believe, was the intention of Elvetham's unusually ambitious iconographical programme.[8] This was to feature, notably, a lively exchange between dramatic embodiments of the four elements and give rise to one of the earliest images of an emergent national and maritime identity, one strikingly inscribed in the very land itself. In this respect the Earl – presumably at the instigation of his brother-in-law, the first lord of the Admiralty who was present, and other leading counsellors concerned with England's role at sea – proved himself adept at seizing the occasion, the opportune moment, to represent such concerns dramatically. Renaissance writing, particularly political writing, shows considerable interest in the question of timing and though Hertford's dramatic landscape was by far the most brilliant of the occasional texts presented to her Majesty on progress, most of her hosts showed a keen sense of what the Greeks called *kairos* and the Romans venerated in the deity *Occasio*. When he writes of the need to "cross the vast quarry of time to reach the heart of occasion" Balthasar Graçian exactly catches the essence of the '*kairic* moment', a temporality which Evanghélos Moutsopoulos has defined by a binary rather than the usual tertiary structure of past, present and future.[9] More prosaically Francis Bacon warned that "occasion (as it is in the common verse) 'turneth a bald noddle after she hath presented her locks in front and no hold taken...'. There is surely no greater wisdom than well to time the beginnings and onsets of things... The ripeness or unripeness of the occasion... must ever be well weighed."[10] And unlike that Renaissance prince who spends a whole play pondering the ripeness or unripeness of the occasion, Hertford unhesitatingly and wittily seized the one the Queen had so unexpectedly offered him.

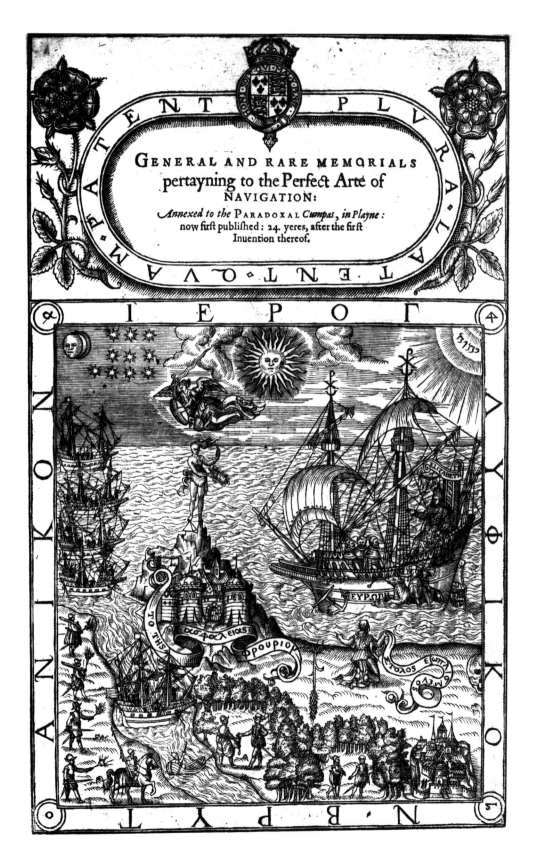

Figure 1

Frontispiece to
John Dee,
*General and Rare
Memorials
pertayning to the
Perfect Arte of
Navigation*
(1577) 48.h.18
By permission
of The British
Library

Jane Avner

Figure 2
Engraving of
Elvetham lake,
John Nichols,*The
Progresses and
Public
Processions of
Queen Elizabeth*
(1788-1821)
599.i.3-5.
By permission
of The British
Library

On learning that the Queen intended to stay with him during the course of her 1591 summer progress Edward Seymour, the Earl of Hertford, was faced with several seemingly insoluble problems. Unlike his other estates tiny Elvetham in Hampshire was quite unfitted to accommodate, let alone entertain, the sovereign and her court on progress. Though the Earl undoubtedly had pressing personal reasons for not letting the occasion slip through his fingers, the distinctly topical nature of the entertainment he offered Elizabeth suggests that political considerations arising from the particular conditions of that year's progress, were of equal, if not paramount, importance in determining the theme and above all the extraordinarily ambitious nature of the programme devised for her visit.

Under renewed threat of Spanish invasion the Queen had decided to inspect coastal fortifications and her itinerary was arranged in consequence. She also hoped that in keeping relatively close to the coast, Henri IV – who was militarily engaged in Normandy – would be persuaded to cross the channel to meet with her and discuss common policy. Elizabeth had sent English troops to aid the Protestant cause in France and was impatient at what she perceived as delays in attacking Rouen. Though her *"très cher bon Frère & Cousin Le Roy très chrestien"* sent emissaries to apologise for not being able to come himself he was, in fact, too fully occupied at Rouen ever to do so. Charles, Lord Howard of Effingham, First Lord of the Admiralty who had directed operations against the Spanish Armada in 1588 was on progress with the Queen that summer. The admiral's cousin, Lord Thomas Howard, was commander-in-chief of what the English were pleased to call an 'expeditionary force' then in the Azores, to which the Queen, rather uncharacteristically, had contributed the fairly substantial sum of around £19,000. News of the naval battle, or rather *débâcle*, in which Thomas Howard's force had been routed just a few weeks previously, Sir Richard Grenville had lost his life – thereby becoming a national hero overnight – and Howard's own conduct been seriously, though unfairly, called into question, was still very fresh indeed at the time of the Queen's visit to Elvetham in September. It was scarcely calculated to persuade her of the opportunity of founding a permanent navy, a step which a number of prominent counsellors – and none more so than the First Lord of the Admiralty himself – had long been urging her to take. It seems not unreasonable to imagine that it was the admiral, whose sister, Frances Howard, was married to the Earl of Hertford, who suggested that England's maritime destiny be placed at the centre of the Earl's royal entertainment. But the form Hertford was to give this entertainment was an elegant combination of *realpolitik* and that peculiarly Elizabethan brand of sexual politics the Virgin Queen so delighted in.

The imperial theme so resoundingly developed during the Queen's visit partakes of both. Whether or not John Dee's emblematic frontispiece to his *General and Rare Memorials Pertayning to the Perfect Arte of Navigation* published in 1577 (figure 1) and dedicated to Sir Christopher Hatton, a firm supporter of naval endeavour, inspired the Elvetham landscape scenography, similar imperial sentiments certainly inspired its dramatic interludes. The last of these featured a "garland made in fourme of an imperiall crowne" around which a Fairy Queen danced with her maids, apparently delighting the live Queen who asked that their dance, performed to the music of an "exquisite consort", be repeated three times.[11] In his drawing, Dee, keen promoter of a permanent British fleet, presents the figure of Britannia pleading with Elizabeth, seated in the vessel Europa, to seize Occasion (poised on the rocky promontary) by the forelock and found the Royal Navy, both as a way of assuring British sovereignty of the waves but also as a first step towards the protestant Empire of which he dreamed.

Throughout the sixteenth century imperial dreams, were being revived, gripping the imaginations of most European powers. But as Frances Yates pointed out many years ago, such hopes were "never politically real or politically lasting: it was their phantoms that endured and exerted an almost undying influence".[12] It is doubtful whether many in England shared Dee's almost messianic fervour but the founding of a permanent navy as a means of assuring British sovereignty and prosperity was another matter, and it is in this respect that mention is usually made of Dee's text by naval historians. The dense and highly symbolic drawing which serves as its frontispiece features what Roy Strong believes to be in fact the first representation of Britannia.[13] 14 years later the distinguished designers of the Elvetham progress cast Elizabeth as a "Sea-borne Queen... the wide Ocean's Empresse" and, following Sir Walter Ralegh's courtly conceit, as the moon goddess Cynthia who commands the waves, as well as the hearts of her courtiers. Spenser's *Faerie Queene*, which was published the year preceding the progress, was also addressed to "fairest Cynthia" whose image the poet promised to shadow "in mirrours more than one". It too develops the doubly imperial theme of a regal Cynthia who "In wider ocean... her throne doth reare/That over all the earth it may be seen".[14] In the late 1580s, supposedly at Ralegh's initiation, a whole cult to Elizabeth as Cynthia had grown up at court, where it had become fashionable to sport crescent-shaped jewels and to exchange emblematic gifts which bore this form.[15] Such, briefly, is the background to the water pageants with which Elizabeth was entertained from the 20 to 23 September, 1591.

Though the courtly cult of Elizabeth as Cynthia had found abundant expression in such diverse domains as poetry, painting, and garden ornament as well as the sartorial fashions of her courtiers, the Earl of Hertford's ingenious decision to emblazon her emblem in the very land itself by creating an artificial crescent-shaped lake was undoubtedly the most extravagant homage ever paid to the Elizabethan Cynthia. In the weeks preceding her arrival at Elvetham hundreds of men worked feverishly to cut "a goodly Pond to the perfect figure of a half-moon" and equip it with various islands and boats as illustrated in the two woodcuts published at the time.[16] (figure 2) The islands or 'grounds' were firstly the so-called *Ship Ile*, "a hundred foot in length and four-score foote broad, bearing three trees orderly set for three masts".[17] The second was a fort and the third, the so-called *Snayl Mount*, an amusing borrowing from contemporary garden ornament, was to symbolise Spain: during the second night's firework display its horns 'fired' at the English fort in a replay of the victory against the armada. Diverse boats were "prepared for musicke".[18] A rather elaborate pinnace was to be the focus of much of the dramatic action.

The Earl's witty solution to the problem of entertaining the Queen in a park whose circumference measured less than two miles, was simply to turn the problem on its head and make its very smallness the central conceit of Elvetham's theatrical landscape. The crescent-shaped lake, a miniature emblem of the ocean over which she supposedly held sway, became the stage upon which Elvetham's tiny park was refigured as microcosm. On the lake's surface dramatic embodiments of the four elements, Water, Earth, Fire and Air, entered into symbolic combat, recomposing an imaginary geopolitical order of an altogether more satisfactory nature than recent events had presaged. A burlesque sea skirmish – a rather light-hearted version of the *naumachia* then fashionable in the Italian and French courts – and a firework 'battle' re-presenting the 1588 Armada victory, wittily enacted that *concordia discors* which, in classical cosmology, figured the Creation. Re-creation was to be the *maître mot* at Elvetham and Elizabeth, very much as in John Case's well known *Sphaera Civitatis* emblem in which she wears an imperial crown, its 'prime mover'.[19] (figure 3) In medieval and Renaissance cosmologies (derived from classical mythologies such as Ovid's) the elements were arranged in concentric spheres with the earth at the centre, enclosed in turn by the spheres of water,

air and fire. These are themselves encircled by the next sphere – that of the moon – significantly positioned between the earthly and the celestial where she may influence the affairs of men. Elvetham's elemental dramas were designed, of course, to be overlooked by that contemporary moon goddess, the Queen herself.

Hertford's elegant Petrarchan homage to a Queen whose courtiers were, as George Gascoigne put it, constantly "tossed to and fro on waves of wan hope", must surely have charmed the royal mistress whose favour he hoped to regain.[20] It was presented to her, with something of a flourish, soon after her arrival: summoned to her casement windows by a gun salute fired from the *Ship Ile*, she first looked down upon this mirror-like blason which returned an ideal, unchanging image to an ageing Queen whose motto was *Semper Eadem* (*Always the Same*). However in the water tableaux of the second day's entertainment she was, in a manner of speaking, invited in "mirrours more than one, herselfe to see": the reflections so discretely proffered during the rest of her visit were addressed – rather in the manner of the textual *speculae* in the *Mirror for Magistrates* tradition – to the prince. I propose now to focus on the way the second day's entertainment (represented in the woodcut reproduced in figure 2) fashioned the cosmic and imperial themes developed at Elvetham. It was then – and in the face of all evidence to the contrary – that Cynthia's maritime supremacy was celebrated in a boisterous *naumachia*.

As the elements Water and Earth prepared to confront each other in the shape of Tritons and Nymphs versus Sylvanus and his woodland folk, the sea-god, Nereus, addressed this barely veiled reproach to a Queen whose memory seemed, regrettably, to be a little short. It was, after all, he reminded her, thanks to *his* waves that her Majesty's enemies had been vanquished – a reference of course to the routing of the Spanish armada in 1588.

> I watry Nereus hovered on the coast,
>> To greete your Majesty with this my traine
>> Of dauncing Tritons, and shrill singing Nimphs,
>> But all in vaine: Elisa was not there;

Naturally it is that good-for-nothing Earth that is to blame for this sorry state of affairs:

> Therefore impatient that this worthless earth
>> Should beare your Highness weight, and we Sea-gods,
>> (Whose jealous waves have swallowed up your foes,
>> And to your Realme are walls impregnable),
>> With such large favour seldom time are grac't:
>> I from the deeps have drawn this winding flud,
>> Whose crescent forme figures the rich increase
>> Of all that sweet Elisa holdeth deare.[21]

Upon which he called on his train of Tritons to sound their trumpets and call out the denizens of the Earth, lusty Sylvanus and his companions. The satyr-like Sylvanus – "attired from the middle downwards to the knee in kiddes skinnes with the haire on… his head hooded with a goats skin and two little horns over his head" – was accompanied by a merry band of wild men carrying fire-brands.[22] No need for the sea-gods "ayr-enforcing shells" to awaken *them* to their duty they cried testily.[23] A comic water skirmish ensued in which Water and Air confronted Earth and Fire, the sea-gods sounding their war horns, the earth-bound folk throwing their fire darts until they were put to rout and retired, amidst general laughter to the woods.

The rough and tumble of the popular mock fighting in this 'satyrical' scene effectively functions as a foil to the oblique allusions to current misfortunes which follow.[24] It falls to Her Majesty – "alwaies friend to Peace and ennemy to Warre" – as Nereus put it, to reconcile the combatants.[25] According to the theory derived by Plato and Aristotle from Empedocles, the elements are shaped by two conflicting forces, Love and Combat, which alternately combine and separate them. The element personified by the sea-god, Nereus, emerges victorious, as of course it must do, in the various sea battles staged in Elvetham's microcosmic theatre. But the real and fictive spaces thrown into play, and which are pulled together by a series of verbal and visual, musical and choreographic echoes and symmetries, effectively seek to arrest, to stabilise Elvetham's ambitious but ephemeral landscape. It is Love of course who must heal the breach between Earth and Water, land and sea. And Love's task turns out to be partly specular, partly performative, and not a little bound up with that "history of wish fulfilment" which the Elizabethans, John Pitcher writes, were so consciously spinning.[26]

Cast as the harbinger of Spring in the Botticelli-like tableau of the Hours and Graces who greet her arrival, Elizabeth is constantly attributed with the power of infusing new life into the 'spectacular' Hampshire landscape. It is her gaze, she is constantly assured, that can bring about the longed for

Figure 4
*Aerial
photograph, 1981*
Photography by
Cambridge
University
Collection of Air
Photographs.
First published
Antiquity,
vol. LVI, no. 216,
March 1982,
p. 46

renewal and restore harmonious relations between the various elements that compose it.[27] But
the royal gaze is, of course, staged. And as Freedman points out, such theatrical looking implies "a
fractured reciprocity whereby beholder and beheld reverse positions in a way that renders a steady
position of spectatorship impossible".[28] Elizabethan designed landscapes of this kind delight in
"fractured reciprocity" and Hertford's was no exception: it effectively made designs upon its royal
reader. Again and again, as the landscape took shape before her eyes, receiving, as Nereus the sea-
god put it, "life from verdure of (her) looks" the text playfully repositioned the spectator-Queen as
'genius' of Elvetham's emblematic landscape, cannily blurring the distinction between spectator and
performer, suspending that between political reality and imaginative fiction.[29] At one particularly
striking moment Elizabeth was called upon to perform something very much akin to one of Austin's
speech acts, by giving the sea-god's pinnace "some prosperous name".[30] It is the sea-nymph Neara
who asks the Queen to "view it with her life-inspiring beames" and "name it with a blisfull word".[31]
Elizabeth obliged by ceremoniously baptising it *The Bonadventure*. It was a pointed choice. For the
real *Bonadventure*, which had once been Drake's flag-ship was, as everyone present was well aware,
still at sea with Howard's ill-fated expedition in the Azores under the command of Robert Cross.
Unlike Elvetham's gay pinnace it was to limp home some three weeks later, unable even to defray
the cost of its voyage.

It is only from written accounts such as those collected by Nichols that we can form any idea of what these theatrical landscapes actually looked like. Inevitably epideictic in nature these fascinatingly hybrid texts purport, one and all, to give "A true account of all that passed at...." And that is the crux. They are not exactly 'play texts' for they also claim to record an actual occasion, a performance, and as such are shot through with what Paula Johnson has called "the rhetoric of presence".[32] Much like royal pageants and Entries they embody both dramatic fictions and historical reality: a real sovereign was there witnessing and responding to the entertainments prepared for her, and those entertainments rarely, if ever, failed to make political designs upon her.[33]

I have argued that Elvetham's microcosmic landscape reached to the very heart of occasion projecting there an image of an incipient national identity that was, even then, inextricably bound up with imperial ambition. It would no doubt be a mistake however, to dismiss such shaping fantasies too readily or consign them too quickly to an Elizabethan history of 'wish fulfilment', for as W J T Mitchell has suggested in *Landscape and Power*, landscape might well be viewed as "something like the dreamwork of imperialism".[34] From a somewhat similar perspective, Jacqueline Rose has argued that far from being private and regressive, fantasy plays a key role in the formation of modern states and nations. In Freud's account fantasy is projective, progressive: "Freud links fantasy to what makes group identities possible and impossible at the same time. There is no way of understanding political identities and destinies without letting fantasies into the frame.... Far from being the antagonist of public, social being, (fantasy) plays a central, constitutive role in the modern world of states and nations.... Like blood, fantasy is thicker than water."[35]

Four hundred years on, in these so-called post-colonial times, the water in Hertford's ingeniously "conceited" lake, whose crescent form projected England's "rich increase", has long since drained away. But curiously enough the traces of this eminently fragile, occasional landscape can still just be discerned, visibly etched in the Hampshire soil, as an aerial photograph taken in April 1981 by David R Wilson reveals.[36] (figure 4)

Several of the ideas developed here were first outlined briefly in my article "English Renaissance Landscapes and their Readers" in *Esthétiques de la Nouveauté à la Renaissance*, Laroque, François and Lessay, Franck, eds., Paris: Presses de la Sorbonne Nouvelle, 2001.

1   Swift, Graham, *Waterland*, London: Picador, 1992, p. 17.
2   White, Hayden, *Tropics of Discourse*, Baltimore and London: John Hopkins University Press, 1978.
3   Montrose, Louis, *The Purpose of Playing: Shakespeare and the Cultural Politics of the Elizabethan Theatre*, Chicago and London: University of Chicago Press, 1996, pp. 5-6.
4   Nichols, John, *The Progresses and Public Processions of Queen Elizabeth*, London: Printed by and for J Nichols, vols. 1, 2, 1788; vol. 3, 1807; vols. 1-3 republished 1823. Like most of the Queen's progress visits, accounts were published almost immediately. The first version of the Elvetham entertainment was published within a week of the Queen's departure by John Wolf. There are three separate editions. I have quoted from the third in the edition compiled by Jean Wilson: *Entertainments for Elizabeth I*, Woodbridge: Brewer, 1980, pp. 96-118. Both the musical and the literary quality of the Elvetham entertainment is considerably

higher than that of most (in my opinion all) other progress texts. Though this remains conjectural, R W Bond has attributed the text to John Lyly; see his edition of the *Complete Works of John Lyly*, Oxford: Clarendon Press, 1967 (1902), vol. 1, p. 404.
5   Cole, Mary Hill, *The Portable Queen*, Amherst: University of Massachusetts Press, 1999. I borrow the phrase "cunning passages" fron Jeremy Hawthorn. See his *Cunning Passages: New Historicism, Cultural Materialism and Marxism in Contemporary Literary Debate*, London: Arnold, 1996; in particular his introductory overview of textuality and historicism.
6   Edward Seymour (1539-1621) was the eldest surviving son of Edward Seymour, 1st Duke of Somerset (Protector Somerset). He was educated with Prince Edward and knighted at Edward's coronation on 20 February 1546. Two months after Elizabeth's accession he was created Baron Beauchamp and Earl of Hertford and in November or December 1560 he secretly married Catherine Grey. Following the execution of her eldest

sister, Lady Jane Grey, Catherine stood next in line to the throne after the succession of Queen Mary and Queen Elizabeth. The marriage, contracted without the Queen's permission, was treasonous and the couple were both committed to the Tower where Catherine gave birth to two sons, Edward (1561) and Thomas (1563). The marriage was declared nul by a royal commission on the 12 May 1562. Catherine died in 1568. Seymour married again twice but on his death in 1621 he was buried with Catherine in Salisbury Cathedral. He again incurred the Queen's wrath in November 1595 by petitioning to have the declaration of the invalidity of his marriage set aside. He was once again briefly committed to the Tower. The relative leniency with which Hertford was treated following his first imprisonment is attributed to the support of Cecil, Ralegh and William, Lord Howard of Effingham (d.1573). At the time of the Elvetham entertainment Hertford had been married to Effingham's daughter, Frances Howard, for about ten years.

7 Gadamer, Hans Georg, *Truth and Method*, trans. Barden, G and Cumming, J, New York: Seabury Press, 1975. See section entitled "The Ontological Foundation of the Occasional and the Decorative".

8 Freedman, Barbara, *Staging the Gaze*, Ithaca: Cornell University Press, 1991, p. 1.

9 Gracian, Balthasar, Maxime 55, in *L'Homme du Cour*, cited by Michel Field, *Excentriques*, Paris: Editions Bernard Barrault, 1987, p. 57 [translation mine]. Moutsopoulos, Evanghélos, *Kairos – La Mise et l'Enjeu*, Paris: Vrin, 1991, pp. 105-106. Moutsopoulos opposes the static trilogy 'before, during and after' and its homologous 'past, present and future' to what he regards as the more dynamic "restructuring and restructurable" binary order of "*pas-encore*"(not yet) and "*jamais plus*" (never again). See also pp. 73-81, 107-114.

10 Bacon, Francis, *Essays*, "On Delays", London: Macmillan, 1927, (1597), p. 53.

11 Wilson, *Entertainments for Elizabeth I*, p. 116.

12 Yates, Frances, *Astraea – The Imperial Theme in the Sixteenth Century*, London: Routledge and Kegan Paul, 1975, p. 1. For a discussion of Dee's emblematic frontispiece see Peter French, *John Dee – The World of an Elizabethan Magus*, London, 1872, pp. 183-185.

13 Strong, Roy, *The Tudor and Stuart Monarchy: Pageantry, Painting, Iconography*, vol. 3: Jacobean and Caroline, Woodbridge: Boydell Press, 1998, pp. 139-140.

14 Spenser, Edmund, *The Faerie Queene*, Thomas P Roche Jr, ed., Harmondsworth: Penguin Books, 1978. (Books 1-3 first published 1590; Books 4-6 first published 1596). Bk. 3, Proeme, 5; Bk. 2, ii, 6, 7.

15 Strong, Roy, *Gloriana – The Portraits of Queen Elizabeth I*, London: Thames and Hudson, 1987, pp. 101-103.

16 Wilson, *Entertainments for Elizabeth I*, p. 100

17 Wilson, *Entertainments for Elizabeth I*, p. 100

18 The various musical interludes and accompaniments which, by all accounts, were exceptionally fine, were composed by Thomas Morley, John Baldwin and Edward Johnson. See Wilson, *Entertainments for Elizabeth I*, pp. 162 and 164-166, and Ernest Brennecke, "The Entertainment at Elvetham, 1591," in *Music in English Renaissance Drama*, Lexington: University of Kentucky Press, 1968.

19 This emblematic diagram is the frontispiece to John Case, *Sphaera Civitatis*, Oxford, 1588. See Andrew and Catherine Belsey's discussion of this drawing, "Icons of Divinity: Portraits of Elizabeth the 1st", in *Renaissance Bodies: the Human Figure in English Culture c. 1540-1660*, Gent, Lucy and LLewellyn, Nigel, eds., London: Reaktion, 1995 (1990), pp. 22-25.

20 From "A Hundreth Sundrie Flowres" (1573) in Jones, Emrys, ed., *Sixteenth Century Verse*, Oxford: Oxford University Press, 1992, p. 207.

21 Wilson, *Entertainments for Elizabeth I*, p. 109.

22 Wilson, *Entertainments for Elizabeth I*, p. 111.

23 Wilson, *Entertainments for Elizabeth I*, p. 111.

24 Of Vitruvius' three canonical theatrical scenes the last, composed of a rural, mountainous or pastoral decor, and featuring its wild denizens is called 'satyric'. (Vitruvius, *Ten Books of Architecture*, Morgan, Morris Hicky, trans., New York: Dover, 1960, Bk.5, ch.8). On the Elizabethan conflation of satyr and satire see O J Campbell "The Elizabethan Satyr-Satirist" in *Satire*, Paulson, Ronald, ed., Eaglewood Cliffs: Prentice-Hall, 1971.

25 Wilson, *Entertainments for Elizabeth I*, p. 112.

26 Pitcher, John, in *The Oxford History of English Literature*, Rogers, Pat, ed., Oxford: Clarendon Press, 1987, p. 90.

27 Wilson, *Entertainments for Elizabeth I*, pp. 106, 109, 111, 112, 116, 117.

28 Freedman, *Staging the Gaze*, p. 1.

29 Wilson, *Entertainments for Elizabeth I,*. p. 109.

30 Wilson, *Entertainments for Elizabeth I*, p. 113.

31 Wilson, *Entertainments for Elizabeth I*, p. 112.

32 Johnson, Paula, "Jacobean Ephemera and the Immortal World", *Renaissance Drama*, n.s. 8, 1977, pp. 151-171. Cited by David Bergeron "Stuart Civic Pageants and Textual Performance" in *Renaissance Quarterly*, vol. LI, no. 1, 1998.

33 See Bergeron, "Stuart Civic Pageants and Textual Performance", pp. 163-183.

34 Mitchell,W J T, "Imperial Landscape", *Landscape and Power*, Mitchell, W J T, ed., Chicago: University of Chicago Press, 1994, p. 7.

35 Rose, Jacqueline, *States of Fantasy*, Oxford: Clarendon Press, 1996, pp. 3-5.

36 "The Site of the Elvetham Entertainment", Notes & News section of *Antiquity*, vol. LVI, no. 216, March 1982, pp. 46-47. David Wilson is Curator in Aerial Photography at Cambridge University.

vérité fabuleuse: the *Rocher* at Lunéville 1743-1745
Renata Tyszczuk

Je suis aussi roi des Polaques; j'ai perdu mon royaume deux fois, mais la Providence m'a donné un autre état, dans lequel j'ai fait plus de bien que tous les rois des Sarmates ensemble n'en ont jamais pu faire sur les bordes de la Vistule; je me résigne à la Providence; et je suis venu passer la carnaval à Venise.[1]

In 1757, Stanislaw Leszczynski – father-in-law of Louis XV and twice-exiled king of Poland – appears in Voltaire's *Candide* as one of the 'forsaken' kings spending carnival in Venice. He had in fact, already established himself as *roi bienfaisant* in the duchy of Lorraine and Bar alluded to in the citation as "another realm". Voltaire's fictional introduction to this enigmatic monarch recalls Jaucourt's entry "Pologne" in the *Encyclopédie* which refers to "Un Roi, qui l'a gouverné quelque tems, & qui nous montre dans une province de France, ce qu'il auroit pu éxécuter dans un Royaume."[2] The landscape of Lorraine underwent many changes during Stanislaw's nominal reign, which took place in the transitional period between the Baroque and the Enlightenment. Both its physical and intellectual topography were altered through his endeavour to do 'more good' which included the establishment, patronage and reform of local industries and arts. In 1737, at the beginning of his nominal reign in the Duchy, Stanislaw also initiated a series of building programmes transforming his newly acquired ducal residences, the châteaux or *maisons du roi*.[3] Lorraine presented the possibility of refuge not only from Stanislaw's actual exile, but from the cultural dilemma exemplified by the perceived inadequacies of the political and moral order. As king, albeit only in name, Stanislaw treated his exile as an opportunity to explore the issue of benign governance, earning the title *roi bienfaisant* in recognition of both the character of his intentions and the ambiguous nature of his court.[4]

Figure 1
The *Rocher* at Lunéville, view from Emmanuel Héré, *Recueil des plans, élévations, et coupes tant géometrales qu'en perspective des châteaux, jardins, et dépendances que le Roy de Pologne occupe en Lorraine, … Le tout dirigé et dedié à Sa Majesté par M Héré etc.* (Engraved by J C François), Paris, 1750-1753. ©Inventaire Général Nancy

Figure 2
The painting of Lunéville originally in the Einville gallery and until recently at the Musée du Château, Lunéville. ©Inventaire Général Nancy

Stanislaw's court and activities need to be understood as a kind of testing ground within which he pursued an agenda that not only explored courtly life, but also formed a vivid counterpart to the deliberations of the academies. His court tends to be portrayed as more carnival than academy. This is because it adopted the character of the developing *salon* culture in which leisure activities were not at odds with intellectual pursuits. Stanislaw hosted and corresponded with many of the key thinkers of the eighteenth century such as Voltaire, Mme du Châtelet and Rousseau, and there is no doubt of the seriousness of his involvement in both contemporary debates and the well-being of the Duchy. At the same time, in his own body of work, he explored a range of representational strategies: these included prolific writings which traversed utopian fable, political tract and instruction on agricultural economy.[5] His original and somewhat capricious material creations ranged from the invention of the *baba au rhum* – a rum-soaked pastry – to *faux-marbre* paintings on glass and a three-wheeled chariot or *calêche*. Stanislaw's various interests were described at the time by the Duc de Luynes as "recherches curieuses" and have since often been regarded as symptomatic of the games and amusements of a dissolute court.[6]

Similarly, Stanislaw's embellishments of the châteaux gardens – which included the earliest *kiosque* structures in Europe, as well as elaborate waterworks and open-air theatres – tend to be seen as a peripheral exercise when compared to the urban projects for Nancy that were carried out in the last

Figure 3
*Carte
Topographique
du Château Royal
de Lunéville et
des Bosquets,* by
Joly, July 1767.
©Inventaire
Général Nancy

15 years of his reign. The ambitious series of urban interventions in Nancy were considered exemplary even in their own time, and portrayed as a realisation of Stanislaw's utopia.[7] In fact, the enigmatic and ephemeral architecture of the various châteaux gardens took on its own significance within Stanislaw's enterprise in exile, in which governing, writing, and play-acting were all part of the landscape of, and for, the architecture. Consequently, the connections between kingship, utopia, and theatre were attended to with particular ingenuity in Stanislaw's gardens: here his initial efforts to exploit the new Enlightenment conditions to create an exemplary 'kingdom' resulted in a domain that was part theatre and part experiment.

The *Rocher* grotto, an automated village, created between 1742 and 1744 at the château of Lunéville, was the central artefact of this episode. It hosted a collection of 86 life-size automata of people and animals in an artificial landscape moved by clockwork and hydraulic mechanisms. Emmanuel Héré, Stanislaw's architect, included an engraving of the *Rocher* in his *Recueil* which was presented to Louis XV in 1753 and distributed throughout Europe.[8] (figure 1) The *Rocher* itself no longer exists and is known only from Héré's engraving, from two paintings, and from a few descriptions by visitors to Stanislaw's court.[9] The *Rocher* eludes classification and has, more generally, posed a problem for interpretation, not only because it has not survived, but also because of the notable absence of explanatory drawings and writings on its mechanisms and meaning. Most importantly, we lack any direct testimony from Stanislaw. Yet it remains as an extraordinary record of a singular Enlightenment enterprise, displaying in one arena the ambiguous exchange between illusionism and technology, between fantasy and system, prevalent in this transitional period.

In Héré's engraving the Rocher appears as a compendium of village life, which suggests an encyclopaedic viewpoint. This is symptomatic of more general developments within European culture: in particular the new classifying impulse commonly associated with, and exemplified by, Diderot and d'Alembert's *Encyclopédie*.[10] The distinguishing characteristic of the *Rocher* in this respect, however, may be grasped by comparing Héré's engraving to the series of plates describing *Ouvriers,* familiar from the *Encyclopédie*. It is evident that the representation of the *Rocher* is primarily concerned with the *mise-en-scène* of the action (*praxis*), as if life's activities gained clarity through being seen as theatre. A long caption appended to the engraving reads as stage directions, giving brief details of each individual automaton's movements. Héré's engraving clearly does not display the over-riding interest in the details of technique and equipment common to the encyclopedists.[11]

The *Rocher*'s miniature kingdom of loyal subjects is aligned in the engraving with the apartments of the king in the château. Indeed the *Rocher* may be readily compared with Stanislaw's visions of an ideal realm as demonstrated in his political treatise *La Voix Libre* and also in his utopian writings, *Entretien*.[12] The connections between the construction of automata and of an idealised social order in the Enlightenment period substantiate such an interpretation.[13] However, it is important to recognise Stanislaw's efforts in the gardens at Lunéville as not merely an illustration of a social or political programme of 'beneficence', most visible in his writings, nor simply the laconic background to events narrated or played out in history. Stanislaw's capacity for metaphoric thinking shown in his various writings requires that the *Rocher* be understood in the context of the whole of his enterprise – governing, writing, playacting, creating. Moreover, if his enterprise is understood as a type of compendium, it is of the various spheres of representation which Enlightenment culture will find necessary or appropriate to engage with in order to deliver a plausible reality.

On voudrait rendre la vérité fabuleuse comme on se sert de la fable pour exprimer la vérité.[14]

As Stanislaw's own aphorism suggests, an engagement with the worlds of fiction and fable provides a way of accessing truth. It is as if 'doing more good' needed fiction to bolster the enterprise. The fictional contingency of eighteenth century intellectual endeavours is the most prescient way of understanding the complex representational world of Stanislaw's creations.[15] His efforts combined the experimental with the theatrical, and were prone, like the popular science demonstrations of the eighteenth century, to labels of charlatanism and affectation. Stanislaw is known to have experimented with collage and painting techniques, contrived illuminations and tricks of light for garden entertainments and devised mechanical contraptions such as a chariot, gondola and plough. His library held books on all kinds of marvellous inventions and artifice including developments in hydraulics, automata, perspective and optics. It is pertinent that contemporary techniques were treated not only as tools for the advancement of artistic and scientific knowledge but also as devices whose potential to manipulate and distort reality was equated with fantasy and artificial magic.

The *Rocher* presents a multiplication of the nuances of the fact/fiction problem encountered in the painting, theatre and game-playing of the period.[16] Just as fiction was needed to ground what otherwise appeared capricious, uncertain and irrational, it could also fix the limits of the utopian and the hypothetical. The *Rocher* comprises the setting for an elaborate experiment such that, to borrow Baltrušaitis' phrase, "science unfolds in a fairy tale atmosphere".[17] What seems to be at stake in the *Rocher* is the possibility that the fabulous *be* actual.

Inspection of the *Rocher* frequently marked both the beginning and the culmination of an instructive/entertaining journey around the gardens for Stanislaw's courtiers and visitors. The curiously unfolding *tableau* of scenes from village life followed an ambulatory around one cross arm of the newly created canal of the *Bas Bosquets*. On the opposite bank of the canal, Stanislaw had another village built on an island, *L'Île Belle*, called the *Chartreuses* after the monastic model. This was a group of cottages inhabited by 'real villagers' chosen from among his courtiers during *la Belle Saison*. The two ideal villages or miniature kingdoms, the *Rocher* and the *Chartreuses,* delineate an experimental territory in the garden, which was the setting not only for elaborate theatrical events, game-playing and promenades, but also for intellectual discourse and an exploration of courtly life. (figures 2-3)

The idea for the *Rocher* is attributed to Stanislaw. Héré and François Richard, the clockmaker, were responsible for its realisation.[18] It is as if Stanislaw had asked Richard to take one of his intricate clockwork *tableaux* and magnify it to lifelike proportions. The scale of this ambition surpassed any hydraulic garden grotto, musical clock or mechanical toy that had been created in the past, but involved techniques and motifs inherited from all of them.[19] Automata, caught (after Descartes) between philosophy, experiment, and courtly theatre, occupied the precise territory that fascinated Stanislaw: and indeed, the *Rocher's* automated village exemplified the eighteenth century attempt to bring nature, technology and society to a single horizon of understanding. Its mechanical marvels deftly displayed the contemporary conflict between fact and fiction, science and magic, flitting between the parallel worlds of the *foire,* salon and court.

The *Rocher* was composed of 86 life-size figures, birds and animals arranged in a series of rural vignettes within a carefully constructed landscape of sandstone, minerals and stalactites from Mont

Vosges, and vegetation collected from the surrounding area. The figures were made of wood and cloth and their heads were modelled after the inhabitants of Lunéville. Descartes' suggestion that men might masquerade as automatic machines was brought uncannily and literally to life.[20] The importance of such detail in juxtaposition with physiognomy, pattern, and collection recalls the conventions of travel writing, early anthropology, and botany, as well as the curiosity cabinet or *Wunderkammer*. The *Rocher*'s artificial landscape harboured not only a microcosm of Lorraine, but presented a microcosm of Nature itself. It elicited a distortion of values, a neutralisation of time and scale: it was simultaneously a miniature village and a giant clock. As such, it is indicative of the power afforded instrumental reason over time and history; that is, the belief in the capacity to conceive and construct a 'model' village aligned with a clockwork universe. The virtuous rural labour, natural sites and implements of the *Rocher* recall the providential and proportional distribution of talents of Leibniz' *théâtre de la vie humaine*, and equally Bacon's promotion of human industry.[21] In presenting artisans, artificers and labourers as the mainstay of humanity, "ordinary life" is exalted.[22] In these conceptions the formerly 'lower' professions not only contributed to science but also held the key to scientific demonstration. (figures 4-6)

Among the automated scenes were a shepherd playing his bagpipes, a peasant carving a piece of wood, a boy pushing a swing, a cat preparing to pounce on a rat that bared its teeth, men working at a forge, and above them a solitary violin player. It included figures smoking pipes, drinking and singing in a tavern, women making butter and washing linen, a monkey being taunted by a small boy with an apple on a pole and a hermit praying in his cavernous cell. The *Rocher* was unique, in not merely imitating the activities of the villagers, but simulating sounds, smells and textures in a *tour de force* of artificial effects. The relation of the senses was often described in paintings with rural themes in this period; however, the *Rocher tableau* offered an immediate experience. When set in motion the cries of animals, human voices, and automated instrumentals mingled with the thunder of cannon and the lightning of pyrotechnics during spectacles on the canal. The artificially disjunctive motions and fragmented gesticulations of the self-propelling automata found their counterpart in the movement of tools, farm implements, the cycle of water, and the turning of wheels. The *Rocher* landscape acted as a working diagram of the whole enterprise of irrigating, planting and preparing the land of not only the *Bas Bosquets*, but King Stanislaw's greater undertaking in his contrived garden of Lorraine. The material transmutations and illusionism of the Rocher and its corresponding ambiguities are thus set against the controlled transformations of a real landscape and society.

Qu'il est triste que le bonheur humain ne se rencontre qu'en des pays inconnus, et qui nous sont inaccessibles![23]

Stanislaw's writings on utopia and politics are imbued with a concern for securing the happiness, or *bonheur* of his subjects, leading from more philosophical musings on peace to projects for agricultural economy that have the flavour of a nascent physiocracy. Stanislaw's association of *bonheur* with the emerging ethic of 'ordinary life' presents happiness as an attribute of a benign realm, indeed an agricultural paradise, in which the *bienfaisance* of each toiling individual is reciprocated by the *bienfaits* or gifts of nature. Stanislaw's advocation of husbandry in his writings is re-presented as a quasi-symbolic motif throughout the Lunéville château garden, summarised in the setting of the *Rocher* and re-enacted in the greater landscape of Lorraine. His utopian novel, the *Entretien*, complements both the *Chartreuses* and the *Rocher* as a demonstration of an idyllic and natural collective culture presided over by a *bienfaisant* king. Indeed, with the *Rocher* acting

Figures 4-6
Details of the
Rocher from
Héré's *Recueil*,
1751
©Inventaire
Général Nancy

as the backdrop, the *Chartreuses* cottages lined up along the canal provided the setting for a theatrical exploration of utopia set against the highly cultivated court culture.

Stanislaw chose the 'tenants' of the *Chartreuses* from among his favourite guests and courtiers. They were supposed to tend their gardens, and, at short notice, occasionally play host to the king so that he could sample dishes prepared from the produce they had grown. This theatrical game involved several inversions, including the king as guest of an actual guest, the guest as a forced resident of an ornamental pocket utopia, and the courtier as a gardener serving food. It indicates also a quasi-ritualistic attitude to the land wherein the passage of the day was marked by the transformation of the *chartreux'* labours into a simple repast. One can well imagine the inhabitants of this new dispensation uttering Abbé St Pierre's much used phrase, "Paradis aux bienfaisants!"[24]

The nostalgic desire to present the lower classes, peasant life, or the cultural other within an arrested time and incontaminable miniature form – of the *tableau*, the collection, or the utopia – is symptomatic of the desire to manipulate reality. The anthropological model approximates clockwork, and the past and present meshed is the time of both the pastoral and the utopia. Like the *Rocher*, the *Entretien* approximates both instruction manual and story. The need to situate the social engineering of the utopia within a narrative structure inevitably produces several levels of representational ambiguity.[23] The *Entretien* displays the contemporary confusion between narrative and conceptual understanding: it is presumably the same 'reason' which is engaged both in working out a programme of benign efficiency and indulging in the ludic and dramatic possibilities of a story or a play.

The dominant characteristic of the *Rocher,* however, is its presentation of several modalities of *theatrum mundi*, wherein life's activities are explored through their involvement in theatre. The theatre of the eighteenth century provided a setting for the progressive blurring of the paradigm, the model, the hypothesis, and the scientific or educational demonstration.[24] And it was often automata that were the celebrated actors of the linked stages of court, *foire* and scientific demonstration, dominating the *cabinets de physique* as well as the *salles d'expositions*. The crossovers between their performances are illustrated by the well-known example of Vaucanson's migrating fluteplayer, drummer and duck.

Le monde présente sans cesse de nouveaux spectacles, où les mêmes acteurs ne jouent pas toujours les mêmes rôles.[27]

This remark by Stanislaw points to the continuity between ludic theatre, the possible reality of the utopia and the psychological experiment. Indeed, Locke's thought experiments such as the account of the prince waking up in the body of a cobbler, bear striking resemblance to both the scenarios of the *Chartreuses* and those re-performed by automata in the *Rocher*.[28] Role-playing at the level of mental activity can also be compared to the *commedia dell'arte* or the *Théâtre de la Foire* performances. In *foire* productions the characters were often deliberately confused with 'unsuitable' characters, for example *Arlequin* playing the hero of traditional French drama. Another ruse was the replacement of the real actors with canvas and wood marionettes, or *comediens du bois,* if the authorities, who championed the *comediens du roi,* introduced restrictions on the *foire* performers.[29] Such reversals and role-playing dominated eighteenth century deliberations on the place of the individual in society as is shown in the attention given to the status of the actor in the writings of Diderot and Rousseau.[30] The theatre of the eighteenth century provided not only a target for ridicule and satire but was also a vehicle for speculation regarding alternative social orders.

The popular theme of the inverted or upside-down world is a useful case for understanding the nuances of this ambiguous domain and the confluence of psychological experiment, stagecraft and perspectivity. The plot of *le monde renversé*, derives from the carnivalesque tradition of turning the world, with its preconceptions and expectations, literally upside down. A *monde renversé,* furthermore, alludes to a speculation on the speculative order, mimicking the structure of experimental thought.[31] The *Rocher*, as a type of *monde renversé* needs to be understood as both an experiment, a setting *for* experiment, and an exploration *of* experiment.

The court at Lunéville was often described as an enchanted realm, or fairyland, acting as a refuge not only for Stanislaw, but also for *philosophes*, scientists, and artists escaping problems with censors and critics. Simultaneously, it carried with it a critique of the court etiquette of Versailles, the prevailing context or *monde*, suggestive of a movement towards not only fiction but more significantly the *monde renversé* and an importation in the manner of the *foire* performances. The role-playing most evident in the *Chartreuses* with its comic protocol, was endemic to the life of the court at Lunéville. If Stanislaw's court can better be understood as a species of *Versailles renversé,* and consequently a fictional counterpart to Versailles, this blurs its distinction from contemporary fictions which took on this role, such as Voltaire's *Zadig*. The possible and fabulous is thus *made* actual.

In the *Rocher*, the tradition of the theatre-grotto is transformed into a curious fusion of satyric and comic stage sets, placed against the 'tragic' vision of the Lunéville château and town. This *theatre renversé* exhibits a series of inversions beginning with that of an ideal world set in the *Bas Bosquets* at the foot of the château. The massive foundations of the château are replaced by a hollow tableau of *papier-maché*, wood and carefully contrived boulders, apparently in danger of collapsing. Moving from left to right the peasants and artisans are followed by the depiction of 'real' nobility in the loggia, and finally by a hermit, thus conveniently situating all three estates in reverse order. The grotto and the inevitable presence of water evoke the traditional garden themes of renewal, regeneration and metamorphosis, with the Muses as animations of the landscape. However, rather than a classical rendering of this material taken from Ovid's *Metamorphoses,* within a setting that adequately refigures the mountainous sanctuary of the Muses, the scene approximates that of a *foire* transformation. The dawning of a new age becomes more like the repopulation of the earth after the flood in *Arlequin-Deucalion*, enacted by Arlequin throwing down rocks and stones which grow into people.[32] And just as it is presented in the *Rocher*, the order of people in this *foire* performance inverts that of the traditional hierarchy such that the peasant is now the first of the progeny, then the artisan, and the nobleman, followed only by the priest. The real inhabitants of Lunéville – as their simulacra, the *comediens du bois* – are disguised and simultaneously exalted as peasants. Ultimately the gardens of Lunéville as a whole are exhibited as a version of the *théatre renversé* with the actual cultivation of the surrounding landscape, 'off-stage', now providing part of the scenery. The ingenious demiurgic production inevitably has as its correlate the mechanical improvement of the landscape and society.

Souvent une chaumière est un abri plus sûr contre les orages de la fortune que le plus brillant palais.[33]

This aphorism of Stanislaw recalls the scene-making familiar from both Rousseau – whose oak tree provides the shelter for happy peasants in *The Social Contract* – and Fénelon whose 'happy swains' convey a rural paradise in the *Télémaque*.[34] The *Rocher* presents a self-invoking fiction at several levels. The representation of artisanal labour is itself constructed by artisans under an architect-king's supervision and is mirrored in the *Chartreuses* opposite. It approximates a species of self-narration, whereby the *Rocher* can be contemplated as a version of the king's own experiences of passing in disguise between social roles, described in his account of escape to exile from Poland, the *Départ de Dantzick*. Alternatively, given Stanislaw's predilection for an entertaining and demonstrative education informed by the writings of Fénelon and Locke, the *Rocher* can be read as presenting an extreme manifestation of the set pieces that Stanislaw advocated in his programme for the education of the French royal princes, his grandchildren.[35] Stanislaw was inspired by the account of the staged rural scenes that Fénelon, as tutor, had fabricated for the Duke of Burgundy's education. This was also a precedent for Rousseau's episode of Emile's schooling in the artisan's workshop. Like the utopia of the *Entretien*, both the *Chartreuses* and the *Rocher* have the character of demonstrations in a fictional landscape. With their didactic pretensions, they are difficult to distinguish from either the domain of the experiment, the working diagram or Fénelon's entertaining theatrical procedures for the instruction of youth.

The *Rocher*'s miscellaneous spectacle and unpredictable connections shuffle within a single landscape semblances of the *foire*, carnival, Vaucanson's *salle d'exposition*, the amateur collector's cabinet, artisan's workshop, Nollet's laboratory and Fénelon's cottages. The syncretic and consuming landscape maintains an ambiguous existence between entertainment, spectacle, dramatic performance and practical instruction. Above all, the hydraulically operated village indicates a desire to animate and not simply to know. In the eighteenth century animation occupied a spectrum which ranged from inherited Aristotelian notions of the soul, *anima,* in movement, through mechanics, 'the clockwork universe', to the debate on the passions. The Enlightenment justification of the passions acknowledged that a state of pure reason could result in the undesirable 'motionlessness' of human beings. The successive scenes of village life could be set in motion whenever desired. The creation of fictions, a concern with the synthesis of knowledge and subsequently the bringing to life of the whole enterprise, so that everything could be experienced simultaneously, was presented within a synaesthetic version of 'the world as theatre'.

Lunéville could be compared at the time to a "painted and corrupt Vauxhall" and the *Rocher* was received with both admiration and contempt by contemporary visitors.[36] One visitor described the *Rocher* as "one of the most flagrant perversions of taste" which degraded the "real pastoral objects and rustick images" much in evidence in Lorraine with its "wooden cows and canvas milkmaids".[37] The garden structures built for Stanislaw at Lunéville did indeed display an irreverent and playful use of materials, borrowing techniques associated with the theatre and pleasure grounds (the painted scenery of the *Cascade* at the other end of the canal, for example, or the *trompe l'oeil* brickwork of the *Chartreuses* cottages). In keeping with a theatrical tendency (and indeed the *monde renversé*) the scale, choice of material and mechanisms of the *Rocher* would, however, have been intentional. The durability and artifice of these creations was appropriate to the tradition of garden ephemera and the related notions of mistake and contrivance – the halfway world between creative illusion and fictional error which Stanislaw cultivated throughout his enterprise.

The most telling aspect therefore of the *Rocher* landscape is its provisional quality and ephemeral character – as if it had become nervous about its own existence. It seems that the only way to be credible in the new Enlightenment context was by displaying irony or wit, with an element of undermining that testified to one's self-awareness. The *Rocher* was intentionally created as if on the verge of collapse; its fountains and grottos in a state of dissimulation, a stability that depended on *papier-maché,* canvas and make-believe. The makeshift constructions of Stanislaw's châteaux gardens seem to have deliberately exhibited the fact/fiction ambivalence prevalent in the literature and theatrical *renversements* of the period. Stanislaw's investigations into the world of artifice and experiment, theatrical illusion, and utopia cannot be dissociated from the hazy materiality of his built ephemera. These were conceived as an intensely artificial structuring of the world – and as such an appropriate setting for the games, entertainments, role-playing and *divertissements* of his court.

A peculiar combination of dramatic and systematic structures is revealed in the *Rocher's* agitated landscape, veering between stage set and utopia. The artificial landscape of the *Rocher* oscillates between the illusionism of the Baroque, and the relativity and delusions of an Enlightenment *micromegas*. Under the new Enlightenment conditions, history, technology, and scale are manipulated as material for autonomous and demonstrable creation. The *Rocher* represents the high-point of the culture, an experiment both future-oriented in the manner of a demonstration, and self-critical in the manner of a self-directed satire. The seductive and playful world of the *Rocher* reveals an elaborate representational structure capable of fusing speculative science, play, quasi-myth, and fiction. Its unstable mixture of fantasy and actual experience attempts to capture the elusive quality of not only a real landscape but a real world with all that concerned, baffled, intrigued and unsettled the Enlightenment. In this experiment, the simple farm and watch technology is put at the disposal of an 'automatic' setting. The power of the automata in this setting then resides in the paradoxical notion of the mechanical soul and not in its achievement of a convincing simulation. The use of automata and the ensuing tension between mind and matter, automation and handwork, conception and technique, confers an uncertain existence on material things. It reverses the status of human and machine, ultimately rendering the maker obsolete. This strange and powerful moment resides in the mode of embodiment. The *Rocher* provokes the question as to whether its designer discovered a way of advancing a cultural paradigm, or simply encapsulated the range of subterfuges and stratagems necessary to promote the dream of one's own making as a *roi-bienfaisant*. The theatrical and experimental landscape so much in evidence at Lunéville eventually becomes a generality with the emphasis being placed on the structure of seeing, like the role of epistemology in believing/historical veracity. The *Rocher* anticipates this phenomenon in its effort to correlate scientific and traditional meanings into a single representation that heralds the isolation of a spectacle. In its conception and making however, its distinction resides in the continued blurring of the possible and the actual. The *Rocher's verité fabuleuse* maintains the creative tension between speculative and dramatic possibilities in an artificial landscape.

1   Voltaire, François Marie Arouet de, *Candide, ou l'Optimisme* (1757), René Pomeau ed., *Les Oeuvres Completes de Voltaire*, V 48, Oxford: The Voltaire Foundation, Taylor Institute, 1980, pp. 240-241. "I, too, am King of Poland. I lost my kingdom twice, but Providence gave me another realm, in which I have done more good than all the kings of the Sarmatians were ever able to do on the banks of the Vistula. I also submit to Providence and have come to Venice for the carnival." Voltaire, François Marie Arouet de, *Candide, or Optimism*, Butt, John, trans., West Drayton: Penguin 1947, p. 127.

2   "A King, who ruled there some time ago, and who shows us in a province of France what he would have done in a Kingdom." Diderot, Denis and d'Alembert, "Pologne", *Encyclopédie; ou Dictionnaire raisonne des sciences, des arts et des métiers*, Paris: Briasson 1761-1772, p. 931 [my translation].

3   Stanislaw's embellishments of the ducal estates of Lunéville, Einville, Jolivet, Commercy and Malgrange are detailed in Pierre Boyé, *Les Châteaux du Roi Stanislas en Lorraine*, Réimpression de l'éditon de Paris-Nancy, 1910, Marseille: Lafitte Reprints 1980.

4   The subject of this paper is drawn from my PhD thesis (University of Cambridge:1998) which explored the connections between Stanislaw's writings and his architecture in Lorraine: "*in spem melioris aevi*, The Architecture and Writings of Stanislaw Leszczynski, roi

bienfaisant, 1737-1766".

5   These writings were published collectively towards the end of his life in 1763 as *Oeuvres du Philosophe Bienfaisant*. Stanislaw was one of the patrons of the first volumes of the *Encyclopédie*, but later withdrew his support. He also published his own compendium of inventions the *Nouvelles Découvertes pour l'Avantage et l'Utilité du Public*, Nancy: Haener (n.d.).

6   "curious investigations": Luynes, Duc de, *Mémoires sur la Cour de Louis XV (1735-1738)*, Dussieux, L and Soulié E eds., Paris: Firmin-Didot 1860-1865, 17 vols.; Octobre 1751, Paris, Luynes, XI, p. 249, my translation. For contemporary reports on Stanislaw's court in Lorraine see, Luynes, *Mémoires,*. More recent works include: Boyé, Pierre, *La Cour de Lunéville en 1748 et 1749 ou Voltaire chez le Roi Stanislas*, Nancy: Crépin-Leblond, 1891; Maugras, Gaston, *Dernière Annèes de la Cour de Lunéville*, Paris: Plon, 1906, and *La Cour de Lunéville au XVIII Siècle*, Paris: Plon, 1904; and Cabourdin, Guy, *Quand Stanislas Régnait en Lorraine*, Paris: Librairie Artheme Fayard, 1980.

7   In 1755 the second edition of Leszczynski's utopian novel included two reviews which explicitly made the connection with the urban projects, one of them saying: "... all of this is being realised not in Dumocala, but in Lorraine, following the order, and under the direction of a great king." *Entretien d'un Européen avec un Insulaire du Royaume de Dumocala*

[1755], Versini, Laurent, ed., Nancy: Presses Universitaires de Nancy, 1981, p. 147.

8 Héré, Emmanuel, *Recueil des Plans, Elévations, et Coupes tant Géometrales qu'en Perspective des Châteaux, Jardins, et Dépendances que le Roy de Pologne Occupe en Lorraine… Le Tout Dirigé et Dedié à Sa Majesté par M Héré etc.*, [engraved by J C François], Paris: J C François, 1750-1753.

9 A painting of the Rocher by Joly may be seen in the Musée Historique Lorrain, Nancy. The painted panel of the gardens at Lunéville (figure 2) which originally formed part of a series in the Einville Gallery, no longer exists as it was destroyed in a recent fire at the Musée du Château, Lunéville on 2nd January 2003. Apart from the duc de Luynes, *Mémoires*, contemporary sources for description of the Rocher include the writings of visitors such as Delespine, Billardon de Sauvigny, Fillion de Charigneu and Dom Calmet.

10 Foucault, Michel, *The Order of Things: an Archaeology of the Human Sciences*, London and New York: Tavistock Publications, 1986.

11 On the engravings in the *Encyclopédie* see Sewell, William H, "Visions of Labor: Illustrations of the Mechanical Arts Before, In, and After Diderot's *Encyclopédie*", *Work in France, Representations, Meaning, Organization, and Practice*, Kaplan, Stephen Lawrence, and Koepp, Cynthia J eds., Ithaca: Cornell University Press, 1986.

12 Ostrowski, Jan, "Rocher, Teatr Automatow Stanislawa Leszczynskiego w Lunéville", *Pamietnik Teatralny*, XXI, 1972, pp. 309-315; and Middleton, Robin, "Boullée and the Exotic", *AA Files*, 19, 1990.

13 Schaffer, Simon, "Enlightened Automata", *The Sciences in Enlightened Europe*, Clark,William, Golinski, Jan and Schaffer, Simon, eds., Chicago, London: University of Chicago Press, 1999, pp. 126-165.

14 "One would like to make truth fabulous, just as one uses fable to express truth." Stanislaw Leszczynski, "Réflexions sur divers sujets de morale", *Stanislas Leszczynski, Duc de Lorraine et de Bar, Inédits, Plans de Paix, Réformes Politiques, Economie et Société, Réforme de l'Eglise Affaires de Lorraine, Oeuvres Morales*, Taveneaux, René, and Versini, Laurent, eds., Nancy: Presses Universitaires de Nancy, 1984, p. 321 [my translation].

15 Referring to the eighteenth century and the blurring of styles of narration, Koselleck speaks of a "compulsion to use fictional narrative to render available a reality whose actuality has vanished". Koselleck, Reinhart, *Futures Past: on the Semantics of Historical Time*, Cambridge, MA and London: MIT Press 1985, p. 217.

16 On this problem see Hobson, Marian, *The Object of Art: the Theory of Illusion in Eighteenth Century France*, Cambridge: Cambridge University Press, 1982.

17 Baltrušaitis, Jurgis, *Anamorphic Art*, Strachan, W J, trans., New York: Abrams, 1977, p. 39.

18 Boyé, Pierre, *Les Châteaux du Roi Stanislas en Lorraine* [Paris-Nancy 1910], Marseille: Lafitte Reprints 1980, pp. 29-30.

19 On the history of automata see Chapuis, Alfred and Droz, Edmond, *Les Automates: Figures Artificielles d'Hommes et d'Animaux*, Neuchâtel: Griffon, 1966; also Beaune, Jean-Claude, "Classical Age of Automata: an Impressionistic Survey from the Sixteenth to the Nineteenth Century", *Fragments for a History of the Human Body: Part One*, Feher, M, et al, eds., New York: Zone, 1989, pp. 431-480.

20 Descartes, R, "Second Meditation", *The Philosphical Writings of Descartes*, Cottingham, John, trans., Cambridge: Cambridge University Press, 1984, vol. 2, p. 21.

21 Manuel, Frank E and Fritzie, P, *Utopian Thought in the Western World*, Oxford: Blackwell, 1979.

22 Taylor, Charles, *Sources of the Self: the Making of the Modern Identity*, Cambridge: Cambridge University Press, 1992, p. 240.

23 "How sad it is that human happiness can only be found in unknown countries, which are inaccessible to us." From the "Avertissement" to the *Entretien*, Versini, L, ed., p. 1 [my translation].

24 Keohane, Nannerl O, *Philosophy and the State in France: the Renaissance to the Enlightenment*, Princeton: Princeton University Press, 1980, p. 365.

25 A good bibliography and summary of the profuse utopian literature of the eighteenth century is given in Choay, Françoise, *The Rule and the Model: on the Theory of Architecture and Urbanism*, Cambridge, Mass. and London: MIT Press, 1997.

26 See for example Stafford, Barbara Maria, *Artful Science, Enlightenment Entertainment and the Eclipse of Visual Education*, Cambridge, MA and London: MIT Press, 1994.

27 "The world continuously presents us with new spectacles where the same actors do not always play the same roles": Stanislaw Leszczynski, "Penseés Diverses", *Oeuvres Choisies De Stanislas, Roi de Pologne, Duc de Lorraine, de Bar, etc.*, St Ouën, Mme. De, ed., Paris: Carez, 1825, p. 344 [my translation].

28 On Locke's "disembodied self" and his thought experiments see Taylor, *Sources of the Self*, p. 172; also Ricoeur, Paul, *Oneself as Another*, Blamey, Kathleen, trans., Chicago and London: The University of Chicago Press, 1992, p. 126.

29 On French theatre and *foire* productions see Rex, Walter E, *The Attraction of the Contrary: Essays on the Literature of the French Enlightenment*, Cambridge: Cambridge University Press, 1987.

30 See Sennett, Richard, *The Fall of Public Man*, London: Faber and Faber Ltd., 1986, pp. 110-122.

31 "a kind of 'upside-down world' to borrow Hegel's famous expression": Taylor, Charles, "Preface", *Philosophical Arguments*, Cambridge, MA: Harvard University Press, 1995, p. viii.

32 On this performance see: Rex, *The Attraction of the Contrary*, pp. 64-66.

33 "Often a humble cottage provides more certain shelter against the storms of fortune than the most brilliant palace": Leszczynski, "Penseés Diverses", *Oeuvres Choisies*, p. 376 [my translation].

34 Fénelon, François de Salignac de la Mothe, *Telemachus, son of Ulysses* [1699], Riley, Patrick, trans. and ed., Cambridge: Cambridge University Press, 1994, pp. 23-25.

35 Leszczynski, "Réponse de Stanislas au Dauphin contenant un Plan d'Education pour les Jeunes Princes", *Oeuvres Choisies*, pp. 213-240.

36 Wiebenson, Dora, *The Picturesque Garden in France*, Princeton: Princeton University Press, 1978, p. 12.

37 Stuart, James, *Critical Observations on the buildings and improvements of London* London: J. Dodsley 1771, pp. 11-12.

Landscape: a Discussion of Certain Scopic Regimes in Theatre
Ewa Kębłowska-Ławniczak

The notion that landscape provides grounding for a considerable amount of poetry and novels, rather than for drama and theatre, is recognised with few reservations even if it is hard to establish a distinct mode of criticism within this perspective. However, literary texts – whether novels or not – are never simply 'grounded' in a specific landscape that is already there. Landscape as a mental-cultural arrangement, as opposed to simply a material artefact, is actualised in processes of writing and reading and, in this light, the once sociologically definable and certain concept of 'being rooted' or 'being uprooted' requires reconsideration. For example, Arnold Wesker's idea of "being uprooted" assumes the tangibility of an 'out there' whose anchoring function for a long time remained unquestionable to both authors and critics.[1] In contrast to this, the notion of landscape constituted in the process of writing and reading presupposes a permanent undecidability consisting in a fragile equilibrium of imposing and revealing. Additionally, the present problematisation of maps and photographs as media rendering the real landscape prior to the 'fictional' necessitates a consideration of the discourses that purport to mediate between the actual and the literary. As a result, doubts arise as to the very possibility of any extratextual 'it'.

A case in point is Tom Stoppard's *Arcadia,* which excels in creating a landscape collage by juxtaposing fragments from various garden studies the author consulted in the course of his research. These dispersed descriptions, in turn, convey diverse ideas, concepts and controversies personified by the gardens themselves. Inevitably, these references lead to further textual and visual layers, such as the Virgilian tradition, mythology, and certain paintings, as well as impressions and real or fake sketches brought from travels. Here, even undecidability itself becomes thematic the moment the question of the genius of the place is raised. While finding and uncovering buried designs is sponsored by archeological and scholarly pursuits, the architectural, mechanical and scientific endeavours attempt to impose, to give measure and decisiveness. Following the proposition of J Hillis Miller, such a landscape can become a "generative prosopopoeia" and, in my view this holds good, not only for novels and poetry but also for drama and theatre.[2] If landscape is treated as such a complex generative rhetorical figure, characters – by analogy – become also figures of some kind and borrow or arise from this linguistic construct. A landscape defined in this way is no longer subservient in relation to character; that is, it does not function as a backdrop in the process of establishing selfhood. In her discussion of Gertrude Stein's dramatic output, Elinor Fuchs perceived interesting but different advantages of introducing landscape into theatre. Accordingly she argued that Stein's landscapes consist of a "liberating democracy of 'things'" which erases the culture/nature opposition.[3] This surrealist demand to focus on and enjoy things – rather than patterns – requires a visual landscape response which comes to be fully appreciated, later, by Robert Wilson.

Theatre, in the most general terms, and theatre buildings or interiors in particular, assume definite conditions of viewing and thus promote or support specific scopic regimes often either implementing the current power relations or showing resistance to them. The seventeenth century masks and the long-standing tradition of box-theatres subjected the stage to the powerful gaze of the auditorium, often separating the two worlds by a solid obstacle such as a moat. Evening performances and the use of artificial light promoted a limited convergent focus rather than a dispersed – for example, medieval – organisation that would foreground the primacy of characters and marginalise the already conventional sets. The textually unhindered and visually unimpeded reception enables the eye and the ear to absorb the entire *mise-en-scène* at once.

Performing landscape entails a diffused landscape response. The concept seems intelligible when applied to Barrie Wexler's *Tamara* in which the consumerist visual regime totally reorganises the familiar physical staging conditions.[4] The literally mobile spectatorship is entirely dispersed and the optical stability of the Cartesian subject position non-existent. The scene, comparable to a shopping facility, becomes multi-focal. The darting, diffuse and heterogeneous gaze is fragmented by being allocated to the individual consumers whose aleatory discoveries lead them from one 'department' to another and, additionally, encourage them to keep an eye on fellow-buyers. The distance/difference between stage and audience is collapsed and neither the eye nor the ear is able to embrace the landscape-like *mise-en-scène*. Unlike Stein's landscapes, however, Wexler's commercial enterprises prevent any instantaneous absorption, any perception 'at one go'. It is with this condition that Stoppard's *Arcadia* could be associated. Although the productions of *Arcadia* do not encourage physical mobility on the part of the audience, the play does engender the new, diffused, scopic regime. This paper interrogates the ways in which Stoppard's play might be said to provoke 'landscape viewing' and it raises the question of what this particular mode of viewing consists.

The very title of Tom Stoppard's play refers the spectator to the ancient landscape of Arcadia with all of its potential ambiguities (which span the poles of the hostile woodland in Greece – where Pan seduces nymphs with the music of his flute – and the elegance of mannerist and Renaissance shepherds who pursue love and poetry contests in a sophisticated courtly atmosphere). What the whole spectrum shares is nostalgia and a sense of loss and thus a dominant tendency to look backwards, and this is quite explicitly evoked in the opening scene of Stoppard's play: "Britons live on milk and meat."[5] Now the stability of the Arcadian and pastoral life and landscape is obviously gone and the images of certainty give way to change.

The secondary text informs the reader that the play opens with the view of "a room on the garden front of a... large country house in Derbyshire in April 1809".[6] Architectural details do not betray its style and thus cunningly hide the visual implications. Several doors and French windows are enumerated in *didascalia* but, apparently, they refuse to provide any clear access to the garden. The park is supposed to be the "typical English park of the time" and the only open window registers "a bright but sunless morning".[7] Although characters leave through the French window and enter from the garden, ostentatiously cleaning their muddy shoes (perhaps to confirm the physical existence of the off-stage landscape) the actual view remains obscured by carefully staged obstacles: "I bet she's in the hermitage, can't see from here with the marquée...."[8]

Stoppard evidently takes advantage of poetic licence but he also sets traps to tease the audience. More diligent investigations show that *Arcadia's* country house – whose mistress, Lady Croom, appears to be the mother of Thomasina – is less likely to be in Derbyshire than it is to be (Croome Court) in Worcestershire.[9] The historical Croome Court experienced changes similar to those we find in Stoppard's play. Painted by Richard Wilson (1714-1764) in 1758, the house still shows a 'Brownian landscape' although, as in the play-text, it was not designed by Lancelot Capability Brown himself. Moreover, the same Richard Wilson was involved in the re-painting of Brocket Hall, another marker emerging from Stoppard's landscape in connection with Caroline Lamb's garden investigated, here, by Hannah Jarvis.[10] It points to the existence, around 1740, of an earlier formal Italian garden later re-designed according to the subsequent fashions.[11] Whether the playwright's landscape really follows the change experienced by any of the historically existing residences, or is a palimpsest of sources derived from several locations, is archaeologically interesting but, ultimately, of lesser importance: the emerging pattern remains the same.

The new designs, replacing the former Italian garden, undermine the commonplace seventeenth century association of knowledge with vision. The unity of the seeing eye and the seeing intellect, questioned earlier by Descartes, undergoes a final split. And thus the spectator enters a room whose eyes/windows are already blind and even the single, opened French window is metaphorically obscured. Chloe's assuring "I bet" is dissociated from "I see". Moreover, if one considers the location of a hermitage, according to contemporary designs, the marquée becomes a poor excuse. The house does not comply with the designs favoured by politically orientated residences. Therefore the foreground for viewers disappears and so does the centrally placed window customarily overlooking the central alley or the avenue terminated in an obelisk or other 'eye-trap'. The long-ranging perspective inspected by the immobile eye is now blinded and short-sightedness becomes a privilege. By defining Croome Court or Sidley Park as a typically English park of the time, Stoppard provokes the spectator to assume this generalising long-distance perspective – just to 'watch' the audience stumble over this surprise. The relation between the house and the landscape the playwright conjures appears to follow Richard Payne Knight's suggestions from his *Inquiry*, 1805, rather than from his earlier *The Landscape*, 1794, in which he remarked that: "few persons ever look for compositions when within doors. It is in walks or rides through parks, gardens or pleasure grounds that they are allowed to and become subjects of conversation."[12] The viewers are encouraged to follow the clues provided by the library's stocks and to enter the garden. Otherwise the audience is granted the limited voyeuristic position of 'inside the house' with the view from the French window curiously obscured. Thus Chloe's inability to see the hermitage from 'here' is a more important anticipatory message than the marquée (which is just a temporarily installed obstacle that is more likely to afflict with blindness the spectators and ignorant visitors, like Bernard Nightingale).

Arcadia's landscape problematises the 'correct' place of viewing as defined in terms of the theory of linear perspective. Eighteenth century criticism, without foreknowledge of later developments in mathematics, did not, itself, question the theory of perspective.[13] Therefore disruptive statements the spectators discover in Stoppard's comedy derive partly from the palindromic walks into the twentieth century where the new physics and computer science provide markers of future change. The late eighteenth century confusion derives from aesthetic theory rather than science, even if the two appear in Stoppard's play as interrelated. Consequently, the curtained windows at Croome Court do not overly challenge the mathematical rules but their blindness prevents them from establishing the true Point of Sight of both the figures already in landscape and for the spectators who will enter it. A trope based on the Albertian scheme claims that the best plane of representation is transparent and like "a window through which the viewer looks on to the real world".[14] The result the artist/viewer attains is the framed landscape with firm boundaries that Richard Payne Knight rejects in his *Inquiry* and Stoppard in his landscape play. The disappearance of the former Point of Sight suspends the theory legislating the acts of viewing that have operated thus far, and so also the position of the viewer.

Perspective restricts the viewing subject to the proper place by defining the *authorised*, that is socially accepted, position as well as the *authorial,* which implies participation in the author's insights and authority. Both exclude private viewing. A character seated in the correct viewing point becomes the privileged – albeit limited – focaliser whom the spectators can trust or whose position they can assume themselves. Evidently, Chloe is not the privileged focaliser – the subject – and her pastoral name denotes the short-sightedness of a textual shepherdess figure placed in the already picturesque landscape. In order to see anything Chloe has to move, thus temporalising the viewing experience by walking. The requirement of taking a walk leads to truly polyvalent points of view and to a plurality of relations between the viewing subject and the object of sight, no longer supervised by the general perspectival legislature. As opposed to playful but precisely rule-governed anamorphosis, true polyvalence leads further on to a liberation and privatisation of the viewing experience. This liberation of viewing may derive from the growing impact of the variously motivated and defined concept of the 'private' on garden and architecture designs. Controlled visuality suspended, the new mode of viewing and visiting requires a guide, either in the form of the *Switzers* employed in Wörlitz, 1794, or a printed *Ambulator*.

And so the Sidley Park we enter through the dialogues of its inhabitants and employees is in the process of such changes. The architect hired by Lord Croom enters with his theodolite to take the bearings of the garden and to propose its new geometry. The identity of Mr Noakes is not clearly defined. Although he enters with Humphrey Repton's *Red Books* of *before* and *after*, for Septimus Hodge he remains "a jumped up jobbing architect who sees carnal embrace in every nook and cranny of the landskip!".[15] This seems more reminiscent of William Chambers, a pushy and ambitious architect, who claimed knowledge of the genuine Chinese style. In place of Brown's ideas, Chambers' designs sought to agitate the mind by a variety of opposing passions. The canonical division of the garden: *locus amoenus,* the *melancholy,* the *romantic* and the *ceremonial,* slides into the confusion Thomasina (followed by the audience) spells out in her closing question: "Does carnal embrace addle the brain?"[16]

The figure of the architect in Stoppard's play is highly confusing.[17] The formal garden demands geometrical optics: and a stable point of view, straight lines and powerful perspectives required what Richard Payne Knight unflatteringly called the "mind and hands of a mechanic".[18] The new landscape however admitted a poet, a philosopher and a painter who refused to see nature in terms of cones and pyramids. Stoppard's Mr Noakes wants all and in Septimus' words "He puts himself forward as a gentleman [i.e. a poet], a philosopher of the picturesque, a visionary [i.e. a God-like painter] who can move mountains and cause lakes, but in the scheme of the garden he is the serpent."[19] Noakes' slimy character doubles and triples as, during the course of the play, the audience is encouraged to associate him with the names of various architects. The serpent-like quality of Lord Croom's architect manifests itself in the destruction of the first paradise, Arcadia, the land of ancient Britons he enters in the Brown-like guise to trace the new *line of beauty*. In his book, *The Picturesque*, Christopher Hussey recounts that an anonymous "friend" of Sir Uvedale Price once referred to Capability Brown as a snail which crawls all over the ground and leaves his cursed slime wherever he goes.[20] By this he meant that roads and paths, as well as lakes and belts of planting in his designs assumed a winding shape; and this in turn displaced the paradisiacal visual centrality and divine sanction normally granted to the owner. The static long-range visuality of the former geometry was replaced by the short-sightedness of a strolling private reader of landscapes who needs a pair of glasses rather than binoculars. Even Septimus Hodge realises that "we must stir our way onward mixing as we go, disorder out of disorder...".[21] Taking a walk becomes indispensable.

The new protocols of seeing – that is, reading the landscape – are revealed to the spectators from the very beginning and affect the scopic regimes of stage and audience. The grand narrative lost, the garden and the play offer a palimpsest of viewpoints, a collection of things/inscriptions turning the place into a museum "brought home in the luggage from the grand tour".[22] Accordingly, the collection comprises a landskip architect, views stolen from the paintings of Claude Lorrain and Nicolas Poussin, Salvator Rosa's renderings of Italian landscapes, and Mrs Ann Radcliff's and Horace Walpole's literary landscapes, as well as Virgil's. With the play unfolding, the collection grows and the table displays more and more objects interrelating past and present.

As well as paintings and literary works, the collection also includes follies and the gazebo. Originally, the function of a gazebo was to provide a place from which one could *see* and *look at* the view. It effectuated the gaze, the long and steady look of the immobile eye constituting the landscape. For these particular reasons the gazebo is the first pavilion to be affected by Mr Noakes' improvements. Thomasina announces the change: "Mrs Chater was discovered in carnal embrace in the gazebo": the enunciation betrays genuine surprise and according to Septimus is simply "absurd".[23] The absurdity consists in the fact that the *point of correct sight* becomes the object of viewing in the manner that the country house becomes an adjunct to the picturesque landscape. Mr Noakes, here obviously the voyeur and not the authorised visionary, sees the pair through his spyglass while taking measurements in the garden. The irreversibility of changes in visuality is confirmed by the later discovery of Lady Croom and Lord Byron in the gazebo: at this point no longer a surprise.[24] The slimy rhetoric of indirectness, turning down all chivalry, as well as the pre- and proceeding incidents makes the spectators aware of the new order introduced by the serpent architect. The status and arrangement of follies changes irrevocably. Architectural form and function are no longer correspondent. The display of follies in the landscape reveals designs relying on additive pastiche. The gazebo is *superposed*, to use Lady Croom's geometric expression, by what she calls a "hovel", or a cowshed, and what Mr Noakes names a "hermitage".[25] Places of public reception where statements of political and financial power are made are transferred to the marquée with its pseudo-democratic annual masked ball. In the late 1780s, however, masquerade only pretends to reconstruct carnival; it becomes a form of simulation within a safely contained spectacle. Any serious reference to an outer, focalising 'it' is lost.[26]

The hermitage, replacing the gazebo, signals the reversal of visual relations. The correct Point of Sight, its privilege of placing and subjecting nature "as God intended", is dislodged, surrenders to a palimpsest of points of view, and becomes an item in the collection.[27] Having completed the belt walk, the stranger pays a visit to the hermit. The 'anchorite' remains a mute inscription, one of the numerous in the garden collection: John the Baptist at Sidley Park, the philosopher J-J Rousseau at Ermenonville, the poet Shenstone, or just a pottery gnome like Gus. The hermit epitomises the museum landscape whose reading remains fragmented, like that of the early collections, notably the Hermitage in St Petersburg. Apparently, the eighteenth century idea of landscape as literary text appealed also to Brown. Hannah More's memoirs provide an interesting illustration of this peculiar bent: "He [Brown] told me he compared his art to literary composition. Now there, said he... I make a comma, and there, pointing to another part... a parenthesis – a parenthesis – now a full stop, and then I begin another subject."[28] Thus looking and reading become an inseparable aspect of the late eighteenth century art of landscaping and so the following items share the cultural, social and physical environments distinguished by DeBolla: the landscape garden, the country house and the exhibition of pictures.[29] Stoppard borrows this concept of landscape and introduces it into his twentieth century theatre inducing the spectators to accept the proposed scopic and textual field.

Apart from the characters banished from Croom Court, the remaining inhabitants become part of the landscape as if emphasising prospects rather than portraits, a fashion found in the novels of Ann Radcliff and referred to as "landscapes with figures". Figures and not portraits make personifications. Therefore the idea of landscape as an extended prosopopoeia surfacing, on stage, in the form of figure-personifications seems more adequate. Characters become inscriptions in the landscape they read and in which they dwell as actors and spectators. The *textualisation* of such a theatrical event results in the impression of watching characters – quotations reading quotations. In Tom Stoppard's play-text the prosopopoeia of landscape becomes painfully complex. The time span it covers requires shuttling within the temporally split landscape: from the eighteenth to the twentieth century. Even a cursory understanding of the concept of the 'typical English park of the time', foregrounded in the opening lines of the play, requires a knowledgeable and mobile spectator. For example, the discussion on landscape improvements in *Arcadia* might be a paraphrase of analogous dialogues in Thomas Love Peacock's *Headlong Hall*, 1816.[30] Thomasina, like Tenorina in T L Peacock's text, is literally buried in the park becoming one of its monuments. Hence her question in the first scene of *Arcadia* becomes ominous: "How is a ruined child different from a ruined castle?"[31] Thomasina's ruin and memorial belong to the landscape and have numerous historical counterparts. The garden at Ermenonville is host to one of the most famous follies, the tomb of J-J Rousseau who lived hermit-like in the park for several weeks before his death in 1778 when he was buried on the Poplar Island. He became one of the most famous follies in the park formerly dedicated to his writing.[32] Similarly, Hagley, Lyttleton's country estate, has a monument dedicated to James Thomson, the Scottish poet who anticipated the romantics' feeling for nature and praised in *The Seasons (Spring)* the beauty of the very landscape which, later, welcomed his symbolic tomb. According to the same controversial tradition of real and fake garden burials, Tom Stoppard's young heroine, Thomasina, is buried in her garden at Croom Court. Among other characters, Septimus becomes a hermit while the speechless Gus is already inscribed in the landscape as a pottery gnome offering the new apple of knowledge to Hannah. On the outskirts of Arcadia/*Arcadia*, Lord Croom is placed in his hunting park – one of the oldest forms of garden art – where we hear him shooting and then 'read' him transferred into the hunting books.[33] Hannah Jarvis is buried alive in the design of the garden, reading the landscape and thus burying herself gradually in the pleasures of archeological pursuits, immersed in a close study of detail. Finally, Hermione Croom recalls the Shakespearean *(The Winter's Tale)* queen-statue, supposedly sculpted by Giulio Romano and bearing the same name as Tom Stoppard's character. Like her "textual prototype", miraculously brought back to life, the nineteenth century figure is also granted a new life-chance in the twentieth century. By now the spectator may have reached the point of assuming that the author himself is buried somewhere in the landscape thus eliminating the remaining authoritative point of view.

Arcadia contains exceptionally numerous scenes of, and references to, reading and writing. It juxtaposes two pragmatics of reading: silent private reading and its public counterpart. The privacy of the former grants more freedom to the reader who moves forwards and backwards turning the pages and skipping less interesting passages. Á K Varga recognises this more aleatory perception as topographically close to the reception of paintings in a gallery where the onlooker is granted the physical freedom of distance and angle. This particular visual/textual nexus makes it possible for the diffused scopic regime to constitute itself in Tom Stoppard's landscape play. Varga terms this particular case of visual/verbal relations, in which texts are hidden beyond visual images, *la coincidence cachée* (covert coincidence).[34] Focusing on the visual the onlooker discovers the texts, which, in turn, enable him to understand and appreciate the visual. Public reading, on the contrary, like most theatrical events, remains linear and metonymic. Although the body enjoys limited freedom, the public reader attempts to impose his reading upon a public expected to follow his point of view.

Thomasina and Septimus practice private reading in Scene One by being separately occupied with the study of mathematics and poetry, the former reading letters and making inscriptions. The garden is introduced via the pseudo-Reptonian books of sketches. Both Hermione and Valentine emerge as ardent if peculiar readers of garden books and hunting registers – "a calendar of slaughter" instead of *The Shepherd's Calendar* – which they study in private. Hannah Jarvis writes garden books and wonders whether there is any book "in Chater", the unsuccessful poet. Thomasina is rebuked for reading too many of Mrs Ann Radcliff's books. Papers, magazines and newspapers as well as books, doubled by time, fill the table at Croome Court as well as the hermitage. These reading scenes are prevailingly private and silent. This alternative reading, pursued by most characters in Stoppard's *Arcadia,* displays an attempt to move the activity from the public to the private: from a socially constructed subject controlled by the mirror audience to a self-produced subject – or a text-produced subject – escaping accepted legislation. Both Fordyce and Sheridan, in the 1770s and 1780s, warned against illicit private reading, "the silent perusal of texts", which destabilises discourse and rearranges the text/reality relation allowing the fantasy to "seep into the real".[35] A reader/spectator overmastered by the text perused in silence is the *transported* reader who becomes part of the text, part of the landscape. Apparently, the eighteenth century legislation of reading procedures contradicts the new protocols of seeing, reading and visiting the textual space of landscape and picturesque gardens.

A scene of public reading is offered by Bernard Nightingale. Bernard's reading of the lecture is an *event* with a professional lecturer who requires an equally professional or willing audience, which the master of the ceremony realises only too late: "It's no fun when it's not among pros, is it?".[36] As a reader, Nightingale is mainly governed by the legislated manoeuvres defining the body language of an eighteenth century orator as described by Gilbert Austin in *Chironomia*.[37] Pacing around he is reading aloud to keep the audience hanging on every word, maintaining eye contact and public tone of voice. Bernard's performance, with its patronising forms of address, demand for respect, and theatrical show of pages is a demonstration of the power the new landscape rejects.[38] The failure of his show to subject the audience through a centralising visuality and the imposition of a single interpretation on the factual material reveals itself in a gradual displacement and deterioration of visuality and voice. From a baleful stare the lecturer passes on to a suspicious glance, a glint, and a failure to see well: "Look at the mote in your eye."[39] He ends up in 'boggle-eyed' desperation. His body language amounts to acrobatics – presumably, both visual and mental.[40] The centrality of his voice is brutally dislodged by Hannah, whose attention he cannot win: like the radio playing in the background he can be turned off or marginalised.

The palimpsest-like scopic regime introduced by Tom Stoppard into his *Arcadia* suspends the once dominant protocols of oculocentrism and perspectival unity by introducing catoptric visuality, a combination of gaze and glance, by placing both actors – that is, figures personifying the textualised landscape – and spectators on the stage within the premises of the constituted mental, scopic mapping and putting them in the double roles of those who see/watch and are seen/watched. The garden-in-process invites actors/spectators as enfranchised interpreters walking with the *Ambulator*/Programme, almost an exemplary spectator with a guide for the eye. Perception in *Arcadia* consists in watching and reading in our private compendium of recalled texts that the landscape evokes. No public reading/guiding focaliser is provided by the landscape itself. Even the author secures a place for himself within the garden. The motto greeting visitors to the landscape created by Stoppard could be borrowed from an obelisk in the famous Vauxhall gardens: *Spectator fastidiosus sibi molestus.* The inscription warns the viewers that they will harm themselves, deprive themselves of aesthetic pleasure, understanding and freedom, if they resist entry into the visuality constituted by the landscape/play.

1   See, for example, Michał Misiorny who comments on Wesker in his *Współczesny teatr na świecie. Sylwetki pisarzy.* Warszawa: Wydawnictwo Artystyczne i Filmowe 1978, pp. 145-146; Christopher Innes, *Modern British Drama 1890-1990,* Cambridge: Cambridge University Press 1992, pp. 114-117.

2   Hillis Miller, J, *Topographies,* Stanford: Stanford University Press, 1995, p. 25.

3   Fuchs, Elinor, *The Death of Character: Perspectives on Theatre After Modernism,* Bloomington and Indiana: Indiana University Press, 1996, p. 94.

4   Gertrude Stein's approach was certainly liberating and avant-garde in its acknowledgement of the set as a character's partner rather than an inert piece of painted canvas. However, Wexler's and Wilson's experiments establish landscape as, potentially, the active performer and subject 'being performed'. This, in turn, draws the spectators into an entirely different experience; in the case of Wexler's version it assumes physical involvement. The spectator, who is not given the chance to appreciate the totality of the production, is thus exposed to dispersed fractions of the event spreading in a multiplicity of directions (limits are purposefully obscured). The projected and actual response is diffused, then, in the sense of being an unfocused, often chance-governed reception. This 'physical' condition can be transferred onto more abstract material. If performativity matters, competence or the various prosthetic instruments such as binoculars should aid our/spectators' ability to appreciate the intellectually constructed landscape. However, the confusing amount of data and absence of a clear scopic regime resist subjection to any system or sense of performative efficiency. Any attempts to master the dispersed and multi-layered generative idea by imposing focalisation are inevitably frustrated.

5   Stoppard, T, *Arcadia,* London and Boston: Faber and Faber, 1993, p. 2.

6   Stoppard, *Arcadia,* p. 1.

7   Stoppard, *Arcadia,* p. 1.

8   Stoppard, *Arcadia,* p. 16.

9   Hunt, J D and Willis, P, *The Genius of the Place. The English Landscape Garden 1620-1820,* London: Paul Elek, 1975, p. 1.

10 Stoppard, *Arcadia,* p. 24.

11 Hussey, C, *The Picturesque. Studies in a Point of View,* London: G P Putnam, 1927, p. 253.

12 Hussey, C, *The Picturesque,* p. 181.

13 DeBolla, P, *The Discourse of the Sublime. Reading in History, Aesthetics and the Subject,* New York: Basil Blackwell, 1989, p. 187.

14 DeBolla, *The Discourse of the Sublime,* p. 195.

15 Stoppard, *Arcadia,* p. 10.

16 Stoppard, *Arcadia,* p. 14.

17 More information on the confusing figure of Mr Noakes, the garden architect, can be found in J D Hunt's article tracing the garden history in Stoppard's play. The Stoppardian character appears as a conflation of the Brownian and Reptonian concepts even though the audience might not be competent enough to recognise these aspects, especially p. 59. Hunt, J D, "'A breakthrough in dahlia studies': on *Arcadia* by Tom Stoppard", *Landscape Journal,* vol. 15, no. 1, September, 1996, pp. 58-64.

18 Knight, R P, *The Landscape: a Didactic Poem in Three Books Addressed to Uvedale Price, Esq.,* London, 1795, p. 11.

19 Stoppard, *Arcadia,* p. 4.

20 The material may be of anecdotal value only: the anonymous "friend," otherwise referred to as "a fellow" is quoted in Hussey, *The Picturesque,* p. 141.

21 Stoppard, *Arcadia,* p. 5.

22 Stoppard, *Arcadia,* p. 25.

23 Stoppard, *Arcadia,* p. 2.

24 Stoppard, *Arcadia,* p. 36.

25 Stoppard, *Arcadia,* p. 12.

26 Jervis, J, *Exploring the Modern. Patterns of Western Culture and Civilisation,* Oxford: Blackwell, p. 26ff and p. 148ff.

27 Sławek, T, "The Spirit of Luxury: Shenstone, Delille, and the Garden Theory" in Rachwał, T and Sławek, T, eds., *Word Subject Nature. Studies in Seventeenth- and Eighteenth-Century Culture,* Katowice: Wydawnictwo Universytetu Śląskiego, 1996, p. 66.

28 More, H, *Memoirs of the Life and Correspondence of Mrs Hannah More,* Roberts, William, ed., 2 vols., London, 1834. See a letter to Mrs More's sister from 31 Dec 1782 in vol. I, p. 267.

29 DeBolla, P, "The Visibility of Visuality: Vauxhall Gardens and the Siting of the Viewer", *Vision and Textuality,* Melville, S and Readings, B, eds., London: Macmillan, 1995, p. 282.

30 Peacock, T L, "Headlong Hall", *Headlong Hall and Gryll Grange,* Slater, M and Baron, M, eds., Oxford: Oxford University Press, 1987, chapter VI.

31 Stoppard, *Arcadia,* p. 11.

32 Dams, B H, and Zega, A, *Pleasure Pavillions and Follies in the Garden of the Ancient Regime,* Paris: Flammerion, 1995, p. 147.

33 Rottermund, A, *Ogród-symbol-marzenie,* Warszawa: Zamek Królewski, 1998, p. 120.

34 Varga, Á K, "Entre le Texte et l'Image: une Pragmatique des Limites", in Heusser, M, Hanoosh, M and Hoek, L, eds., *Text and Visuality. Word and Image Interactions 3.* Atlanta, GA: Amsterdam, 1999, pp. 77-92, pp. 78, 88-89.

35 Sheridan, T, *Lectures on the Art Of Reading,* 2nd edition, 2 vols., London, 1782, vol. I, p. 187. Fordyce, J, *Addresses to Young Men,* 2 vols., Dublin: 1777, vol. I, pp. 115-116.

36 Stoppard, *Arcadia,* p. 62.

37 Austin, G, *Chironomia; or, a Treatise on Rhetorical Delivery,* London, 1806, p. 528.

38 Stoppard, *Arcadia,* p. 57-58.

39 Stoppard, *Arcadia,* p. 58-59.

40 Stoppard, *Arcadia,* p. 65.

Ewa Kębłowska-Lawniczak

Landscapes and Bodies

Landscapes and Bodies
Gillian Rose

The most familiar coupling of bodies with landscape, perhaps, is the landscaping of 'the female body'. Given the way that Western culture has so often claimed that women's bodies are governed by natural instincts, and that Nature herself is feminine, it is hardly surprising that a continuing trope of the Western art canon is to show women's bodies as landscapes. Nude, most often, a female body, stripped of any individuality, is turned into a terrain for visual exploration.[1] The critique of this way of seeing is now as well-established as the visual trope itself is tired.

It is hardly surprsing, therefore, that all the essays in this section ignore this particular conjunction of the natural and the feminine. Instead, they turn their attention to other landscapes and other bodies, suggesting that consideration of the relationships between bodies and landscapes also needs to shift towards a wider range of configurations. Amy Sargeant looks at just one part of the body – the brain – and at how it was figured as landscape by certain Soviet scientists and filmmakers. Marcus Idvall and Jenny Iles both take bodies and disperse them analytically across various landscapes. Idvall explores the landscapes through which the science of xenotransplantation is imagined, while Iles examines the landscapes of cemetry gardens and tourism in what was the Western Front of the First World War. Idvall's is a paper that looks forward, temporally, as it were; his landscapes are those that their practioners see as producing a future. Iles, on the other hand, explores the pull of the past in her essay, and the way that pull is having very material effects on the landscapes of the present.

Charlotta Malm and David Crouch focus very much on those pulls in and on the present, in their discussion of landscape. They argue that the only way to understand these tensions that riddle landscapes – between inside and outside, materiality and representation, past and present – is to consider the production of landscape as itself an embodied practice. Always in process, landscape becomes through its performance by embodied subjects. Their bodies are neither dismembered nor dispersed, but complex and creative. If the idea of landscape itself is mutable, then it seems to have similar effects on those concepts it is made to work with. Just as there is no one landscape, so there is no one body with which it may work.

1   See Adams, S and Robins, A G, eds., *Gendering Landscape Art*, New Brunswick: Rutgers University Press, 2001.

Mapping the Brain and the Soviet 'Conquest of the Soul'
Amy Sargeant

Hamlet: That skull had a tongue in it, and could sing once; how the knave jowls it to the ground, as if it were Cain's jaw-bone, that did the first murder! It might be the pate of a politician, which this ass now o'er offices, one that would circumvent God, might it not?

Horatio: It might, my lord.

Hamlet: Or of a courtier, which could say 'Good morrow, sweet lord! How dost thou, good lord?' This might be my Lord Such-a-one, that praised my Lord Such-a-one's horse, when he meant to beg it, might it not?

Horatio: Ay, my lord.

Hamlet: Why, e'en so, and now my Lady Worm's chapless, and knocked about the mazzard with a sexton's spade. Here's fine revolution, an we had the trick to see't. Did these bones cost no more the breeding but to play at loggats with 'em? Mine ache to think on't.

[*Hamlet, Prince of Denmark* Act V sc.1]

Throughout the history of Western materialism, the interior space of the human brain has been posited as a territory susceptible to exploration and mapping, equivalent to exterior domains and landscapes. Furthermore, this inner space has been a site as vigorously contested amongst and between competing ideologies, both materialist and non-materialist, as any final frontier in the distant universe. This paper is concerned with the particular case of Soviet mechanism although, as will be shown, there is much here which is inherited from a far more ancient tradition, traceable through Hippocrates and Aristotle. The equivalence I seek to demonstrate is evident in the metaphors applied and in the structures and methods employed. I shall be especially concerned here with the use of film as "Created Geography" and "Created Anatomy", and as a means well suited to the exposition of the brain as a navigable topography.[1] Specifically, I shall discuss Vsevelod Pudovkin's popular documentary film about the eminent physiologist, Ivan Pavlov, *The Mechanics of the Brain: the Behaviour of Animals and Men,* 1926. I shall be concerned also with the appropriation by Soviet ideology more generally of a scientific practice established and developed elsewhere.

'What, exactly', asked Pavlov, 'is the concept of a reflex?':

> The theory of reflex activity is based on three fundamental principles of
> exact scientific investigation: 1) the principle of determinism i.e. an impulse;
> 2) the principle of analysis and synthesis i.e. the initial decomposition of the
> whole into its parts or units and subsequent gradual re-establishment of the
> whole from these parts or elements; 3) the principle of structure i.e. the
> disposition of activity of force in space, the adjustment of dynamics to
> structure.[2]

Rodchenko's photomontage portrait of Mayakovsky seems pertinent to our theme in a number of
ways: Mayakovsky is depicted staring intently forwards, a modern visionary genius, his brain
bestriding the world like a colossus. (figure 1) Equally, the globe is mapped over his brain as though
identifying relationships of time and space governing the topology and circumnavigation of both.
Significantly, the picture appeared as the back cover to the 1926 publication *A Conversation with a
Tax Inspector about Poetry*: even those activities which had been previously ascribed to divine
inspiration were now to be subjected to mechanical enquiry:

> [......]
> My labour's
>   akin
>   to the labour
>   of any other.
> [......]
> All poetry
>   is a journey
>   into the unknown.
> Poetry's
>   also radium extraction.
> Grams of extraction
>   in years of labour.
> For one single word,
>   I consume in action
> thousands of tons
>   of verbal ore.
> [......]
> And what
>   if during these last
>   fifteen years
> I've ridden
>   to death
>   a dozen Pegasuses?![3]

Figure 1
Aleksandr
Rodchenko,
*Razgovor c
fininspektorom
o poesii*, 1926
Moscow:
Knizhnyi skal
izd-va <gudok>

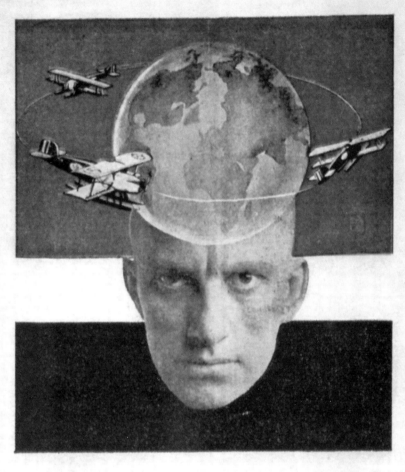

In 1927, René Fülöp-Miller observed the facile appropriation by Bolshevism of the work of Pavlov:

> The fact that Pavlov's 'conditioned reflexes' seem to demonstrate the transition from purely physiological automatism to association of ideas and primitive forms of thought, was utilised by the Bolsheviks in the most grotesquely exaggerated way in order to represent that all spirituality whatever, even in its highest forms, art and science, is an expression of mere mechanism, as it were the output of a more or less complicated factory...
>
> Thus, if it is regarded as proved that every expression of human spirit, emotion or thought is in the last resort to be traced to purely material, physiological, mechanistic causes, it follows immediately that all apparently autonomous intellectual phenomena must be fundamentally of a material nature.[4]

The account delivered by this foreign correspondent was corroborated by those near to Pavlov himself. Boris Babkin, an assistant in his laboratory, recalls:

> Very soon after the accession of the Bolsheviks to power, Pavlov's teachings on conditioned reflexes were recognised by them as affirming that the intellectual life of people can be radically reconstructed and that a proletarian revolution world-wide would create a new human society.[5]

The force of such contemporary reports was much enhanced in subsequent Cold War mythology by the status which Pavlov was accorded posthumously: after a brief fall from grace in the 1930s he was granted a privileged place amongst the alumni of Soviet science, and deviation from the path which he had directed was deemed inexcusable.[6] However, the later official version has served to mask a number of important features of the Soviet scene in the 1920s – for instance, the fact that many of Pavlov's major discoveries had been made before the revolution unheeded by politicians; also, the fact that Pavlov was, like many of his generation, for much of his life, for as long as was possible, staunchly opposed to Marxism (or, more specifically, Marxist intervention in the practice of science);[7] and, furthermore, the fact that the scientific community was divided not only by political allegiance and the extent of the materialism to which factions subscribed, but also by controversy over procedures, results and the scientifically correct interpretation thereof, notably by the various disputes between Pavlov and his fellow reflexologist, Vladimir Bekhterev, and amongst members of the Communist Academy (whose courses in physiology were widely regarded as grossly inferior).[8] Given that all areas of culture were distinctly marked by 'Scientism' in this period, it seems worth investigating why Pavlov attained such a prominent and exemplary position.

I am interested here less in the intricacies of these internecine feuds than in the grounds to which Pavlov's followers appealed in an attempt to secure validation and support. What public expectations of scientific method rendered Pavlov's practice attractive as a paradigm? Given that Marxism was born of a particular mid-nineteenth century world-view and that the experimental tasks set out before Pavlov were similarly the product of nineteenth-century science, was the nature of the imbrication anything other than a grand syllogism, effected through an easy equivalence of a shared scientistic vocabulary? Marx and Engels, it must be remembered, were adherents of Darwin.[9] Perhaps the assertion of identity through common naming in scientistic terminology indicates an attractive aspiration towards a meaningful endeavour, a means of placing a particular practice within a consolidating self-justifying whole, rather than providing a substantive truth. "The splitting of a single whole and the cognition of its contradictory parts", says Lenin in *On the Question of Dialectics*

... is the essence... of dialectics...

In mathematics: + and -, differential and integral.

In mechanics: action and reaction.

In physics: positive and negative electricity.

In chemistry: the combination and dissociation of atoms.

In social science: the class struggle.[10]

In 1904, Pavlov was awarded the Nobel prize for his work on the digestive system in dogs. Two years later he began to work more intently on conditioned reflexes. Pavlov's fundamental theoretical conception was that the functional properties of the nervous system and the cerebral cortex were based on two equally important processes: excitation and inhibition, two sides of one and the same process always existing simultaneously but their proportion varying in each moment. The international acclaim accorded Pavlov was to be important to the young Soviet state, all too aware of its inadequacy in other areas. A number of nascent national schools of objective psychology were competing for recognition at the turn of the century, but in many respects Pavlov and Bekhterev were followers in an established line of enquiry and not its initiators. Pavlov was especially familiar with the work of Darwin and Lewes in Britain, of Helmholtz in Germany, and of Bernard in France; Bekhterev with that of Darwin and Spencer. Both, following Hippocrates, regarded man's behaviour as the product of, and productive of, his environment, and located him within an animal continuum, opposing the use of anthropocentric descriptions: "unconditioned and conditioned reflexes serve as the basis of behaviour not only of animals but also of mankind", reads an intertitle in Pudovkin's film.[11] Both followed the work on frogs (also demonstrated in *The Mechanics of the Brain*) of the pioneering Russian physiologist Ivan Sechenov.

Throughout the nineteenth century, radical literary and political movements in Russia had allied themselves with perceived progress in science. Their shared concerns were partly utilitarian (a desire for improved public health and welfare) and partly political: the discoveries of natural science challenged simultaneously the authority of the Orthodox Church and of an absolute monarchy. Indeed, acknowledging the threat, the Tsarist state had sought to suppress publication of many major scientific texts.[12] The fact that physiology had aroused such strong opposition from the old régime encouraged its facile characterisation as a fundamentally revolutionary force, and Pavlov found himself yoked to a 'progressive' political cause in spite of his own protestations. The suggestion that learning (as the acquisition of habit) was a mechanical process independent of the prescriptions of inheritance was commensurable with an ideology of egalitarianism and with the internationalist thrust of Soviet policy in the early 1920s. The ideological imperative to found a vision of society on a scientifically authorised model was made manifest in literature and the visual arts. The theme of 'Darwinism and Marxism' was present in all academic programmes of the Commissariat of Enlightenment. "This", notes Sheila Fitzpatrick, "gave the progressive secondary school teacher the chance to work on the formation of a materialist world-view in his pupils, to inculcate scientific-atheistic views of the world, and to make them active transformers of nature."[13] The education programme continued throughout the 20s in apparent disregard of Pavlov's later work in typology which obliged him to admit, ultimately, that some dogs were simply born more intelligent than others.[14] "All life, all culture is wholly made up of reflexes", reads a title in]*The Mechanics of the Brain*; "The study of conditioned reflexes serves as the basis of materialist understanding of the behaviour of animals and man." Reviewing the film, *Pravda* declared triumphantly that the notion of 'Soul' had been decisively extinguished, although Pavlov, meanwhile, suggested that it was as yet premature to announce its demise.[15]

Bekhterev was altogether more ready to seize upon the social applicability of Pavlov's research and recognised that it afforded endorsement of theories which he had thus far advanced only speculatively. The division of Bekhterev's Psycho-Neurological Institute in Leningrad into medical, pedagogical and juridical faculties indicates the scope and interdependence of enquiry with which he was concerned. In 1924 the Leningrad Congress of Psychoneurology passed a resolution to introduce instruction in the science of behaviour of animals and man, studied from an objective standpoint, and the fundamental content of this science, it was said, "must be the investigation of those internal (biological, physico-chemical) and external (physical and social) factors which determine the development of the human being and his behaviour".[16] But, here again, such debates and associations had frequently informed the literature of the nineteenth century. Whereas Bekhterev complained that spiritual dogmatism and the concept 'Freedom of Will' were an obstacle to the eradication of evil, Tolstoy referred to theories of brain reflexes disparagingly as denoting a failure of personal responsibility. Dostoevsky, too, pondered whether crime was born of nature or nurture and in what measure punishment, charity and forgiveness were to be meted out accordingly. Sechenov was the model for the radical doctor, Bazarov, in Turgenev's *Fathers and Children*:

> All men are similar, in soul as well as in body.... It is enough to have one human specimen in order to judge all others.... We know more or less what causes physical ailments; and moral diseases are caused by the wrong sort of education, by all the rubbish people's heads are stuffed with from childhood onwards, in short by the disordered state of society. Reform society and there will be no diseases.[17]

Bekhterev couches his theory in a wide swathe of cultural reference, including the psychologist Münsterberg (who moved from Germany to work with William James at Harvard), the philosophers Christiansen, Bergson and Schopenhauer, and the philologist Potebnaia; most often however he refers to himself. Pavlov, on the other hand, expresses little interest in material not immediately germane to his field. But, paradoxically perhaps, Pavlov's general refusal to engage with such extraneous questions, his disaffection for the international conference circuit and disdain for journalistic treatment, fuelled even, by his own disinterest in matters political, lent his position weight as an impartial, scientifically objective witness whose experimental findings coincidentally endorsed Soviet ideology.

Both Bekhterev and Pavlov were concerned to put within the realm of experimental science phenomena hitherto thought insusceptible to objective enquiry and to discover which areas and activities of the brain were responsible for what particular mental states and processes. Mind, for Bekhterev and Pavlov, is actually – and not just metaphorically – what the brain *does*. "Pavlov insisted", says Babkin, "that the study of the conditioned reflex mechanism permits one to reduce the problem of the activity of the central nervous system to the study of space relations, something psychology is unable to do: 'You must', Pavlov said, 'be able to point to where the excitation process was at a given moment and where it has gone'."[18] In an address to the Petrograd Philosophical Society in 1916, Pavlov described the psyche as a function of a mechanical system, as timekeeping is of a watch; elsewhere he was wont to picture the brain as a telephone exchange.[19] Both Bekhterev and Pavlov reject Gestalt psychology's preoccupation with 'wholes' as actually undemonstrable: "it believes the brain to work in large patterns, by 'closing gaps'... rather than by the operation of nerve paths linking this and that little centre in the brain" and "lacks grounding in physiology" (it has neglected, Pavlov says, to acquaint itself thoroughly with Helmholtz).[20] Both find that Freud's theories fail to offer a fulcrum of analysis (this is to say, that they lack anything so strikingly specific or readily isolated as the reflex) but Bekhterev is more equitable and conciliatory.[21] Bekhterev also comes dangerously close to accepting a hieroglyphic thesis of perception (posited by Plekhanov, the father of Russian Marxism, but rejected by Lenin) and declares himself sympathetic to Mach and by association to Dühring, in turn roundly rejected by Engels. Here again, I think, such equivocation cast him as something of a maverick. Certainly he was even less likely to secure a favourable reputation after his pronouncements against Stalin in 1927, when Bekhterev died under sudden and allegedly suspicious circumstances....

But Bekhterev was not above censuring Pavlov for lapses from the straight and narrow path. In an address of 1918 in which he criticised communism, Pavlov also cited centuries of slavery as the cause for the waning of the aim reflex amongst Russians while the Anglo-Saxons, he claimed, freely developed this characteristic to a high degree. Bekhterev retaliated:

> Now the question is: do the reduction of the most complex biological activities to such a simple scheme... afford a solution of the problem in the sense of explaining the given biological phenomenon? It is scarcely necessary to point out that very little is gained in this way and that the adversaries of the objective method... are given a weapon.[22]

Bekhterev attacked Pavlov's interpretation of his results and the methods by which he obtained them. Pudovkin's film, *The Mechanics of the Brain*, uses animated diagrams to show the formation of a conditioned motor reflex in a dog, although this was, in fact, a procedure favoured by Bekhterev while Pavlov preferred salivation. (figure 2) This latter method, said Bekhterev, presented all sorts of practical difficulties which cast doubt on Pavlov's work. Sometimes Bekhterev's complaints sent Pavlov into a sulk, when he would lock himself away then, after re-trials, occasionally reluctantly concede the point; and sometimes he would expose the work to public scrutiny. Both Bekhterev and Pavlov were keen to show off the apparatus employed: the 1923 edition of Bekhterev's *General Principles of Reflexology* contains numerous diagrams and photographs; Pudovkin's film shows us white-coated lab-technicians in control booths, petri dishes, test tubes and needles jigging on cylinders.

Although Pavlov preceded Bekhterev in his experiments in reflexology, Bekhterev was the first to publish extensively and to be translated abroad. Bekhterev formed general opinions before endeavouring to substantiate these with experimental evidence while Pavlov, as a follower of Newton in both his physics and his methods, was at pains to show that his conclusions were strictly drawn from experience: "What is a theory? It is experience codified." Contrary to Bekhterev's sniping, Pavlov maintained that his experiments were conducted under model, uniform conditions over an extensive period of time: Pavlov would not announce a theory until results had been consistently verified for six months at least and was cautious about leaping into print. Unhesitatingly, he would amend a theory if experience required it. Indeed, when Pudovkin made *The Mechanics* the work which it represents had yet to be fully published and his assistants had to make sense of it themselves from notebooks and laboratory records.[23] Even when Pavlov's *Lectures on Conditioned Reflexes* appeared in 1927 he chose to publish his findings in sequence, in order that the methodical working through of a problem could remain apparent. "In this manner", he said, "the reader is placed in a position to obtain a much clearer idea of the natural growth of the subject."[24] Pavlov was initially opposed to the making of *The Mechanics of the Brain*, says Pudovkin, for fear that popularisation would necessarily vulgarise his work.[25] It seems to me that Bekhterev and Pavlov nicely characterise two strands in scientific methodology, the former deductive, the latter inductive. But the fact that Pavlov was appropriated so wholeheartedly demonstrates, I think, that it was the style as much as the content of the proof that the Soviet state found expedient.

Lenin famously declared cinema the most important of the arts for the Soviet state.[26] However, there was disagreement as to how this instrument of vision was to be most effectively employed, even in the scientific field where films had been made and imported before the Revolution. The controversy over procedures, results and interpretation between Bekhterev and Pavlov is matched in the disputes of Eisenstein, Pudovkin, Vertov and their contemporaries. Sometimes one has the sense of an argument manufactured for an audience (Eisenstein accused Vertov of making mischief with his polemical tracts), but often the differences are substantial (Pudovkin, when planning *The Mechanics of the Brain*, repudiated absolutely Vertov's method of 'seizing life unawares'). In effect, Pudovkin attempts to reconstitute in filmic construction a process of cognition which Pavlov's experiments had investigated:

> It is generally known that the essence of proper montage consists in correctly connecting the attention of the spectator. If I photograph a thing whole, then the spectator will perceive that thing in its entirety, whereas the closer I approach it with the camera, the more the spectator will grasp only selected details. This applies both to the filming of a static object and to the filming of a dynamic process. An observer following a demonstration guides his attention sometimes here, sometimes there, then he pursues some detail, then he occupies himself with the whole. As a result of which the attentive observer secures a clearly delineated impression of the thing. He will endeavour not to disregard any characteristic point whatever, nor will he lose sight of them whilst concentrating on the particular features.... It depends on the director whether the spectator becomes a good or a bad observer. It is clear that the shifting here and there of concentration – corresponding to montage – is a strictly regular process. Such laws of observation, which are required for correct understanding, must be fully and completely transferred onto the montage structure.[27]

Eisenstein, Pudovkin and Vertov all agreed that theory was a required concomitant to practice and that it should serve to facilitate making: theoretically, at least, mere idle speculation was condemned. In general, the terminology of the workshop or laboratory became fashionable. Contemporaneously, Nikolai Punin formulated artistic creation, T, as the sum of an infinite number of principles, together multiplied by intuition; the theatre director Vsevolod Meyerhold found that the actor, N, comprised A^1 (the artist who conceives the ideas and issues the instructions necessary for its execution) *plus* A^2 (the executant who executes the conception of A^1) and Timoshenko, in his 1926 *The Art of Cinema*, represented Lev Kuleshov's system of montage by means of geometric figures.[28]

Eisenstein and Pudovkin differ in their understanding of instrumentation and in their response to the scientific example provided by Pavlov. When Eisenstein speaks of the work of art as "a tractor ploughing over the audience's psyche in a particular class context" the rhetoric reminds one of Bukharin's intention to "put our stamp on intellectuals, we will work them over as in a factory".[29] However, Pudovkin, less antagonistic as ever, contents himself with the psychological guidance of his audience. Pudovkin, theoretically, often indicates that montage should follow the 'natural' flow of an observer's attention, as if the observer were watching a scene played out before him, and presents worked examples which are clearly organised in terms of spectator motivation. But although Pudovkin, as a trained chemist, was in a position to understand Pavlov's work thoroughly, he never refers to it directly nor seeks to underpin his own theorising by recourse to Pavlov's authority. He

Figure 2
*Mekhanika
golovnovo mozga*
(Vsevelod
Pudovkin, USSR,
1925), animated
sequence, NFTVA
London

never explicitly equates his model of correct film construction as differentiation followed by integration with Pavlov's principle of analysis and synthesis. Nor, furthermore, does his writing of the 20s connect this with Lenin's exposition of the dialectic. Pudovkin's editing of *The Mechanics of the Brain*, designed for easy comprehension by a lay audience, emphasises connectedness between shots and within sequences, by means of such devices as repetition and directional continuity of movement from mid-shot to close-up. After the intertitle at the end of reel 1, "unconditioned reflexes are innate", Pudovkin begins reel 2, "What is a conditioned reflex?"; "It's simply demonstrated in the digestion of animals." Pudovkin's predeliction for a preconceived editorial plan, referring to an actual or notional profilmic event described by the scenario, lends itself to the analogy with calculus. The famous experiments in "Created Geography" and "Created Anatomy", in which Pudovkin assisted Kuleshov, demonstrate precisely both functions of the process. The geographical or anatomical plan identifies elements drawn from different sources which are subsequently integrated into a newly fabricated whole, the entire construction residing conventionally in the imagination of the observer. It is important not only that the episode is broken down for the sufficient assembly of a logical sequence but also that this montage sequence can be adequately constructed from individual bits shot independently.

To say that art could be regarded as the product of a factory or workshop, as did Fülöp-Miller by way of criticism, was to bestow high praise. The image celebrates vision, unmediated, just as Rodchenko's monochrome poster for Cinema-Eye celebrates the power of the lens. (figure 3) Vertov championed Pavlov for demolishing out-worn superstitions and for envisioning the world with a new clarity, and urged that cinema follow suit:

Figure 3
Aleksandr
Rodchenko,
Poster for *Kino
glaz* (Dziga
Vertov, USSR,
1924), Russian
State Library

Not 'Pathé' nor 'Gaumont'
Not this, not about this
The apple should be seen as Newton saw it.
Open eyes to the Universe.
So that the ordinary dog
By Pavlov's eye can be seen.
We go to the movies
To blow up the movies
In order to see the movies.[30]

Pavlov's science was proclaimed by Bolshevism to supersede partisan restrictions: in the objectivity and universality of abstraction, the brain was no longer deemed simply to mediate between the individual and the external social and natural world but to correspond in its material articulation with the mechanism of that world. Nothing of the natural world lay beyond the cognitive capacity of the brain and the interpretation of neuro-science; neuro-science discovered in the brain a metonym for the order of that world. Paradoxically, Bolshevism in the 1920s sought in Pavlov's science independent impartial validation for its ideological tenets – but it was equally a particular modernist scientism which placed faith in science as supremely authoritative.

1   Kuleshov, L, "Art of the Cinema", in Levaco, R, *Kuleshov on Film*, Berkeley, CA: University of California Press, 1974, pp. 52-53.
2   Pavlov I P, *Selected Works*, Moscow: Foreign Languages Publishing, n. d., p. 426.
3   Mayakovsky, V, "A Conversation with a Tax Inspector about Poetry", in Marshall, H, ed., *Mayakovsky*, London: Dennis Dobson, 1965; see also Mayakovsky, V, *How Are Verses Made?*, [1927], Bristol: Bristol Classical Press, 1960.
4   Fülöp-Miller, R, *The Mind and Face of Bolshevism*, London: GP Putnam's Sons, 1927, p. 58.
5   Babkin, B, *Pavlov: A Biography*, London: Gollancz, 1951, p. 162.
6   Joravsky, D, *Russian Psychology: A Critical History*, Oxford: Oxford University Press, 1989, p. xvi; Graham, LR, *Science and Philosophy in the Soviet Union*, London: Allen Lane, 1973, pp. 375-394.
7   see transcript made by Gantt, W H, of address given by Pavlov in 1923, *Integrative Physiology and Behavioural Science*, vol. 27 no. 3, 1992, p. 271.
8   Joravsky, D, *Soviet Marxism and Natural Science*, London: Routledge and Kegan Paul, 1961, p. 67.
9   Marx requested permission from Darwin for the dedication of *Das Kapital*, but Darwin declined the invitation, being unfamiliar with Marx's work and for fear of causing offence to some members of his family; see Joravsky, *Soviet Marxism and Natural Science* and Beer, G, *Darwin's Plots*, London: ARK, 1985.
10 Lenin, V I, *On the Question of Dialectics* [1915], Moscow: Progress Publishers, 1980, p. 10.
11 Frolov, Y P, *Pavlov and His School* [1938], London: Johnson, 1970, pp. 238 and 261.
12 see Todes, D P, "From Radicalism to Scientific Convention", PhD thesis, Michigan University, 1981
13 Fitzpatrick, S, *Education and Social Mobility in the Soviet Union*, Cambridge: Cambridge University Press, 1979, p. 23.
14 Teplov, BM, "Problems in the Study of General Types of Higher Nervous Activity in Man and Animals", in Gray, JA, ed., *Pavlov's Typology*, Oxford: Oxford University Press, 1964.
15 *Pravda*, 14 Dec. 1926; *Sovetskoe iskusstvo*, 20 Dec. 1933
16 Bekhterev, V M, *General Principles of Human Reflexology* [1923], London: Jarrolds, 1933, p. 206
17 Turgenev IS, *Fathers and Children*, Edmonds, R, trans., Harmondsworth: Penguin, 1979, p. 160.
18 Babkin, *Pavlov*, p. 310.
19 Joravsky, *Russian Psychology*, p. 158.
20 Pavlov I P, *Selected Works*, pp. 578-595.
21 Pavlov I P, *Lectures on Conditioned Reflexes*, London: Martin Lawrence, 1928, p. 219.
22 Bekhterev, *Human Reflexology*, p. 141.
23 Pudovkin, VI, in *Kino*, 26 Apr. 1927.
24 Pavlov I P, *Conditioned Reflexes*, Oxford: Oxford University Press, 1927, p. xi.
25 Iesuitov, N, *Pudovkin*, Moscow: Iskusstvo, 1937, p. 54
26 Lunacharsky, A, "A Conversation with Lenin", in Taylor, R, and Christie I, eds., *The Film Factory*, London: Routledge and Kegan Paul, 1988, p. 57.
27 Pudovkin, V I, *Kinozhurnal ARK*, no. 9, 1925.
28 see Braun, E, *Meyerhold on Theatre*, London: Methuen, 1969, p. 50; Punin's "First Cycle of Lectures", in Bowlt, J E, ed. *Russian Art of the Avant-Garde*, London: Thames and Hudson, 1988, p. 171; Timoshenko, S, *Iskusstvo kino i montazh fil'ma*, Leningrad: Akademia, 1927.
29 Bukharin, quoted by Fitzpatrick, *Education*, p. 84
30 quoted by Petric, V, *Constructivism in Film*, Cambridge: Cambridge University Press, 1987, p. 30.

Death, Leisure and Landscape: British Tourism to the Western Front
Jenny Iles

Physically, land is the oldest of all archives. As Christopher Tilley observes, embedded in its earth are personal biographies, social identities and memories of previous movement.[1] It is the most widely shared *aide-memoire* of a culture's understanding of its past and future and is, as Rob Shields remarks, the "memory bank" of society.[2]

One place that has remained a key site in the British memory bank is the landscape of the Western Front. Today the area occupies a more central place in the British psyche than at any other time since the end of World War II. This essay focuses on the commemorative landscape of the Western Front and the ways in which tourism has become intricately bound within the nationalistic narratives of its cemeteries and memorials. Throughout the year, hundreds of thousands of tourists travel across the Channel to visit cemeteries and memorials of these Great War battlefields. As one of the most catastrophic and traumatic wars in history passes out of living memory, the "war to end all wars" continues to hold our fascination.

Tourists in the landscape: the search for satisfying scenes

What connection do tourists have with memory banks? Why should an activity such as tourism, often perceived as being superficial, be employed to try to unlock "the spirit of a landscape"? Even tourists dislike being regarded as tourists. Most tour companies taking out coach loads of people for weekend sightseeing trips prefer to call their clients travellers, which neatly distances them from the shallowness for which the tourist role is often condemned. Until relatively recently the study of tourism has been traditionally avoided by scholars, except to criticise it or to suggest its often negative impact on environments, local cultures and economies. The historian Daniel Boorstin believed tourism to be an aberration and considered the tourist to be a poor cousin of the traveller.[3] Travel offers action, not just the passive superficial appreciation of sightseeing. "People", he wrote, "go to see what they already know is there. The only thing to record, the only possible source of surprise, is their own reaction."[4]

However, while tourism does often involve stereotyped, superficial behaviour, despite its widespread denigration it remains an important activity. As the sociologist John Urry has observed, tourism is not only a substantial industry, it is also a part of our contemporary culture and is an important way in which people today can relate to their society.[5] Along the same lines, Dean MacCannell has aimed to endow the tourist role with a new dignity by comparing tourism to a religious pilgrimage.[6]

Tourism and war

The Western Front was the setting of one of the main theatres of fighting in the Great War and consisted of a line of earthworks or trenches which stretched from the Channel to the Swiss Frontier. Four years of fighting over the same areas of ground left millions of servicemen dead and a devastated, torn-up landscape, described in a Belgian guidebook as "nothing but a deserted sea, under whose waves corpses are sleeping". In 1917 John Masefield wrote that "It is as though the place had been smitten by the plague."[7] Whole villages vanished, reduced to what he described as "handfuls of smoke-grimed dust". On the land, entire sections of top-soil disappeared, exposing the limestone substratum underneath. After the Armistice in November 1918, the dead were gradually cleared from the battlefields and reburied in military cemeteries; towns, villages and roads were rebuilt; trenches and craters were filled in; and crop cultivation and natural re-growth slowly returned the Western Front area to the local communities. The area also became a magnet for tourists.

Even from the very outset of the War, interest in the fighting was so great that tourists were venturing out there on sightseeing expeditions while the guns were actually still blazing. As early as 1915 the travel company, Thomas Cook and Sons, felt obliged to run an advertisement in *The Times* warning people that there would be no conducted tours until the war was over.[8] Although tourism remained buoyant right up until the eve of the Second World War, during the 1950s and 60s public interest in the area dwindled away and commercial battlefield tours almost ceased to exist. The military historian, Martin Middlebrook noted that during a visit to the battlefields in 1967: "My friend and I met no other visitors on our travels and there seemed to be no organised tours."[9]

The Front gradually re-emerged as a tourist attraction during the 1970s, when it was almost accidentally kick-started back into life by a couple of military enthusiasts, Major Tony and Mrs Valmai Holt. The Holts, along with several other operators I have talked to, expressed surprise about the continued demand for these tours and see themselves as responding to a demand no one could have predicted. There are now at least nine fairly substantial travel firms offering tours, including a relative newcomer, Leger Holidays, which in 2001 took ten thousand people to the area. There is also a growing number of 'one man band' operators driving around in transit vans with names like "Bert's Battlefield Tours" literally crayoned on bits of paper and stuck in front of the driver's steering wheel.

In tandem with the region's growing appeal, new monuments are still being built, new ceremonies to honour the dead are still evolving and within the last ten years, at least six museums have opened. All kinds of people are attracted to this area, ranging from military enthusiasts and family historians, right down to the merely curious who want a different type of holiday. As a result of the English national curriculum requirements, tens of thousands of school children also make the trip out there.

So what is the power of this place? At first glance the sleepy market towns, the new industrial parks and intensely farmed rolling landscapes of the Ypres Salient and the Somme region could hardly be described as tourist honey pots. In addition, the hundreds of memorials and cemeteries situated within a poisoned landscape that remains saturated with decaying bodies and ammunition do not exactly offer themselves as feasts of sensual pleasure either. Yet, as sociologists such as Valene Smith and Tony Seaton have observed, where there is war, tourism is bound to follow.[10] Although at first glance tourism and war may appear to be at the polar extremes of cultural activity, it seems that we have a compulsion to revisit sites of conflict.[11] The battlefields of Flanders and Picardy have been no exception to this trend and they belong to a form of attraction which has been variously called 'thanatourism' or 'dark tourism'.[12]

However, not all wars remain as firmly fixed in our historical imagination as the battles on the Western Front. The psychological, emotional and intellectual investment of the British in that conflict is enormous.[13] Although historians might point out that its attraction is obvious simply because it was *the* great military and political event of its time which brought the life and values of Victorian and Edwardian England to a sudden end, this explanation alone does not account for its success as a popular and growing tourist attraction. As Seaton explains, the answer lies more in the actual nature of the tourism process itself and the way in which it is constructed and sustained.[14] He points to the work of MacCannell who offers some interesting insights into how sights evolve and continue to mature into quasi-religious, sacred attractions by way of a marking process resulting in 'sight sacralisation'.[15]

One of the most important processes of this sight sacralisation is the initial phase of naming. It is through this stage that places become invested with meaning and significance, transforming the physical and geographical into something that can be experienced historically and socially.[16] While Verdun remains the focus of French memory of the War, and the Trench of Death at Dixmuide is deeply symbolic for the Belgians, the names of the Somme and Passchendaele are key sites in British memory. For over 80 years they have remained synonymous with images of stalemate and the slaughter of thousands of young men across shell-torn wastelands of thick, glutinous mud. In fact, the carnage that took place on those battlefields during 1916 and 1917 have indelibly shaped our perceptions of the entire War. If the last year is remembered at all it is not for the Allied armies successes on the battlefields that led to the German surrender, but only for the Armistice itself.

Although a number of historians are presently re-appraising many of the traditionally accepted versions of the conduct of the War, the 'butchers and bunglers' myth and Blackadder's buffoon-like General Melchett are still uppermost in the public imagination and certainly in the media's presentation of the War.[17]

The itineraries of all organised battlefield tours reflect this trend by including trips to these sites. Just outside the village of Passchendaele is Tyne Cot, the largest British military cemetery in the world and the most frequently visited cemetery in the Ypres Salient. Throughout the year there are lines of coaches and cars parked outside its entrance and it is almost impossible to find a day when it is devoid of figures wandering up and down the rows of headstones. Lack of interest in the British armies' actual successes, however, has meant that the majority of guided tours still only cover the Somme and Passchendaele areas. Few cover the battles of 1918.

Today there is still an almost tangible sense of ownership over these areas of the Western Front where thousands of soldiers fought and died in appalling conditions. This sense of British appropriation of a foreign landscape began during the War and has continued off and on ever since. Writing about his wartime experiences at the Front, Mottram remarked that it "became a part of Britain, to be defended".[18] A sign put up at a cemetery in the Somme shortly after the War which captures this sense of ownership reads "The Devonshires held this trench; the Devonshires hold it still."

In addition to the thousands of military cemeteries which were ceded to Britain in perpetuity as the 'free gift' of the French and Belgian governments, other portions of the Western Front have since been acquired by the British.[19] In 1929 Lord Wakefield bought Talbot House in Poperinghe, Belgium for the Toc-H Organisation, and purchased the near-by Spanbroekmolen Crater a year later.[20] More recently Lochnagar Crater at La Boiselle on the Somme was purchased by Richard Dunning in 1978 and is now permanently preserved as a memorial; in 1990 the Western Front Association purchased the Butte de Warlencourt, an ancient burial ground which was the scene of fierce fighting in the 1916 battles on the Somme.

Yet the sense of shared inheritance between Britain, France and Flanders is more than just one of human agency. As Baker asserts, a landscape needs to be situated within its own natural ancestry and upbringing if it is to be properly understood.[21] Places have their own geographical personalities and their own biographies.[22] Until about 8,000 years ago, geologically Britain was still part of the European continent. Before the retreat of the last Ice Age, there was no English Channel. The Dogger Bank was a low ridge of peaty land lying below the great Chalk Down which extended from the South Downs to join the chalk in France.[23] Consequently, the tall cliffs on the Picardy coast look similar to the 'White Cliffs' of Dover, and both sections of shoreline have pebble beaches lying at the base of high walls of chalk. There are further resemblances inland. The French countryside around the Somme region was often compared to the Kent and Sussex landscape by veterans returning to the battlefields. In 1930 Henry Maskell wrote that "it was a typical Wealden landscape.... The hedgebanks were yellow with primroses and in the spinney, around the litter of bundled faggots, the bluebells mingled into a dreamy sapphire glow... I woke out of my reverie and remembered that this was not southern England, but the very heart of Picardy."[24] More recently, the military historian, Paul Reed, writes in his guide to the Somme that:

The land is rolling, and similar in texture to the Sussex Downs, where I grew up. Large fields are cut by dusty tracks in summer, and muddy lanes in winter. Birdsong is everywhere; the beauty of this place often belies the tragedy that unfolded here in 1916.[25]

Still intertwined in the historic and spatial configuration of the terrain are traces of the soldiers' vernacular landscape. Much of the Western Front still abounds with the wartime names the soldiers gave to particular places, ensuring the enduring British presence in the region. With the hundreds of Commonwealth War Grave Commission signs pointing to cemeteries which have names such as Owl Trench, Windy Corner, Hyde Park Corner, Bedford House, Blighty Valley, Flat Iron Copse and Dartmoor, it is often fairly easy to forget that you are not on British soil when driving around the French and Belgian countryside.[26] In history books and tourist guides too, English names for places and land features are habitually used. Tour guides will routinely gather their clients at Lochnagar Crater in the Somme, for example, and point out the Sausage and Mash valleys which lie on either side of it. At Ypres, a typical tour will take in Hell-Fire Corner, Clapham Junction and Sanctuary Wood. Recently, more and more signs have been cropping up to direct tourists to particular features which give the English wartime name along with the official French and Belgian ones.

Also helping to maintain British links to the area was the custom of twinning many of the ruined villages and towns in France and Flanders to British towns and cities, especially those places which had raised Pals battalions. In the Somme the village of Serre was adopted by Sheffield, Thiepval by Tonbridge, Beaumont-Hamel by Winchester, Peronne by Blackburn, Mametz by Llandidno and Albert by Birmingham, which has a street name called "rue de Birmingham". Even today there are strong links between the towns and cities of the Somme and Britain. The Salford Pals Memorial in Authuille, which stands next to the village's own local war memorial in the main street, was unveiled in 1995 with much pomp and ceremony in the presence of the Mayor and other town dignitaries. In July 2000 a memorial to a Victoria Cross winner, Lt Donald Bell of the Yorkshire Regiment, was erected in the village of Contalmaison with the co-operation of the mayor who said: "The people of Contalmaison have not forgotten the sacrifice of those young and brave soldiers and in particular, those in our small corner of France, the Somme."

In addition to place names, the individual names of the dead have also been planted on the landscape. Thousands of names, on headstones in cemeteries, on monuments to the missing, thread their way down the contours of the Front. As Laqueur observes, "the pyramids pale by comparison with the sheer scale of British commemorative imposition on the landscape – let alone the German, French, Belgian [and] Portuguese".[27] The desire to list the names of the fallen has also acted to continually reinforce their memory. Take any name from a telephone directory and it can be found inscribed somewhere on a memorial to the missing or on a headstone. The cemeteries, or silent cities as they are sometimes called, contain the bones of whole communities. The ever-growing distance in years from the conflict has led to a widening and stretching in the level of family connections and today most people, if they go back far enough, will discover a relative who fought or died in the trenches. According to the military historian and tour guide, Paul Reed, at least 50% of his clients have come out specifically to find a grave or to trace the footsteps of a relative who fought there.[28]

A seemingly infinite number of names are carved on the memorials to the missing at Ypres and at Thiepval on the Somme. The panels of the Menin Gate carry the names of nearly 55,000 British Empire soldiers who disappeared on the Ypres Salient from the outbreak of war in 1914 to August

1917.[29] The massive Thiepval Memorial to the Missing commemorates approximately 73,000 British and South African men who died in the Somme from July to November 1916.[30] After the sites were unveiled in 1927 and 1932 respectively, they became the focus of the thousands of pilgrims and tourists who travelled to the Front from across the Channel during the inter-war years and today they remain key sites of memory for British visitors. In Ypres, it is not unusual at any time of the year to see at least a hundred people gathered under the Menin Gate to listen to the nightly Last Post ceremony. On the Somme, the Thiepval Memorial to the Missing is more frequently visited than any other site on the Somme. In 1998 it attracted over 140,000 people, 70% of whom were British.[31] The sites also incorporate formal expressions of commemoration. Every year the Armistice Day ceremonies are held at the Menin Gate and are attended by various dignitaries and representatives from Britain, Europe, and Commonwealth countries as well as thousands of visitors from Britain. On 1 July at Thiepval a smaller, but increasingly popular annual memorial service is held to commemorate the first day of the Battle of the Somme. Until the early 1990s the service was organised by the Ministry of Defence but it has now been taken over by the Royal British Legion, Britain's *de facto* custodian of remembrance. Both ceremonies used to be traditionally attended by veterans of the War, but very few are now able to make the journey.

Fields forever England

Although tourists are taken on 'battlefield' tours, it is the cemeteries, rather than the battlefields themselves, which form a central part of their experience. The 'sacred islands of Empire' are lovingly kept by the Commission's gardeners and their work constantly evokes expressions of admiration from visitors. Their design was under the overall direction of Sir Frederic Kenyon, Director of the British Museum, who was appointed Adviser to the Commission in 1917, "with a view to focussing, and, if possible, reconciling the various opinions on this subject that had found expression among the Armies at the front and the general public at home...". Kenyon recommended that the cemeteries should recreate a pastoral idyll, reminiscent of a mixture between an English country garden and a village churchyard. Their planning was carried out by the Commissions' principal architects who worked alongside Gertrude Jekyll and horticulturists from the Royal Botanic Gardens.[32] The Commission intended that their basic styling should be dignified and respectful to soldiers of all ranks, from privates to generals, and irrespective of race, creed or civilian status. The plots of graves with their uniform headstones, were deliberately positioned to create the image of an army unit on parade, symbolic of soldiers still serving. To ensure that the inscriptions on the headstones were not obscured, it was decided that the borders should be typically planted with a mixture of low growing, hardy cottage garden plants such as herbaceous perennials, alpines and floribunda roses. Most cemeteries contain yew trees, which in some sites are clipped in shapes which resemble the tips of artillery shells.

The Commission's intentions were achieved with remarkable success. A veteran who returned to the battlefields in 1938 wrote: "the headstones are becoming dulled by time, roses and tree lupins adorned each little plot and in every sense it was an English garden".[33] Comments written in the cemetery visitor books indicate that present day visitors experience the same sentiments:

A beautiful English garden, rest in peace.

Fields forever England.[34]

Tyne Cot
British Military
Cemetery

Yet as Morris observes, the decision to make all soldiers lie in "... some corner of a foreign field, That is forever England" as Rupert Brooke's lines, written in 1914, uncannily predicted, has to some degree negated the identities and involvement of the former colonies.[35] Although there has been a limited planting of 'native plants' in some sites – Canadian graves in France are planted with maple trees; Australians with blue tree gums and wattle; Indians with marigolds and cypresses – other graves that belong to West Indian, West African and South African soldiers have no plants typical of their countries because the area's cold and inclement winter weather will not support them.

However, as Mabey points out, landscape has traditionally been used by nations to promote patriotism and the national landscape which has symbolised Britain is usually English in character.[36] Further, it is a rural English landscape, even though England has been an industrial and urban nation since the nineteenth century. The terrain of the Western Front has embodied this trend. As Spender commented, what men were fighting and dying for was some very green meadow with a stream running through it and willows on the banks – freedom was at heart "a feeling for the English landscape.[37] Yet despite the promotion of "a little bit of England over there" in the design of the cemeteries it has generally attracted little criticism, even from Commonwealth countries themselves. Comments in the visitors book at Adanac Cemetery on the Somme, which contains over 1,000 Canadian burials, express only positive responses towards the soldiers' resting-places, for example:

> A proud day to be a Canadian soldier.
> Visiting and remembering with
> respect and thanks.
> A fitting place to honour Canada's
> soldiers on the 56th anniversary.[38]

Tourism and the eroding landscape

Finally, how has the Front stood up to the ever-growing influx of throngs of British tourists? The success of the sight sacralisation process is now beginning to have a negative impact in some areas. Most tourist guide books remind their readers to be aware that the terrain they are travelling through is a working one and that some landowners may not welcome the sight of tourists tramping over their fields, looking for the remnants of war. Yet although the farmers are usually very tolerant, an increasing number of difficulties are occurring. Access to the cemeteries is a growing problem. A few farmers who are under financial pressure to make use of every square inch of their land, regularly plough up the cemetery *chemins*, leaving the tourists and Commission's gardeners to beat a path through the crop. One farmer who owns property that adjoins the Sheffield Memorial Park in the Somme has had enough of tourists, their cars and their coaches and has periodically blocked off the road to the Park with his tractor. The Commission has now put up a notice asking people not to drive to the site, but to walk instead.

The tramping of thousands of feet has also resulted in considerable wear and tear in some of the more prominent sites. Cemeteries such as Tyne Cot and Ramparts on the Salient have suffered considerable damage to their fabric, most notably the lawns, which in some sections have been completely worn away. Some of the memorial parks are also showing signs of erosion and damage to their fabric. The Newfoundland Memorial Park on the Somme, managed by the Canadian Department of Veterans Affairs, has recently undertaken conservation measures to prevent any further deterioration to the site. Much to the disappointment of regular visitors and tour guides, the entire area known as Y Ravine which contains a network of dugouts and tunnels, has now been placed out of bounds.

In other areas, it is not only the earth which is being worn down. The evocative ambience of the landscape is also being eroded. The Last Post ceremony at the Menin Gate in Ypres is now starting to suffer under the weight of crowds who gather to listen to the buglers. The ceremony is often applauded, which the buglers feel is embarrassing and inappropriate because they are not giving a performance. Some tour guides ask their clients not to clap, but as one of them remarked: "all it takes is one wally to start and everyone thinks they should follow". Due to recent financial cutbacks, the Ypres town council is not always able to provide police to stop the traffic during the playing of the Last Post. On these occasions the buglers are forced to play on the steps of the Gate, out of sight and earshot to many of the people who have come to witness the event.[39]

In conclusion, MacCannell's sight sacralisation model can provide valuable insights into the evolution of contemporary tourist attractions. Tourism is use of leisure time, and seeing, rather than participating, is the essence of touristic experience. Yet beneath its bland and shallow surface, tourism is political territory. Against the ever-present detritus of death, the Western Front landscape still has the power to evoke an imagined community of British nationhood. As Nigel Fountain remarked in his article in *The Guardian* about touring the Belgian battlefields: "Everybody should go to Flanders. It is what the old country is all about".[40]

1 Tilley, C, *A Phenomenology of Landscape: Places, Paths and Monuments*, Oxford: Berg, 1994, p. 27.

2 Shields, R, *Memory and Place: The Importance of Attending to Absence in Place-Based Research*, unpublished conference paper, 2000.

3 Boorstin, D J, *The Image: A Guide to Pseudo-Events in America*, New York: Harper and Row, 1964.

4 Cited from Jakle, J A, *The Visual Elements of Landscape*, Amherst: The University of Massachusetts Press, 1987, p. 153.

5 Urry, J, *The Tourist Gaze: Leisure and Travel in Contemporary Societies*, London: Sage, 1990.

6 MacCannell, D, *The Tourist: A New Theory of the Leisure Class*, London: MacMillan, 1976.

7 Masefield, J, *The Old Front Line*, London: W. Heinemann, 1917.

8 For an in-depth study of tourism and pilgrimage to the Western Front during the inter-war years please see Lloyd, D W, "Battlefield Tourism: Pilgrimage and the Commemoration of the Great War in Britain, Australia and Canada, 1919-1939", Oxford: Berg, 1998.

9 Middlebrook, M and Middlebrook, M, *The Somme Battlefield: A Comprehensive Guide from Crecy to the Two World Wars*, London: Penguin, 1994.

10 Smith, V L, "War and Tourism: An American Ethnography" in *The Annals of Tourism Research*, vol. 25 no. 1, 1998, pp. 202-227. Seaton, A V, "Guided by the Dark: from thanatopsis to thanatourism" in *International Journal of Heritage Studies*, vol. 2 no. 4, 1996, pp. 234-244. Seaton, A V, "War and Thanatourism: Waterloo 1815-1914" in *Annals of Tourism Research*, vol. 26 no. 1, 1999, pp. 130-158.

11 Diller, E and Scofidio, R, eds., *Back to the Front: Tourisms of War*, FRAC: Basse-Normandie, 1994, p. 19.

12 Foley, M and Lennon, J J, "JFK and Dark Tourism: Heart of Darkness", in *Journal of International Heritage Studies*, vol. 2 no. 2, 1994, pp. 195-197.

13 McPhail, H, "La Grande guerre – ressentiment et ignorance britanniques", Report for the *Historial de la Grand Guerre*, Peronne, pending publication, 2001.

14 Seaton, A V, "War and Thanatourism: Waterloo 1815-1914", p. 140.

15 MacCannell, D, *The Tourist: A New Theory of the Leisure Class*. MacCannell suggests five distinct stages of marking: naming – this marks the sight as being worthy of preservation; framing and elevation – this involves the display of an object or the opening of a sight for visitation. With elevation comes the need for framing the sight, i.e. putting it on display or placing an official boundary around it; enshrinement – the framing material, i.e. buildings erected to house important works of art or relics, such as museums, which themselves become attractions; mechanical reproduction – the reproduction of the attraction through the printed word, photographs, illustrations, etc.; and social reproduction – representation of the attraction in everyday practice away from its place of origin – e.g. from the Western Front we now have trench coats, wristwatches, the naming of suburbs and streets, sayings such as 'bombing along' etc..

16 Tilley, *A Phenomenology of Landscape*, p. 18.

17 See Bond, B and Cave, N, eds., *Haig: A Reappraisal 70 Years On*, Barnsley: Leo Cooper, 1999; Beckett, Ian F W, *The Great War 1914-1918*, Harlow, England and New York: Longman, 2001.

18 Mottram, R H, *Through the Menin Gate*, London: Chatto and Windus, 1932, p. 72.

19 France granted land 'in perpetuity' for British military cemeteries in 1915, Belgium in 1917.

20 Talbot House was a rest house behind the lines for soldiers of all rank, begun by Padre Tubby Clayton. It was named after Gilbert Talbot, son of the Bishop of Winchester, who was killed in the Salient. The soldiers shortened the name in Army signallers' language to 'Toc H'. In 1919 Clayton founded the Christian movement Toc H and the house has remained open as one of its branches.

21 Baker, A R H, and Biger, G, *Ideology and Landscape in Historical Perspective*, Cambridge: Cambridge University Press, 1992, p. 2.

22 Samuels, M S, "The Biography of Landscape" *The Interpretation of Ordinary Landscapes*, Meinig, D W, ed., Oxford, 1979.

23 Colvin, B, *Land and Landscape: Evolution, Design and Control*, London: John Murray, p. 19.

24 Maskell, H P, *The Soul of Picardy*, London: Ernest Benn Ltd., 1930.

25 Reed, P, *Battleground Europe. Walking the Somme*, Barnsley, South Yorkshire: Leo Cooper, 1997, p. 6.

26 Hereafter referred to as the 'Commission'. Before 1960 the Commission was known as the Imperial War Graves Commission. For a history of the Commission please see Longworth, P, *The Unending Vigil: A History of the Commonwealth War Graves Commission 1917-1984*, London: Leo Cooper/Secker & Warburg, 1985.

27 Laqueur, T, "Memory and Naming in the Great War" *Commemorations: The Politics of National Identity*, Gillis, J R, ed., Chichester: Princeton University Press, 1994, p. 155.

28 Interview, 12 April 1999.

29 The Menin Gate was designed by Reginald Blomfield. It was too small to include the names of the soldiers who died after August 1917. The remaining 34,888 names are inscribed on Herbert Baker's memorial at the rear of Tyne Cot cemetery.

30 Missing soldiers from Australia, Canada, India, Newfoundland and New Zealand are commemorated on national memorials to the missing at Villers-Bretonneux, Vimy Ridge, Neuve Chapelle, Beaumont-Hamel and Longueval respectively.
According to Vincent Scully, author of "The Terrible Art of Designing a War Memorial", in *The New York Times*, 14 July 1991, p. 28, Maya Lin drew the inspiration for her 'statement of intention' required to accompany her design for the Vietnam Veterans Memorial in Washington DC, from a lecture at Yale College on Lutyen's monument to the missing.

31 C D T Somme, "La Fréquentation Touristique de l'Espace Historique des Batailles de la Somme", (avec la collaboration de l'Historical de la Grande Guerre et du Musée des Abris et de la DDE de la Somme), May 1999 (unpublished).

32 Edwin Lutyens, Reginald Blomfield, Herbert Baker and Charles Holden.

33 This is quoted from an article, "Roses for memory" and signed 'C.W.P.' which first appeared in, *The Ypres times* in January 1938. It was reproduced under the heading "War Scenes Re-visited" in *The Western Front Association Bulletin*, June 2000, no. 57, pp. 30-31.

34 These comments were written in the Thistle Dump Military Cemetery visitors' book, April 2001.

35 Morris, M, "Gardens 'For Ever England': Landscape, Identity and the First world War. British Cemeteries on the Western Front", in *Ecumene*, vol. 4 no. 4, 1997, pp. 411-434.

36 Mabey, R, "Landscape: Terra Firma?", *Towards a New Landscape*, N. Alfrey et al, London: Bernard Jacobson Ltd, 1993, pp. 63-68, p. 64.
See also Lowenthal, D, "British National Identity and the English Landscape" in *Rural History*, vol. 2, no. 2, 1991, pp. 205-230.

37 Spender, S, *Love-Hate Relations*, London: Hamish Hamilton, 1974.

38 Adanac is Canada backwards. These comments were written in the visitors' book, March 1999.

39 Cited from correspondence in *The Western Front Association Bulletin*, no. 60, June 2001, pp. 42-43.

40 Fountain, N, "Fields forever England", *The Guardian*, Travel Section, p. 9, 1998.

Imagining Xenotransplantation: the Global Cultural Economy of an Emergent Biotechnology
Markus Idvall

A Landscape Terminology

In his book *Modernity at Large* the anthropologist Arjun Appadurai describes the contemporary global cultural economy as an "order" characterised by being "complex, overlapping, [and] disjunctive".[1] This particular order is, moreover, apprehended as distinctly new. As such it is also designated as in need of a new type of analytic model capable of countering some of the more established theories of the global economy which are preoccupied with strictly economic models of global development and the role of individual nation-states.[2] Appadurai offers a framework for realising a more thorough investigation of how disjuncture and difference have become major elements in the global cultural economy. Five dimensions, each one outlining a specific aspect of its cultural flows, are included in the framework: 1) ethnoscapes, 2) mediascapes, 3) technoscapes, 4) financescapes, and 5) ideoscapes. "The suffix *-scape*", Appadurai explains,

> allows us to point to the fluid, irregular shapes of these landscapes, shapes that characterise international capital as deeply as they do international clothing styles. These terms with the common suffix *-scape* also indicate that these are not objectively given relations that look the same from every angle of vision but, rather, that they are deeply perspectival constructs, inflected by the historical, linguistic, and political situatedness of different sorts of actors: nation-states, multinationals, diasporic communities, as well as subnational groupings and movements (whether religious, political or economic), and even intimate face-to-face groups, such as villages, neighborhoods, and families.[3]

Central to this landscape terminology is what Appaduari calls "the imagination as a social practice".[4]

> No longer mere fantasy (opium for the masses whose real work is elsewhere), no longer simple escape (from a world defined principally by more concrete purposes and structures), no longer elite pastime (thus not relevant to the lives of ordinary people), and no longer mere contemplation (irrelevant for new forms of desire and subjectivity), the imagination has become an organised field of social practices, a form of work (in the sense of both labour and culturally organised practice), and a form of negotiation between sites of agency (individuals) and globally defined fields of possibility.[5]

Cultural constructions based on a multitude of perspectives in combination with different kinds of situatedness – historical, linguistic, political – are the very essence of the concept of imaginary landscape. Imaginary ethnoscapes, for example, are in this respect a way of recognising that even the most peaceful and calm community is "everywhere shot through with the woof of human motion".[6] Still, a main point of using a landscape terminology is its stabilising effect. The imaginary landscapes make it possible to frame the manifoldness of an existence where everything is in motion: people, information, technology, money, and ideologies.

Appadurai concludes that the imaginary landscapes are "the building blocks" of what he describes as "imagined worlds".[7] What these imagined worlds can be seen as, I will return to in the end of this paper. A comparison will then be made between Appadurai's concept and two other analytical concepts: the sociologist Pierre Bourdieu's "field" and the social scientist Benedict Anderson's "imagined community".

However, having come this far I must now consider the possibilities of applying this framework of imaginary landscapes to my own empirical field of investigation – an emergent biotechnology called xenotransplantation. How will the theory of global imaginary landscapes withstand the empirical reality of this (generally not very well-known) phenomenon? And, what aspects of xenotransplantation can be developed on the basis of the theoretical model? Let me first give a sketch of the sort of matters with which I am dealing.

Studying an Emergent Biotechnology

Xenotransplantation is a scientific practice that preoccupies several medical centres around the world, mainly in the rich countries of North America, Europe and Asia. Technically speaking, it concerns the transplantation of solid organs and other tissue across species borders. The concept includes a number of different technologies with different aims. No standardised clinical methods of treatment exist. Xenotransplantation is still a quest for scientific models whose value depends on their potential to become a clinical success. As for organs, transplantation from animals to humans is seen as a possible solution to the critical shortage of human hearts, lungs, livers, and kidneys – a shortage which presently inhibits transplantation surgery in many countries. Regarding animal cells, there is a hope for therapies both for diabetes and Parkinson's disease. The former approach involves transplants of insulin-producing cells from the pig's pancreas into humans, the latter transplants of brain tissue from a pig foetus into the human brain.

There are, however, several medical problems connected to the development of xenotransplantation technology. One is the immunological barrier between humans and animals. If there is no effective way of suppressing the reaction of the human immune system, animal transplants will always be rejected by the human body. Scientists are attempting to neutralise the barrier in different ways. One approach has been to modify the animal transplants genetically by adding human genes and thereby making them less susceptible to rejection.

Another medical problem is the risk of animal viruses spreading among humans. In 1997 a virological study showed that a so-called endogenous retrovirus of the pig is able *in vitro* (in test tubes) to infect human cells.[8] Since such a virus is a hereditary part of the genome of the pig, the difficulties of avoiding infections became evident. Experts started to discuss the possibility that an animal virus of this sort would spread among humans in the future and, at worst, cause new incurable diseases. In 1999 a new study revealed that out of 160 patients, who all had been treated with various living pig tissues up to twelve years earlier, none showed any sign of being infected by an endogenous retrovirus of the pig.[9] However, the debate about the risk of infection was not settled, since the incubation period is expected to be much longer than the 12 years upon which the study of the xenotransplanted patients was based.

Various ethical and cultural problems can also be anticipated. Several studies dealing with these issues have been presented. Some have discussed the public perceptions of the specific research.[10] Others have focused on the debates between scientific experts and their opponents.[11] The individual attitudes and experiences of patients, university students, and nurses have also been studied.[12] An overall ambition has been to understand how scientific knowledge is perceived and received by different social groups in society.

In my own research I concentrate on the social network of some potential recipients of xenotransplants and their interlocutors at the hospital and in the family. I have carried out 37 in-depth interviews with scientists, doctors, nurses, staff nurses, patients, and relatives, all having a connection to the Department of Transplantation Surgery at Huddinge University Hospital/Karolinska Institute in Stockholm, Sweden. The aim of the project has been to describe and analyse, from a cultural and ethical viewpoint, the different attitudes and perceptions of xenotransplantation among some subjects which, either by personal plight or professional involvement, are engaged in the xenogenetic research of the clinic – a research programme aiming at treating diabetic patients clinically by transplanting insulin-producing cells from the pancreas of the pig into humans. Basically it has been a question of understanding how an acceptance of scientific methods is created and maintained in medical environments distinguished by an oscillation between the everyday routines of care and the determined activities of hard science.

The Imaginary Landscapes of Xenotransplantation

By using specific landscape terminology it is possible not only to visualise the disjunctive character of the global cultural economy surrounding the development of xenotransplantation, but also to establish the leading part that imagination plays in the social processes in question. It is generally known that material conditions vary a great deal in the world. But even when groups and individuals share the same material conditions, their imaginary participation in activities cannot be taken for granted as being identical. In this regard the imagination contributes effectively to cultural complexity. Here I want only to focus on two of the five imaginary landscapes that were presented above. Giving priority to imaginary ethnoscapes and mediascapes seems, nevertheless, to be in correspondence with Appadurai's own intentions. In the introduction to *Modernity at Large* he gives, at any rate, special attention to the global flows of migration and media. These are, he says, "two major, and interconnected, diacritics" when analysing "the work of imagination as a constitutive feature of modern subjectivity".[13] Below I will first focus on the imaginary ethnoscapes of xenotransplantation and the cultural meanings of the immense travel industry that encircles this particular biotechnological development: the imaginary practices of the researchers can, here especially, be distinguished. Secondly, I will deal with the imaginary mediascapes and their effects on the relationships and performances in the medical wards.

Scientific Journeying

Central to the imaginary ethnoscapes is the urge of the individual researcher to make claims about some aspect of the big puzzle of xenotransplantation and thereby become known as the one who liberated the world from a widespread and particularly painful disease. Embodying this urge, the researchers are prone to liken their work to a journey which has only begun, but which, eventually, will open up for new and better conditions. In the meantime a number of discoveries, in the shape of milestones along the narrow road of science, can be expected. This imaginary of saving the population of the world from diseases that cause pain and early death, has lately turned into a conviction that the most effective way of distributing the results of science is to start a company on the basis of the researcher's own discoveries. To gain patent rights is both a goal and an instrument in this imaginary process.

From a material perspective, the imaginary ethnoscapes of xenotransplantation are rooted in international air traffic and the constitution of attractive scientific meeting spots (conference buildings, universities, cities). This infrastructure makes possible the personal interaction between like-minded researchers from different parts of the world. Being present at an international conference, together with individuals who envision the world in a similar way, becomes important for how the individual researcher pictures his/her scientific work in relation to what is possible or probable. Young and upcoming researchers are, in particular, exposed to the imaginary atmosphere of the international conference.

The imaginary ethnoscapes of xenogenetic research also have a sedentary character in the sense that the individual researchers, to a great extent, are dependent on the global networks of electronic interaction. The practice of sitting in front of the personal computer, looking at websites and reading electronic mail, forms not only the base of the scientific travel industry. It also creates spaces which, by themselves, are shaping the dreams of the researchers.

Thus, as a participant in the imaginary ethnoscapes the researcher has a good possibility of becoming a creative dreamer and inventor. He or she may, however, also appear as an eccentric in his/her own local contexts. The self-sacrificing engagement in scientific practice seems odd in the eyes of the local others – the nurses as well as the patients and their relatives. Surprisingly, the researchers in this respect share more with the opponents of xenotransplantation than with their collaborators in the local hospital or in the laboratory. Being a member of an animal activist group and a champion of the prohibition of xenotransplantation, is in a way to participate in the same type of inspiring dreamscapes that researchers engage in. In order to achieve the goal of saving the animals from experimentation, the activists take part in a global imaginary landscape that has many features in common with how researchers interact. As in the world of science, international conferences and web sites attract a lot of attention among the animal activists. By striving for legislation that will stop what is seen as a cruel utilisation of the animals, the activists are, symbolically, fighting in the same type of legal arena as the researchers do when struggling for patent rights.

Anticipating Change

The imaginary mediascapes of xenotransplantation haunt the medical ward and its different social actors whom they provide with a multitude of different mass media images. The possibilities for taking up a principled stance vary. Sometimes mass media offer quite neutral explanations of scientific data; sometimes they focus on the patient and promises of an imminent remedy; and sometimes they attend to questions relating to animals and assumptions that suffering cannot be avoided. The kaleidoscope of media images frames the way in which the social actors of the ward – the medical personnel as well as the patients and their relatives – relate to the scientific quest. Despite the loose connections that these groups often have to the scientific activity, we are here confronted with a significant cultural power regarding the legitimacy of the research being undertaken. The social actors of the medical ward are not only the potential executers of what is anticipated will come true, but also kinds of moral witnesses in an ethically difficult situation.

In this context the media images of xenotransplantation are filtered through a multitude of malfunctioning but, very likely, improvable everyday life activities and, under the influence of this filtering, they are converted into visionary emblems. What appears is a clinically biased image of xenotransplantation which, in my study, has mainly positive connotations for the social actors, but which, depending on the situation, also can materialise as disillusionment and opposition.

Regarding the medical personnel, the nurses of the ward, because of their large numbers and their tendency to dominate the social interactions in the ward, are central to how mass mediated images of xenotransplantation are received. In general, nurses have limited possibilities for becoming full members of the scientific community. They might know a great deal about the conditions of the research in the particular clinic, but they never really participate whole-heartedly in the practice of science. Instead the nurses are the ones who most originally contribute to the clinically biased imagination of xenotransplants. As a cultural force they become representatives of a growing wish within the health sector that certain diseases and injuries be remedied. An emergent impatience with particular types of suffering is created.

The patients and their relatives provide the clinical imagination with a personal rather than a professional air. The growing impatience is here embodied in concrete life situations which are significant not only in the hospital, but in society in general. In this regard, the media images of xenotransplantation are experienced as both more general and more private and distressing in comparison with how they act upon the medical personnel.

Thus, in the midst of the mediascapes surrounding the medical ward, the imagination of the social actors, despite the differences that have been discussed above, circles around a mutual anticipation of change. How this potential change is experienced varies from time to time and from situation to situation. In my study different versions of a success story dominate. But also representations of a forthcoming disaster may, under certain circumstances, take hold of people's beliefs in the future. Struggling for patent rights or legal restrictions is, in this regard, matters of less importance for the social actors of the medical ward. Instead, attention is given to the malfunctioning therapeutic situation and the possibility that things, in one way or another, can change and, hopefully, improve. Through the mass media images of xenotransplantation the expectations of change taking place in one direction or another become higher and higher.

The Body Economy of the Xenotransplant

From the perspective of the individual actor – inside, what Appadurai calls, "the last locus of this perspectival set of landscapes" – imagining xenotransplantation becomes a struggle around the animate body.[14] Several more or less antagonistic images of the organs and the tissue within the expected xenogenetic programme are formed. The antagonism describes a social process where scientific ideas, rather than clinical practices, stand in the forefront. The opposing body images are generated by the fact that the project of realising animal-to-human transplants is associated both with great achievements for mankind (the elimination of the organ shortage and common diseases like diabetes and Parkinson's), great risks (the spread of new and incurable diseases), morally charged issues (the transcendence of the species border between humans and animals, the experimental utilisation of animals), and the possibility of great personal gains (heart patients being 'given a new life', diabetic patients being cured of what was believed to be a chronic disease, scientific entrepreneurs making big money). In the midst of all this, the living body exists as an intermediary between good and bad, between what is seen as ethical and unethical.

Thus, transplanting across species' borders involves a body economy that is constituted by a number of animate categories and their varying exchange rates. Promises of benefits as well as premonitions of suffering are articulated within the frames of this body economy. A number of motivational structures or movements are formed and transformed on the basis of how the images of the different human and animal categories are valued. Among the social actors these movements create, through their corporeal foundations, both a total engagement in the present and a strong hope, or alternately distrust, in the future. Here I will discuss some of these imaginary movements which are caused by and are causing the struggle around the living body.

Transplanting from Animals to Humans – the Clinical Vision

Moving transplants from animal to human clinically and routinely is what many researchers and doctors want to achieve in the relatively near future. But before this, one will have to solve the problems concerning the rejection of animal grafts and the risks from viruses by doing experiments also on humans. Xenotransplantation then raises questions about the procedures being followed when patients participate in tests. What will be needed in order to make the individual patients well-informed and highly motivated test subjects? What are the limits if one does not want to create human guinea pigs?

Authorities in several Western countries want to create a frame of consent around xenotransplantation research and its relationship to patients. A concept called "informed consent" has been introduced in Sweden and other countries. It aims at providing science with appropriate test subjects without the patients feeling that they are being exploited or maltreated. The key word is "information". By giving the patients information that is truthful, unabridged and comprehensible, it is expected that they – after taking their so-called voluntary decision – will accept being made a test subject without suspicion, and attendant negative thoughts, that they are possibly being taken advantage of.

However, practising this informed consent will be more difficult than mapping its principles. Put into practice the concept of informed consent will be part of that complex balancing act between pros and cons that each patient has to perform before saying yes or no to participation in an experimant. In my interviews the nurses especially, as intermediaries between science and care, are conscious of the ambivalent situation of the patients and the personal risk that they run every time they participate as test subjects. Giving an illustration of how it should *not* be, one nurse refers to the controversial xenotransplantation case of the newborn Baby Fae who, in 1984, received a heart from a baboon and died after 21 days. Another nurse makes a reference to the Polish heart patient who in 1992, according to Swedish mass media, received a pig heart and died after just 24 hours.

In the movement from animal to human, the animals are represented as donor animals or source animals. A way of legitimising these still not fully realised transgenic animals, whose only task in their short life will be to sacrifice their organs and tissue to humans, is by reference to animals slaughtered for food. Since we have always eaten animals, the use of source animals, one thinks, should not, logically, be anything unethical. But in times when the meat industry is questioned by many and when people choose to become vegetarians and even vegans, any reference to animals raised for slaughter is understandably never unproblematic.

Justifying xenotransplantation by referring imaginatively to slaughtered animals makes, nonetheless, the pig, rather than the monkey, into the appropriate xenogenetic animal. Accordingly, several of my interviewees classify the pig as an industrial product. Another aspect of this is their firm belief that no individual or personal ties will develop between a human and a pig after a xenotransplantation. Still, some interviewees ponder on the possibility that eating pork would be more difficult in the future for a person transplanted with a pig organ or pig tissue. Regarding the possibility of having monkeys as donors, the interviewees feel, with a few exceptions, that this should be avoided. Monkeys are seen as wild animals, and the possibility that man could start hunting these wild monkeys – which, like humans, nurture families and have family related feelings (as a nurse explains to me) – to collect fitting transplants is a discomforting thought for many of the interviewees. The monkeys are, in this respect, seen as morally similar to humans, while the pigs are taken as morally dissimilar.[15]

Moving from Humans to Animals – a Future Threat?

Regarding the motivation structure "from human to animal", the plots of the fairy-tales that we read for our small children come to mind. In these half real, half virtual spaces we are confronted by individuals which are animals, but also owners of human legs, human arms, human brains and motivations and so on. Only under these circumstances do humans seem willing to endow the particularities of their own species on creatures of another.

However, fairy-tale figures are surprisingly crucial when appreciating how the issue of xenotransplantation is perceived among different groups in society. Fairy-tale figures have in particular become part of organised resistance to biotechnology. In my interviews any reference by me to them – viz. creatures being more animal than human – was often comprehended as a reference to the popular critique of xenotransplantation.

Besides being part of the resistance movement, fairy-tale figures are an expression of how xenotransplantation has come to be experienced as a possible threat to the human species, even among some of its defenders. In my interviews the experience of this threat manifested itself particularly when individuals, who were basically positive to the xenogenetic approach, had reservations – albeit in different ways – concerning the ongoing biotechnological development. A nurse, who distinguished herself by being a strong adherent of xenotransplantation research, told me for example that "gene manipulation" is good "as long as we use it in a way that is not absurd": xenotransplantation, she added, is not absurd. Also one very research friendly patient that I interviewed felt that he could not speak affirmatively about biotechnological development without some kind of reservation. Although a proponent of "DNA research", he felt obliged to emphasise that such research has to be supervised, "so we do not start to switch brains". His wife, being interviewed at the same time, replied that genetic modifying is something good if one attempts to eliminate serious diseases, but this does not mean that researchers are allowed to create "elite humans".

The Imagined Worlds of Xenotransplantation

As suggested in the introduction, when studying xenotransplantation as a question of imaginary landscapes we come across something called imagined worlds. These can be seen as the effect of the imaginary landscapes. As such they consist of all those mixed feelings that are generated by the imaginary landscapes and which have been discussed above: the feelings of creativity, anticipation, risk, and threat. Theoretically, the concept of imagined world aims at understanding the processes whereby cultural identities and integration are formed and transformed in modern society. Compared with the aforementioned theories of Pierre Bourdieu and Benedict Anderson, an analytical framework of imagined worlds offers a different and more globally orientated perspective. Here I want, very tentatively, to challenge some facets of these two extremely influential theories by pointing critically to a sort of incapacity with regard to the attention they give to the imagination as a cultural force.

The concept of field is pivotal to Bourdieu's theory of class society. A field is, in many regards, a materialisation of how class society works through the production of class-related beliefs. It may be defined as a structured space of socially and hierarchically related positions, in which the different agents of the field – on the basis of their individual resources or cultural capital – are engaged in a struggle against each other, but also for a common and, in relation to other fields and classes, distinguishing goal.[16] A prerequisite for the constitution of the field is autonomy. Without autonomy *vis-à-vis* its surroundings, the field cannot exist, and, in principle, neither can the classes, since their existence is to a great deal dependent on the interactions in the social field. An analysis of imagined worlds does not dispute the existence of class struggle and class related beliefs. It questions, however, the assumption that these social forms are produced within autonomous fields of legitimatising interaction. Dealing with the imagination as a social practice implies rather an interest in the mutual interdependence and continuous overlaps between different spheres of social and cultural agency. In the discussion above it has been demonstrated that the different social categories of xenotransplantation – researchers, nurses, patients, relatives, and even activists – cannot be held apart concerning their contribution to how the specific biotechnology is valued in society. On the contrary, these different categories seem to be continuously exposed to each other's performances and attitudes.

In Anderson's theory of nationalism, the concept of imagined community is absolutely indispensable. According to Anderson all kinds of communities, "larger than primordial villages of face-to-face contact (and perhaps even these)", are founded on imagining and creation.[17] With regard to the nation, the imagination has three aspects: limitation, sovereignty, and community. In Anderson's own words:

> The nation is imagined as *limited* because even the largest of them, encompassing perhaps a billion living human beings has finite, if elastic, boundaries, beyond which lie other nations.... It is imagined as *sovereign* because the concept was born in an age in which Enlightenment and Revolution were destroying the legitimacy of the divinely-ordained, hierarchical dynastic realm.... Finally, it is imagined as a *community*, because, regardless of the actual inequality and exploitation that may prevail in each, the nation is always conceived as a deep, horizontal comradeship.[18]

The aspects of sovereignty and community appear crucial for capturing a specific historical reality: the idea of the nation was created in the end of the eighteenth century, and it has been realised – deeply and horizontally – for more than two hundred years all over the world. However, the aspect of limitation, *territorial* limitation, must be questioned. It is built on the false assumption that the imagination would obey territorial boundaries. But a territorial autonomy of the nations is, like the social autonomy of the classes, not possible considering the imagination as an empowering force. In that sense the imagined worlds of xenotransplantation involve territories that are boundless rather than bounded. Those images of possibilities and risks that have been discussed above may, for example, have their origin within the frames of my local study. Analytically, they are still symptoms of global flows rather than anything else.

Looking at xenotransplantation from the perspective of imagined worlds is, thus, a way of critically scrutinising two key concepts in social and humanistic theory: the concepts of class and nation. Regarding the emergent phenomenon of xenotransplantation, the theory of imaginary landscapes demonstrates the non-existence of those autonomous platforms of social agency or national sentiments that other theories often take for granted. These imaginary landscapes therefore confirm the importance of social and cultural theory that can appraise the work of imagination and its visionary, but at the same time practical, influence on society.

1   Appadurai, A, *Modernity at Large: Cultural Dimensions of Globalization*, Minneapolis and London: University of Minnesota Press, p. 32.
2   Appadurai, *Modernity at Large*, p. 32.
3   Appadurai, *Modernity at Large*, p. 33.
4   Appadurai, *Modernity at Large*, p. 31.
5   Appadurai, *Modernity at Large*, p. 31.
6   Appadurai, *Modernity at Large*, pp. 33-34.
7   Appadurai, *Modernity at Large*, p. 33.
8   Patience, C, et al, "Infection of human cells by an endogenous retrovirus of pigs", *Nature Medicine*, vol. 3, 1997, pp. 282-286.
9   Paradis, K, et al, "Search for Cross-Species Transmission of Porcine Endogenous Retrovirus in Patients Treated with Living Pig Tissue", *Science*, vol. 285, 20 August, 1999, pp. 1236-1241.
10 Durant, J, et al, eds., *Biotechnology in the Public Sphere: a European Sourcebook*, London: Science Museum, 1998.
11 Brown, N, "Debates in Xenotransplantation: on the Consequences of Contradiction", *New Genetics and Society*, vol. 18 no. 2/3, 1999, pp. 181-196. Brown, N and Michael, M, "Switching between Science and Culture in Transpecies Transplantation", *Science, Technology, & Human Values*, vol. 26 no. 1, 2001, pp. 3-22.
12 Lundin, S, "The Boundless Body: Cultural Perspectives on Xenotransplantation", *Ethnos*, vol. 64 no. 1, 1999, pp. 5-31. Hagelin, J, et al, "Students' Acceptance of Clinical Xenotransplantation", *Clinical Transplantation*, vol. 14, 2000, pp. 252-256. Mohacsi, P J, et al, "Attitudes to Xenotransplantation: Scientific Enthusiasm, Assumptions and Evidence", *Annals of Transplantation*, vol. 3, 1998, pp. 38-45.
13 Appadurai, *Modernity at Large*, p. 3.
14 Appadurai, *Modernity at Large*, p. 33.
15 Brown and Michael, "Switching between Science and Culture in Transpecies Transplantation", pp. 3-22.
16 Bourdieu, P, *Language and Symbolic Power*, Cambridge: Polity Press, 1991.
17 Anderson, B, *Imagined Communities: Reflections on the Origin and Spread of Nationalism*, London and New York: Verso, 1991, p. 6.
18 Anderson, *Imagined Communities*, p. 7.

Landscape Practice, Landscape Research: an Essay in Gentle Politics
David Crouch and Charlotta Malm

This paper explores aspects of the webs of everyday life through which, we argue, landscape is practiced and figured. Through this exploration we intend to reveal, or better, to make sense of, processes and meanings that are simultaneously shaped and communicated through social interaction and engagement between human subjects and what is called landscape. To go further, we suggest that landscape is constructed and constituted in the embodied practice, or performance, of space. We consider this engagement, or encounter, in a number of contexts and scales. The discussion engages the dynamic relationship between representations of landscape and their practice. Central to this discussion are the potentials of non-representational, or embodied, geographies presented as a possible way of addressing and accessing lay knowledges of landscape.[1]

Our concern is to access knowledges constituted through practicing, or performing, landscapes, both as a means for the researcher to make active, useful and positive contributions to people 'out there', as well as adding to and challenging academic discourse on landscape.

Recent developments in so-called bodily aware, sensuous and expressive theory in terms of lay, everyday geographical knowledges provide new orientations for theorising landscape.[2] We outline some of these perspectives as complementing and developing the prevailing interpretations of landscape as 'text'. Furthermore, we argue that strictly textual approaches to landscape tend to make it difficult for the researcher to engage the ways in which meanings and everyday knowledges of landscapes are grasped. We regard these 'everyday' dimensions of landscape encounter as important in making sense of what landscape is. Thus, landscape is about much more than vision – despite the importance of vision.[3] Following a brief exploration of some recent theoretical developments we turn to a consideration of how such ideas may inform the politics of landscape and, in particular, the politics of landscape research that follows from such a theoretical re-orientation.

In this paper, the politics of landscape is considered in terms of two orientations. First, as a micro-politics of human subjectivity through which landscape is (re)figured in relation to identities. We argue that engaging recent debates on embodied practices or performances of landscape will contribute to a fuller understanding of the micro-political practice of landscape and its representation. We suggest that the bundle of so-called non-representational geographical theory offers a deeper possibility to engage aspects of this lay micro-political practice. And second, as a research politics of the 'in-between' relations between researcher and researched, in which insight is also enabled by the possibility of rethinking landscape as bodily encounter.

Our discussion will be elaborated through references to two projects in which the co-authors are involved, as researchers. These are, first, a project investigating landscapes in Shetland, Scotland, represented, two-dimensionally, in photographs as something pretty, primordial and 'empty', detached from local understandings and yet in which everyday life is politically embodied. Our second project works around an interpretative encounter between researcher, photographer, landscapes and people living in Upper Weardale, County Durham, England, using photography and forms of ethnographic interview in order to develop a discourse of embodied landscape. We conclude with a discussion on ethnographic research methodologies, focusing in particular on various implications of fieldwork, in an attempt to respond to the potential that our discussion of theoretical orientations suggests.

Embodying Landscape

The individual encounters landscape in complex, multi-dimensional practices. Thomas Csordas argues that the subject lives her body and lives the world through her body.[4] In these terms, our contact with the world can be considered a multi-dimensional encounter that expresses emotion and relationship through inter-subjective body-communication.[5] The individual moves, speaks and experiences space through and in relation to her body and its space – the space of the world around her body as the immediate material and metaphorical space of action. The feeling of being together, for example, can animate space through the meaning of the physical encounter with other bodies: such encounters are also inter-subjective.[6] Space, and by extension, landscape, is given character by the expressive performance through which the individual encounters it. For the individual this constitutes a feeling of doing, an act of space-ing, constituting landscape anew in a multi-sensual patina, provoking imagination and its translation into different sensual feelings and spatial intimacies.[7] Landscape is thereby performed in a process of flows, where combinations of memory, action and meaning are complex and performed together.[8]

This is a knowledge made sensual through doing, in particular places and times whose inscriptions are refigured into an individual embodied semiotics, making sense in terms of individuals' lives and contributing to the ways in which life may be made sense of.[9] The semiotic process becomes problematised, in consequence, and further investigations would benefit from the application and development of Anne Game's autobiographical account of materialist semiotics:

> … my desire has indeed been to know the place, to be able to read the codes of, for example, the public footpaths and bridleways; to have a competence with respect to this landscape, to be local and party to its stories, in a sense there is a desire to 'know' what cannot be seen….[10]

What emerges is a practical, ontological knowledge as space is engaged in the ongoing processes of the individual, in what Tim Ingold terms a process of dwelling.[11] It is in this sense, too, that practical knowledges, anchored in reflexivity, emerge as embodied processes. Indeed, as Nick Crossley argues, people inhabit and constitute spaces of power relations, and embodiment provides "necessary grounds through which to rethink them."[12] Such encounters enable a negotiation of relations. What appears to be happening is both pre-discursive and discursive. The apparently pre-discursive sensuous/expressive is made by subjects already embedded in a cultural world; they may act pre-discursively, but reflexively and discursively re-figure their sensuous/expressive and poetic encounters. But in this process they are also refiguring the so-called mediated 'contexts' of that world. Discursivity and subjectivity are further complicated by simultaneous pre-discursive encounters. In effect, landscape is practised and signified in relation to an expressive and sensuous embodied practice. Inscribed contexts (such as tourist brochures or heritage reports) can pre-dispose forms of expression, but they can also be disrupted.

Figures 1-4
From *A Landscape Assessment of the Shetland Isles by Scottish Natural Heritage* 1998, prepared by Gillespies, pp. 77, 81, 99, 109

It is possible to argue that landscapes become a process of reflexivity, of identity and inter-subjectivity. Their 'character' is constructed, by the subject herself, from numerous 'things', and her own encounter, physically, with bits of landscape. These become engaged as fragments of a wider everyday visual culture, 'there', though her embodied and reflexively-embodied encounter may be most significant. Material features so encountered are rendered meaningful through our personal engagement with them.[13] What emerges is a geography of spatialisation: a process. Understood in this way, landscape, place and space, are never ontologically given but developed through practices, discursively grasped in an embodied way. The subject in landscape is spacing, practising, producing, doing things in and with space.

Landscapes Empty and Contested

Different approaches to landscape – different understandings of what landscape is and how it should best be studied – will produce radically different stories. So far we have mainly discussed landscape as processes, as a multitude of relationships between inner and outer geographies. Yet, a longstanding tradition in landscape studies still deals with landscape as a predominantly objective enterprise, where landscape is understood as something detached and 'other' from the encountering subject. It is perhaps in these contexts, too, that representations such as maps and photographs are most frequently drawn upon to communicate landscape 'value'. Here, we will consider a so-called landscape character assessment of the Shetland Islands, published a few years ago by the Scottish Natural Heritage (SNH), in order to discuss the adequacy of such representations in relation to some of the perspectives touched upon in the introduction to this chapter.[14]

Scottish Natural Heritage is a government body, and as such its brief is to promote good management and enjoyment of the Scottish countryside, as well as to provide certain executive services to government. The landscape character assessment is explicitly aimed at those concerned with land management and landscape change on a professional basis. More specifically, it is intended to provide a 'landscape context' for council officials and SNH staff based in the islands, responding to planning and land use related issues. However, it soon becomes evident that the text speaks not only to planners, council officials and SNH staff. For instance, we may claim the text for our own ends, as academics, or as individuals interested in Shetland landscapes, just as it could be drawn upon and appropriated by many others for a number of different motifs. Of course, this is nothing unique to this particular text. Practices and contexts surrounding any text, in terms both of where it is displayed and by whom it is and is not viewed, will inevitably have effects on the text, its authors as well as its readers. [15]

The assessment primarily works around a systematic identification of areas regarded as currently being under threat, together with suggestions for ways of safeguarding such areas through special landscape initiatives, often through the enhancement of certain features considered to contribute to landscape character. [16] On the basis of this, a set of guidelines is formulated, aimed at indicating how certain identified, and potentially threatened, landscape characteristics may be conserved, enhanced or developed as considered appropriate. [17] Or, more precisely, as considered appropriate by the Scottish Natural Heritage.

In addition to functioning as a working tool for the SNH staff in the islands as well as for officials at the local council, the assessment informs us that it, in line with the National Programme of Landscape Character Assessment, also "aims to improve the knowledge and understanding of the contribution that landscape makes to the natural heritage of Scotland." [18] In this sense, Shetland becomes, or better, is made into, a pristine wilderness, where local everyday understandings of landscape are made into something 'other' and distinctly elsewhere. It is also, as such (a wilderness) that the islands are taken to represent a valuable – proper – natural Scottish heritage. Thus, implicit in the representations used in the assessment – whether in the form of written text, maps or photographs – is a set of definitions of what Shetland is and, indeed, what it should be.

We suggest that the written text, the maps and the photographs presented in the assessment, on their own, but even more so when viewed together, come across as what could be termed a 'resolute listing of the real'. Adding to this notion of completeness is also a fair amount of repetition with regard both to text and image. This becomes especially obvious in terms of the photographs, where unbroken horizons, the interplay of sea and sky, and land in various shades of greens and browns reappear and make landscape into something outside, pristine and 'other'. (figures 1-4) Again, this mode of representing the landscape, together with the use of repetition, points to a set visual agenda, or practice of vision, in which certain modes of representation are made, and made use of, to represent the world around us. [19]

Although there are only very rarely any direct references made in the written text to the illustrations used, and the illustrations typically lack textual descriptions to go with them, they nevertheless seem to enhance one another. This effect is largely achieved through a reliance on the rhetoric of descriptive facts, and is further aided by a strong faith in the objective recording of any chosen scene below or in front of the observing eye/I. Thus, when viewed together, the written text, the maps and the photographs appear to become *matter of fact*. Everything is covered – all is there. Or, is it? None of the photographs show any people in them.

This outside, or detached, approach to Shetland landscapes lay claim to material as well as imaginative resources that have their specific (but by no means uncontested) meanings within the islands. In other words, not only does the assessment describe the landscape – through its appropriation of Shetland as a material and imaginative resource, and represented through a particular scientific and visually biased approach to what landscape is – it also prescribes the landscape.

However, the resolute listing of the real, as referred to above, can be challenged, and is challenged. This is perhaps most clearly exemplified in the various kinds of local engagement that the landscape assessment and the policies related to it have given rise to. It may therefore not come as a surprise that over the years the involvement of the SNH in a series of planning issues has prompted some considerable unease among people in the islands, or that the SNH lately has come to spend some considerable amount of time trying to anchor its policy locally. We argue that at the heart of these disputes are different and contested views from 'within' and 'outwith' Shetland, shaped by and further reproduced and communicated in myriad ways of using, encountering and repeatedly making the landscape.

These conflicts tie in with themes relating to a widespread discrepancy between landscape perceived of as consisting mainly of visual qualities – to be looked at and to be depicted in accordance with certain dominant regimes of aesthetics and beauty – and landscape understood as something still highly visual, but becoming and gaining significance through everyday practices. In turn this also relates to questions of ownership and power, and to how such notions are expressed, or played out, in the makings of landscape.

New Representations of Landscape

People of the Hills is a continuing photographic and oral documentary project begun in 1994 to interpret landscape in terms of embodied practice or performance.[20] (figures 5-6) The experimental project is developed by one of the present authors with a professional photographer, Richard Grassick of Amber Films, Newcastle Upon Tyne. The hills in question are located along the eastern Penninies that dominate the northern spine of England. The area has been familiarly branded as 'Land of the Prince Bishops' by way of reference to the large-scale ownership of land in this area during the late Middle Ages and a presumption of its significance in making the landscape what it is today. The project contests that presumption.

The project seeks to respond to one dominant representation of the place as 'Land of the Prince Bishops', whose landscapes are depicted in regional, and in particular in tourism literature, as a large empty space signified in the barely-evident marks of land owners of the twelfth century and in rare flora unknown to most people. The subjects of the Hills project include mineworkers, small farmers and allotment holders, caravan-tourists, mothers taking their children to school and working in the local factories. There is a picture of a youth who lives at a farm walking with a kettle through partly-cleared snow track to unfreeze water pipes. The photographs of these subjects seek to represent their encounter with space in a version of landscape. Individual photographic images are combined with passages of text that represent the voices of the photographed. Both seek to avoid presenting the subjects and their lives as *tableaux*, rather as moments, actions, encounters.

Figure 5
Silver Band
Stanhope Silver Band crossing the river Wear in Stanhope. The band, 175 years old, play distinctive silver instruments to signify their links with lead mining. The more common brass bands play in the coal villages to the east. ©Richard Grassick 1996.

The voices complement that visual representation of this landscape and, together, they provoke a consideration of complexity and flow of the encounter the individual makes with space/landscape in performance. The text is directed at both people who live in the area and visiting tourists. It thus engages the tourist, too, in the embodied encounter she makes.[21] Indeed, the encounter of the tourist and the individuals living in the area are mutually implicated in the landscape they constitute and construct in performance.[22] Their depiction in the images and text were discussed with each individual.

> I used to climb over there when I was a child. I don't think there's anywhere as pretty as this. I love the Dale, but particularly here. You stand outside at night in the summer, … it's magic to watch the planes going over to the airport (Newcastle)… I can't say where our land stops and the valley begins….

> I like to be out in the open at work. I work right in the quarry, I drive the machine: you tend to take the countryside for granted… up on the hilltops you can look all the way up and down the Dale. It's a wonderful view.

> Caravanning and cycling makes me smile inside. Here in the morning you open the door and feel you're breathing air into your living. People come down to the stream and stand and watch life go by. It's amazing how you can have such pleasure from something like that.

> To be a visitor to the Dales can be a complex experience. The place surrounds you, and this is felt whether in working or in wandering a footpath or just walking around the car visiting the Dale for the first time. The senses are aware and alert, perhaps relaxed, perhaps sweating in effort, in a rush. You have discovered some more things first-hand of the way this environment, like others, is made by people's lives, and continues to be so.[23]

Figure 6
Frozen Kettle
William Betton
fetching hot
water to unfreeze
pipes. The more
remote farms
can go for weeks
without running
water. Waters
Meeting, Harwood
in Teesdale.
©Richard Grassick
1995.

Gentle politics

Of course the power of representing landscape is the power of the text, whether written, photographed, filmed or otherwise produced.[24] Landscape may be important in a number of everyday practices, related to ownership and access and determination of use. However, we have also argued that there is more to the power of landscape and that it can be used in making sense of people's lives, identities and relationships. We have suggested that the values and significances that surround landscape, and which can be negotiated in terms of access, ownership and determination of use may be informed by this discussion, thereby bringing to the fore more complex encounters that people make with, in and through landscape.

In this section we translate the performance of the embodied individual to that of the researcher. Our focus is upon the reflexive researcher. To be a reflexive researcher in this situation means to invest oneself as an individual in the making, encounter and dwelling of landscape. Whilst the researcher can never be the same as the researched, inter-subjective encounters play a central role in this discussion of research performance and practice.[25]

What is suggested here then is a more interactive and engaged mode of landscape research that offers a possibility for the researcher to reveal and take into account everyday and 'lay' meanings of landscape. Such an embodied and reflexive landscape research implies a process like a series of movements in and between fields with blurred boundaries, whereby the researcher has to repeatedly rethink both her own project and objectives, and how these relate to, or perhaps fail to relate to, the people and communities that are in one way or another involved in the research project.

In order to do this we argue, with Spivak, that there is a strong need to further explore and take into account our "somewhere elses"; that is, all those political, emotional and other spaces that are excluded from academic work.[26] However, an investing of ourselves, as persons, into our roles as academics, is not a call for navel-gazing, or pure introspection. Rather, such investments make for a potentially more active and interactive research process. Investing more of ourselves, as well as recognising the subjects of our work as rounded and multifaceted individuals with involvements, experiences, stories, fears and desires reaching far beyond any research project, may indeed help putting the politics of research practice and its claims to knowledge more firmly on the academic agenda.[27]

However, such inter-activity and inter-subjectivity also raises a number of questions regarding the give and take involved in 'doing research', questions which indeed apply to any social situation. There is a wide range of ethical issues involved here, in representational as well as in so called non-representational work.[28] Some of these issues will be addressed here, by working through a number of aspects of the more recent debates on fieldwork, and notions of how the field is constructed, encountered and made use of in the research process.

Home and Away

Fieldwork has traditionally been regarded as something of a trademark within certain academic disciplines. In effect, the applications of different observational techniques in the field still today form a stepping stone for much contemporary academic research. Landscape studies are by no means an exception. We will consider possible ways of making landscape research more human-centred, through a discussion of alternative notions of fieldwork and what 'the field' might be.

The field is still today mainly treated as a physical assignation, out there, preferably far away, different, distanced and detached from the everyday, or 'home', of the researcher. It perhaps comes as no big surprise, then, that various outward signs of transit – from one place to another – have been widely drawn upon by many writers in relation to their fieldwork. It has been suggested elsewhere that such references to strictly outward movements mark (and, indeed, hide) what is much more crucially a cognitive, emotional and experiential set of movements rather than a strictly physical 'change of places'.[29]

Supporting such emphases on outward movement, to an unknown and uncharted elsewhere, the field is frequently presented as having clear-cut boundaries, in spatial as well as temporal terms. This framing of the field also implies that fieldwork is something that is conducted there, rather than here, and during a specific moment in time, distinctly cut off from 'normal' time and space, almost as a sacralisation of the research practice. In this context it can also be argued that fieldwork becomes imbued with a certain kind of macho ethos, as it is often understood to be 'character building' and, therefore, should not be made too easy.[30] In effect, the researcher appears to be moving in and out of the field at her own will and choice. The field is there for the researcher, wherever she wants it to be, whenever she wants to make use of it.

Several feminist contributions to the research debate inform ways in which we can 'get closer' to interpreting and interacting with people in relation to landscapes.[31] This, we argue, offers a means whereby academics can be better able to engage in debates over the treatment of places, landscapes, and through their efforts be better able to assist in the articulation of conflicts by providing a discursive space that speaks and acts also outside of a rather more local context.

At the same time, the idea of the field as a discrete, bounded geographical locale or as a distinct or neatly bracketed culture has become increasingly outdated and untenable. In addition, it has been suggested by several writers that fieldwork be viewed as a unique form of research, especially in terms of better understandings of how knowledges are made, contested and transformed by the body, the mundane and the everyday.[32] Here, the field emerges as critically located and defined in terms of specific political objectives that cut across time and space, rather than representing a clear-cut or fenced off 'other' or 'elsewhere'. When approached in this way, the field becomes a predominantly social terrain in which we, in our roles as researchers, have the opportunity to forge bonds between the academy and the world at large.[33] Or, as Tim Ingold suggests in his description of the value of participant observation: "to become a participant observer means developing the knack of joining in and keeping at a distance".[34]

Still, no matter how well aware we are of both the obstacles and the possibilities of fieldwork, work in the field more often than not raises questions of how the relationships and friendships that develop through these encounters may also be both potentially, and mutually, exploitative. Moreover, the notion of multiple, and at times contrasting or competing, positionalities on behalf of the researcher, must be taken into account. Such multiple positionalities are of course not unique to the researcher, or even to the researcher/researched situation. Everyone is, complexly, part of the ongoing makings of the world.

Karin Norman has suggested that we do not learn about others solely by observing and participating in their realities, but that we must also go by way of how we experience and embody our own understandings of the world around us.[35] The attention the researcher directs towards categories of informants, or towards particular individuals, while being in the field, and her modes of thinking about them, is closely related to understandings of the world embodied in herself. Thus, the construction of a field involves efforts to accommodate and interweave sets of relationships and engagements developed in one context with those arising in another. In effect, the distinctions between where 'home' ends and 'field' begins will become increasingly blurred, as one spills over into the other.[36] Another aspect of this, pointed out by Cindi Katz, refers to the field as a site of betweenness where, she argues, we are always already in the field as multiply positioned actors, and as such cannot be separated from it.[37]

It can be argued that the field, as well as the fieldworker and everybody else involved in the makings of landscape, are constantly shuttling between many positions. The drawing up of boundaries between home and away, inside and outside, is thus not quite as easy and straight forward as it may initially have appeared to be.

Fielding the landscape

It is becoming increasingly clear within different strands of academic debate that interpreting landscape through strictly visual and textual methods is incomplete. Relying on visual interpretations of landscape alone runs the risk of reifying the landscape as an object of appropriation and, as such, making it into something detached and 'other' from the researcher. In contrast, we have suggested that landscape be considered as engaged, encountered and worked in body-performance. Understood in this way, landscape is known and made sense through and in relation to processes through which the individual subjectively encounters the world.

Our main argument, then, is that landscape, as a site of practice and of spatialisation, is one of active identity. It is possible to find ourselves in a landscape and seek out those inscriptions which are prompted by pre-given abstractions of what those landscapes may mean. However, we suggest that it is possible to consider and to explain landscape in other ways too. Our experience of being in a landscape may travel along pre-figured channels but may be disrupted by our encounter with it, as active, mobile and reflexive human beings dwelling in space. The particular contexts through which landscapes may be conveyed can be disrupted by our own actions and feelings. They can be experienced less in terms of linear proportion, horizon and perspective, and more as kaleidoscopes and patinas of space and time: less resonant with inscription and more inscribed through our own process of embodied practice and performance. There are consequences for researching landscape.

It is in this vein, too, that Catherine Nash has suggested a more integrated performative research process, refiguring and rethinking social and cultural practices as theorisations of the world in themselves rather than merely serving as raw material for theoretical processing.[38] In line with this, we suggest that fieldwork – and landscape research – is a fundamentally social rather than solitary experience, mediated by and constituted through relationships between ourselves and others.

When ideas such as these are worked through and incorporated into the landscape research agenda, they would seem to suggest a rather more embodied and reflexive research strategy. Instead of producing set agendas for the research process, such as entering and exiting a definite, or fixed, field of landscape, the practice of research must reckon with landscape understood in terms of spatially and temporally overlapping and intertwined fields of relationship: always here and now. As such, landscapes become complex sites of encounters and performances, rather than presenting themselves to the researcher as a given set of views, vistas, or representations.

We have suggested that we are always already inside our object of study – unable to cut ourselves off – and in effect there is a constant blurring of subject-object positions. We have also argued that landscape is moving, or shuttling, between many positions or meanings, forging the material and the imaginary, mind and body, nature and culture. Understanding landscape as a set of processes, that is both contested and shared, will have consequences for how landscape research is conducted. Thus, arguing that we make up the landscape as we go along, as we think and do our daily lives, rather than representing something that we can stand back from and address from 'on high', adds dimensions to what landscape research can be – and do.

1 Nash, C, "Performativity in Practice: Some Recent Work in Cultural Geography", *Progress in Human Geography*, vol. 24 no. 4, 2000, pp. 653-664. Thrift, N, *Spatial Formations*, London: Sage, 1997. Thrift, N, "Steps to an Ecology of Place", *Human Geography Today*, Massey, D, Allen, J and Sarre, P, eds., Cambridge: Polity Press, 1999, pp. 295-322.

2 Crouch, D, "The Intimacy and Expansion of Space", *Leisure/Tourism Geographies*, Crouch, D, ed., London: Routledge, 1999, pp. 257-276. Crouch, D, "Spatialities and the Feeling of Doing", *Social and Cultural Geography*, vol. 2 no. 1, 2001, pp. 61-75.

3 Jay, M, *Downcast Eyes: the Denigration of Vision in Twentieth-Century French Thought*, Berkeley, CA: University of California Press, 1993.

4 Csordas, T J, "Embodiment as a Paradigm for Anthropology", *Ethos*, vol. 18, 1990, pp. 5-47.

5 Merleau-Ponty, M, *The Phenomenology of Perception*, London: Routledge, 1962. Radley, A, "The Elusory Body in Social Constructionist Theory", *Body and Society*, vol. 1 no. 2, 1995, pp. 3-23.

6 Crouch, "Spatialities and the Feeling of Doing". Nielsen, N K, "The Stadium in the City", *The Stadium and the City*, Bale, J, ed., Keele: Keele University Press, 1995, pp. 21-44.

7 Crouch, "Spatialities and the Feeling of Doing".

8 Csikszentmihalyi, M and Rochberg-Halton, E, *The Meaning of Things: Domestic Symbols and the Self*, Cambridge: Cambridge University Press, 1981.

9 Crouch, "Spatialities and the Feeling of Doing". Shotter, J, *The Cultural Politics of Everyday Life: Social Constructionism, Rhetoric and Knowledge of the Third Kind*, Buckingham: Open University Press, 1993.

10 Game, A, *Undoing Sociology*, Buckingham: Open University Press, 1991, p. 184.

11 Ingold, T, *The Perception of the Environment: Essays in Livelihood, Dwelling and Skill*, London: Routledge, 2000.

12 Crossley, N, "Merleau-Ponty, the Elusive Body and Carnal Sociology", *Body and Society*, vol. 1, 1996, pp. 43-61.

13 Radley, A, "Artefacts, Memory and a Sense of the Past", *Collective Remembering*, Middleton, D and Edwards, D, eds., London: Sage, 1990.

14 Gillespies, "A Landscape Assessment of the Shetland Islands", *Scottish Natural Heritage Review*, no. 93, 1998.

15 Hall, S, ed., *Representations. Cultural Representations and Signifying Practices*, London: Sage, 1997.

16 Gillespies, "A Landscape Assessment of the Shetland Islands", p. 5.

17 Gillespies, "A Landscape Assessment of the Shetland Islands", pp. 59-65.

18 Gillespies, "A Landscape Assessment of the Shetland Islands", Preface.

19 Jay, *Downcast Eyes*. Rose, G, *Feminism and Geography*, Cambridge: Polity Press, 1993. Daniels, S, *Fields of Vision: Landscape Imagery and National Identity in England and the United States*, Cambridge: Polity Press, 1993.

20 Grassick, R and Crouch, D, *People of the Hills*, Newcastle: Amber Side, 1999.

21 Crouch, "The Intimacy and Expansion of Space".

22 Crouch, D, "Tourist Encounters", *Tourist Studies*, vol. 1 no. 3, 2001.

23 Grassick and Crouch, *People of the Hills*.

24 Crouch, D and Lubbren, N, eds., *Visual Culture and Tourism*, Oxford: Berg, 2003.

25 Katz, C, "Playing the Field: Questions of Fieldwork in Geography", *Professional Geographer*, vol. 26 no. 1, 1994, pp. 67-72. Rose, G, "Situating Knowledges: Positionality, Reflexivities and Other Tactics", *Progress in Human Geography*, vol. 21 no. 3, 1997, pp. 305-320.

26 Spivak, C G, *The Post-Colonial Critic: Interviews, Strategies, Dialogues*, Harasym, S, ed., New York: Routledge, 1990, p. 14.

27 Amit, V, "Introduction: Constructing the Field", *Constructing the Field: Ethnographic Fieldwork in the Contemporary World*, Amit, V, ed., London: Routledge, 2000, pp. 1-18.

28 See Nash, "Performativity in Practice", for further implications and applications of theory, and especially the potential limitations of non-representational theory.

29 Rapport, N, "The Narrative as Fieldwork Technique: Processual Ethnography for a World in Motion", *Constructing the Field: Ethnographic Fieldwork in the Contemporary World*, Amit, V, ed., London: Routledge, 2000, pp. 71-95.

30 Callaway, H, "Ethnography and Experience: Gender Implications in Fieldwork and Texts", *Anthropology and Autobiography*, Okley, J and Callaway, H, eds., London: Routledge, 1992, pp. 29-49.

31 Bridgman, R, Cole, S and Howard-Bobiwash, H, eds., *Feminist Fields: Ethnographic Insights, Peterborough*, Ontario: Broadview Press, 1999. McDowell, L, "Multiple Voices: Speaking from Inside and Outside 'the Project'", *Antipode*, vol. 24 no. 1. 1992, pp. 56-72. Nast, H, Katz, C, Kobayashi, A, England, K V L, Gilbert, M, Straeheli, L A and Lawson, V A, "Women in the Field: Critical Feminist Methodologies and Theoretical Perspectives", *Professional Geographer*, vol. 46 no. 1, 1994, pp. 54-102. Rose, G, "Situating Knowledges: Positionality, Reflexivities and Other Tactics".

32 Nast, et al, "Women in the Field". Nast, H, "The Body as Place: Reflexivity and Fieldwork in Kano, Nigeria", *Places Through the Body*, Nast, H and Pile, S, eds., London: Routledge, 1998, pp. 93-116.

33 Nast et al, "Women in the Field".

34 Ingold, *The Perception of the Environment: Essays in Livelihood, Dwelling and Skill*, p. 3.

35 Norman, K, "Phoning the Field: Meanings of Place and Involvement in Fieldwork 'at Home'", *Constructing the Field: Ethnographic Fieldwork in the Contemporary World*, Amit, V, ed., London: Routledge, 2000, pp. 120-146.

36 Norman, "Phoning the Field", p. 124.

37 Katz, "Playing the Field".

38 Nash, "Performativity in Practice".

Haunting The City:
Industrial Ruins And Their Ghosts
Tim Edensor

In the economic convulsions of the 1980s, manufacturing realms were radically transformed into service space. Nineteenth century factories and warehouses were erased and replaced by retail parks, housing estates and new leisure sites, were converted into flats, or demolished. Yet in urban areas where boosterism was less successful, old industrial buildings continue to linger and decay. Gradually falling apart they become neglected, often feared spaces in the shiny new urban fabric, fenced off and policed, imagined as venues for illicit behaviour. Such ruins do not mesh with the visions of bureaucrats, imagineers, heritage personnel and property developers.

In ruins, boundaries collapse, the process of decay erasing lines of demarcation. Factories are intimately concerned with ordering space, things and people, but once disused, such elements fall out of their assigned contexts to mingle in unplanned juxtapositions. Traces of banal order fade and nature intrudes: pigeons lay claim to roof space and plants blur boundaries between outside and inside.

The factory was a locus for movement, flows of goods, money, transport and people. As ruins, they have been dropped from the networks into which they were installed but the traces remain. Would-be-commodities lie dormant in loading bays or on conveyor belts, boxes are piled up for export but will never be sent, chits and receipts are made out but never filed, parts of manufactures lie separate and will never be joined together.

Tim Edensor

The things found in ruins are also ghosts of that which they once were, for their status as separate objects is revealed to be merely an aggregation of parts and fragments, a mass of molecules. Things are wrapped around and inside each other; they merge to form weird mixtures, gradually becoming something else. Fungus replaces wood and wallpaper; gaps appear, are gnawed by beasts and worked upon by bacteria; moss grows on brick. Intricate patterns of warping, peeling, mouldering and rotting change the form of things. They become transparent, diaphanous, and finally give up their solidity, becoming distributed in an indiscernible mulch.

Ruins bear the traces of the people who made, designed, inhabited, worked in, passed through, and decided to abandon them but can tell no kind of coherent story. The shreds and silent things that remain can conjure up only the half-known or imagined. There is a profusion of vestigial signs that people worked here – overalls, hobnailed boots, gloves and hardhats, odd implements, bills, posters, paperwork and noticeboards.

The form of knowing available in ruins is not like that of the heritage industry which collects and organises particular fragments. Selected and carefully arranged, these displays disguise the excess of matter and meaning of which they are part. Conversely, ruins are sites where we can construct alternative stories which decentre commodified, official and sociological descriptions, producing an open-ended form of knowing which is sensual and imaginative, which resides in chaotic arrangements, fragments, indescribable sensations and inarticulate things.

Tim Edensor

Contested Landscapes

Contested Landscapes
Gillian Rose

Given the productivity of landscapes – the way they seem to articulate many issues, in various registers – it is hardly surprising that many landscapes are contested. Their meaning and significance may be debated, their implications challenged. Indeed, even the definitions of landscape worked with by academics are contested. J B Jackson challenges the usual etymology of the term landscape, noting for example that 'scape' has connotations not only of view but of pattern.[1]

The essays in this section – but also many others in this book – all explore landscapes that are in some way contested. Andrew Kennedy's discussion of a late eighteenth century English print series demonstrates clearly the way that many landscape images articulate the viewpoint of the powerful, in this case both military and cultural power. He also points out, however, that at this rather unstable moment in British history, the very forcefulness with which that view is imposed suggests that other views may be possible. The repeated representation of lower class and non-English loyal subjects inevitably raises the ghosts of the many non-loyal subjects of the time. Kirk Hoppe's essay looks at a much more brutal imposition of a landscape by a powerful military and cultural presence, the British in Tanzania in the mid twentieth century. In its effort to eradicate sleeping sickness by removing the vegetation and people believed to carry its vector, the tsetse fly, huge swathes of land were reshaped into landscapes of eradication and containment. But these landscapes were failures; boundaries were breached, movements continued, and other landscapes continued to be made as a result.

Given the powerfulness of so many productions of landscape, it is often easier to acknowledge that they are or were contested than to actually explore a contestation. In contrast, Adrian Ivakhiv's paper examines directly what the other two essays imply: the existence of very different interpretations of landscape drawing on the same physical environment. In his discussion of the rock formations around Sedona in Arizona, Ivakhiv shows both that the visualised landscape of a pristine nature perspectively seen continues to exert a powerful influence, but also that a quite different relation to that land is articulated through a different sense of landscape, one that is not particularly ocularcentric but rather depends on 'a baroque profusion of tongues'. Liam Kelly also explores the relation between words and images in his discussion of recent Northern Irish art. He argues that central to an artistic practice that sees the representation of landscape as a directly political act is the questioning of representation itself; in this case, by putting words and images into an uneasy relationship. Writer and photographer Patricia Macdonald also offers here, in a paper that works in conjunction with her photo essay which appears earlier in this book, words and images. Both of these show landscapes exploited and degraded but also in regeneration through what she suggests are new modes of perception and practice.

The contestation of landscape can thus be examined in a number of ways. Landscapes may be representationally unstable, they may be practiced in different ways, and the same materiality may enable very different relations to human subjects, among many other possibilities. However, as Kate Soper suggests in her essay, there may be one commonality to these contested versions of landscape, and that is that landscape always invites an aesthetic response. The contest over landscape, then, is also always a contest over aesthetics, as well as much else.

1   Jackson, J B, "The Word Itself", *Discovering the Vernacular Landscape*, New Haven: Yale University Press, 1984, p. 7.

Representing the Three Kingdoms: Hanoverianism and the *Virtuosi's Museum*
Andrew Kennedy

The elevated landscape viewpoint has been the subject of a number of scholarly investigations since the 1970s, particularly in relation to the long or prospect view in Europe from the sixteenth century onwards, and the panorama from the late eighteenth century.[1] More recently, Michael Charlesworth and Denise Blake Oleksijczuk have focused on the implications of the elevated viewpoint in the context of Hanoverian rule in eighteenth century Britain.[2] Drawing upon Foucault's analysis of the panopticon in *Discipline and Punish*, Charlesworth, in particular, has linked the panoramic type of prospect used by Thomas Sandby, and at times by his younger brother Paul, to characteristic forms of state surveillance. Surprisingly, however, given the importance of the Sandbys for this area of study, there has been little written about the political meanings of the imagery of the *Virtuosi's Museum*. This print series, largely comprised of views after Paul Sandby, is probably the most comprehensive attempt in the late eighteenth century to construct a visual statement about George III's realm in terms of topographical landscape.[3] I will argue that the series represents Hanoverian hegemony through an intriguing combination of references to overt military control and invocations of more subtle forms of domination.

The *Virtuosi's Museum*, published between February 1778 and January 1781, was the first topographical print series to give substantial coverage to all of the three kingdoms (and four countries) that made up the British state. Most other contemporaneous print series with pretensions to representing more than one country tended to focus on one kingdom, England and Wales.[4] There are 108 views in the series, 33 of which are of Ireland, 26 of Scotland, 32 of England and 17 of Wales. There would typically be an English, an Irish and either a Scottish or a Welsh view in each monthly number or part. At this time there was a range of major perceived threats, both internal and external, to the Hanoverian state, namely the revolution in the American colonies (1775-1783), the entry of France (1778) and Spain (1779) into the conflict, the Gordon Riots in London (1780) and the Irish Volunteer Movement (1778-1784). Arguably, it is at least partly in response to such dangers that the series depicts the three kingdoms as enjoying the benefits of Hanoverian rule and the Protestant succession within a unified framework.[5]

The Sandby brothers had many ties of obligation to the Hanoverians. Paul's elder brother Thomas maintained a long association with the Duke of Cumberland. Between 1747 and 1751, Paul Sandby was chief draughtsman for the Military Survey of Scotland. His main brief was to assist with the making of comprehensive maps of the Highlands which would be of use in combating any future rebellion, but he also made wide-angle prospect views of Scottish castles, towns and landscapes which in many instances would have had a cartographic and thus a military intelligence function.[6]

Not surprisingly, given their connections, both brothers became founder members of the Royal Academy in 1768; also in that year, Paul was appointed to the post of First Drawing Master at the

Royal Military Academy at Woolwich. Drawing was taught in this context first of all as a practical military tool – allowing one to analyse and record the lie of the land and thus to ascertain offensive and defensive options. Yet it was in this case also a means of giving the young sons of the gentry and aristocracy, aged between 12 and 16, a polite accomplishment (dancing was apparently also taught at the Academy).[7] An important part of Sandby's landscape practice was thus situated at the intersection of military control and cultural forms of power. This is reflected in the *Virtuosi's Museum*. An elevated viewing position is deployed repeatedly in these images, but care is taken to soften the connotations of power and surveillance by the judicious use of the aesthetic devices of polite culture and at times by an unusual admission of the non-genteel to the privileged vantage point.[8]

The *Virtuosi's Museum* was marketed by its publisher, George Kearsley, to a wide audience among the respectable 'middling sort' as an economical form of the visual refinement normally available to their betters. It was therefore very much an example of the workings of cultural hegemony, in which the middle class audience would identify with a ruling-class viewpoint.[9] The title evokes the private experience of a connoisseur or man of taste – a virtuoso – who has a collection – a museum.[10] The Preface even goes so far as to claim (falsely) that Kearsley is providing a printed version of the views painted on Wedgwood's famous Dinner Service for Catherine the Great. More truthfully, it then compares the price of each monthly number (three shillings), to the price of entrance to the pit of the theatre, which would have connoted sober middle class respectability as against the ostentatious splendour of the boxes or the vulgarity of the gallery.[11]

A keynote image for the series, published in an early number, explicitly celebrates the military control of non-English territories within the British state and the Protestant succession this guarantees. I refer to the view of the *Obelisk in memory of the Battle of the Boyne.* (figure 1) Sandby's drawing for this view was based on a sketch by John Dawson (1744-1798) a member of the Anglo-Irish Protestant Ascendancy.[12] As the letterpress tells us (quoting the inscription on the monument) the obelisk was erected on the banks of the river Boyne in 1736, from the contributions of both English and Irish Protestants, to commemorate the victory in 1690 of the forces of William of Orange over the Catholic army of James II. The letterpress describes the Battle of the Boyne as that "glorious and important victory... by which the revolution [the Glorious Revolution of 1688] was finally established, and the happy constitution of the three kingdoms in church and state preserved from impending ruin". The text also, however, notes the existence of the "delightfully situated house" of Mr Codrington, and the image allows a sight of the pleasing, well-maintained grounds in their riverine setting. We are meant, I think, to see that it is the temporary violence of the Boyne battle that has put a halt to endemic Irish instability and has created the peaceful conditions within which landowners may improve their estates. As Philip Luckombe wrote in his *Tour through Ireland*, 1780, referring to the Williamite triumph: "this island, till within these ninety years, has been a continual field of blood, which must have greatly prevented its improvement, as we see what a vast progress it has made in almost everything for the better, in so short a space of time".[13] We therefore find an organic link postulated in this image between the order imposed militarily and the subsequent order of polite, commercial, Protestant civilisation.

The activities of the sightseeing party constitute a kind of instructive narrative progression, from the finding of a Catholic cross and rosary to the reading of the moralising anti-Catholic inscription, at a higher viewing position than the one we occupy. The domination permitted by military victory is thus re-enacted in a ritual which combines playfulness and seriousness. Such regulated, aestheticising play, epitomised not only by the visiting of this significant site, but by the consumption of the engraved view itself, is also the product of this free, affluent and cultured Protestant civilisation, as, in its own way, Kearsley's Preface to the *Virtuosi's Museum* asserts.[14]

At this time, however, the legal and constitutional basis of Ireland's place in the united British state was being severely examined under the pressure of the avowedly loyal and Protestant Irish Volunteer Movement. In 1779 and 1780 the London Parliament conceded the demand of the Dublin House of Commons that the unjust restrictions on Irish trade should be removed, and in 1782, against the background of Britain's international isolation and its armies' impending defeat in America, Ireland's Parliament was granted legislative independence.[15] Not a whisper of this constitutional turmoil, it

Figure 2
The *View of the Copper-Works at Neath*, (published 1 March 1779; engraved by W Walker and W Angus). Witt Library, Courtauld Institute, University of London

Figure 3
View of the Encampment in the Museum Gardens, August 5th 1780, (published 1 October 1780, engraved by James Fittler). Witt Library, Courtauld Institute, University of London

might be said, is apparent in the *Virtuosi's Museum*. But perhaps, as we shall see when we consider the Scottish views, the very idea that the non-English nations of the British Isles should be accorded due prominence in the series was itself an attempt to assuage anxieties about the coherence of a state already faced with the revolt of its Protestant American colonies.

In its aesthetics and its politics, the view of the Boyne monument sets the tone for much of the series. Fertile and productive landscape often combines with mildly picturesque scenery, presenting a portrait of the united, peaceful and prosperous realm from an elevated situation, thus satisfying both the tourist and the improver. Military topography often also focused on this type of scenery. Combining gently hilly and flattish terrain, such landscapes were viewed as battlefields, whether potential or (as in the above case) actual, allowing some room for manoeuvre but also the possibility of attaining commanding positions. Subtler undulations in the land surface were of interest as potential areas of cover and concealment, as well as offering points for rangefinding. One would therefore wish to be somewhat raised above the general level of the landscape, with as unobstructed a view as possible. Clear outlines took precedence over broadly brushed effects.[16]

The *View of the Copper-Works at Neath*, (figure 2) in the *Virtuosi's Museum*, displays some of the above characteristics. Both the approach of military topography and the particular aesthetic approach adopted here laid stress on order, clarity, control and the subtle interrelationship of features. The South Walian copper works, seen from a highish, distant viewpoint, are placed in a wooded, fertile landscape which partakes of the beautiful, in Edmund Burke's terms (smooth, small-scale features, undulating, feminine), but combined with a mildly picturesque variety and irregularity.[17] The smoke of the copper works, white and curving, signifies both beauty and productivity. Disposed around the engraved internal frame, dancing figures, horns of plenty and agricultural products further reinforce the connotations of prosperity and contentment.

John Barrell has characterised the high, wide-angle prospect as the prerogative of the man of 'extensive views' whose social position and education gives him the ability to consider a myriad of particulars before he comes to his conclusions.[18] Denise Blake Oleksijczuk elaborates on the implications of such a viewing position in her account of the visit in 1793 by George III and Queen Charlotte to Robert Barker's panorama of the Fleet at Spithead. For her, the "stationary viewpoint" maintained by the King (though not by the Queen) "aims at consensus and order" and produces a unified subject who is able to exercise mastery over both the self and the prospect before it – just as the Fleet itself, of course, will act as the instrument of sovereign power.[19] She characterises this viewpoint as Cartesian: it is based on the geometrical abstraction of one-point perspective, and is disembodied, situated outside the prospect it surveys. Military drawing was similarly based on a one-point perspective, and was expected, where possible, both to benefit and to derive help from a surveyor's geometrical measurements and calculations. Its resultant cool clarity denied the consequences for fragile human bodies of its effective use – in, for example, rangefinding.

The Sandby image of the river Neath also constructs a stable, masculinised viewing position, overseeing and controlling an ordered (and, here, feminised) landscape, from which the reflective, disembodied, viewing self is differentiated. It might be pointed out, however, that the lively working class bodies in the foreground have at least partially occupied the space of the genteel. One of the sailors is even dancing on top of the sober, monumental, classical block into which the title of the view has been 'carved'. Strictly speaking, in the panoramic field of military topography, there can be "no interplay with local people", as Charlesworth points out.[20] But such an interaction is facilitated here through the device of the vignette-type internal frame, which, in helping to make the elevated prospect into a prospect/'view' hybrid, licenses two kinds of pleasure – the unthinking merriment of the lower class figures and the refined, aesthetic pleasure of the viewer. The playful, limited form of transgression of the dancer and his comrades merely demonstrates that Britons are not 'slaves', that this is no land of Popery and wooden shoes.[21] These are loyal subjects (the fiddle-player has no doubt been injured whilst serving in the Navy).

In any case, they are not equipped to derive instruction from the view behind them, in contrast to their social superior, the viewer, for whom the aestheticised format of the image eases and makes cheerful his patriotic reflections on Britain's blessed state. Overt connotations of military surveillance, associated with the unadorned prospect, are thus rendered unnecessary.

Even after major civil unrest, surveillance is palliated by the rituals of refined play in order that the the right, normalising note should be struck. Between the second and the ninth of June 1780, the Gordon Riots occurred. Starting as a sectarian Protestant protest, they developed to include elements of social insurrection: there were attacks on the Bank of England and prisons were burnt. Dozens of rioters were eventually killed by the military. The Virtuosi's Museum includes three images depicting, respectively, the military encampments in St James and Hyde Parks and the British Museum gardens, all of which were in place for some months after the suppression of the Riots. The three engravings were published in late 1780, only a few months after the Riots.[22] I show here the plate entitled *View of the Encampment in the Museum Gardens, August 5th 1780*. (figure 3) I have previously referred to the intersection of military and of cultural forms of power in Sandby's practice, and significantly the letterpress for this and the other two plates presents these camps as embodying a victory over the mob by a combination of the threat of force and the assertion of polite values. We are told that the camps were a great attraction for respectable Londoners:

Officers of every rank seemed to vie with each other in attention to their... visitors, entertaining them all (the ladies particularly) with variety of refreshments....

Furthermore:

... it is universally acknowledged that the gentlemen of the army take the lead of all others in acts of politeness....

In the image, women and children and male civilians stroll about under the protection of the soldiers with the ordered, classical façade of the British Museum presiding in the background. And thus, according to the letterpress:

These camps had the desired effect upon the misguided wretches which gave occasion to them. Alarmed at the appearance of such a force, they were happy in returning to their humble habitations....

Polite sociality is, then, deployed symbolically alongside military power to assert the cohesiveness of genteel society against the dangerous rabble. The confidence that order has been reimposed is signalled here partly by the higher viewpoint, with its connotations of surveillance and control, and partly by the nonchalantly cross-legged pose of the officer as he entertains a lady. In the view of the copper works near Neath, (figure 2) the sailor is similarly cross-legged, though his posture is associated with uninhibited dancing, not with elegant repose. In both cases, then, certain freedoms are available to the loyal subject, although how this freedom is exercised and recognised appears to depend crucially upon one's social class. In the image of the encampment, for example, certain of the genteel foreground figures, including women, are turned toward the scene below them, but then they would be regarded as more likely to derive instruction and benefit from such viewing than the unreflective working class figures in the view of the river Neath.

The most serious internal threat to the Hanoverian regime in recent decades had originated in the Scottish Highlands, in the form of the 1745-1746 Rising. It therefore became important for government supporters to stress the loyalty of Scots and particularly Highlanders during the American War of 1775-1783. As Linda Colley points out, "many influential Scots... seized on the American war as a means to underline their political reliability to London, deliberately contrasting their own ostentatious loyalty with American disobedience, and with the anti-war activity of English radicals".[23] Two regiments of Highlanders were among the four regiments of Fencibles raised in Scotland in 1778 to counter the threat of American privateers. Highlanders also served in the British Army in America, following their successful use in the Seven Years' War.

In the images and letterpress of the *Virtuosi's Museum* that relate to the Highlands, associations of Jacobitism and disloyalty have been not so much erased, as neutralised, as though to demonstrate the extent of the transformation that has taken place since the Forty-Five. Thus in the caption and letterpress to the *View of Fort George and Town of Inverness, as it was in the year 1744*, (figure 4) the need for military domination is firmly located as prior to the Jacobite Rising: the letterpress explains that the "old Fort St George [sic]... was... blown up by the rebels in 1746". The old Fort appears in the image in its pre-Rising state, dominating the town and the hills around, and fulfilling its historical function of defending what the letterpress calls the "opulence" of Inverness against the "plunder" of Highland clans. The new Fort, which replaced it, situated some distance from Inverness, was a large, modern complex, able, unlike the old Fort, to withstand artillery sieges.[24] But it is not represented in the series: not only were its forms notably less picturesque than those of the previous structure, it would have stood for the kind of overt control of the Highlands by force which was officially no longer judged to be necessary in a politer, more prosperous and more united Britain.[25]

The majority of the Highland views in the series represent what would have been seen as the most civilised and loyal parts of that region, and show places on the 'petit tour' of the Highlands, which included the lands of the wealthy, historically pro-Hanoverian clan chiefs, especially on Tayside, in Argyll and around Loch Lomond, rather than the 'grand tour', which took in the Great Glen and the wilder territories of the western Highlands, with their lingering associations of lawlessness and Jacobitism.[26] Thus *The Earl of Breadalbane's Seat at Killing*[sic](figure 5) shows a Highland estate on the 'petit tour' belonging to the powerful Breadalbane Campbells, and situated at the western end of Loch Tay. John Campbell, the third Earl, began improving this part of his possessions in the 1730s and only died in 1782, the year after the *Virtuosi's Museum* completed publication. In this view, a Highland family survey rich, sunlit pasture and planted belts of trees. To emphasise the benefits accruing under the family's overlordship, the sunlight accordingly picks out the large modern granary in the middle distance, just off-centre, which the Earl had had built for his tenants. His own modest residence, placed some way back in the view, to the left, discreetly superintends these improvements. Further away, a sharp division is visible between productive grazing land and the barren mountainside.

Figure 4
*View of Fort
George and Town
of Inverness, as it
was in the year
1744* (published
1 February 1780,
engraved T
Cook). Witt
Library,
Courtauld
Institute,
University of
London

Figure 5
*The Earl of
Breadalbane's
Seat at
Killing*[sic]
(published 1
August 1779,
engraved by W
Walker and W
Angus). Witt
Library,
Courtauld
Institute,
University of
London

It is appropriate that the letterpress for this and most of the other Scottish views is to a great extent plagiarised from Pennant's *Tour in Scotland in 1769*. For example, Pennant notes that the town of Perth, "as well as all Scotland, dates its prosperity from the year 1745...."[27] In the improvements being carried out by the clan chiefs in the Tay valley and adjoining glens, Pennant sees the further beneficial consequences of the defeat of the Jacobites. The letterpress to the view of Killin, based on Pennant, accordingly points up the Earl's relationship with his supposedly populous and well-managed estates:

> The abundance of inhabitants on this side surpasses that of any other place in Scotland of equal extent; ... there are not fewer than 1780 souls, happy under a humane chieftain.[28]

In the full context of the *Tour*, the Earl is a "humane chieftain" partly because he can have no recourse to the institution of "feudal tenures, or vassalage". Pennant notes that before the government abolished these tenures, "the Strong oppressed the Weak, the Rich the Poor".[29] These remarks may be set against the comments of Patrick Stuart, Killin's minister, and loyal to the Earls, writing in the mid 1790s. Referring to the Breadalbane family's "wise plans for [the country's] improvement", he observes approvingly that "the sober and industrious among the people were supported and encouraged; and the turbulent and irregular expelled the country".[30] He also has to admit, however, that parts of the parish had been depopulated over the previous 60 years by "the union of farms and the number of sheep introduced".[31] This process would have been well underway when Sandby visited Killin sometime between 1747 and 1751.[32]

The Highland couple in the view are evidently sober, industrious and loyal. They occupy a slightly raised position and, interestingly, are allowed to reflect on the fortunate condition of post-Jacobite Scotland. The woman indicates the fertile portion of the prospect with its cows and sheep. The man, whose body is turned towards the wilderness, seems, with his gun (which he may be licensed to carry as a gamekeeper of the estate), to be guarding against it and the various types of vermin (including, perhaps, disloyal subjects) that it engenders. He adopts the confident, cross-legged pose we had previously associated with the officer in the British Museum view. (figure 3) He also wears a plaid, an article of clothing which had been banned in 1746, except for those serving in the Highland regiments. The kilt/plaid was to be unbanned in 1782, not long after this print was published, but it is evident that here the Jacobite meanings of Highland dress have already been defused, partly because for several decades this dress had been associated with the service of the Crown, and partly because the Jacobite cause had long since been defeated. The British state is thus presented as a broad, inclusive entity which tolerates cultural diversity. In reality, British Army intolerance of Highland traditions and culture led to four mutinies among Highland regiments in 1779, the year this plate was published.[33]

In the *View of Ben Lomond near Dunbarton*, (figure 6) another Highlander, wearing a plaid, actively surveys the rich prospect before him, that of the vale of the river Leven, which here includes a ploughed field, cattle in pasture and a cottage – perhaps his own – fitting snugly into the side of the hill on which he stands. He indicates all this to the redcoat standing next to him. The balance, again, is both aesthetic and political: mountainous distance and rich farmland are harmonised, as are soldier and Highlander, cottage and (on the right) military encampment. Furthermore, this composition has been adapted from a longer prospect view made during Paul Sandby's time with the Military Survey of Scotland and thus embodies an accommodation between military and polite cultural modes of viewing.[34] The clear outlines, attention to gentle undulations, the elevated

Figure 6
View of Ben Lomond near Dunbarton (published 1 October 1778; engraved by W Walker and W Angus). Witt Library, Courtauld Institute, University of London

Figure 7
View of St George's Chapel, and the Town Gate of Windsor Castle (published 1 January 1780; engraved by W Walker and W Angus). Witt Library, Courtauld Institute, University of London

viewpoint, even the motif of the encampment, have been carried over from the earlier prospect drawing to the engraved image, albeit the angle of vision is narrower and the mountains are raised in height in the engraving.

The vale of Leven had been celebrated in the "Ode to Leven Water" by Tobias Smollett, a poem which first appeared in his novel *Humphrey Clinker*, 1771, and was thereafter frequently cited in published picturesque tours.[35] The poem's catalogue of pastoral delights ends on a serious, patriotic note, in lines which, as in the Sandby image, combine georgic and military themes:

> And hearts resolv'd, and hands prepar'd,
> The blessings they enjoy to guard!

In both of the above Highland views, (figures 5-6) we see these "hearts resolv'd and hands prepar'd". We also, however, see reflecting minds at work in the humble figures who survey the view and by their gestures acknowledge their blessings. Another Scot, David Hume, had previously derided "the narrow views of a peasant, who makes his domestic economy the rule for the government of kingdoms", but that is precisely what is allowed in these cases.[36] At a time when the American War put a premium on genuine loyalty, Sandby's Highland peasants (including, in figure 5, a woman) are permitted to draw general conclusions, about the benefits of the Hanoverian state as a whole, based at least partly in their particular experience of their own ameliorated circumstances – although the elevated vantage point in each case ensures that these conclusions are based on fairly extensive, not narrow, views.

My final image is the plate *View of St George's Chapel, and the Town Gate of Windsor Castle*, (figure 7) which shows English and Scottish soldiers mingling with children and civilian adults of both sexes, at what is, significantly, the town gate of the royal castle. There is no fear of a disloyal population in this securest of environments, with which both Sandbys were intensely familiar, and there is thus no need for the raised, controlling viewpoint associated with military topography. This image can be read as an updated version of Hogarth's famous patriotic composition, *Calais Gate, or the Roast Beef of Old England* (painted 1748, engraved 1749). In that depiction, the old English town gate of Calais is frame, backdrop and witness to the poverty of a land (France) ruled by a priestly tyranny. On the right-hand side, an exiled Jacobite Highlander, wearing tartan, gnaws on a head of garlic. In the Sandby image, in contrast, the tartaned Highlanders relaxing in the gateway are off-duty soldiers, serving the rightful monarch. Sandby's English sentry is armed with a musket, in contrast to his Scottish comrades, but he refrains from strutting self-importantly like the French sentry on the left of the Hogarth image. Instead, as an indication of his confidence, he has vacated his box in order to have a chat, leaving it to be occupied by a child. Such belief in the present internal security of the realm must have been comforting to the viewer in the midst of a largely unsuccessful war with America, France and Spain.

The *Virtuosi's Museum* contains a good deal of evidence about the political, military and aesthetic processes by which the landscape of the British Isles/Atlantic archipelago was domesticated and made into a fit object for the touristic gaze.[37] Indeed, the series itself played a role in this historical process. However, it is likely that the way in which the publication schedule of the series was organised so as to showcase the multi-national and diverse character of Hanoverian Britain reveals a certain anxiety about the state's integrity in this period. That the realm is not felt even to be *internally* secure in its entirety is indicated by the frequency with which lower class and non-English figures in these images have to declare themselves as loyal subjects. And it is noteworthy that in the potentially problematic metropolitan context of the British Museum encampment after the Gordon Riots, the polite only intermingle with people like themselves. Fortunately, the corruptions of the metropolis have not apparently touched Windsor and other more rural English locations, or Scotland and Wales (and Ireland). Here, the common people are often enabled to occupy the foreground of the view. In the *Virtuosi's Museum*, therefore, a number of ways are found to express a political hegemony, which thus takes the series' pictorial vocabulary well beyond that of mere military surveillance and control. In one or two cases the lower class foreground figures (figures 5-7) are even permitted to reflect upon the benefits of Hanoverian rule. Through their loyalty, indeed, they have become self-surveilling, whilst not ceasing to be the objects of the gaze of their superiors. But that is also true of the middle class viewers of the *Virtuosi's Museum*, who have designated themselves as 'polite' in order to feel a community of interest with the ruling class of the Hanoverian state.

1 In a British context, see Turner, J, *The Politics of Landscape: Rural Scenery and Society in English Poetry 1630-1660*, Cambridge, MA.: Harvard University Press, 1979; Daniels, S, "Goodly Prospects: English Estate Portraiture, 1670-1730", *Mapping the Landscape: Essays in Art and Cartography*, Alfrey, N, and Daniels, S, eds., Nottingham: Nottingham University Art Gallery and Castle Museum ex. cat., 1990, pp. 9-12; Barrell, J, *The Idea of Landscape and the Sense of Place, 1730-1840*, Cambridge: Cambridge University Press, 1972, and "The Public Prospect and the Private View", *Reading Landscape: Country-City-Capital*, Pugh, S, ed., Manchester: Manchester University Press, 1990.

2 See Charlesworth, M, "Thomas Sandby Climbs the Hoober Stand: The Politics of Panoramic Drawing in Eighteenth Century Britain", *Art History*, vol. 19 no. 2, June 1996, pp. 247-266, and Blake Oleksijczuk, D, "Gender in Perspective: the King and Queen's Visit to the Panorama in 1793", *Gendering Landscape Art*, Adams, S, and Gruetzner Robins, A, eds., Manchester: Manchester University Press, 2000, pp. 146-161.

3 This article has been developed from the second chapter of my PhD thesis, *British Topographical Print Series in their Social and Economic Context, c. 1720-1840*, University of London, Courtauld Institute, 1998.

4 The one series of the time with a similar claim to comprehensiveness, Thomas Hearne and William Byrne's, *Antiquities of Great Britain*, which also began publishing in 1778, covered Scotland as well as England and Wales, but did not cover Ireland. On this series, see Morris, D, *Thomas Hearne and his landscape*, London: Reaktion, 1989, chapter 3.

5 See the useful essays in Bradshaw, B, and Morrill, J, *The British Problem c. 1534-1707: State Formation in the Atlantic Archipelago*, Basingstoke: Macmillan, 1996, esp. Pocock, J G A, "The Atlantic Archipelago and the War of the Three Kingdoms", pp. 172-191.

6 As official draughtsman, Thomas Sandby had accompanied the Duke of Cumberland, son of George II and brother of George III, on the campaign against the Jacobites that ended with their defeat at Culloden in 1746. He was appointed the Duke's private draughtsman in 1750. See, on the brothers' careers, Herrmann, L, *Paul and Thomas Sandby*, London: Batsford, 1986, and Ball, J, *Paul and Thomas Sandby, Royal Academicians*, Cheddar, Somerset: Charles Skilton Ltd, 1985; also Christian, J, "Paul Sandby and the Military Survey of Scotland", in Alfrey and Daniels, eds., *Mapping the Landscape*, pp. 18-22.

7 See the letterpress to the view of *The Royal Military Academy at Woolwich*, engraved by Michael Rooker after Paul Sandby and published in Kearsley's *Copper-Plate Magazine*, 1 December 1775.

8 Charlesworth, "Thomas Sandby", p. 260, notes e.g. Paul's use of Claudean composition in this context.

9 On this kind of identification, see Charlesworth, "Thomas Sandby", p. 257, and the discussion in Fabricant, C, "The Literature of Domestic Tourism and the Public Consumption of Private Property", *The New Eighteenth Century; Theory, Politics, English Literature*, Nussbaum, F, and Brown, L, eds., New York and London: Methuen, 1987, pp. 254-313.

10 The example of this usage of 'museum' given in the Oxford English Dictionary actually brings the two words of the title together: "He waited on the virtuoso, and was finally admitted to an audience in his museum". See Johnston, C, *Chrysal, or the Adventures of a Guinea* (1760), London: J F and C Rivington, etc, 1783, vol. 1, chapter 16, p. 92.

11 Harrison and Company later used the same theatrical frame of reference to market a cheaper periodical, with a different sales pitch: "the judicious Managers take care that their joyous friends in the Galleries shall have a share of the evening's entertainment, as well as the splendid occupiers of the Boxes, and the sober criticks in the Pit." See *The Pocket Magazine; or Elegant Repository of Useful and Polite Literature*, 5 vols., London: Harrison and Co., 1794-1796, vol. 2, January-June 1795, pp. 1-2, Preface. See also chapters 2 and 3 of my PhD thesis for a more extensive discussion of these metaphors.

12 See Cokayne, G E, *The Complete Peerage*. "The Honourable Mr. Dawson" disappears from the letterpress and "the Lord Viscount Carlow" appears in it after 22 August 1779, the date John Dawson succeeded to the peerage (he was created first Earl of Portarlington in 1785). Most of the other Irish views were also based on sketches by Dawson/Carlow and other members of the Ascendancy, Sandby never having set foot in Ireland. He may have met some of these men through his friendship with the Irish architect James Gandon who, for example, designed Emo Park, Co. Laois, for Dawson. See Gandon, J, and Mulvany, T J, *The Life of James Gandon*, Dublin: Hodges and Smith, 1846.

13 Luckombe, P, *A Tour through Ireland in 1779*, London, 1780, p. viii.

14 Kearsley's Preface refers to "a universal taste for every species of elegant luxury that can add to the comfort, or increase the pleasures of social life" and advocates "the direction of this national taste to the most innocent and refined amusements" such as the *Virtuosi's Museum*.

15 See e.g. Lecky, W E H, *A History of Ireland in the Eighteenth Century*, 5 vols., London: Longmans, Green and Co., vol. 2, 1908, p. 236 et seq.

16 See e.g. Richards, W H, *Text Book of Military Topography*, London: HMSO, 1883, p. 7. See also the lucid discussion in Charlesworth, "Thomas Sandby", pp. 255-256.

17 See Burke, E, *A Philosophical Enquiry into the Sublime and Beautiful (1757, 1759)*, Harmondsworth: Penguin, 1998, part iii, sections xiii-xv, pp. 147-149.

18 Barrell, "Public Prospect and Private View".

19 Blake Oleksijczuk, "Gender in Perspective".

20 Charlesworth, "Thomas Sandby", p. 262.

21 See the discussion of the English labouring classes as "true sons of liberty" in Barrell, J, *The Dark Side of the Landscape: the Rural Poor in English Painting 1730-1840*, Cambridge: Cambridge University Press, 1979, pp. 112-117; also Colley, L, *Britons: Forging the Nation 1707-1837*, New Haven and London: Yale University Press, 1992, esp. chapter 1.

22 Sandby also exhibited three views of the encampments at the Royal Academy in 1781 and issued related aquatint engravings.

23 Colley, *Britons*, p. 140.

24 See McIvor, I, *Fort George*, Edinburgh: HMSO, 1983.

25 See for example, Pennant, T, *A Tour in Scotland in 1769*, Chester, 1771, p. 136, on Fort George in 1769: "it is kept in excellent order, but by reason of the happy change of the times, seemed almost deserted."

26 See Womack, P, *Improvement and Romance: Constructing the Myth of the Highlands*, Basingstoke: Macmillan, 1989, p. 63, and Pennant, *Tour in Scotland*, p. 85.

27 Pennant, *Tour in Scotland*, p. 70.

28 Pennant, *Tour in Scotland*, p. 86.

29 Pennant, *Tour in Scotland*, p. 87.

30 Stuart, Rev. P, account of the Parish of Killin, *The Statistical Account of Scotland*, Sinclair, Sir J, ed., 21 vols., Edinburgh, 1791-1799, vol. 17, p. 380.

31 Stuart, in Sinclair, *Statistical Account*, p. 384.

32 When William Gilpin visited Killin, in 1776, he was somewhat nonplussed by the tales of emigration he heard: "a discontented spirit got abroad, even in those parts, where no oppression could be complained of; particularly in the domains of the earl of Breadalbane; the happiness of whose tenants seems to have been among the principal sources of the happiness of their lord." See Gilpin, W, *Observations relative chiefly to Picturesque Beauty, made in the year 1776, on several parts of Great Britain; particularly the High-lands of Scotland*, 2 vols., London: R Blamire, 1789, vol. 1, p. 169.

33 See Prebble, J, *Mutiny: Highland Regiments in Revolt 1743-1804*, Harmondsworth: Penguin, 1977, chapter 2.

34 The depiction is derived from the middle portion of a large pen and wash prospect drawing inscribed "View near Dunbarton", from the late 1740s (16.5 x 97.8cm, National Library of Wales). This is discussed and partially reproduced in Joyner, P, *Some Sandby Drawings of Scotland*, Aberystwyth, 1983, reprinted from *National Library of Wales Journal*, vol. 23, 1983-1984, pp. 1-16 (cat. no. 4, pp. 9-10).

35 See, on the novel's generally loyalist standpoint, Keymer, T, "Smollett's Scotlands: Culture, Politics and Nationhood in *Humphrey Clinker* and Defoe's *Tour*", *History Workshop Journal*, no. 40, 1995, pp. 118-132.

36 Or at least these views are derided by Hume's character Philo, in Hume, D, "Dialogues Concerning Natural Religion" (written in the decade before 1761) in Eliot, S, and Whitlock, K, *A206: The Enlightenment, Texts*, II, Milton Keynes: Open University, 1992, p. 19.

37 See, on Wales as a "refuge" of loyal "tranquillity", Solkin, D, *Richard Wilson: the Landscape of Reaction*, London: Tate Gallery, 1982, pp. 102-103, and, on similar perceptions of Ireland, Cullen, F, *Visual Politics: the Representation of Ireland 1750-1930*, Cork: Cork University Press, 1997, p. 17.

Illegal Living and Planned Community: Forced Depopulations and Resettlement by British Colonial Sleeping Sickness Control in Tanzania, 1920-1960
Kirk Arden Hoppe

British colonial sleeping sickness control in Tanzania was a powerful mechanism for environmental and social engineering that defined and delineated African landscapes and reordered people's mobility and access to resources. Beginning in the early 1920s, sleeping sickness control officials forcibly depopulated areas infested with tsetse fly or threatened by it, and resettled Africans into carefully located and planned communities. They simultaneously organised African labour to cut and burn large swathes of land as barriers to the spread of tsetse fly between the depopulated zones and resettlements. Tsetse avoided these open spaces, needing the shade and moisture of brush-cover.

This massive campaign, that depopulated thousands of square miles and involved tens of thousands of Africans, lasted until the end of British colonial rule in 1962. British scientists and officials considered the spread of tsetse fly, the insect vector of human and animal trypanosomiasis, a threat to the occupation and productivity of Africa. Sleeping sickness officials sought to separate people from tsetse: any human presence within the depopulated fly zones except that of colonial scientist-administrators and their African agents, was illegal. Within the defensive positions of (theoretically) tsetse-free sleeping sickness settlements, local people were to be re-educated to live and produce as modern rational farmers and pastoralists before spreading back out to reclaim their lands from tsetse in a healthy and orderly manner.

This paper is a social and environmental history of sleeping sickness control that examines depopulations, resettlement and brush clearing as environmental engineering. It mounts three arguments. Firstly, that sleeping sickness control as environmental engineering was a central component in the colonial organisation and occupation of economically and politically marginal areas in Tanzania. Colonial scientists first made the connection between tsetse, protozoan parasites known as trypanosomes, and sleeping sickness in Southern Uganda in 1903 during a major sleeping sickness epidemic. Sleeping sickness officials depopulated the Lake Victoria shore and islands, sending people inland. After World War I, the epidemic in Uganda abated, and the British continental focus of sleeping sickness research and control shifted to the new British protectorate of Tanganyika. In 1924, colonial officials considered two-thirds of the territory tsetse infested or threatened by infestation.

My oral and archival evidence focuses on the corridor in north central Tanzania, between Lake Victoria and Lake Tanganyika, which was a primary locus of colonial sleeping sickness control.

Figure 1
Map of Legally
Designated
Settlement Areas
in Northwest
Tanganyika, 1939

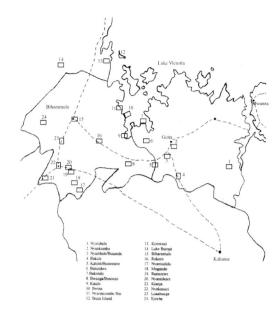

Occupied by Ha, Zinza, Sumbwa, Sukuma groups, the area was remote from the centres of colonial political and economic power. By 1934 colonial officials had relocated at least 130,000 people into over 70 sleeping sickness settlements in this area.[1] Close to 80% of the total tsetse territory officially reclaimed in Tanzania by clearing was in the Lake Victoria Basin – in the Lake, Central, and Western Provinces.[2] Colonial officials on sleeping sickness tours were often the first whites to visit villages, and sleeping sickness control intervention was often the first colonial policy to attempt to directly regulate this area. (figure 1)

The second argument is that the emerging cultural and political authority of natural and medical science informed the logic, organisation and meaning of colonial sleeping sickness control.[3] As colonialism shifted from conquest to occupation, scientists and those appropriating scientific methods and language had a great deal of leverage and freedom of action at moments when administrations were uncertain about the role and future of colonial rule.[4] European military forces were eliminating primary African resistance, and Western imperial nations needed new manifestations of power to stabilise occupation and construct morally defensible, economically and administratively viable colonial systems. Colonial science moved into and was structured by this opportunity. Borrowing a term from the scholar of travel literature Mary Louise Pratt, science served as a form of "anti-conquest". Science was by definition not exploitative but impartial, absolute, and humanitarian claiming to serve the greater human good simply by revealing universal truth. Science provided colonialists with languages and methods of conquest that constructed themselves and their employers as having only to do with the rational pursuit of empirical evidence, as having nothing to do with the politics and appropriation of conquest. As Pratt demonstrates, science presented itself as non-imperial, "claiming no transfomative power whatsoever".[5]

Sleeping sickness control appropriated African environments by creating three distinct landscapes: pristine (if diseased) human-free nature, reorganised human settlement, and man-made natural barriers in between. These were scientifically-defined landscapes, which conveyed colonial practices as anti-conquest: moral questions of forced depopulation and land alienation were rendered mute beneath over-arching and allegedly transcendent global values of science. For colonial scientist-officers these were areas in which relatively unrestricted experimentation and observation could take place. Sleeping sickness control offered researchers from various fields – biologists, entomologists, geologists, botanists, zoologists, as well as colonial disease control policy makers and enforcers – a broad range of opportunities. In the fly zones, a first generation of professional natural scientists allied and merged with colonial administrators.

The third argument is that Africans' actions shaped systems of Western scientific knowledge and policy in colonial contexts. Sleeping sickness control is an early example of a high-modernist state project of rationalisation and standardisation, organising people and environments, as James Scott argues, according to "state maps of legibility" for efficient surveillance and control.[6] But environmental engineering was not a straightforward exercise of colonial power. In practice, the process of sleeping sickness control compelled negotiation. African elite, farmers, and fishers, and British administrators, field officers, and African employees, all adjusted their actions according to on-going processes of resistance and compromise. Interactions between colonial officials, their African agents, and other African groups informed African and British understandings about sleeping sickness, sleeping sickness control and African environments, and transformed Western ideas in practice.[7]

Colonial regulations neither effectively limited the spread of tsetse or controlled local Africans' activities. Both tsetse and their wildlife food source flourished in depopulated areas and consequently most local people did not accept the logic of the colonial argument for land alienation and restrictions on African movements and activities. This paper contrasts colonialist imaginings of sleeping sickness control with local peoples' understandings of, experiences with, and responses to control policies. The heterogeneity of the African responses show the limits of colonial power to order people and environments. From a colonialist perspective, the more tsetse spread, and the less effective sleeping sickness control was, the more necessary scientists and unrestricted action by scientists became.

Ordered living

> Like newborn babies, sleeping sickness settlements must be very carefully handled at first if they are to grow and keep in being.[8]

Sleeping sickness scientists claimed that scattered populations living in tsetse-infested environments were at high risk of contracting disease, were high-risk carriers because of their mobility, and were settled too remotely from each other to clear enough contiguous land to create fly-free communities. But in contrast, higher population concentrations of Africans farming in a centralised area would, the argument went, establish "cultivation steppes" – areas of brush-free and therefore tsetse-free farm lands. Sleeping sickness control in Tanganyika was based on this approach. While a great deal of literature was published making recommendations and suggesting guidelines for resettlement, there was no fixed pattern to the process itself. Resettlement was ad-hoc and depended on the interests and expertise of local officials and on the responses of local people.

In general, a first stage to resettlement involved disease control officials identifying tsetse-infested areas, populations to be moved, and safe and defensible resettlement sites. Tsetse Control Department sleeping sickness surveyors, employing Africans known as "fly-boys" to catch and count tsetse, mapped where tsetse were and were not present, and the direction fly were spreading.

In the 1920s, officials gave local people relatively vague resettlement directions to move near or away from a geographic landmark, to pull back behind a road or stream, or to move to the vicinity of a specific established community.

But from the 1930s, mapping and resettlement became much more sophisticated, intrusive and comprehensive. Fly maps identified where medical examinations had found sleeping sickness cases while surveyors compiled detailed information on the movements of individuals, road and path systems, political boundaries, topography, vegetation and soil types, water sources, wildlife, crops, markets, and livestock.[9] The Tsetse Control Department then targeted areas according to those over-run by tsetse, the spread of fly, the routes people were travelling, and where infected individuals had lived and worked. Resettlement sites were determined according to soil fertility, water access, distance from fly fronts, and access to main roads, markets and political authorities.

An important determination was size: how much land each household in sleeping sickness settlements needed and was capable of keeping clear in order to maintain a fly-free environment. Too few people on too much land meant bush growth and tsetse encroachment, while too many people on too little land would result in too few crops to meet people's needs, land conflicts, erosion, soil degradation, and ultimately in out-migration.

Between 1935 and 1945, scientists and officials developed a standard statistical guide that the minimum population necessary was 1,000 families, with each family receiving from 5 to 15 acres.[10] Colonial scientists adjusted and debated this figure throughout the colonial period. Equations involved changing variables that were both agronomically – such as soil fertility and sustainable land use – and statistically determined, such as average family size and livestock population densities.

Through the early 1930s, sleeping sickness control programmes did not define the structure of new settlements, but by 1935 British officials began to conceive of sleeping sickness settlements in terms of an inclusive vision of public health and scientific management in which all aspects of settlers' lives would be re-ordered and controlled. This was part of a shift toward more active and interventionist strategies of development and local administration.[11] Colonial authors argued that health could not be isolated from issues of social organisation, behaviour, and economics. In sleeping sickness settlements, officers presented all aspects of development through the link between order and health: "With better agriculture, more crops and therefore more money, it will then be possible to start propaganda for better housing, better hygiene and better health in the fullest sense of the word."[12]

In the new settlements local labour was organised to clear ten-foot 'traces' demarcating the outer perimeter of the settlement, and boundaries between homesteads and between fields and pastures. In Shinyanga district, settlement regulations required all farmers to set three foot posts at the corner of plots, to dig six foot wide trenches along property lines, and to register their crops and livestock on the property with the local native authority.[13] Settlements were usually geometrically shaped. In theory, as settlement populations and abilities to keep land cleared increased, settlement officers would extend boundaries to include new land. Regulations made it illegal for local people to live or herd livestock outside demarcated areas, and limited travel in and out of settlements to main roads or paths. (figure 2)

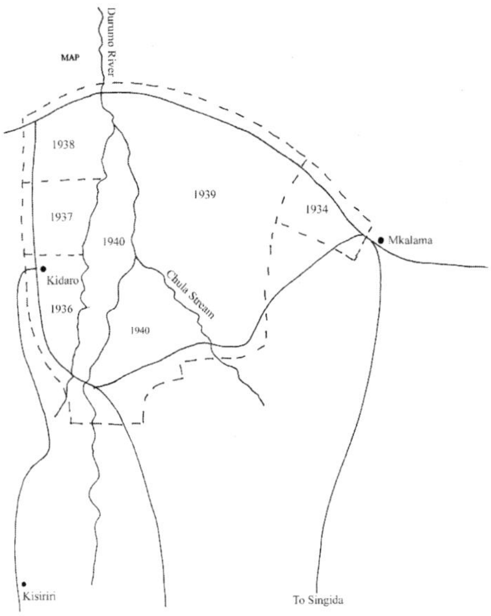

Figure 2
Map of the Legal
Boundaries of
Mkalama
Sleeping Sickness
Settlement, 1940

Each settlement was planned, at least on paper, to have a medical clinic, a mission and school, and a central market. An agricultural and a veterinary advisor would "rationalise" pastoralism and African agriculture; settlement officers were to organise the construction of dams and wells to assure dependable water supplies; but native authority would set up a court and an administrative centre. In the 1950s, settlement plans even included soccer fields and tennis courts.[14] Development, the argument went, would attract further economic investments while markets, churches, schools and clinics would draw people out of dangerous scattered homes in tsetse brush. The schools and central markets were to serve as vehicles for the dissemination of information about health and tsetse control.

As part of the re-ordering of African production systems in sleeping sickness settlements, attempts were made to identify, restrict and regulate African industries that involved a high risk of exposure to tsetse.[15] Information was gathered on African work patterns and technologies involved with honey, wood and mushroom collecting, iron smelting, fishing, fish curing, transportation, trade, hunting, salt mining, and charcoal production – in short, any productive activity that involved travel, by Africans, through tsetse areas.[16]

Colonial sleeping sickness rules required Africans in high-risk occupations in the settlements to register, receive medical examinations and carry permits and identification. The administration in Tanganyika in the 1940s called for a permit system for honey collectors, hunters, and fishers who then had to carry medical passes to gain access to forests and fishing areas.[17] Passes were good for one month, and settlement guards took blood for blood-slide tests from everyone as they returned.[18]

At any one time between 1923 and 1963, there were between 50 and 100 sleeping sickness settlements throughout Tanzania, most located to the south of Lake Victoria. The number of people who relocated in each depopulation action varied: sometimes small groups of 50 to 500 moved into pre-existing settlements; on other occasions officials dissolved and combined settlements.[19] Between 1935 and 1955, the number of people in sleeping sickness settlements was probably between 100,000 and 150,000 annually.[20]

While the British considered sleeping sickness controls a necessary and humanitarian health policy, local oral histories and an analysis of African responses show how removed colonial rhetoric was from Africans' understandings of sleeping sickness control. Local people consistently rejected, or never considered, these colonial policies as disease control. While Africans did not necessarily believe colonial agents were lying, most communities were not experiencing a sleeping sickness epidemic. What they did experience was the British expropriation of land and labour, the loss of investments in homes and farms, and the denial of access to resources.

Local men in Butundwe remember being told not to cross a ten-foot perimeter they themselves had cleared around their greater village, and only to travel by designated main paths: "The British said this was to keep sickness from getting in, but we were the ones kept from going out."[21] Africans did not separate science and medicine from the broader historic context of colonial violence and coercive power.

In the face of enforced resettlement, many people moved deeper into 'illegal' fly areas, or waited until it was complete, and then filtered back to their previous home areas.[22] This kind of unregulated migration was referred to by the colonial authorities as desertion. In 1933, of 16,700 families resettled in Kigoma District, settlement officers reported that 18% had moved out of the district to other areas, either to other settlements or to non-sleeping sickness control areas, and another 16% were unaccounted for.[23] In Bukoba in 1935, 24% of the families ordered resettled from Nyabionza and Nyaishozi areas did not show up in designated settlements.[24] In 1943, the Provincial commissioner of Lake Province wrote that a 15% desertion rate from settlements was normal.[25]

Local responses were not simply resistance to colonial coercion, but involved local power relationships. For example, there was a generational and gendered element to out-migration as a response to the threat of resettlement. In Katoro, Salvatory Kalema spoke of young men taking orders to relocate as an opportunity to migrate on their own: "Older people with families could do nothing, but many younger men, even some with wives and young children, would leave."[26] Men in Biharamulo remembered, in contrast, that families with labour and material investments in farm land and buildings often refused to move: "Sometimes a man's father had been born on the same land, and a family had buildings and businesses and animals. To force people to leave was theft."[27]

There was a history of the colonial administration establishing, dissolving and re-establishing settlements as tsetse officials re-evaluated sizes and locations according to the most recent scientific conclusions and survey reports.[28] Responding to shifting populations, officials closed and reconstituted settlements, repeatedly moving groups of people around. Chief Selemani Ikamazya of Ussangi in Western Province complained that a sleeping sickness officer had relocated him in 1938, another official had allowed him to return to his original lands in 1948, and then in 1950 granted him an exemption from moving yet again. Finally a third officer was ordering him to relocate in 1953: "Since 1938 the government has been shifting people and ever since I have never rested."[29] Cycles of resettlement, out-migration and re-resettlement reinforced local people's beliefs that sleeping sickness control was politically motivated and ad-hoc.

Burnt Brush

Tsetse barriers were produced by bush clearance carried out by (usually unpaid) African labour. Throughout Tanganyika, barriers of various sizes and shapes were constructed. Different kinds of clearings had different environmental and socio-economic effects and reflected particular British ideological relationships to Tanzanian lands and people.

The idea of clearing barriers was based on the understanding that tsetse were advancing along huge fronts into fly-free areas. Colonial scientists believed that clearing vegetation (which provided tsetse with shade and cover) ahead of these fly advances would stop their spread. Strategically placed barriers should, they reasoned, render large areas safe for human and animal occupation.

The Tsetse Research and Reclamation Department generated plans for various types of clearings depending on the species of tsetse involved, on environmental conditions, and on different colonial visions of African environment. Various clearing methods created three types of clearings – sheer clearing, densification, and discriminative clearing – each having different environmental impacts. When colonial scientists initiated tsetse control clearing schemes in the early 1920s, they proposed sheer clearing as a standard method. Areas of land would be completely cleared by African labour through cutting down trees and brush and controlled burning. Charles Swynnerton, the first director of tsetse research and control in Tanganyika, argued that thorough, well-organised and controlled burnings late in the dry season would destroy smaller trees along with dry underbrush, kill tsetse pupae, and deprive tsetse of shade.[30]

Adult male workforces were raised under the auspices of community labour requirements. African labourers used machetes and axes to clear-cut trees and vegetation in demarcated areas, and then set controlled fires. Workers dragged cut vegetation into piles and left the piles to dry, burnt them, then moved through areas in the wake of controlled burns to clear-cut surviving vegetation.

Conversely, tsetse scientists also observed that flies avoided areas with dense vegetation and conjectured that in such areas, fly movement was hampered, or there was too little food, or flies could not see their food clearly. Thus, the logical flipside of cutting and controlled burning was to

Figure 3
Aerial Photograph of a Sheer Tsetse Clearing, 1935 (upper left corner)

Figure 4
Map of
Discriminative
Clearing near
Arusha, 1943

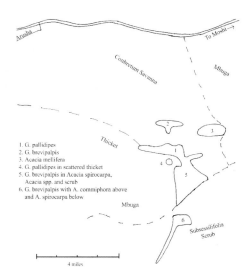

grow vegetation that was too thick for tsetse habitation. This second type of approach was called 'densification' by fire exclusion. The problem with it was that, although densified barriers were maintenance-free in theory, in fact firefighting and fire prevention policing proved labour-intensive and expensive. Furthermore, such lands were not easily reoccupied.[31]

In between these two landscaping extremes – sheer clearing and uninterrupted growing – lay a third approach: 'discriminative clearing'. Over time clearing strategies became increasingly sophisticated, targeting specific kinds of vegetation and combinations of plants and trees that promoted the spread of certain tsetse species. Sleeping sickness officials found that they could deploy African labour more effectively by using precise mapping and focusing on small 'surgical' interventions to create safe, navigable, 'latticework' environments. From the 1930s to the end of the colonial period, scientists advocated a variety of methods that cleared discriminitively, targeting 'vital' vegetation communities.[32] These methods involved the selective destruction of 3% to 10% of total vegetation cover in various clearing shapes.[33] These options, and their combinations, allowed tsetse officers flexibility in considering issues of labour availability and costs (discriminative clearing was cheaper than sheer clearing), local topography, erosion control, and conservation. (figure 3)

British scientists emphasised that discriminative clearing, which became the primary focus of research in the 1930s and the method of choice after World War II, was the most sophisticated and advanced means of tsetse control. It required the greatest degree of entomological and botanical knowledge, the most detailed surveillance (mapping), and the most precise use of African labour. Discriminative clearing also addressed British ideological hesitations about sheer clearing. An East African Tsetse and Trypanosomiasis Research and Reclamation Organisation Report from 1949 argued sheer clearing was a mistake as "the general aspect is one of ghastly desolation".[34] Discriminative clearing was an expression of aesthetic and conservationist ideas in tsetse control, as it left nature partially intact and accessible. (figure 4)

From the 1920s through the 1950s throughout Tanganyika, African labour cleared hundreds of tsetse barriers in a myriad of sizes and shapes, and type-combinations. These ranged from long, two-mile wide, swatches of sheer-cleared land, to ten-yard wide strips along riverbanks, to

Figure 5
Map of Cleared
Tsetse Barriers,
Northwest
Tanganyika, 1949

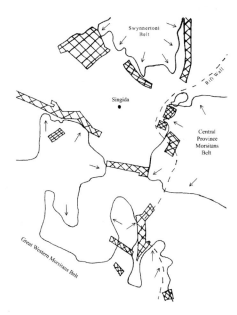

discriminative clearings of five-acre stands following the contours of particular kinds of vegetation growth.[35] Colonial scientists debated the minimum width and length of variously shaped clearings necessary to stop the spread of tsetse. The first tsetse control clearing in Shinyanga was on the Mwanza-Tabora road where colonial officials directed African labour in clearing a seven-mile long barrier that fluctuated from 400 to 1,000 yards wide.[36] In another example, the idea of the dumb-bell clearing was in response to researchers conjecturing that tsetse might fly parallel to a barrier until its end and then come around the flank. Flies confronted with round clearings at the ends of rectangular clearings (thus the dumb-bell shape) would theoretically change direction and veer back towards where they came from. Colonial reports estimated the amount of land cleared according to estimates of labour per man per day. According to statistics for Tanganyika, by 1944 African men had worked 2,250,000 man-days to clear approximately 500 square miles, resulting in the reclamation of a total of 1,000 square miles.[37] By 1960, tsetse barriers had reclaimed an additional 1,000 square miles.

The schemes required much more clearing than was ever accomplished and more labour than could be raised. The Singida Hexagon plan begun in 1936 called for an eight-mile combination of barrier types around the nineteen-mile hexagon perimeter involving 250,000 man-days. (figure 5) As tsetse bush in Tanganyika continued to expand in spite of clearing efforts, so too did the scale of proposed clearing schemes and consequent labour demands. In 1947, the Tanganyika colonial labour commission complained that sleeping sickness labour requested by clearing scheme plans in Central Province alone was 10% of the total territorial force working on sisal plantations, and 50% of that employed in mining.[38]

Clearing work was dangerous and difficult. Camps were uncomfortable. Men were separated from their families and from their own farms and regular occupations. Falling trees injured and occasionally killed workers and axe and machete injuries were common.[39] Coletha Francisco recalls welcoming men returning from tsetse labor in the 1930s in Geita: "We felt as if they were returning from war. We would dance and yell. It was very dangerous work, like war, and men were hurt or killed."[40]

As with resettlement, people resisted conscription by temporarily or permanently fleeing, and not reporting for work.[41] When the proposed clearing site was not in the immediate vicinity, tsetse officials experienced particular difficulties gathering workers and winning the co-operation of chiefs.[42] Deserters from labour sites, who sometimes took camp supplies with them – axes, machetes, and blankets – were a constant problem.[43] Bazage Kanumi joked, "Tools sometimes were payment for work. The whites had no use for tools without workers."[44] Deserters risked arrest and punishment, but in fact colonial and native authorities caught and returned few deserters.[45]

Empty lands

Depopulated fly zones provided colonialists with space to imagine and observe nature, and to conduct research. Although access to them was limited to colonial scientists and officials, their African agents, and travellers with passes from sleeping sickness officers, local people worked and lived illegally throughout them.

An example of the importance of depopulated lands for colonial science was the Tsetse Research Department headquarters and research station at Shinyanga, south of Lake Victoria. Founded in 1930, the department had environmental control over the entire 3,600 square miles of Shinyanga district. By 1933, the research station itself consisted of 13 irregularly shaped blocks of land encompassing 800 square miles of supposedly African-free nature. After 1945, the department created four new blocks adding over 600 more square miles of alienated land for research. Tsetse officials tried to strictly control fly, animal and human access in and out of the blocks. They considered the blocks to represent on a small experimental scale what might be done to huge regions of Tanzania. Researchers used the blocks for experiments in clearing, game-fly relations, tsetse behaviour and habitat observation and, after World War II, for experiments in insecticide use, game destruction and crossbreeding sterile tsetse. Tanzanian workers counted animal and fly populations and charted movements. Researchers tried to separate animal species and drove certain species in and out of tsetse areas to observe the effects of contact and separation.[46]

Some African movement through fly zones was necessary to provide access to colonial mines and plantations, for commerce, and to allow for the policing, supplying and administration of settlements. As the state didn't wish to eliminate migrant labour from fly areas, and could not eliminate interactions between communities, sleeping sickness officials sought to at least regulate African travel through fly zones. Certain routes between sleeping sickness settlements, and in and out of fly areas were deemed essential and legalised: all other roads and paths were illicit. Tanzanian labour turnouts cleared legal roads, and African fly guards barricaded, policed and patrolled both legal and illegal travel routes.[47]

Travel was regulated by a system of roadblocks and inspection stations. Fly pickets (two-man inspection stations at the border of fly areas, or near major population centres) guarded legal routes.[48] Guards stopped and checked all motorised vehicles, bicycles, people and their animals using the road. If flies were found, cleansing chambers were used in which fly guards used smoke to drive the insects off vehicles and people (in the 1950s insecticide sprays were also used).[49] Tsetse officials used fly-picket counts to determine the spread of tsetse and road use. They regularly shifted the location of posts, closing pickets on less-travelled roads with few tsetse, and picketing roads which surveys identified as heavily used, fly infested, or near recently discovered cases of sleeping sickness. In 1950, there were 40 operational fly pickets in Tanzania, and nine cleansing chambers.[50] Fly guards also inspected for medical passes and sometimes for tax certificates.

Sleeping sickness officials experimented with the treatment of vehicles as they passed through pickets. Beginning in 1924, fly guards applied 'rat varnish', a mixture of resin and castor oil, to a limited number of cars, bicycles and people. Reports argued that this application both protected people from tsetse bites and served as an effective way to monitor fly numbers (not only did the mixture kill the fly, but as they remained adhered to it, they were easy to count).[51] For African travellers, fly inspections at fly pickets and inside cleansing chambers were moments of surveillance and physical discomfort. The system drove many travellers to avoid legal routes and move illegally.

While the logic and planning of colonial sleeping sickness control depended on effective depopulation, local people were always accessing officially human-free areas. Africans avoided resettlement and moved in and out of settlements illegally to work and travel in fly zones. They ignored and circumvented pass systems, sneaking in and out or claiming they had lost their passes. Fishers operating illegally in fly zones shifted to marketing dry fish. They would leave their catch on drying racks at landings, return at night to collect the processed product, and claim at market that the dried fish was imported from a legal fishery.[52] Settlement guards arrested and fined people for illegal hunting, honey and wood collection, and for being in depopulated areas, but as with labour desertions, colonial officials found their powers of enforcement limited.

Conclusion

Sleeping sickness control as environmental engineering was a means of direct colonial intervention into remote areas of colonial Tanzania. Under the rubric of health, British officials attempted to control the exact location of people, to regulate behaviour, mobility, and productivity, and to re-order relationships between people and nature. Sleeping sickness control policies were articulations of British visions of African environments and Africans' place in those environments. British colonialists imagined African-free, fly-infested wilderness distinctly separated from cleared tsetse barriers and healthy, controlled villages. Depopulation, resettlement and brush-clearing policies were meant to promote tsetse-free environments, sustainable agriculture, and longer-term African investment in land and community. But African responses, combined with limited colonial investments and mechanisms of control, resulted in cycles of out-migration and resettlement, planned villages which were never under effective colonial control, and depopulated fly zones which were never really depopulated.

Sleeping sickness control was important to local people's understandings of and experiences with the colonial state. These experiences involved violence, struggles over land and resources, and a seemingly haphazard application of ever-changing regulations, all under the rubric of health. For colonialists, these imagined landscapes of disease control were important in centering professional scientists in the colonial state, and in legitimising colonial occupation as "anti-conquest", an altruistic and scientific re-ordering of African space.

1   Kjekshus, Helge, *Ecology Control and Economic Development in East African History*, London: James Currey, 1977, pp. 170-172.

2   Swynnerton, C F M, *The Tsetse Flies of East Africa*, London: Royal Entomological Society of London, 1936; Ford, John, *The Role of the Trypanosomiasis in African Ecology*, Oxford: Clarendon Press, 1971, p. 202; Napier

Bax, S, "A Practical Policy for Tsetse Reclamation and Field Experiment", *East Africa Agricultural Journal*, 9, 1944; Tsetse Research and Reclamation Department Reports, 1949-1960, Zanzibar Archives (ZA), Zanzibar Town.

3   Comaroff, Jean, "The Diseased Heart of Africa: Medicine, Colonialism, and the Black Body", *Knowledge,*

Power and Practice: The Anthropology of Medicine and Everyday Life, Lindenbaum, Shirley, and Lock, Margaret, eds., Berkeley: University of California Press, 1993, p. 306; Vaughan, Megan, *Curing Their Ills: Colonial Power and African Illness*, Stanford: Stanford University Press, 1991; Lyons, Maryinez, *The Colonial Disease: A Social History of Sleeping Sickness in Northern Zaire, 1900-1940*, Cambridge: Cambridge University Press, 1992.

4   Grove, Richard, *Green Imperialism*, Cambridge: Cambridge University Press, 1995, p. 7; also see Vaughan, Megan, *Curing Their Ills*, p. 21.

5   Pratt, Mary Louise, *Imperial Eyes*, New York: Routledge, 1992, pp. 38-39.

6   Scott, James C, *Seeing Like a State*, New Haven: Yale University Press, 1998, p. 3.

7   White, Luise, "'They Could Make Their Victims Dull': Genders and Genres, Fantasies and Cures in Colonial Southern Uganda", *American Historical Review*, vol. 100 no. 5, 1995, pp. 1379-1402.

8   Draft Memorandum on the Establishment of Controlled Settlement Areas, Provincial Commissioner, Western Province, 4 May 1951, Tanzanian National Archives (TNA), Dar es Salaam, 215/660.

9   Report on Karagwe Chiefdom, 15 June 1935, TNA, 215/660; Preliminary Survey of Uzinza, May, 1937, TNA 25102; Ikoma Area Sleeping Sickness Area Survey, 1 July 1942, TNA 463.

10 Tsetse Research Department Report, 1935-1938, TNA; Director Tsetse Research to DC Musoma, 24 April 1944, TNA 32535.

11 Anderson, David, "Depression, Dust Bowl, Demography, and Drought: The Colonial State and Soil Conservation in East Africa During the 1930s", *African Affairs*, 83, 1984, pp. 321-343.

12 Fairbairn, H, "The Agricultural Problem Posed by Sleeping Sickness Settlements", East African Agricultural Journal, vol. 9 no. 1, 1943, pp. 17-22

13 7 June 1932, TNA 20763.

14 Settlement Officer Report, July 1957, Biharamulo, TNA T5 vol. III.

15 Draft memorandum on the Establishment of Controlled Settlement Areas, PC Western Province, 4 May 1951, TNA 192/251.

16 Nguruka Survey, July 1953, TNA P4/66 vol. II.

17 PC Lake to District Officers, 30 July 1949, TNA 192/215.

18 Provincial Office Meeting Tabora, 28 November, 1950 TNA P4/61; Sleeping Sickness Report, Western Province, November, 1954, TNA P4/64, vol. II.

19 Fairbairn, "The Agricultural Problem", 20.

20 Sleeping Sickness Officer to Director of Medical Services, 14 November 1945, TNA 11771, vol. II.; Sleeping Sickness Meeting Notes, Tabora, 17 July 1933, TNA 21712.

21 Interview with men in Butundwe, Geita District, Tanzania, 11 December 1994.

22 PC Lake to Chief Secretary, 12 July 1949, TNA T5/1.

23 Uha and Kahama Development Report, 1933, TNA 21712, vol. II.

24 District Officer, Bukoba, to Provincial Commissioner, Mwanza, 29 December 1935, TNA 215/660, vol. III.

25 Provincial Commissioner Lake Province to Chief Secretary, 8 June 1943, TNA 28446.

26 Interview with Salvatory Kalema, Katoro, Tanganyika, 16 September 1994.

27 Group Interview, Biharamulo, Tanganyika, 10 November 1994.

28 Sleeping Sickness Officer to Director of Medical Services, Dar es Salaam, 1 September 1945, TNA 28446; C Macquarie to Sleeping Sickness Officer, Tabora, 22 November 1939, TNA 192/251; Anti-Sleeping Sickness Measures, Provincial Commissioner, Western Province, 23 July 1940, TNA 192/251.

29 Selemani Ikamazya to District Commissioner Tabora, 10 June 1953, TNA P466, vol. III.

30 Swynnerton, Charles F M, "An Examination of the Tsetse Problem in North Mossurise, Portuguese, East Africa", *Bulletin of Entomological Research (BER)*, XI, 1921, pp. 325, 382-385.

31 Glasgow, J P, "Shinyanga: A Review of the Work of the Tsetse Research Laboratory", *East African Agriculture and Forestry Journal*, vol. 26 no. 1, 1960, p. 25.

32 Tsetse Department Report for 1955, ZA.

33 Director Tsetse Research to DC Musoma, 24 April 1944, TNA 32535; Director Tsetse Research to PC lake Province, 11 February 1953, TNA 215 T5/3.

34 East African Tsetse and Trypanosomiasis Research and Reclamation Organisation Report from 1949, TNA 37791.

35 Department of Tsetse Research Report, 1935-1938, 18, TNA; Department of Tsetse Survey and Reclamation Annual Report, 1955, TNA.

36 Swynnerton, Charles F M, "An Examination of the Tsetse Problem", p. 320 and p. 323.

37 Tsetse Research and Reclamation Department Report, 1949, ZA; Labor Commissioner to Chief Secretary, 2 June 1947, TNA 12698.

38 Clearing Schemes, Agricultural Officer to DC Shinyanga, 12 April 1948, TNA 32555.

39 Bush Clearing Accidents and Fatalities, Biharamulo, 14 March 1955, TNA 201 T5/2; Tsetse Guard to DC Mpanza, 18 October 1955, TNA 20321.

40 Interview with Coletha Francisco, Katoro Village, Geita, Tanzania, 17 September 1994.

41 DC to PC Lake, 7 May 1955, TNA 24/5 vol. II.

42 Director Tsetse Research to PC Northern Province, 5 August 1946, TNA 287/5.

43 Director Tsetse Research to PC Northern Province, 5 August 1946, TNA 287/5.

44 Interview with Bazage Kanumi, Biharamulo, Tanzanian, 30 September 1994.

45 Director Tsetse Research to PC Northern Province, 5 August 1946, TNA 287/5; Native Authority Order 14 June 1954, Nguruka, TNA P4/66 vol. III.

46 Harrison, H, "The Shinyanga Game Experiment: A Few of the Early Observations", *Journal of Animal Ecology*, 5, 1936, pp. 271-293; Glasgow J P, "Shinyanga", pp. 28-29.

47 Sleeping Sickness Report Mwanza, June-August 1932, TNA 20909; G. Maclean, Sleeping Sickness Memorandum 8 September 1927, TNA 19357.

48 Uganda Protectorate Annual Medical and Sanitary Report, 1936, ZA.

49 Acting Director of Tsetse Survey and Reclamation, 2 February 1953, TNA 29315; Tanganyika Tsetse Survey and Reclamation Department Annual Report, 1951, 15-16, TNA.

50 Tsetse Survey and Reclamation Department Annual Report, 1950, ZA; Acting Director of Tsetse Survey and Reclaimation, 2 February 1953, TNA 29315.

51 Swynnerton to Chief Secretary, 17 November 1924, TNA 2702, vol. II.; Swynnerton to PC Tabora, 20 January 1927, TNA 2702, vol. II.

52 Group Interview, Biharamulo, Tanzania, 10 November 1994.

Seeing Red and Hearing Voices in Red Rock Country
Adrian J Ivakhiv

Over the past few decades, the American West has been transformed from a landscape dominated by resource extraction centred on the mining and energy industries, agriculture, and ranching, into one that is widely valued for its contrast to the urban metropolis, but which increasingly resembles the very suburban centres from which the 'New West's' newest immigrants arrive.[1] With the growth of exurban counterstream or 'reverse migration' from urban to rural areas, shopping strips, subdivisions, and gated communities increasingly fill the terrain surrounding sunbelt and skibelt towns and cities. Small western towns have reinvented themselves as postmodern tourist centres, 'new art towns,' and 'adventure playgrounds' for enviro-sentimental urban expatriates; they have become resortified, 'Aspenised' and 'Californicised'.

The north-central Arizona city of Sedona, an enclave of some 10,000 with another 6,000 in its immediate vicinity, epitomises the postmodern tourist centre. Unlike other hubs of the New West, Sedona did not begin its life as an extractive reserve; the town didn't grow much beyond 400 residents until the 1950s, so the gold rushes and resource booms that scoured other places left Sedona largely unscathed. Its reinvention in the last 30 years has been sparked by a different kind of gold rush, however, a postmodern or postindustrial one in which the gold is the red rock landscape that cradles the city, and the miners are the real estate agents, resort developers and entrepreneurs, who buy, package, market, and sell it. Sedona is nestled at the mouth of the box canyon the Oak Creek has carved out of the Mogollon Rim, the 300 metre high escarpment that makes up the southern rim of the Colorado Plateau. In this 'red rock country', reddish brown and vermilion, copper, orange and magenta sandstones and shales have been sculpted by wind and water over millions of years into spectacular mesas, buttes, spires, columns, domes, and arches. With such dramatic visual possibilities, the engine of the town has become the demand to produce, stage manage, and market visual pleasure. The landscape has been thematised as the historical Old West of Cowboys, Indians, rugged settlers, and explorers; transformed into an adventure playground for climbers and latter-day explorers; and sold as an upmarket destination resort, a picture-postcard haven for exurban second-homers and retirees, and a photographer's paradise. Underlying all of these transformations has been the visual commodification of the landscape, an activity that has proceeded largely on the basis of well-worn traditions of visual representation, which will be examined below.

Like many such places, Sedona has become a site of struggle between these forces of growth and development and, on the other side, local conservationists who have come to see the tourist dream, at best, as a 'devil's bargain' and, at worst, as environmental ruin.[2] In what follows, I will examine representations of Sedona produced by its developers, by those defending it against development (though I will not dwell at length on this group), and by a third group which can be considered as situated somewhere between the former two, overlapping at both ends, if somewhat closer in spirit to the second. This third group is the town's comparatively sizeable 'New Age' or 'metaphysical' community, which has established itself as an undeniable presence in the area over the last 20 years. Comparing these will reveal surprising convergences and divergences, with interesting implications for the understanding of visuality, modernity, and postmodernity. While developers have most obviously constructed Sedona as an object for the possessive 'magisterial' gaze, environmentalists have, for pragmatic reasons, drawn on the same visual practices to defend the landscape from development. In contrast, the New Age community de-emphasises the visual sense altogether, opting instead for a *listening* – an attempt to hear and 'channel' the soundings of cosmic wisdom believed to be circulating in the surrounding canyons. New Agers thereby renarrativise the landscape, rendering it much more active than the mute object of the dominant visual gaze. With their emphasis on transformative spiritual experience – *becoming* rather than *being* – they also challenge the Cartesian assumptions underlying the commodification of Sedona.

Yet New Age discourses show some of the same pitfalls as did an earlier tradition of Southwest representation, that of the late nineteenth and early twentieth century writers and artists who first turned the region into a "mythological holy land", but in so doing paved the way for tourism and industry.[3] Like today's tourist and real estate developers, New Age devotees can be seen as 'postmodern miners' seeking a kind of gold, but this gold is not material, nor even visible: it is the experience of power or of contact with the 'energies' of the Earth, energies that are said to be highly concentrated in Sedona's red rocks. Though the New Age community shares with environmental conservationists a respect for the earth and a critique of overdevelopment, it has also come to depend on a kind of commodification of the landscape – the spiritual commodification of Sedona as a sacred site – which, arguably, is very much a part of what Hugh Urban has called the "spiritual logic of late capitalism".[4]

Modernist Visuality and the American West

Several cultural historians and philosophers have argued that the dominant mode of Western modernist visuality has been rooted in Cartesian perspectivalism, the tradition according to which a coherent, distinct subject gazes out at an empirical, discrete object, with no inherent connection between the two and neither changing in the process of seeing or being seen.[5] In the Cartesian relation, the seeing subject is active, viewing the objects of the world on his or her own mental representational screen, whilst the object seen is passive, simply there to be viewed. In the words of visual historian Martin Jay, the ascendancy of classical linear perspective in the Renaissance meant that the "participatory involvement of more absorptive visual modes was diminished, if not entirely suppressed, as the gap between spectator and spectacle widened".[6] When this gaze fell on objects of desire, "it did so largely in the service of a reifying male look that turned its targets into stone". This visual order produced a "de-narrativisation or de-textualisation", with the rendering of the scene becoming an end in itself for the artist.[7]

In the eighteenth and early nineteenth centuries, European artists and critics elaborated several distinct visual modalities atop the (generally) Cartesian substrate of perspectival landscape art: most notably, those of the *beautiful*, the *sublime*, and the *picturesque*. Where neoclassical beauty emphasises smoothness and delicacy, giving rise to benevolent feelings of pleasure and affection, sublime forms evoke powerful feeling, from awe and admiration to fear and horror. With its extremes of magnitude or power, the experience of the sublime, according to Edmund Burke, subverts order, coherence, and rational organisation, exceeding the limits of human comprehension and inducing feelings associated with religion and the sacred. Eighteenth century versions of the picturesque typically place it in the middle ground between the beautiful and the sublime: "artfully designed so that it [can] be read like a picture", the picturesque mode presents landscape as a series of views apprehended through the apparatus of a picture frame.[8] But in their transmission to the North American continent, these visual discourses were adapted and remoulded into ones more appropriate to the western landscape, with its vast spaces, high plateaus, endless prairies, and deserts, but also more appropriate to the needs of an emerging national mythology and its ideological project of continental colonisation. The result, by the 1830s or 1840s, was a fusion which Conron has called the "picturesque sublime", in which the ineffable and overpowering "delightful horror" of the Burkean sublime becomes subordinated to the pictorial requirement (among others) of national iconicity.[9]

The intersection of Cartesian perspectivism and picturesque sublimity is epitomised in the *magisterial gaze*, a mastering and panoramic view from on high, which constructs nature as scenic vista and spectacle, to be gazed at and admired for its sweeping visual beauty and to thereby be possessed by its viewer.[10] In American pictorial practice, the Western landscape became the prime site for this project: celebrated and sanctified as the mythic destiny of the American people, the conquered West served both as the "psychic trophy" and the *sipapu* or "emergence place" for the new nation.[11] As a colonial strategy, however, the magisterial gaze serves as a prelude to the appropriation of land and the extraction of resources. "To colonise", as Dorst puts it, "was to occupy a position from which the colonial object could be seen coherently as an artifact available for appropriation."[12] The development of photography strengthened the oculocentrism, or hegemony of the visual, of Western culture, making possible the birth of the "world picture" and the "conquest of the world as picture," which Martin Heidegger saw as the fundamental event of the modern age and which allowed the natural world to be transformed into a "standing reserve" to be surveyed, unlocked, and transformed into usable energy.[13] At places which have been pictorially sanctified as reserves of sublime Nature, Americans have shown a marked ambivalence about activities other than recreation or spiritual rejuvenation. Where 'resourcification' has proved problematic and contested, however, 'resortification' has succeeded in turning Western landscapes into consumable commodities.

Seeing Red Rock Country: Constructing the 'Spell'

In the terms of dominant Euro-American visualities, Sedona's landscape presents itself as highly photogenic: its 'imageability' has been evident to visitors at least since 1895, when archaeologist Jesse Walter Fewkes described the rock formations outside Sedona in religiously sublime terms, as "weathered into fantastic shapes suggestive of cathedrals, Greek Temples, and sharp steeples of churches extending like giant needles into the sky", adding that "This place, I have no doubt, will sooner or later become popular with the sightseer."[14] By the 1920s and 1930s, Hollywood had begun to make use of the red rock landscape (in black and white) in its mythic portrayals of the American West; since then, in fact, over 60 feature films, including many classic Westerns, have been shot in the area. By the 1940s, visual artists including Surrealist Max Ernst and Egyptian sculptor Nassan Gobran arrived in the area after seeing its photographic or filmic portrayal (in Gobran's case, in the movie *Broken Arrow*). In the 1960s, a more sedate visual appropriation of the landscape was launched with the founding here of the Cowboy Artists of America, a group of artists who set themselves the goal of celebrating the memory and culture of the Old West.

The connection between Sedona and Western and/or Southwest artistic representation is thus a well established one, and the rise of the real estate and tourist industries has been closely connected to this tradition. The development potential of Sedona has been somewhat restrained by the fact that nearly half of Sedona's land (and 90% of land in the Greater Red Rock Area) is held by the Forest Service for open space and conservation, while only about 30% of the city is privately held and developable. The Forest Service plays a key role in the tug of war between conservationists and developers, and the main mechanism by which land is added to the private land base is through controversial forest service land exchanges. Significantly, the 2001-2002 *Sedona Visitor's Guide*, in its section on Real Estate, boasts that "Today, due to the *diligence* of *courageous* developers who found parcels of land *previously not known to be for sale*, and who were willing to 'pay the price', so to speak, Sedona and Village of Oakcreek are sporting a selection of the finest, new residential communities found anywhere in the world".[15] Touting the "magnificent, panoramic views", the guide continues, "Almost every choice of lot imaginable is available, from those that sit on high hills or blend into rolling ridges, to the ones that are hidden in cozy little canyons or hug the cliffs of Oak Creek." The guide notes that an investment in Sedona real estate "will appreciate more than stocks and bonds", and characterises its main market as those who "have had a sufficient number of years to accumulate the means necessary to enjoy themselves now, not later".[16] Despite its status, then, as, in large part, publicly managed land, Sedona is being sold as a self-consciously upmarket Valhalla, a garden of the gods for successful capitalists.

One of the most effective marketing tools for the selling of Sedona has been the slick and glossy full-colour publication *Sedona Magazine*. (figure 1) Filled with full-page picture-postcard photographs of red rock scenery, resorts and subdevelopments, golf courses, and advertisements for art galleries (with their characteristic Native American and Southwest kitsch), the magazine, which is available on news-stands across the United States, attempts to elicit a kind of open-jawed excitement in its target audience. The back cover of a typical issue can be taken as an example of its visual strategy. It features the caption "Ah... isn't this why you came to Sedona?" above three rectangular-framed, wide-angle images of high-contrast reddish rock formations majestically looming above a forest-green landscape and set against the blue and grey of the sky. Each of them presumes a viewing subject positioned magisterially well above ground level at a panoramic distance from the monuments portrayed: three windows onto a scenic landscape viewed from an invisible panoptic location hovering in mid-air somewhere above Sedona. The advertisement is for Casa Contenta, "Sedona's premier residential community", yet there is no residence in sight nor any sign of human habitation at all. Clearly, this is one reason why people come to Sedona: to see views that can only be captured by camera – in fact, the redness of the landscape is often accentuated through the use of colour filters – because they carefully omit the signs of human activity that have made them possible.

Figure 1

The advertisement, like so many others, offers a promise that completely effaces its own materiality, a God's eye view from everywhere and nowhere, and the prospect of living in a place uncontaminated by living itself.

Unlike many similar advertisements, the Casa Contenta one presents three small photographs rather than a single panoramic view. Yet this is in microcosm what the magazine does as a whole: it presents a kaleidoscope of views, a series of peephole-like glimpses to be gazed at longingly, intimating that the real landscape from which these photographs are derived is endless. Of nine photograph-laden advertisements for residential communities or real estate in this issue, five show only the red rock landscape with no sign of the residences being sold and two of the others show residential buildings only as small inserts within a larger panoramic backdrop. And though particular views and scenes are presented in juxtaposition with each other, competing for the attention of readers and potential clients, the magazine's overall effect is to create a view of Sedona as a place where all these things happen at once, to be enjoyed for the price of admission. Admission, meanwhile, is presented as something that is rising in price (the median price of homes selling in Sedona in 1997 was $285,000), and is ever threatened by the possibility that, with so much of the land under forest service control (and carefully watched by environmentalists), the 'gates' may soon be closed.[17] Some advertisements, jumping the gun on zoning and land-use decisions, cautiously acknowledge this possibility directly: an ad for the future subdivision La Barranca informs its readers that "Within this epic landscape resides the last preserve of large estate lots in a secluded canyon. Jacks Canyon Rd in Sedona. Priced from $150,000 to over $300,000." But tiny fine print at the bottom of the page adds that "No offer to sell may be made or accepted prior to the issuance of the final Arizona Subdivision Public Report." (The Jacks Canyon land exchange involved a bitter struggle between conservationists and developers).

The dominant optical regime in Sedona, then, has followed in the tradition of the magisterial and panoramic gaze at nature. Among visitors this gaze becomes effected through the taking of photographs, while among those who stay it mediates the buying and selling of land. Extending that gaze deeper into the surrounding hills and canyons, however, has required the more penetrative approach of jeeps, helicopters, and other off-road vehicles. Since the first Sedona jeep tour in 1959, tour companies have evolved in Darwinian fashion to carve out distinctive and specialised niches within a diversified market, and in the process have contributed to the thematisation – or 'theme-park-isation' – of the landscape. Red Rock Jeep Tours, which calls itself "Sedona's cowboy tour company", provides a Broken Arrow tour, named for Jimmy Stewart's movie and the part of Sedona in which it was shot; Time Expeditions (now part of Pink Jeep Tours) focuses on the history and archaeology of the area; Sedona Photo Tours provides ample opportunities for shooting the red rocks, while Pink Jeep Tours (figure 2) at least offers an appropriately coloured vehicle from which to view them. Others offer nature excursions, horse adventures, trolley tours, couple's tours, 'brew tours', 'earth wisdom tours', and 'vortex tours' (more on them below).

The Struggle over Red Rock Crossing

Arriving in Sedona, a visitor joins some three to six million others who pass through the town every year, which amounts to an average of sixteen to twenty thousand cars crossing the lone bridge over Oak Creek at the axial centre of town, daily.[18] To deal with this traffic, a group called Citizens for an Alternate Route (C-FAR) has been arguing that a new bridge be built further down the creek at a point known as Red Rock Crossing. For the purpose of getting cars across at this point, nothing less

Figure 2

You gotta do it!

than a large suspended 'monster bridge', at an estimated cost of nearly thirty million dollars, would do. C-FAR argues that residents of the Village of Oak Creek need an alternate route to get to the closest hospital, in nearby Cottonwood, in case of emergencies and for simple convenience; and the city's business elite and 'old guard' of media owners and wealthy families have been strong supporters of the bridge.

The bridge proposal has been vigorously contested by environmentalists, led by the local Sierra Club chapter and by the Responsible Residents of the Red Rocks (or '4 R's', formerly the Retirees and Residents of the Red Rocks). Bridge critics fear that building a highway bridge here will open up a large swath of land to development, put further pressure on an already vulnerable creek, and ruin one of the remaining environmental and recreational treasures of the area. To garner the public support environmentalists have needed to fight the bridge, however, they have come to rely on the same representational strategy as that used in selling Sedona. One of the main – and most successful – tactics used to stop the bridge and to save Red Rock Crossing from development has been the argument that this is the "most photographed spot in Arizona" and, some say, in all of North America. Red Rock Crossing runs directly below a rock formation known as Cathedral Rock, a highly distinct 'signature monument' that graces photographs, postcards, and tourist brochures for Sedona more frequently than any other. (figure 1) This 'photogenicity' argument cuts to the heart of the paradox of the American West, and can be seen as a kind of historical reversal whereby the landscape's role in the creation of the mythic West has now become part of its own defense. Film and photography create imagined geographies; appropriating elements from the real world, they create decontextualised images and 'stars'. This defense of Red Rock Crossing, though it helps garner attention to that particular struggle, contributes to a 'mediated' environmentalism that decontextualises visual landscapes from their ecological surroundings, arguably making it easier to ignore the less tangible ecological effects of such an environmental 'star system'.

In contrast to the 'most photographed place' argument, local New Agers defend Cathedral Rock and Red Rock Crossing for the reason that they are among the most potent of Sedona's 'vortex' areas. A local author has written that

> we must do everything we can to make sure that this bridge is never built. We must hold the line. Cathedral Rock is sacred and a highway through this area can not be allowed. *Cathedral Rock is an*

ascension point. [...] Placing a metal bridge over Oak Creek at this place would also interfere with the spiritual energy that flows along the creek.[19]

The same author argues that "many people, myself included, have encountered Angelic entities in this area".[20] Another prominent psychic informs her readers that "two magnificent Archangels stand guard over the 'entrance to the inner sanctum'" at Red Rock Crossing, and adds the claim that Red Rock Crossing is the only "magnetic vortex" in the area, thus vital to the energetic balance of the landscape.[21] For another local spiritual group, the controversial Aquarian Concepts Community, Red Rock Crossing is nothing less than the central "power point" on the Earth's surface.

What are we to make of these arguments about vortexes and spirit guides? In the remainder of this article I will attempt to shed some light on New Age discourses of nature, particularly the idea of energy vortexes, highlighting the ways in which these ideas have been appropriated into dominant representational strategies, but also some ways in which they may aid in resisting them.

Alternative Optics: the Circulating Gaze, Baroque Visuality

In *Looking West*, a perceptive analysis of visual discourses of the American West, John Dorst argues that dominant modes of Western visuality have more recently become supplemented and to a large degree supplanted by an alternative mode, that of the "circulating look", in which lines of sight are multiplied, visual mastery is rendered less certain, objects have become elusive and deceptive, and the apparatus of looking is acknowledged as constitutive of the act of seeing. The traditions of pastoral, picturesque, sublime, and touristic visual representation, according to Dorst, shared an underlying Cartesian assumption of a self-contained, "monocular" viewer "who registers an external reality through an unmediated and essentially unproblematic act of looking".[22] In contrast, the visuality of the circulating look represents the extension of capitalism into new modes of consumption, in which the accumulation of goods and capital "is inseparable from the ceaseless desire to mark semiotic differences and to engage in the endlessly renewable display of identity".[23]

To put this another way, the Cartesian subject-object duality, Dorst argues, has been supplemented by a third set of eyes, a spectator who, with ironic self-awareness, surveys the scene (of subject-object) and is aware of its construction (or artifice), though not necessarily engaged in it. We can distinguish between two moments in this development, which we might call the 'postmodernisation of the gaze'. (The term 'postmodernisation', however, is intended more as a heuristic device than a historical demarcation, since this optic has arguably been an undercurrent within Western visuality for some time.) The first moment follows in the tradition of advanced consumerism, which itself breaks down the strict Cartesian subject-object dichotomy to the extent that it allows the consumer both an active and a passive position: that is, the social order interpellates or 'hails' the individual as a consumer who is *active* in relation to the objects of her gaze, but *passive* in relation to the larger system of production (albeit shaping it minimally through consumptive choices).[24] Dorst refers to the "act of looking that seems to create the very spectacle toward which it is directed", and uses as an example of this the way in which the Devil's Tower (Bear Lodge) rock monument in Wyoming has been turned into a spectacle by the desiring gaze produced in and through Steven Spielberg's film 1977 *Close Encounters of the Third Kind*.[25] (The film portrays a number of seemingly ordinary citizens 'receiving' visions of the monument which, on an inner compulsion, they proceed to visit, once they realise where it is located – arriving in time for the descent of the benevolent and godlike extraterrestrial mothership.) Likewise, the spectacle of Sedona and peoples' experience of it has been created in and through the visual representations of that landscape.

The second, and posterior, moment of the circulating gaze appears when other sets of eyes become visible and enter the network of exchange set up by competing gazes. In the case of Devil's Tower, these 'eyes' represent the Native American presence surrounding the monument. Though Dorst does not elaborate on this point, it is notable that the 'circulating gaze' he describes relies heavily on non-visual (or more-than-visual) practices, including traditional Native American narratives as well as the vernacular array of legends, jokes, folk art, road signs and display environments, and the like. Once this more extensive and pluralistic 'circulation' is set up, however, it becomes possible for the dominant gaze to reassert itself by co-opting the 'new voices' into the discourse of an inclusive liberalism and by appropriating difference into the spectacle itself. At Devil's Tower, for instance, the National Park Service has endorsed and incorporated Native American narratives, but in a way that keeps them safely relegated to the realm of the quaint and the historical, kept separate from the story of the tower's 'real' geological formation and from the more prominently displayed 'ascent narrative', the history of the tower's overtaking by climbers. In the case of Sedona, the Native American presence has been less visible, though the Yavapai-Apache tribe, relocated outside the area in the latter years of the nineteenth century, continues to make religious use of selected sites. At Boynton Canyon, however, one of the places most sacred to the Yavapai-Apache, half of the canyon's mouth has been taken up by a development called Enchantment Resort. (figure 3) In its effort to incorporate the canyon's 'other voices', the resort hired a Native American 'cultural performer' from the Havasupai tribe, seemingly unconcerned that his tribe had no direct relationship to the Sedona area.

Figure 3
Figure 4

A more radical potential of this second moment would involve the opening up of possibilities for participation to the formerly marginalised voices – a participation that can actually change the system into which the new participants have entered. There have been notable instances of such a widened horizon or expanded conversation between different subject-positions (for instance, the cases of co-management between the park service and local Native American tribes, such has occurred at Canada's Gwaii Haanas National Park). In Sedona, the possibilities for such a radicalisation involving the Yavapai-Apache remain remote, mainly because they do not live in the area, though forest service rangers have worked together with Native Americans to set aside or manage specific areas. The other 'eyes' of the circulating gaze, however, can hardly be reduced to those of Native Americans; they are more multiple than that. Even allowing for this second, more radical response, the nonhuman, natural world generally remains passive, still in the position of the gazed-at rather than an acknowledged participant in the circulatory network. This construction of a mute nature is one that many environmentalists have questioned; yet, as shown above, environmentalists often, for tactical purposes, fall back into an objectifying mode whereby they aim to 'save nature' by turning it into an object of visual pleasure. New Age discourses, with their references to earth energies and spiritual beings, can be seen as challenging this Cartesian objectivisation of nature.

Before describing these alternative discourses, however, I wish to introduce another mode of visuality, one which Martin Jay identifies as one of two alternative ocular regimes of modernity: the *baroque*.[26] "In opposition to the lucid, linear, solid, fixed, planimetric, closed form of the Renaissance", Jay writes, "the baroque was painterly, recessional, soft-focused, multiple and open." Rejecting the "monocular geometricalisation of the Cartesian tradition" in favour of a "dazzling, disorientating, ecstatic surplus of images", a distorting and strongly tactile or haptic "madness of vision" with its "palimpsests of the unseeable", the baroque, for Jay, indulges in a fascination for opacity, unreadability and indecipherability, and resonates both with the raptures of Counter-Reformation mystics and with the postmodern reappearance of the sublime.[27] New Age discourses of nature, as I will show, can be seen as a narrative, non-ocular version of such a baroque form of representation: dazzling, disorientating and ecstatic in their surplus of voices and meanings, with the sublime underwriting them through and through.

The New Age Sublime: a Postmodern Baroque Glossolalia?

Sedona's New Age or 'metaphysical' community, one of the most concentrated of such communities in North America, has been growing steadily since the late 1950s, but this growth accelerated dramatically after psychics Dick Sutphen and Page Bryant publicly identified the area's 'power spots' or 'vortexes' in the late 1970s, and especially following the so-called Harmonic Convergence of 1988.[28] Many of the town's New Age devotees arrived in the area because they felt a strange connection to the landscape: like the characters in *Close Encounters,* many followed an inner compulsion, a feeling of being 'irresistibly drawn' to Sedona, or obsessed over it after they first heard about it or saw pictures of it.[29] The community includes a variety of psychics and spiritual counselors, therapists and alternative health practitioners, and others who have left behind better-paying jobs and lives elsewhere and taken on whatever work they can find in the retail or service industries. Local New Age authors tout the vortexes, describe the 'miraculous' experiences they and others have had at them, draw up maps of what they call the "interdimensional landscape", and encourage visitors to meditate and build 'medicine wheels' (circular formations of stone) for prayer at the sites.

The vortexes have contributed to an already long list of types of guided tours of the Sedona area, with vortex maps being given out for the asking at the Chamber of Commerce. To their credit, however, New Agers have organised a Sacred Sites Coalition, which has produced information that attempts to restrict vortex publicity to the small number of already well-known sites. Like hikers, wilderness enthusiasts, and rock climbers (if not more so), Sedona's New Agers celebrate the landscape less for its scenery than for the experiences to be had in it. In their case, what they seek is contact with energies of various sorts (physical, psychic, electromagnetic, or some other kind) or communication with beings they believe to exist in other, non-physical dimensions of the material world. Where most visitors are content with the 'view' – the 'scenery' – New Age pilgrims show a profound distrust for visual representation; instead, they valorise the invisible. Research at New Age sites has shown that spiritual pilgrims rank photography much lower on their list of important activities than non-spiritual visitors; instead, they are much more likely to pray, visit or build shrines, bathe in a creek, or watch for UFOs.[30] New Age activities are directed less at gazing onto an objectified landscape, and more at listening, receiving or 'tuning in' to voices or signs that lurk behind the observable façade of the landscape. The notion of channelling – a term encompassing various forms of mediumship, clairaudience, or 'spirit communication', rooted in the simple effort to 'open up' and listen to the voices that speak from the spiritual ether – exemplifies this effort.

Sedona's more prominent channellers are frequently featured in the locally based magazine *Sedona: Journal of Emergence,* which has become one of the two or three leading venues for channelled spiritual writings in North America. (figure 4) In a streaming heteroglossic stew, the magazine regularly features information about impending 'Earth changes' and galactic shifts, astrological predictions, and endless spiritual and personal advice penned in quasi-scientific jargon by channels with names gleaned from science-fiction (Kryon, Vywamus, Zoosh, the Galactic Council), romantic fantasies about Native Americans (Red Cloud and the Council of Eight), more traditional religious references (Archangel Michael), and even "Mother Earth (Gaia)" herself. Riordan's description of the channelling phenomenon is apt here: a "bewildering cacophony of cosmic voices babble, gossip, and prophesy on every aspect of human and nonhuman life, offering a myriad of ingenious revisionist (and often mutually contradictory) versions of history, theology, and science, and a profusion of clashing – but equally unorthodox – commentaries on current events".[31]

Journal of Emergence bills itself as presenting "the latest channeled information on what to do as humans and the earth move from the third to the fourth dimension – how these energies affect you and the earth". The ambiguous notion of 'energies' plays a crucial function within New Age discourse, serving as a kind of conceptual glue that binds together alternative and non-Western physico-medical theories, ideas inherited from late nineteenth and early twentieth century spiritualism and metaphysical religion, the post-1960s lingo of humanistic and consciousness psychology, and an imagined future in which advanced technology is reconciled with earthly and cosmic ecology. The connection between energy and rocks is one that has been especially pursued within New Age thought, particularly during the crystal craze of the 1980s, and the two together constitute a type of 'New Age sublime' that is readily found in Sedona's looming ancient rock formations. That red rock landscape often serves as a background – but in some cases the foreground as well – for the communicative productivity of Sedona's psychics, yet these voices show little interest in the monumental visuality splayed across the pages of (the rival) *Sedona Magazine.*[32] The few photographs to be found in *Journal of Emergence* tend to be grainy, black-and-white images of inscrutable lights in the sky, mysterious 'flying disks' captured on film surreptitiously in the night sky, and other signs of meaningful life beyond the visible spectrum. The channellers portray the landscape as redolent with invisible and mysterious, but psychically perceivable activity, filled with 'energy portals' and 'interdimensional doorways', dissemination points, stargates, spiritual presences and alien beings. In contrast, then, to the dominant representations of Sedona, *this* landscape harbours far more than the eye can see, making up a neo-magical universe in which particular locations (canyons, rock outcroppings, and so on) correspond to specific stellar constellations, cosmic forces, chakras and body parts, elemental qualities, and spiritual states.

And yet, despite the apparent zaniness of this sublime textual productivity, Sedona's New Agers could be seen as presaging, or at least reflecting, a shift from modern ocularcentrism to a more baroque and postmodern circulation of voices and gazes. Where Sedona's dominant culture of real estate and tourism presents the red rock landscape as purely an object, to be viewed magisterially and appropriated as such, the New Age approach is, at one and the same time, more penetrative – probing into the deepest mysteries of self and cosmos – and less objectifying, finding the object not mute and inert, but filled with a whirling stream of voices. The circulating gaze, in the hands of Sedona's channellers, becomes a profusion of tongues, overlapping and intertextual, wildly connecting between places in the landscape, images, and desires. New Age religion has often been derided as a 'self-religiosity', the spiritual apex of postmodern consumerism; however, though the self remains focal in New Age spirituality, it is a postmodern one, less bounded and more fluid, kaleidoscopic and changeable, a self that seeks openings, if not to the larger human community, at least to the imagined communities of nature, the cosmos, and other 'others'.[33]

Where modernist visuality had emphasised the capacity to organise the world, imposing a clear and well defined logic which allowed the agent-subject to master and subdue the object of vision, the postmodern revival of orality and textuality can lead to a fragmentation and inability to cognitively map the world.[34] For Sedona's New Agers, dreams of ancient wisdom mix with the multiply refracted and contorted languages of an imagined technoscience, and the desires and paranoias of millennial global capitalism scramble and multiply into a kaleidoscope of voices swirling in an electrostatic hum in which it becomes possible to hear anything. The very activity of listening to this hum is perceived as a form of empowering resistance to the dominant modernist order, but, alas, the narrativisation too often leaps off the rails of publicly consensual discourse. If Sedona's New Agers take things too far in the direction of narrativity, then, perhaps this indicates not so much a surfeit of democratisation, as it is merely an inversion of modernist ocularcentrism: as Cartesianism represented a refusal of embodiment, so the hypernarrativised New Age sublime represents a kind of refusal of the directly visual and empirical, the middle-ground between the personal (and inner) and the cosmic (and outer).[35] A more balanced multisensory modality, drawing on the full spectrum of flesh, touch, hearing, and modified, non-aggressive vision, might be that advocated by environmental philosophers and feminists, among others.[36]

There is another sense in which New Age practices present an alternative to the dominant constructions of place, self, and landscape. Both mainstream and New Age representations of Sedona have crafted an alluring 'spell' which channels desire into the landscape: in the first case, this desire is reflected back through capitalist commodity practices related to the consumption of images, while, in the second, it is reflected back into experiences which, following Foucault, can be called "practices of the self". New Age self-making practices are explicitly articulated within a discourse that is critical of modernity. But its potential for challenging the dominant society remains limited by a hazy understanding of that modernity, and by a desire for *personal* transformation which can be readily accommodated within postmodern patterns of capitalist consumption. This is a trait which contemporary New Age ideas share with those of early twentieth century mythologisers of the Southwest, such as Zane Grey, Charles Fletcher Lummis, Henry Brinkerhoff Jackson, and others. For these writers (most of whom came from the Eastern United States), the West played a restorative and redemptive function in American history. To the materialism, artifice, and dissipation of the East, it offered rejuvenation, building moral character, self-reliance, courage, honesty and purity. The early mythologisers of the West created a literature of 'becoming', which while often vested in racist and gendered stereotypes, nevertheless retained an openness to the landscape as an active agent which could change a man (and, more rarely, a woman).

In a similar way, today's New Agers seek an essentialised nature that is equated with romanticised primitives and with truths that must be sought in a 'true self' that lies outside the empire of a fallen modernity. The photographs of the channellers in *Journal of Emergence* betray the tug of an exoticism by which white, middle class faces become *other*: Kryon speaks through Lee Carroll, Ramses through Brent Powell, the Brown-Robed Ones through the heavily lipsticked blonde Joy Lee Larocque, Mother Earth (Gaia) through Pepper Lewis, and so on. The smiling neighbourly whiteness of these faces is all too conspicuous, but focusing on the visual misses the point that it is the verbal message that counts (for readers), just as focusing on the confirmability or 'objective reality' of the message misses the point that it is the message's meaning *for the interpreting listener* that counts. To the outsider, channeled messages may seem a combination of trite platitudes and cosmic nonsense – the equivalent of *glossolalia*, the phenomenon of 'speaking in tongues' which are accepted as meaningful (by the believer) even if the 'words' themselves appear nonsensical. The New Age movement, in this sense, despite its socially or environmentally transformative aspirations, has internalised the privatisation of values and meanings that late capitalism encourages. It is, as Urban argues, or at least is *consistent* with, the "spiritual logic of late capitalism".[37]

Seen in the light of its sensory engagements, New Age religiosity presents an interesting example of the rejection of modernist visuality and its replacement by a baroque profusion of tongues. New Agers follow their desires into a democratised visionary (or oral-auditory) commonwealth, and arrive at a 'dazzling, disorienting, ecstatic' surplus of voices, with its 'palimpsests of the unseeable' and, more broadly, unknowable. As such, they exemplify the kind of excessive postmodernity against which neo-Marxists like Fredric Jameson and David Harvey have warned.[37] Yet, they show that, contrary to Jameson's suggestion that "postmodernism is what you have when the modernisation process is complete and nature is gone for good", neither nature nor, for that matter, religion need be threatened by this proliferation of tongues.[38] Both flourish in Sedona, whether as the object of desire and contention, or as an everpresent background hum. As the first, both nature and the sacred are objectified, thematised, offered for sale or submitted for protective legislation; as the second they are intimately woven into the everyday politics of living. If environmentalists have picked up the strategy of objectifying the land, the better to protect it, from the promoters of the magisterial gaze, the New Age discourse of 'voices' and 'energies' can be seen as a way of pointing at the other focus of environmental concern – the non-objectified landscape, redolent with other sets of eyes and ears (but those of more earthbound nonhumans) and teeming with ecological relations and energetic flows. It is in the articulation of such a landscape that the New Age and environmentalist communities can fruitfully cooperate to generate a more participatory politics of 'landscape beyond the gaze'.

1 Riebsame, W E and Robb, J J, eds., *Atlas of the New West: Portrait of a Changing Region,* New York and London: Norton, 1997; Campbell, N, *The Cultures of the American New West.* Edinburgh: Edinburgh University Press, 2000.

2 Rothman, H, *Devil's Bargains: Tourism in the Twentieth-Century American West,* Kansas: University Press of Kansas, 1998.

3 Weigle, M, "From Desert to Disney World: the Santa Fe Railway and the Fred Harvey Company Display the Indian Southwest", *Journal of Anthropological Research,* vol. 45 no. 1, 1989, pp. 115-137, p. 133.

4 Urban, H, "The Cult of Ecstasy: Tantrism, the New Age, and the Spiritual Logic of Late Capitalism", *History of Religions,* vol. 39 no. 3, 2000, pp. 268-304.

5 Heidegger, M, "Age of the World Picture", *The Question Concerning Technology,* Lovitt, W, trans. and ed., New York: Harper and Row, 1997; Rorty, R, *Philosophy and the Mirror of Nature,* Princeton: Princeton University Press, 1979; Bordo, S R, *The Flight to Objectivity: Essays on Cartesianism and Culture,* Albany: State University of New York Press, 1987; Jay, M, *Downcast Eyes: the Denigration of Vision in Twentieth-Century French Thought,* Berkeley: University of California Press, 1994.

6 Jay, M, "Scopic Regimes of Modernity", *Modernity and Identity,* Lash, S and Friedman, J, eds., Oxford: Blackwell, 1992, pp. 178-195.

7 Jay, "Scopic Regimes of Modernity", pp. 181 and 182.

8 Hyde, A F, *An American Vision: Far Western Landscape and National Culture, 1820-1920,* New York: New York University Press, 1990, p. 14.

9 Conron, J, *American Picturesque,* University Park, PA: Pennsylvania State University Press, 2000.

10 Boime, A, *The Magisterial Gaze: Manifest Destiny and American Landscape Painting, c. 1830-1865,* Washington, DC: Smithsonian Institution Press, 1991.

11 Rothman, H, *Devil's Bargains: Tourism in the Twentieth-Century American West,* Kansas: University Press of Kansas, 1998, p. 14.

12 Dorst, J, *Looking West,* Philadelphia: University of Pennsylvania Press, 1999, p. 195.

13 Heidegger, "Age of the World Picture".

14 Cited in Rigby, E, "Forest Service Working to Stabilise Local Indian Ruin", *Red Rock News,* March 28, 1979, p. 8. For discussions of 'imageability', see Lynch, K, *The Image of the City,* Cambridge, MA: MIT Press, 1960 and Steen Jacobsen, J K, "The Making of an Attraction: the Case of North Cape", *Annals of Tourism Research,* vol. 24 no. 2, 1997, pp. 341-356, p. 351.

15 2001-02 *Sedona Visitor's Guide,* p. 54, (my emphasis).

16 2001-02 *Sedona Visitor's Guide,* p. 55.

17 Cheek, L W, *Sedona Calling: a Guide to the Red Rock Country,* Arizona Department of Transportation, 1998, p. 10.

18 Schill, K, "'Something in This Picture isn't Right': Popularity Overwhelming Sedona", *Arizona Republic,* October 12, 1994, B1.

19 Dannelley, R, *Sedona UFO Connection and Planetary Ascension Guide.* Sedona, AZ: Richard Dannelley/Vortex Society, 1993, p. 62; italics in original.

20 Dannelley, *Sedona UFO Connection and Planetary Ascension Guide,* p. 54.

21 Bryant, P, et al. *Sedona Vortex Guide Book,* Sedona, AZ: Light Technology Publishing, 1991, p. 13.

22 Dorst, *Looking West,* p. 104.

23 Dorst, *Looking West,* p. 111.

24 Note that the feminine pronoun becomes important, and perhaps only for the first time a genuine possibility, with the emergence of sites of active female spectatorship, such as the department store, amusement parks, museums, packaged tours, world exhibitions, arcades, novel reading, and so on.

25 Dorst, *Looking West,* p. 192.

26 Jay, "Scopic Regimes of Modernity". The other is the more descriptive and empirical Northern tradition, which paid detailed attention to the visual surface of the world, and which flourished especially in the Netherlands during the seventeenth century.

27 Jay, "Scopic Regimes of Modernity", pp. 187-189; Buci-Glucksmann, C, *La raison baroque: De Baudelaire à Benjamin,* Paris: Editions Galilée, 1984.

28 See Ivakhiv, A, *Claiming Sacred Ground: Pilgrims and Politics at Glastonbury and Sedona.* Bloomington: Indiana University Press, 2001.

29 Dongo, T, *The Mysteries of Sedona: the New Age Frontier,* Sedona: Hummingbird, 1988; Ivakhiv, *Claiming Sacred Ground,* pp. 187.

30 Huntsinger, L and Fernandez-Gimenez, M, "Spiritual pilgrims at Mount Shasta, California", *Geographical Review,* vol. 90 no. 4, 2000, pp. 536-58.

31 Riordan, S, "Channeling: a New Revelation?", *Perspectives on the New Age,* Lewis, J R and Melton, J G, eds., Albany: State University of New York Press, 1992, p. 107.

32 For example, Bryant, et al., *Sedona Vortex Guide Book.*

33 See Heelas, P, *The New Age Movement.* Oxford: Blackwell, 1996. Kuhling, C, "The Search for Origins and the Desire for Wholeness in the New Age Movement: Transcendental Homelessness as a Symptom of Postmodernity", *Border/Lines,* vol. 31, 1993, pp. 4-9. Ivakhiv, A, "Nature and Self in New Age Pilgrimage", *Culture and Religion,* vol. 4 no. 1, 2003.

34 As Fredric Jameson has famously argued in *Postmodernism: Or, the Cultural Logic of Late Capitalism,* Durham: Duke University Press, 1991.

35 For example, see Leder, D, *The Absent Body,* Chicago: University of Chicago Press, 1990.

36 For example, see Levin, D M, *The Opening of Vision: Nihilism and the Postmodern Situation,* New York: Routledge, 1998; Rodaway, P, *Sensuous Geographies.* London: Routledge, 1994.

37 Urban, "The Cult of Ecstasy".

38 Jameson, *Postmodernism;* Harvey, D, *The Condition of Postmodernity: an Enquiry into the Origins of Cultural Change,* Oxford: Basil Blackwell, 1989.

39 Jameson, *Postmodernism,* p. ix.

Language, Memory and Conflict: Acts of Interrogation
Liam Kelly

The political and violent conflict in Northern Ireland for the past 30 years or so has acted as a catalyst in the shift from a lyrical but potent pastoralism in the work of a previous generation of artists to a more searching intellectual discursive art by the present generation. It has been an intensive period of self reflection and interrogation by artists on issues such as place, tradition and identity within a lingering post-colonial context.

In this paper I will examine how artists such as Willie Doherty, Philip Napier, Shane Cullen, and Paul Seawright have deployed and interrogated language both orally and in written text as a working strategy within the complex 'post-colonial' context of Northern Ireland. What these artists share is the use of words as a way of rinsing up what is invested in the cultural mapping of the psychic landscape of memory.

Figure 1
Willie Doherty
Strategy Sever
Westlink,
Belfast, 1989,
b/w photograph
with text,
122 x 188cm
(detail)

Considerations of language are central to Willie Doherty's practice. In his earlier work he superimposed text over images in a subversive relationship. (see figures 1-2) The overprinting of words on image creates a compound, existential state, where contradictions, ironies, subversions are at work.

In *The Walls,* 1987, (figure 3) the artist arranges text to settle over sections of a horizontal panoramic view of the Bogside area of the city of Derry in daylight and the elevated dark inner side of the city walls from which we/the artist, the colonised/the coloniser, take in the view and take up a position. *The Walls* lingers with the legacy of the colonised and the coloniser in its absences and presences. From the inner, walled city, captioned "Within/Forever" (in loyalist blue), we survey the outer/other, the Bogside, captioned "Always/Without". Jean Fisher points to the fragility of the seeing/being seen relationship in *The Walls*:

As we imagine that, with powerful lenses, we could penetrate the interiors of the facing windows, so we also become aware that those eyes may see us. Indeed, were it not for the presence of this gaze of the other we should not be able to assume the sovereignty of power that this position affords us. The seeing/being seen dyad is a question of both position and disposition: I see you in the place I am not. However, what *The Walls* brings into relief is that this narcissistic relation between oneself and one's other beyond the given boundary is inscribed with a profound uneasiness.[1]

The Walls then deal with inclusion and exclusion, and Derry, in microcosm, reflects a siege mentality that is culturally endemic in Northern Ireland as a whole.

From his audio/slide installation *Same Difference,* 1990, to his acclaimed *The Only Good One is a Dead One*, 1993, the complexities of language mediated in the press and TV and the dangers of stereotyping as a barrier to understanding has compelled Doherty. He has also explored the media role in the all too easy and immediate construction of innocence and guilt in the installation *Six Irishmen*. The dualities of perception, ideology and mediation, was developed in a different way in *The Only Good One is a Dead One*. (figure 4) This work is a double screen, video projection installation. On one screen the artist uses a hand-held video camera to record a night time car journey, while the second screen shows the view from inside a car which is stationary on the street. The accompanying soundtrack relays the interior monologue of a man who is vacillating back and forth between the fear of being the victim and the fantasy of being an assassin.

Paul Seawright's photographic works are another example of the transformative power of text on image. During 1987-1988, he made a series of 15 photographs based on visits to the scenes of various sectarian murders, or the locations where bodies were dumped in the early 1970s – an intense period of sectarian violence. He did not give the series a title, but reviewers have always referred to them as the *Sectarian Murder* series. (figures 5-7)

The time interval of some 15 years between murderous and creative act was important to the artist, not only to ensure the religious anonymity of each victim, but also, in a sense, to indicate that the murdered were victims of being in the wrong place at the wrong time. Using an old diary from his youth, which noted significant political events among the fairly quotidian entries, Seawright spent protracted periods of time at these sites, considering the meanings associated with their location. In some cases, he re-enacted the route taken from the place from which a victim was snatched to the eventual spot of the murder or dumping of the body. Such reconstructions of reality built up tensions within the artist, as well as eliciting the lingering presence of gross transgressive acts from the location. Each scene was photographed in colour from the victim's viewpoint – close to the ground. The lighting of each scene was controlled in a way which paralleled the forensic photographer's dispassionate approach.

These photographs, however, would remain merely interesting formalist studies if their accompanying text was not integral to their meanings. Seawright had researched original journalists' reports of these killings from local newspapers in Belfast, and selected snippets of text from such reports to work with and to discharge their related images of any easy reading. The text ties them down irrevocably to a place, a sub-culture and a value system of violence. In one image, (figure 7) a roadside inn is viewed, low down from the illuminated grassy edge of the road. A general feeling of tension is engendered by the angle of 'shooting', the absence of people, and the hiatus created between the nearside stationary car and the lorry about to pass the inn.

> Saturday, 16th June, 1973. The man was found lying in a ditch by a motorist at Corr's Corner, five miles from Belfast. He had been shot in the head while trying to hitch a lift home.

The blunt factual text tells of the killing of this misplaced victim. It also seems to indict the vehicles pictured as the location becomes perpetually marked and troubled. The essential difference between Paul Graham's photographs dealing with Northern Ireland, *The Troubled Land,* 1987, and Paul Seawright's image and text photoworks, resides in the endorsement of lived experienced. As with TV coverage of such events, there is no reference to sectarian claims of justification or politicians' repudiations. The sparse text, together with the concentrated absences in the photographs, unite to sustain a resounding moral condemnation of political cause and effect on both victim and violator. Philip Napier's art practice is not only an interrogation but a detonation of language around and

Figure 2
Willie Doherty
Strategy Isolate
Divis Flats,
Belfast, 1989,
b/w photograph
with text,
122 x 188cm
(detail)

Figure 3
Willie Doherty
The Walls 1987,
b/w photograph
with text,
61 x 152.5cm
(detail)

Liam Kelly

Figure 4
Willie Doherty
*The Only Good
One is a Dead
One* 1993, double
screen video
projection with
sound, size
variable

through an axis of power. A recent work, *Gauge,* commissioned and developed for the Orchard Gallery, Derry, was conceived as a two part project. Part 1 occurred as an installation in the Orchard Gallery space, (figures 8-9) whilst Part 2 was presented as a temporary site-specific public artwork in the Bogside area of Derry, Northern Ireland.

Initially it was the events of Bloody Sunday almost exactly 25 years before (the 25th anniversary was 30 January 1997) that provided the contextual point of reference for this work. It was conceived against a backdrop of sustained calls for an apology from the British Government for the events of Bloody Sunday on 30 January 1972, when 14 unarmed civilians were shot dead by the British Army.

The project attempts to measure or gauge that apology. In essence the work consists of 14 speakers and a large suspended public address system which relay a continuous spoken apology. This apology is measured through the agitation of the needles on the face of the weighing scales. Mounted taps dribbled water steadily onto the floor of this space forming large shallow pools. The work evolved as a proposition that language alone cannot be adequate; indeed that no measure of language can be enough because it is always contextual and conditional.

In Part 2, this work was reconceived and installed in a derelict Housing Executive dwelling, (figures 12-13) in Glenfada Park in the Bogside in Derry, facing a courtyard (figure 11) which was the site of the shootings and one of the last architectural remnants of the events of 1972, lingering now amidst widespread redevelopment. The work was installed as though in hiding, in this largely unreconstructed derelict house and was encountered through torchlight amidst unsettling blanket darkness.

Saturday 3rd February 1973

'Gunmen using a stolen car shot down five young boys who were standing outside the Glen chip shop on the Oldpark Road. A sustained burst of gunfire wounded four of the youths and killed the fifth.'

Figures 6-7
Paul Seawright
Sectarian
Murder Series
1987-88, colour
C-type print,
101 x 101 cm

22nd September 1972

'The man left home to go to a bar for a drink and never returned. He was found the following morning dumped on waste ground behind the Glencairn Estate. He had been stabbed in the back and chest, and his body showed signs of torture.'

Saturday 16th June 1973

'The man was found lying in a ditch by a motorist at Corrs Corner, five miles from Belfast. He had been shot in the face while trying to hitch a lift home.'

Figure 8
Philip Napier
Gauge,
installation,
Orchard Gallery,
Derry, 1997

Figure 9
Philip Napier
Gauge, detail

The central theme of these differing presentations focuses on the value of an apology. The work echoes with the registers of colonial and post colonial situations and post conflict situations the world over. Importantly it does not specify who is asking for an apology, who is apologising or who is being apologised to. This public and private experience is left to address the cultural and political baggage of its audience. The act of mediation here arises from its local relevance but universal outreach. Tom McEvilley acknowledges this in his catalogue essay on *Gauge*:

> Encountered in Glenfada Park, the piece seemed to refer to the Irish demand that the British apologise for Bloody Sunday. Indeed, its appropriateness to the site – combined with its sense of dark hiddenness was uncanny, almost eery. Still, as one listened, its resonances seemed to pass beyond the specific situation and approach the universal. No only the British relation to the Irish seemed involved, but the relationship of all colonisers to all the colonised peoples everywhere. It reminded me of Hegel's parable of the Master and the Slave, from the second book of the Phenomenology of Spirit, where History is seen as a long slow shift of relationship through struggle, in which the antagonist's attempts to overcome one another through the annihilation culminate in a mutual overcoming through a kind of absorption, a reception of the other as the negation which completes oneself.[2]

Like Napier, Shane Cullen is interested in the ramifications of language – its emotional, psychographic charges. His series of tabula-like texts, *Fragmens sur les Institutions Republicaines IV,* began in Ireland in 1993 and were completed while on residency at the Centre d'Art Contemporain de Vassivière en Limousin, France, where the work was exhibited from 22 February-13 April 1997. (figures 14) The complete ensemble of texts which form this monumental project were in turn exhibited for the first time in Ireland at the Orchard Gallery, Derry in December 1997. (figures 15-16) The title of the work is itself taken from a series of political ideological texts written by Louis Saint-Just at the height of the revolutionary period in France. What appears to be an orthographical error, i.e., *fragmens*, is in fact an accurate detail of the original manuscript of Saint-Just. It is, actually, an archaic spelling of the word *fragments* in common usage prior to the standardisation of the French language.

The work represents secret communications or *comms* written by Irish Republican Hunger Strikers which were smuggled out of the Maze Prison (the so-called H-Blocks) during the highly charged

Figure 10
View from
Bogside, Derry,
N. Ireland

Figure 11
Glenfada Park,
Bogside, Derry

Figures 12-13
Philip Napier,
Gauge,
installation,
Glenfada Park,
Derry, 1997

period of the hunger strikes in Northern Ireland in 1981. These, in which ten participants died, were mounted in an effort to establish political status for IRA prisoners.

In Cullen's representation of these *comms,* the emotional and fragile language of the private, graphically and in a proclamatory way, were introduced into the public domain of the *polis* – that which pervades both the physical and political space. These *comms*, handwritten by the artist, have been monumentalised in the act of representation, by the handwritten process, paradoxically apeing a mechanical process. On one level interjection by the artist is located in this act of transcription.

While the work looks like a public monument it is in fact anti-monumental and as fragile as the language it represents. The strategy of mediation at work here is, in one sense, the opposite of Napier's in that it brings the public domain of the city monument into the contemplative domain of the art gallery. It is also body related – not only to the bodies of those on hunger-strike but also to the body of the artist. Mike Wilson draws our attention to this in his catalogue essay on Cullen's project.

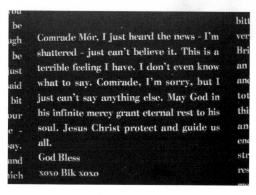

Figure 15-16
Shane Cullen,
*Fragmens sur les
Institutions
Républicaines IV,*
(Details)

This work, this monument which is more a representation of a monument than a monument proper, is marked by the trace of a particular body, the body of the painter, it is further marked by the absent bodies, bodies reduced, erased and superceded by text. It is marked by their words, the words of dead men negotiating the terms and conditions of their death.[3]

In relation to these remarks by Wilson it is worth recalling Maude Ellmann's insightful observation that as the hunger striker's body becomes increasingly emaciated it, at the same time, becomes increasingly loquacious – there is an urgency in the need to communicate.[4]

Tom Paulin, in his essay "A New Look at the Language Question" reminds us "that the history of a language is often a story of possession and dispossession, territorial struggle and the establishment or imposition of a culture".[5] Since cultural identity is laid into language it is not surprising that language can become the cause of a violent interaction between the colonised and the coloniser. In relation to this the critic Seamus Deane cautions:

On the hither side of violence is Ireland as Paradise; on the nether side, Ireland as ruin.
But since we live on the nether side we live in ruin and can only console ourselves with the
desire for the paradise we briefly glimpse. The result is a discrepancy in our language; words are
askew, they are out of line with fact. Violence has fantasy and wordiness as one of its most
persistent after-effects.[6]

The works of these artists examined, beg questions not only about the legacy of violence but about the representation/re-presentation of language and text and its location in myth and in the *polis*.

1   Fisher, Jean, *Willie Doherty, Unknown Depths*, Cardiff: Fotogallery, Derry: Orchard Gallery and Glasgow: Third Eye Centre, 1990.

2   McEvilley, Tom, *Philip Napier, Gauge*, Derry: Orchard Gallery, 1998.

3   Wilson, Mike, *Shane Cullen, Fragmens sur les Institutions Republicaines IV*, Derry: Orchard Gallery, and France: Centre d'Art Contemporain de Vassivière en Limousin, 1997.

4   See Ellmann, Maud, *The Hunger Artists: Starving, Writing and Imprisonment*, London: Virago, 1993.

5   Tom Paulin, "A New Look at the Language Question", *Ireland and the English Crisis*, Newcastle upon Tyne: Bloodaxe Books, 1984.

6   Deane, Seamus, "Brian Friel: the Double Stage", *Celtic Revivals: Essays in Modern Irish Literature*, London: Faber and Faber, 1985.

'Naming' and 'Framing' Land: Labels and Representation in Land-Use Change, Debate and Conflict

Patricia Macdonald

'Naming' and 'Framing'

This paper discusses the significance of verbal labels, and of visual representation, in various situations of land-use change, debate and conflict. The term 'naming' land, is used to cover both the literal meaning: 'applying a proper noun to a piece of land', and also 'descriptive' labelling, which indicates how the namer views it. All peoples have named features of their environment, but have used different approaches dependent upon their culture and world-view. The principal interests here are in the degree of accuracy of the names or labels as descriptors, in the value judgements implied, and in the effects of consequent actions upon the land itself.

'Framing' land signifies the visual equivalent of 'naming': representation presented as a meaningful description or interpretation. A classic example of such imagery is *The Grand Canyon of the Yellowstone*, (figure 1) by Thomas Moran, one of the first painters of the American West to declare himself an 'artist' rather than a 'recorder of facts'. Like other nineteenth century survey-expedition artists, and unexpectedly perhaps in view of the expeditions' official purposes, he "place[d] no value upon literal transcripts of nature" and wished not to "realize the scene literally, but to... convey its true impression".[1] In examples of politically motivated, even less realist, iconography, the term 'framed' may also include its alternative meaning of 'set-up' or 'betrayed'.

The particular historical examples of 'naming' and 'framing' discussed here, from 'Old', 'New' and 'Third' World contexts, all involve ambiguously employed labels or visions of 'wilderness'/'wild land' and of 'emptiness', and their implied opposites, in colonial discourse (although not necessarily in 'traditional' usage), of 'civilization' and 'fullness' or 'plenitude'.

The first example derives from the American philosopher/writer Henry David Thoreau:

> The Musketaquid, or Grass-ground River, though probably as old as the Nile or the Euphrates, did not begin to have a place in civilized history, until the fame of its grassy meadows and its fish attracted settlers out of England in 1635, when it received the other but kindred name of CONCORD from the first plantation on its banks, which appears to have been commenced in a spirit of peace and harmony. It will be Grass-ground River as long as grass grows and water runs here; it will be Concord River only while men lead peaceable lives on its banks. To an

Figure 1
Thomas Moran, *The Grand Canyon of the Yellowstone*, 1872, oil on canvas. National Museum of American Art, Smithsonian Institution. Lent by the US Department of the Interior, Office of the Secretary

Figure 2
Frederic Edwin Church, *Mount Ktaadn*, 1853, oil on canvas. Yale University Art Gallery, Stanley B Resor, BA, 1901, Fund

extinct race it was grass-ground, where they hunted and fished, and it is still perennial grass-ground to Concord farmers, who own the Great Meadows and get the hay from year to year.[2]

In this passage,

Thoreau views 'Musketaquid' – ['Grass-ground'] – as the true name of the river, as a name rooted in a natural and therefore primary rather than merely cultural and thus contingent history.... "Concord"... is merely... an imposition of a recent social order upon natural fact... as 'grass-ground river' the river endures beyond the reign of civilization.... [Thoreau here] achieves a hermeneutical insight into the linguisticality and historicity of the human predicament'.[3]

Thomas Cole's iconically ambiguous painting, *The Oxbow*, brings a contemporary subtle consciousness to a similar (Eastern American frontier) countryside where wildness is giving way to civilization.

Thoreau describes his ascent of Mount Ktaadn in 1846 as a formative encounter with the sublime in a wild place, although, in a powerful aside, he discusses logging, and the philosophical distinction between the words "pine-tree" and "lumber".[4] In contrast, an almost contemporary painting, *Mount Ktaadn* by Frederic Edwin Church, includes an entirely fictional/prophetic, pastoral foreground "like nothing Thoreau could have seen on his travels". (figure 2) This image "defines a... closing moment in the frontier story [:] ... 'the wilderness civilized'... As the frontier recedes, the wilderness ceases to be either an opportunity for progress or an occasion for terror. Instead, it becomes scenery."[5]

Thoreau's 'post-frontier' consciousness scrupulously distinguishes between *"wilderness"*, a *place*, and *"wildness"*, a *quality*, viewing "Man as... a part and parcel of Nature, rather than [merely] a member of society".[6] He saw in wildness, not just 'scenery', but a different value, related to the present-day appreciation of the diversity of life: "I love the wild not less than the good..."[7] and: "... in Wildness is the preservation of the world".[8]

Place-names bestowed by 'traditional' societies, like Thoreau's "Grass-ground River", are often directly descriptive, rather than unrelated cultural impositions. Gaelic mountain names provide examples from Scotland. Although the word for 'mountain' is 'beinn', mountain names are more diverse: *Am Braigh Riabhach* – the Brindled Upland; *Meall nan Tarmachan*, – the (Rounded) Hill of the Ptarmigan (alpine grouse); *Bruach na Frithe* – the Slope of the 'Wild Forest' or 'Wilderness'. The last two names both sound equivalent to 'Grass-ground River', but there is a distinction between them. 'Hill of the Ptarmigan' and 'Grass-ground River' are truly equivalent: descriptions of a place in terms of fullness of non-human inhabitants. But 'Slope of the Wilderness' refers specifically to the *absence* of humans, an uninhabited place – it refers to what is *not* there, rather than to what *is* there, and to the relation of the place to human settlement.

This 'traditional' understanding of 'wilderness' in the Highlands of Scotland is documented by Alexandra Stewart (born in Glenlyon in 1896), who distinguishes between rural countryside inhabited, however sparsely, and however far from centres of population, and 'wilderness', where no people live:

> We were not children of the wilderness, although we were close to natural things. The point of view of the town dweller who talks about 'protecting the wilderness' [of the Highlands] must always be a little insulting to a Highlander [as that 'wilderness' includes her/his home]. The original name of Glenlyon, long centuries before it was settled... was Gleann Fasach, 'Wilderness Glen'. But the modern wilderness in the Highlands is man-made – not, mostly, made by Highlanders but by outsiders who bought whole forests and clear-felled them... or were interested in making money from sheep and deer (or... in the thrill of killing a big animal).

> Everywhere was wilderness once. Seventy years ago the notion of so miscalling Glenlyon, where people have lived [throughout] history, would have seemed without sense. Our childhood happiness was not in the wilderness, although we were always conscious of natural beauty and grandeur. At the end of long lives, we do not look back on a world of wilderness, but on a cheerful, busy and companionable little community that was more fragile than we could know.[9]

Stewart's distinction between 'outsiders'' ideas of 'protecting the *wilderness*', and the appreciation by the 'insider' members of a semi-traditional society of the 'value of *wildness*' as part of the context of their lives, is perceptive. Like Thoreau, she distinguishes between "wilderness", a *place* without human influence, and the *quality* of "wildness", found in varying degrees in inhabited landscapes as well as in those where "man... is a visitor who does not remain".[10] It is crucial, both ecologically and socially, for the current international 'wilderness movement' to recall such distinctions when campaigning to 'preserve wild land' in long-inhabited places. In Scotland, for example, most so-called 'wild land', such as heather moorland, is semi-natural 'cultural landscape', considerably modified by humans.[11] Even iconic 'wilderness areas' like California's Yosemite, which may appear "untrammeled by man", have also been altered by human influence.[12]

While the aesthetic/experiential concept of 'wild-land character' deserves appropriate recognition, ecological or cultural-history distinctions are equally or more significant for future management strategies.[13] The historian James Hunter provides a comprehensive account of how the Highlands of Scotland became "a devastated countryside", and the implications of that process for place and people, quoting both the Highland-based ecologist Frank Fraser Darling and his American mentor Aldo Leopold.[14]

Leopold identified "one of the perils of an ecological education" as being "that one lives alone in a world of wounds. Much of the damage inflicted on land is invisible to laymen." The American Southwest, for example,

> ... when grazed by livestock, reverted through a series of more and more worthless grasses, shrubs and weeds to a condition of unstable equilibrium. Each recession of plant types bred erosion; each increment to erosion bred a further recession of plants. The result today is a

Figure 3
Emanuel Gottlieb
Leutze, *Westward
the Course of
Empire Takes Its
Way*, c. 1861, oil
study on canvas.
Thomas Gilcrease
Institute of
American History
and Art, Tulsa

progressive and mutual deterioration, not only of plants and soils, but of the animal community subsisting thereon … So subtle has been its progress that few residents of the region are aware of it. It is quite invisible to the tourist who finds this wrecked landscape colorful and charming.[15]

Hunter comments:

The tourist finds the typically treeless Highland glen equally charming. The tourist probably considers such a glen to be in its natural condition. But the tourist, as Frank Fraser Darling pointed out,… is wrong. The Highlands… had been stripped of their original vegetation every bit as comprehensively as New Mexico. And the consequences… were just as disastrous for the Highlands as… for those faraway landscapes…: "The Highlands, as a geologic and physiographic region, are unable to withstand deforestation and maintain productiveness and fertility. Their history has been one of steadily accelerating deforestation until the great mass of the forests was gone, and thereafter of forms of land usage which prevented regeneration of tree growth and reduced the land to the crude values and expressions of its solid geological composition. In short, the Highlands are a devastated countryside…."[16]

The details of the loss of forest, and consequently biodiversity, are now considered to be more complex; also, various agencies have begun to address the issues that Darling exposed.[17] Shockingly, however, the main thrust of his conclusions still stands.[18]

Figure 4
Andrew Melrose, *Westward the Star of Empire Takes Its Way – near Concord Bluffs, Iowa*, 1867, oil on canvas. Autry Museum of Western Art, Los Angeles

Figure 5
Alfred Jacob Miller, *The Trapper's Bride*, 1845, oil on canvas. Eiteljorg Museum of American Indian and Western Art, Indianapolis

'Wilderness' and 'Emptiness'

Emanuel Leutze's 'heroic' mural *Westward the Course of Empire Takes Its Way* (figure 3) reminds us of the colonist's vision of the supposedly 'Empty' and 'Promised' Land beyond the frontier. To explore the relationship of ideas of 'wilderness' and 'wildness' to that of 'emptiness', we must situate the literature and iconography of the 'frontier' in a broader context. The Indian scientist/activist Vandana Shiva usefully brings together studies of colonisation, development and biodiversity. She contrasts two concepts which form part, respectively, of two contrasting world-views ('paradigms'): that of Western, industrial/mechanist modernism – the current, obsolescent, paradigm – and that of the new "ecological" or "organicist" paradigm which may be replacing it.[19] Shiva calls her concepts the "Empty Earth Syndrome" (which regards the world's biodiversity as merely a "Genetic Mine"), and the contrasting "Full Earth" concept, related to the new "organicist paradigm", and to *"vasudhiv kutumbam"* (Hindi: 'Earth Family'):

> Third World countries located in the tropics... are the cradle of biodiversity. This [biological] wealth is being rapidly destroyed. In my view there are two root causes.

> The first arises from the 'empty-earth' paradigm of colonization, which assumes that ecosystems are empty if not taken over by Western industrial man or his clones.... The assumption of the empty lands... threatens other species and other cultures to extinction because it is blind to their existence, their rights and to the impact of the colonizing culture.

> The second cause is what I have described as the monoculture of the mind: the idea that the world is, or should be, uniform... that diversity is either disease or deficiency, and monocultures are necessary for the production of more food and economic benefits.... The shutting out of alternative ways of knowing and making leads to the assumption that the dominant knowledge and techniques are the only options. This monoculture of the mind destroys biodiversity by blocking the perception of multiple benefits and uses of biodiversity.[20]

Another frontier image, *Westward the Star of Empire Takes Its Way – near Council Bluffs, Iowa* by Andrew Melrose, (figure 4) depicts, elsewhere, similar processes. Ironically in terms of colonial discourses of 'empty lands', the clear-felled, colonised farm-land and the track-bed of the conquering railroad both appear much emptier than the native forest, bursting with wildlife, that they have replaced.

Patricia Macdonald

Early colonists whose 'manifest destiny' was the filling of a supposedly 'empty earth', found their belief severely tested wherever the prior inhabitants were numerous and organised enough to resist the undesired blessing of fullness being bestowed on them. These prior inhabitants suffered various outcomes: assimilation (as in *The Trapper's Bride* by Alfred Jacob Miller [figure 5]); legal disenfranchisement; destruction of traditional ways of life; decimation by disease; enforced removal from ancestral lands; slavery; genocide; and, finally, canonisation as vanished repositories of lost earth-wisdom (as in Maynard Dixon's elegaic *Earth Knower* [figure 6]).

These activities of emptying the full, masquerading as 'filling the empty', operated on non-human inhabitants and complex ecosystems as well as upon humans. The process applies increasingly to cultivated as well as to wild species: by the incorrect definition of so-called 'new' genetically modified organisms (GMOs) and varieties, together with the inappropriate use of patents and intellectual property rights,

> [t]he right to protect living resources and lifestyles has been reduced to a 'barrier to free trade' … [and] … 'denying the value of indigenous knowledge developed over many generations [as 'empty'], the West is attempting to colonize [not just land, but] life itself… [creating] a new era of bio-imperialism, built on the biological impoverishment of the Third World and the biosphere'.[21]

Alongside this neo-colonial Armageddon, the previous phase of the process continues. In North America, photographers such as Richard Misrach and Peter Goin have deconstructed classic wilderness iconography in their images of recent environmental damage: Misrach's *Desert Cantos* (figure 7) documents:

> [n]ot the pure unsullied wilderness… the desert of Christian purification and American longing, but the real desert that we mortals can actually visit – stained and trampled, franchised and fenced, burned, flooded, grazed, mined, exploited, and laid waste… an awesome witness to our capacity to destroy what we love, and to love what we have destroyed.[22]

Figure 6
Maynard Dixon,
Earth Knower,
c. 1933-1935,
oil on canvas.
Oakland Museum,
bequest of
Abilio Reis

Figure 7
Richard Misrach,
Desert Fire #1,
1983, from series
"The Fires" in
Desert Cantos,
colour
photographic
print, 1987

In Europe, also, a recent school of 'Wasteland' imagery documents environmental abuses. The sites photographed, like those by Wout Berger, (figure 8) often look unremarkable: the menace of such images is not that they appear sinister, but almost *normal*. Only the accompanying text makes clear the horror of the 'wasteland' area:

> Former incinerator where... chemical waste from all over Europe was processed. Perhaps the most severely polluted ground in the Netherlands. Prominent toxic substances: dioxins, PCBs, benzene, xylene.... The soil is a complicated cocktail in which unpredictable chemical reactions occur.... The situation is beyond any 'normal' cleanup methods. Technicians have suggested turning the contaminated soil into glass by passing immense electrical charges through it [to seal the poisons] in the artificial lava created....[23]

There must be few things emptier of life than artificial lava.

Less dramatically caused examples of ecological damage, but significant in terms of the gradual degradation of extensive land-areas which may *appear* to be natural wilderness, are found over much of the Highlands of Scotland, as mentioned above. Despite the ecological facts, many people have become accustomed to these degraded landscapes, emptied of much of their biodiversity. Some writers, for example the eminent Scottish poet Hugh MacDiarmid, have even eloquently celebrated (with a love of nature but in relative ecological ignorance) the biodiversity that remains in the passage that finishes: "'Nothing but heather!' – How marvellously descriptive! And incomplete!"[24] This famous passage is a consummate description of a heather moor. It forgets, however, that, if truly 'wild', such a moor would form only part of a diverse mosaic of plant communities. That varied

Figure 8
Wout Berger,
*Amsterdam,
Diemerzeedijk,
IBS code 025-007,
juni 1986,*
from Gifbelten
(Chemical waste
dumps), colour
photographic
print

Figure 9
Horatio
McCulloch, *Loch
Lomond*, 1861,
oil on canvas.
Glasgow Art
Galleries and
Museums

vegetation would support a richer fauna, more land-based employment options, and thus more vibrant human communities, in which case there would be no need to apologise for, or to celebrate the remnant virtues of, a habitat which is, indeed, at present *almost* 'nothing but heather'.

Highland historical experience over the past few centuries is not technically a colonial one because most of the protagonists have inhabited a single political entity. It shares, nevertheless, many features with colonised experience: lack of self-determination by ethnic/language-minority communities; repeated periods of external military repression, ecological exploitation, and 'emptying' of population through famine, economically driven emigration or enforced 'clearance' from long-established settlements.[25] This experience, fresh in the memories of many Highlanders, has been repeatedly denied by romanticising and/or mystifying external references to much of the Highlands as '(pristine) wilderness', implying that it is *naturally* empty of people and relatively unmodified by human activity. Romantic paintings such as *Loch Lomond* by Horatio McCulloch (figure 9) share features with the American examples discussed above: almost 'empty' landscapes, suffused with a golden glow.

Much of the Highlands, as suggested above, is neither 'natural wilderness', nor 'naturally' empty of people: it is an 'emptied', rather than an 'empty', landscape. Long-term ecological degradation and the loss of natural biodiversity have resulted from a complex range of factors; this degraded state has been subsequently maintained by various land-management/mismanagement practices. This situation has been increasingly researched and debated recently, often acrimoniously and/or disingenuously because of the political implications.

The contributory factors are now thought to include:
- the climate becoming colder and wetter, less favourable to woodland;[26]
- long-standing over-exploitation of native forests;[27]
- widespread overgrazing by (domestic) sheep and goats, and (semi-wild) deer maintained for recreational hunting, preventing regeneration of trees;[28]
- 'muirburn': burning of moorland for sheep and recreational grouse-shooting management;[29]
- the concentration of land-ownership in few hands, limiting diversity of approach. Scotland has "the most concentrated pattern of private land ownership in Europe (more concentrated even than in... Brazil)", exacerbated by absenteeism, and most extreme in the Highlands and Islands, where "half of the private land... is owned by fewer than 100 landowners".[30]

Natural biodiversity, of species, habitats and soils, is the ultimate basis for all livelihoods. Natural woodland habitats in Scotland are generally much richer floristically (often >x10) and faunally than the rough grassland or heath which have often replaced them: woodland is an indicator of biological diversity and ecological robustness.[31] The present-day native-woodland land-cover is extremely low: 2-4%, *cf* an original 50-75%.[32] Levels of biodiversity, natural biological productivity, shelter and soil-quality are correspondingly low in comparison to possible levels.

I have recently documented degraded Scottish landscapes in a series entitled (in homage to Magritte) *This is not a natural wilderness, and it is not a picture of a natural wilderness, either,* with texts similar to those of Wout Berger. A 360-degree, panoramic aerial sequence made in the Highlands provides a graphic demonstration of the native-woodland statistic above (see "Emergent Landscapes", this volume). Surveying the entire horizon below, from Ben Nevis to the expanses of Rannoch Moor, there is hardly a tree in sight; descending lower towards the moor, we see evidence of one of the reasons, mentioned above, for both the loss, and the lack of regeneration, of woodland, namely over-browsing by deer: the moorland surface is criss-crossed by 'deer motorways', and almost the only trees grow on islands in lochs (relatively inaccessible to deer). Environmentally unsustainable numbers of deer persist on many 'sporting (hunting) estates'. The red-deer population estimate in Scotland is c. 400,000, more than double the 1960 statistic, and eight times the estimated sustainable 50,000.[33]

Another major factor also mentioned above, preventing recovery of the degraded ecosystem, is the practice of burning moorland to provide feeding for sheep or game-birds, which depletes soil nutrients and destroys sapling trees. Figure 10 shows controlled 'muirburn' and the resulting landscape, still considered by some, with little ecological justification, 'wild land'.

Shiva's global/'developing-world' concerns with cultural and biodiversity, and 'local' biodiversity problems in a 'developed' country like Scotland, which retains some *relatively* 'wild land', are in some ways equivalent. One shared causal factor is that of reductionist, 'dominator' (rather than holistic) attitudes to the environment, promulgated by mystification in the form of some of the 'naming' and 'framing' processes considered above.

To address such problems, a change in human attitudes appears necessary: one large enough to replace 'dominator' attitudes with approaches more informed by current ecological understanding of the environment, and more appropriate to the self-determination needs of human communities.[34] Such a major change implies radical modification of strategies of 'naming' and 'framing' land and its human and non-human communities. In order to contextualise some of the artwork beginning to employ such strategies, discussed at the end of this paper, processes of 'naming and framing' at the meta-level of change in world-view must next be briefly examined.

Paradigm Shift: Change in World-View

Many commentators consider that we find ourselves at a 'watershed of history' dividing one overarching world-view, or 'paradigm', from another, and they describe this change from one world-view to another, as a 'paradigm shift'.[35] The most recent previous paradigm shift in Western thought took place between the Renaissance and the seventeenth century Scientific Revolution, when the paradigm of mechanist 'modernism' became established (using the term 'modernism' in the wide, Cartesian-Newtonian sense, rather than in any visual stylistic sense).[36] The current change is away from this waning paradigm, towards a new world-view that is 'post-modern' (again using the term in the widest, rather than any narrow, stylistic, sense).

The new world-view is as different from that which preceded it ('modernism' *s.l.*) as modernism was to the previous world-view that *it* replaced between about the fifteenth and seventeenth centuries. It has been termed the 'ecological' or 'organicist' paradigm.[37] Its characteristics, further described below, might be summarised in relation to this publication as follows:

- Matter and 'mind' (cognition) – body/physical world and ideas/perception – land and politics – are not considered separate as in the old paradigm, but as essential complementary aspects of a dynamic, 'living' system. Such a system is an example of an 'emergent phenomenon': one with new, 'emergent' properties, in which the whole is greater than the sum of its parts.[38]
- Physical objects, living or non-living, are not considered as separate, independent entities with fixed boundaries, but rather in terms of their relationships, internal and external, and as occupying flexible areas defined by (conditioned) perception.

The term 'organicist' is shorthand for the characteristics of the new paradigm. The metaphors of the modernist world-view (the 'old paradigm') were 'mechanist': those of the machine, of linear (cause-and-effect-type) logic, of predictability, and of 'progress' envisaged as transformation in a linear, one-directional, sense. The metaphors of the new paradigm, by contrast, are those of (Heisenbergian) 'uncertainty', feedback cycles and networks, and of living organisms – 'organicist', in short. Transformation is still important, but not in a simple sense: in relation to the (new-paradigm) metaphors of living systems, linear transformations lack sufficient complexity.

The emphasis changes as follows:

Old paradigm	New paradigm
– objects; possessions	> relationships; interactions; process
	> "Independence is a political, not a scientific, term."[39]
– parts (reductionist)	> wholes (ecological, holistic)
– hierarchies	> feedback-sensitive networks nested within networks, each successive layer demonstrating 'emergent' properties
– self-assertion; domination	> collaboration; integration
– architectural epistemological metaphors ('foundation and superstructure')	> "a world without ground"[40]

The current paradigm shift might, of course, be considered as simply a change of emphasis rather than a rejection of the modernist world-view. Another sceptical viewpoint might emphasise Lyotard's "incredulity toward meta-narratives", or share Baudrillard's concerns regarding unmasking images; although these ideas have, in turn, been criticised (e.g. by Lotringer).[41] We should also recall that even within Western thought, the ideas emphasised in the new paradigm are not new; artists and scientists have long studied complex, 'non-linear' phenomena such as turbulence.[42] Until recently, however, it has been impossible to provide accurate conceptual/mathematical descriptions of such ideas. What *is* relatively new is that mainstream Western thought is reconsidering its deeply Cartesian principles and, using the recently developed 'mathematics of complexity' and 'cognitive biology', producing precise 'organicist' descriptions of the world, expressed in scientific/mathematical terms.

The types of fractal diagrams – such as 'strange attractors' (figure 11) – which are representations of the non-linear processes involved in natural systems from weather to living creatures, have become visual 'signatures' for new-paradigm thinking. Although motion in the 'attractor' (the diagram's shape) is abstract, as in any graph, it nevertheless conveys the 'flavour' of the motion of the real system that it describes. Such diagrams are not themselves artworks, but their philosophical and symbolic functions in terms of the new organicist paradigm might be considered as being equivalent to those of the 'Platonic forms' and the rectilinear grid for the old modernist paradigm.

Plain-language introductions to these developing fields of investigation are now available.[43] Fritjof Capra argues that if the new paradigm is an ecological/organicist one, in which the most appropriate metaphors are those of living systems, then to understand its implications, we need to understand what is meant by a 'living system'. And to understand the nature of life from a systemic point of view means being able to clearly distinguish between 'living' and 'non – living' systems:

> Since the early days of biology, philosophers and scientists have noticed that living forms, in many seemingly mysterious ways, combine the stability of structure with the fluidity of change. *Like* whirlpools, they depend on a constant flow of matter through them; *like* flames, they transform the materials on which they feed to maintain their activities and to grow; but *unlike* whirlpools or flames, living structures also develop, reproduce, and evolve.

And:

> Throughout the history of biology many criteria [by which to distinguish living from non-living systems] have been suggested, but all of them turned out to be flawed in one way or another. However, the recent formulations of models of self-organization and the mathematics of complexity indicate that it is now possible to identify such criteria.[44]

Capra's synthesis expresses these criteria using three inter-related conceptual dimensions: *pattern*, *structure* and *process*, his shorthand for a network comprising entire fields of investigation. The main points appear to be:
- that the *pattern of organisation* – the 'autopoetic' or 'self-making' network – is inextricably linked to:
- the *process of 'cognition' or 'mind'* (a process more comprehensive than 'consciousness');
- and that these, together, characterise a living system.
- Self-making, cognitive networks are 'embodied' in *'dissipative structures'* which maintain recognisable shapes while both matter and energy flow through them.[45]

The far-reaching implications of this synthesis and its associated metaphors are becoming increasingly clear. The new, wider concept of living/'life-like' systems has been convincingly extrapolated to community, ecosystem and planetary levels: Earth (and the global electronic culture) shows the self-regulating, feedback-mediated properties of a 'life-like' system – not simply a ball of inert rocks covered by a thin layer of slime, the biosphere.[46] The aerial image, 'Blanket bog and felled forest, the Great Glen, Scotland', 1987 (figure 12) conveys the feeling of this new view of Earth in the context of a Scottish landscape.[47]

Creative Practice and the New Paradigm

In the light of these philosophical ideas, I will now discuss briefly the part being played by the specific activities of creative writers and artists ('re-naming' and 're-framing') in the development of this new paradigm. Are such new 'ways of seeing' informing artistic activity and vice-versa, particularly in the context of work dealing with the natural world and the politics relating to it? In terms of 'naming', we have already examined the writing of the archetypal new-paradigm thinker/activist Shiva, and that of Thoreau, an early intimation of the current paradigm shift. We might also consider 'non-anthropocentric' fiction as participating in this change.[48]

And what of 'framing': is visual-arts practice also part of the shift? Much of the mainstream apparently remains preoccupied with the old paradigm, but there are several strands of current practice which explore aspects of the shift. The first of these comprises a range of the 'deconstructive' strategies of post-modern practice, including 'outrage' and 'endgame' art.[49] Recent examples might include the work of artists such as Steven Pippin, Barbara Kruger, Alan McCollum, Zoe Leonard, or Andreas Gursky and Calum Colvin, who attack the façade of the old paradigm or quarry away at its foundations.[50]

The second strand of artistic involvement, the 'reconstructive' strand of post-modern practice, has been extensively explored by Suzi Gablik, who "go[es] beyond [the] framework" of critique of the old paradigm.[51] Some of the artists she mentions work with direct ecologically- and socially-motivated action: Fern Shaffer and Othello Anderson, Dominique Mazeaud, or Mierle Laderman Ukeles. Some utilize process and ephemerality: Robert Janz or Andy Goldsworthy; one might add Chris Drury, Hamish Fulton, Richard Long, Susan Derges and Gabriel Orozco.[52] Others explore

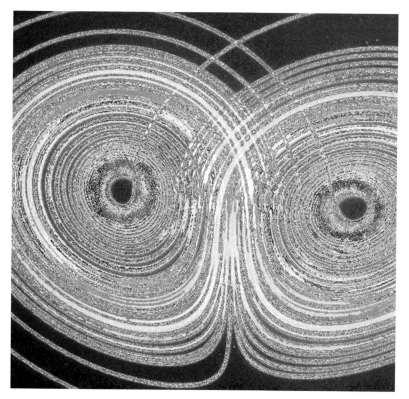

Figure 10
Patricia
Macdonald, in
collaboration
with Angus
Macdonald,
Muirburn,
Scotland, 1999,
Fujichrome print

Figure 11
Fractal diagram
(Lorenz
attractor):
signature of a
complex, non-
linear system,
and therefore
of the new
'organicist'
paradigm

experience and perception (adding again to Gablik's examples): R B Kitaj, Anish Kapoor and Rachel Whiteread, and video/light artists such as Susan Hiller, Mona Hatoum, Bill Viola and James Turrell. All employ "a new connective, participatory aesthetics,… a value-based art that is able to transcend the modernist opposition between the aesthetic and the social".[53]

Emergent Landscapes: Composite Aerial Works (see photo essay this volume, pp 62-69)

This final section considers briefly some of my own recent environmental works using aerial photography which I see as located partly within the *de*constructive, but mainly within the *re*constructive, strand of practice relating to the new paradigm. This work, made in collaboration with Angus Macdonald as pilot, inevitably uses land as its principal subject matter, although the content goes beyond land and its processes. Sometimes, as in our recent joint collaboration with the writer John Berger, *Once in Europa*, closer viewpoints are also used.[54] (figure 13) One of the themes in this book is the socio-ecological effect of the modern(ist) world upon a narrator and a community whose traditional paradigm is very different, and upon their environment.

Our recent aerial work has tended increasingly to be exhibited as large composite photographic pieces. It explores new ways of framing land, and aspects of the meaning of viewpoint and its relation to the nature of the real. It is influenced by our academic interests in perception, in the environment and in the relations between the two. The photo essay, earlier in this volume, includes the triptych: *Change of state* series, no. 1.[55] This piece relates to physical transformation – scientifically, 'change of state' – here, solid to liquid – but also, metaphorically, to perception and to psychological states. This was the first of what has become an increasingly complex series of composite pieces, each forming an 'emergent landscape' in which, in several senses, the whole is

greater than the sum of its parts, dealing with perception and the environment and the relations between the two.

Also shown is a larger, 10-part composite work, *The Sonnets to Orpheus,* related to Rainer Maria Rilke's eponymous poem cycle.[56] My main interests here are in Rilke's vision of the interconnectedness of the natural world, and in his prophetic image of the Orpheus myth as a cycle of 'boundary-crossings' and interrelationships, rather than a linear narrative of transformation in the 'modernist' sense. This is a large piece (3m high) with psycho-kinetic qualities. As the myth requires, it represents a 'descent' to hell, and an 'ascent' back towards life: the 'narrative' proceeds down the left-hand column, suggesting a feeling of falling, and then up the right-hand column with a corresponding feeling of rising. The ends of these movements are linked by the visual relationships between the frames opposite each other at top and bottom of the piece, resulting in a sort of cycle. It may be read as a kind of ecological parable: an ecological 'descent' past systems of enclosure and intensive agriculture to post-industrial wasteland, followed by a 'rise' towards a new beginning.

The final example is the complex composite piece: *The play grounds* series, no. 6.[57] Like *The Sonnets to Orpheus,* it has a psycho-kinetic effect at actual size (c. 2m square). Space allows only a brief exploration of the environmental critique that it contains, or of the various levels on which it functions. Firstly, there is a political level, concerning land-use, on which this piece may be read, particularly in a Scottish context. The component images depict sections of the surface of a grouse-moor, an upland heathland maintained as a habitat for a single species of 'game-bird', the red grouse. The grouse-moor shown here is a deadly board-game, supposedly a 'wild place', where a 'wild' experience may be had by hunters. But the moor is in fact regularly burned to provide food and cover (heather plants of different ages) for grouse, making the striking patterns: black and grey

patches contain heather of different heights, burned at different times in the past; in white areas, snow lies on recently burned ground almost devoid of heather. The moor is as manicured as a golf course. It has a similar low level of biodiversity to a scruffy, small-town football pitch – no mosaic of biodiverse woodland can survive the burning regime, although this would be the natural ecosystem. Far from being a rich and diverse 'wild place', it is an example of human domination of the natural world for one narrow, ecologically and socio-politically doubtful purpose.

The scarred moorland surface is presented simultaneously in various spatial ways and from various points of view, including that of the hunted grouse. So on another layer of operation of the work, it deals with hunting and the experience of being hunted, with freedom and constraint – considered as a vast board game, it shows possible 'sequential' scenarios of escape or of death by the guns of the hunters. The detail from the lower right of the piece shows the 'shooting butts' which conceal the hunters, and near which dead or wounded birds would fall to the ground.

The work strongly relates also, however, to different *modes* of perception, and to parts and wholes: this work is perhaps the clearest example discussed here of what I have termed an 'emergent landscape' piece – one in which, in several senses, the whole is greater than the sum of its parts. It also considers *systems* of perception and knowledge. In a deconstructive way, it contrasts two superimposed versions of the orthogonal grid of the old, mechanist, modernist paradigm: an actual version (the physical reality of the burnt moor) and a conceptualised version (the rectilinear arrangement of the parts of the piece itself) with the complex, non-linear, circling, feedback-loops of the 'strange attractor', one of the mathematical 'signatures' mentioned above (see figure 11) of the new, organicist, paradigm.[58] It therefore functions as a space in which to consider, and to compare, differing perspectives of land and politics.

Expressing Multiple Perspectives

In terms of looking at land and politics, it is to be hoped that future developments will include increasingly effective ways of expressing multiple perspectives – partly as a contribution to land-use debates and their resolution, and partly as a way of understanding and celebrating different types of diversity. These types of diversity would include biodiversity itself, and management practices that enhance it, but also diversity in sustainable cultural and land-use patterns, which tends in itself to protect biodiversity.[59]

As multiple perspectives come to be presented in more accessible forms, ways of naming and framing land may also develop which dispense with not only the narrow terms of either chauvinistic or neo-colonial attitudes, but also the constricted perspectives that echo only our anthropocentric demands. Such ways might reflect more closely the reality of Leopold's description of land as a "community to which we belong", as well as the truth of Thoreau's early insight that: "in Wildness is the preservation of the world".[60]

1   See Anderson, N K, in Prown, J D et al, *Discovered Lands, Invented Pasts*, New Haven: Yale, 1992, p. 16 and pp. 8-12.

2   Thoreau, H D, *A Week on the Concord and Merrimack Rivers*, in Atkinson, Brooks, ed., *Walden and Other Writings of Henry David Thoreau*, New York: Modern Library, 1937, p. 301.

3   Oelschlaeger, M, *The Idea of Wilderness*, New Haven: Yale, 1991, p. 143.

4   Thoreau, H D, "Ktaadn" in *The Maine Woods*, Ticknor & Fields, 1864.

5   Cronon, W, in Prown, et al., *Discovered Lands, Invented Pasts*, pp. 73, 79 and 81.

6   Thoreau, H D, "Walking", *Civil Disobedience and Other Essays*, New York: Dover, 1993, p. 49.

7   Thoreau, H D, *Walden*, London and New York: Dent Dutton, 1972, p. 185.

8   Thoreau, "Walking", p. 61.

9   Stewart, A, *Daughters of the Glen*, Aberfeldy: Leura, 1986.

10 U S Wilderness Bill/Act, 1956/1964.

11 Stevenson, A C and Birks, H J B, "Heaths and Moorland: Long-term Ecological Changes, and Interaction with Climate and People", *Heaths and Moorland: Cultural Landscapes*, Thompson, D B A, et al., eds., Battleby/Edinburgh: SNH/HMSO, 1995, pp. 224-239.

12 US Wilderness Bill/Act; Fox, S, *The American Conservation Movement*, Madison: Wisconsin University Press, 1985, p. 8.

13 *Wildness in Scotland's Countryside*, Battleby: SNH, 2002

14 Hunter, J, *On the Other Side of Sorrow*, Mainstream: Edinburgh, 1995, pp. 149-176.

15 Leopold. A, *A Sand County Almanac*, New York: Ballantyne, 1970, pp. 197 and 242.

16 Hunter, J, *On the Other Side of Sorrow*, pp. 150-151; Darling, FF, *West Highland Survey*, Oxford: Oxford University Press 1955 pp. 192-193.

17 e.g. *Natural Heritage Futures* series, Battleby: SNH, 2002.

18 Warren, C, *Managing Scotland's Environment*, Edinburgh: Edinburgh University Press, 2002.

19 *Paradigm*: "a constellation of concepts, values, perceptions, and practices shared by a community, which forms a particular vision of reality that is the basis of the way the community organises itself" (adapted from Kuhn,T, *The Structure of Scientific Revolutions*, Chicago University Press, 1962), Capra, F, *The Web of Life: a New Synthesis of Mind and Matter*, London: Flamingo, 1997, pp. 5-6.

20 Shiva, V, *Tomorrow's Biodiversity*, London: Thames & Hudson, 2000, p. 27 onwards and pp. 25-26.

21 Shiva, *Tomorrow's Biodiversity*, pp. 25 and 45 onwards.

22 Banham, R, in Misrach, M, *Desert Cantos*, Albuquerque: New Mexico University Press, 1987, p. 1.

23 Berger, W, "Gifbelten", *Perspektief*, Rotterdam, no. 43, 1992, pp. 49-58.

24 MacDiarmid, H, from "Direadh I", *Collected Poems of Hugh MacDiarmid*, Grieve, M and Aitken, WR, eds., vol. 2, Harmondsworth: Penguin, 1985, pp. 1170-1171.

25 Hunter, *On the Other Side of Sorrow*, and Hunter, J, *Last of the Free: A Millennial History of the Highlands and Islands of Scotland*, Edinburgh: Mainstream, 1999.

26 Warren, *Managing Scotland's Environment*, pp. 5-9.

27 Warren, *Managing Scotland's Environment*, p. 9.

28 Staines, R W et al., "The Impact of Red Deer and their Management on the Natural Heritage of the Uplands", *Heaths and Moorland*, Thompson, et al., eds., pp. 294-308.

29 Gimingham, C H, "Heaths and Moorland: an Overview of Ecological Change", *Heaths and Moorland*, Thompson, et al., eds.

30 Wightman, A, *Scotland: Land and Power*, Edinburgh: Luath, 1999, pp. 29 and 30; Wightman, A, *Who Owns Scotland?*, Edinburgh: Canongate, 1996.

31 Burnett, J H, ed., *The Vegetation of Scotland*, Edinburgh: Oliver & Boyd, 1964.

32 Hester, A J and G R Miller "Scrub and Woodland Regeneration", *Heaths and Moorland*, Thompson, et al., eds., p. 140; Mackenzie, N, *The Native Woodland Resource of Scotland*, FC Tech. Paper 30; Warren, *Managing Scotland's Environment*, p. 9.

33 Deer Commission for Scotland, *pers. comm.*, 2001; see also: www.dcs.gov.uk; Staines, "The Impact of Red Deer", pp. 294-308; Darling, *West Highland Survey*.

34 Lovelock, J, *The Ages of Gaia*, Oxford: Oxford University Press, 1988; Manning, R, *Grassland*, Harmondsworth: Penguin, 1997; Pretty, J N and Pimbert, M P, "Beyond Conservation Ideology and the Wilderness Myth", *Natural Resources Forum*, 19, 1, 1995, pp. 5-14.

35 See note 19 and Thompson,W I, ed., *Gaia 2: Emergence*, New York: Lindisfarne, 1991, pp. 11-29.

36 Thompson, *Gaia 2: Emergence*, pp. 11-29, and Capra, *The Web of Life*, pp. 17-35.

37 Capra, *The Web of Life.*, pp. 6 onwards.

38 "C D Broad coined the term 'emergent properties' for those properties that emerge at a certain level of complexity but do not exist at lower levels." (Capra, F, *The Web of Life*, p. 28)

39 Margulis, L and Sagan, D, *What is Life*, New York: Simon & Schuster, 1986.

40 Varela, F, Thompson, E, and Rosch, E, *The Embodied Mind*, Cambridge, Mass.: MIT, 1991, pp. 59 onwards and 143.

41 See Gablik, S, *The Re-enchantment of Art*, Thames & Hudson, London, 1991, pp. 31-40.

42 Kirk, G S and Raven, J E, *The Presocratic Philosophers*, Cambridge: Cambridge University Press, 1964, pp. 187, 191, 196-7, 202 and 214-215.

43 Gleick, J, *Chaos*, London: Sphere, 1989; Prigogine, I and Stengers, I, *Order out of Chaos*, London: Fontana, 1985; Capra, *The Web of Life*.

44 Capra, *The Web of Life*, pp. 172 and 156, my emphasis.

45 Capra, *The Web of Life*, pp. 156-157.

46 Lovelock, J, *Gaia*, Oxford: Oxford University Press, 1979; and Lovelock, *The Ages of Gaia*.

47 See Macdonald, P, *Shadow of Heaven*, London/New York: Aurum/Rizzoli, 1989, p. 85 (accompanying Photographers" Gallery, London, exhibition, 1989); Vowinkel et al., eds., *Kunst Europa*, Bonn: AdKv, 1991, pp. 13, 38-39; Macdonald, P, "To Remain Dissolved: Aspects of Photography and Language" in *Studies in Photography*, Edinburgh: Scottish Society for the History of Photography, 1996, pp. 24-35.

48 e.g. William Golding's *The Inheritors*; Richard Adams' *Watership Down*; Doris Lessing's *Canopus in Argos* series and other titles; Michel Faber's *Under the Skin*.

49 Berger, J, *The Moment of Cubism*: *Selected Essays*, London: Bloomsbury, 2001, pp. 90-92; Gablik, *The Re-enchantment of Art*, pp. 13-40.

50 See Riemschnieder, B and Grosinick, U, eds., *Art at the Turn of the Millennium*, Koln: Taschen, 1999 (Gursky) and Stevenson, S et al., *Light from the Dark Room: a Celebration of Scottish Photography*, Edinburgh: National Galleries of Scotland, 1995, (Colvin).

51 Gablik, *The Re-enchantment of Art*; Gablik, S, *Conversations before the End of Time*, London: Thames & Hudson, 1995.

52 Derges, S, *Liquid Form*, London: Michael Hue Williams, 1999, pp. 76-101; Riemschnieder and Grosinick, *Art at the Turn of the Millennium*, (Orozco).

53 Gablik, S, 1991, *The Re-enchantment of Art*, p. 9.

54 Berger, J and Macdonald, P, with Macdonald, A, *Once in Europa*, London: Bloomsbury, 1999.

55 Macdonald, P, *Order & Chaos: Views of Gaia*, Edinburgh: Stills, 1990; Macdonald, P, with A Macdonald, *Air works*, Edinburgh: Talbot Rice Gallery and London: BCA Gallery, 2001, pp. 12-13; Macdonald, "To Remain Dissolved", pp. 24-35 and Mackenzie, R, in Stevenson et al, *Light from the Dark Room*, pp. 73-87.

56 Macdonald, *Air works*, pp. 20-21; Lawson, J, in Stevenson, et al, *Light from the Dark Room*, pp. 95-104; Macdonald, "To Remain Dissolved", pp. 24-35; Dorrian, M, "The Middle Distance: on the Photography of Patricia Macdonald", *Katalog*, Ødense: Museet for Fotokunst, 1999, pp. 2-11 and Rilke, RM, *The Sonnets to Orpheus*, trans. Mitchell S, Boston, MA: Shambala, 1993.

57 Macdonald, *Air works*, pp. 22-23; Lawson, J, "Patricia Macdonald: "Emergent landscapes" in *Portfolio*, 31, Edinburgh, 2000, pp. 38-43 and Dorrian, "The Middle Distance", pp. 2-11. "Psycho-kinetic" describes a *feeling* of movement, distinct from both "kinetic sculpture" and Joyce's pejorative usage: "kinetic art" (Joyce, J, *A Portrait of the Artist as a Young Man*, Harmondsworth: Penguin, 1992, pp. 221-222).

58 See "Grids", Krauss, R, *The Originality of the Avant-Garde and Other Modernist Myths*, Cambridge, Mass.: MIT, 1996). I employ the grid here in *some* of Krauss's senses; more significantly, however, I also deconstruct modernist attitudes by: using the grid (signature *par excellence* of modernism) to criticise the effects of such attitudes on land-management; offering alternative conceptual structures related to the organicist paradigm; and using the "cheerful schizophrenia" which Krauss attributes (disparagingly, but nevertheless interestingly) to the grid; its paradoxical readings delight me, both *per se*, and in relation to new-paradigm ideas.

59 See note 20.

60 Leopold, A, *A Sand County Almanac*, Oxford: Oxford University Press, 1949/1987, p. viii; see note 8, above.

Privileged Gazes and Ordinary Affections: Reflections on the Politics of Landscape and the Scope of the Nature Aesthetic
Kate Soper

The linking of 'landscape' with 'politics' is subject to two differing, although inter-related, interpretations. Understood in one way, landscape is a matter of politics in virtue of its cultural and socio-economic context. Whether we have in mind actual or imaged landscape it always comes into being and exists within a nexus of power relations whose influence it bears. From this point of view, studies of the 'politics of landscape' would be explorations of the impact of power on the formation and representations of landscapes at differing times and geographical sites. Looked at from a rather more overarching perspective, however, the concern would be with the rationale for directing attention to the political dimensions of landscape in the first place. Is this to be understood as an essentially academic pursuit, a scholarly exchange of views on the 'politics of landscape' construed in the first sense, but conducted without the spur of any concerted political commitment or agenda? Or is there something more in the way of a contemporary critical politics attached to the conjoining of landscape and politics? In other words, is the engagement with the 'politics of landscape' to be viewed as primarily historical and cultural in focus, or does it also encompass the more troublesome and inconclusive issue of why we might want to develop a more politically alert conception of landscape studies, and how this might bear on current political predicaments and possible future transformations?

I do not want to prejudge the answers to these questions. But in raising these issues at the outset, I intend to register a personal sense of the importance of trying to locate the more specifically academic engagement within the larger interrogative framework; and it is this pressure that has been responsible in part for the choice of topic for this paper and the approach I bring to it. My concern here is to place cultural criticism within a broader eco-political setting by considering what the political critique of the landscape aesthetic associated with a 'cultural studies' approach might imply more generally for affective responses to the environment. Although I largely agree with this critique regarding the partial and elitist dimensions of conventional tastes in landscape, I also want to question its implications for the status, attribution and ecological relevance of aesthetic feelings for nature. I am interested, that is, in what is to be inferred from studies which have sought to expose the culturally constructed and politically biased quality of tastes in landscape for the existence of more collective human feelings for nature and their possible role in checking ecological devastation. In the light of the substantial evidence cited by critics for the always culturally relative and shifting quality of the nature aesthetic, one might be led to suppose that it is self-deluding for environmentalists to invoke such collective feeling. If this is the case, however, it must tend to undermine the democratic credentials of any programme of environmental conservation and renewal that seeks public legitimation through appeal to a shared sense of the beauties of nature or gratifications afforded by aesthetically pleasing landscapes. Although I shall here acknowledge the difficulties of arguing for any universal aesthetic of nature, I shall also explore the limitations in the arguments against it, and point to some reasons for continuing to invoke it in support of environmental protection.

I have spoken above of 'nature' and 'environment', as well as of 'landscape', but I want to make clear at the outset that although I recognise that the landscape idea is closely cognate with a number of others, (including nature and environment, but also place, countryside, natural scenery, to name but some) I approach it here as nonetheless distinguishable from all these, and not to be conflated with them. Indeed, I shall be focussing on what many today may feel is an overly narrow and classical conception of landscape. This is not because I regard this as the only appropriate concept, or want especially to defend it (at various points, in fact, I shall indicate its limitations), but because it is the concept most regularly invoked by the arguments with which I am here concerned.

According to this conception – which is very much in line with the original use of 'landscape' (or 'landskip') as a term of representation referring exclusively to pictures of inland scenery – landscape is primarily an object of contemplation and visual aesthetic gratification.[1] Even when the reference is extended to include vistas or expanses of the natural environment itself as well as their pictorial image, 'landscape' in this understanding retains its connotations of art in a number of respects. It does so in part because it refers most usually to a rural or pastoral – hence humanly modified – environment. It is what Cicero termed 'second nature', and all the more so in the case of the contrived landscapes created through landscape gardening and architecture, since the latter are clearly humanly made not simply in the sense that they bear the trace of human agricultural work or contain human artefacts, but in the stronger sense that they are the overall product of human intervention and artifice, and undertaken with a view to improving on what was naturally provided in the first place.[2]

Landscape, moreover, in this narrower and more classical conception has retained a legacy of its origin as a term of art, in two further respects. It has done so firstly because it has been thought of, typically, *as* prospect, in other words as in some sense enframed, as referring to that containable within a human viewpoint afforded from a given vantage; and secondly, and more importantly perhaps, because landscape in this conception is 'scenic', because it carries within it the idea of aesthetic attraction – hence pleasure in the natural environment purely as observed phenomenon. Actual, as opposed to represented, landscapes have been regarded as scenes in nature which are akin to representations in being conceived primarily as aesthetically compelling rather than as instrumentally valuable.

It is an implication of these remarks that this concept of landscape is aesthetic, by which I mean that it comes into being only in virtue of the historical aestheticisation of nature: it depends, that is, on the emergence of a regard for nature conceived as object of beauty or sublime appreciation (as opposed to, or in addition to, viewing it as terrifying, abhorrent, replenishing, useful, productive, fertile, etc.). It is difficult, I would argue, to pronounce with confidence about the arrival in European culture of a more contemplative and purely aesthetic approach to nature, although one can claim evidence of it very early on. This is in part because no history of its development can be offered that is not dependent, at least implicitly, on a prior decision as to what constitutes a distinctively *aesthetic* feeling, as opposed to a more instrumental concern for or interest in or affection for the natural environment – and this decision is, of its nature, philosophically problematic and always contestable. To give but one example of this: Jay Appleton, in his influential 'habitat' and 'prospect-refuge' theory, postulates that the aesthetic pleasure in landscape derives from the observer experiencing an environment favourable to the satisfaction of biological needs and protection against hazards. We respond to landscape (and also, so it is claimed, its representation in painting) intuitively on the basis of its ability to offer both 'prospects' – commanding vantage points – and 'refuges' – places of concealment from which we may command the view without being viewable ourselves.[3] Now 'habitat' and 'prospect-refuge' theories shed a lot of light on how we survey our terrain when playing 'hide and seek' (a game which was surely among our forefathers an indispensable childhood training for adult hunting forays). It also well captures the criteria on which any of us who go in for 'wild camping' select our tent sites. But we may surely question how far such a naturalistic approach informs us about a distinctively *aesthetic* sensibility for landscape given that we might want to define this latter precisely in terms of the disinterested pleasure it affords – which is that of delight in the beauty or sublimity of nature conceived entirely in abstraction from any consideration of its value for other purposes. Adorno, for example, in line with Kant's insistence on the 'pure' and 'disinterested' quality of a properly aesthetic judgement, emphasises the purely visual aspect of natural beauty, hence its closeness to art, and claims that it is the mark of the aesthetic experience of nature that it – like art – is wholly abstracted from self-preservation.[4] In other words, if we are of a Kantian/Adornian frame of mind on this issue, we shall tend to define the aesthetic response to nature in such terms as to rule out the pertinence of Appleton's type of naturalism. Of course, the defendent of the 'habitat' and 'prospect-refuge' theory might then insist that the theory does not deny the aesthetic quality of the *experience* of landscape, but only that it can be explained without reference to self-preservation; to which the Kantian/Adornian response will be that no properly aesthetic experience *is* explicable in those terms, to which the more naturalistic response might be that this is to so define that experience as to rule out the possibility that anyone has it – and so on and so forth.

This does not mean that we should opt for Kant/Adorno rather than Appleton (Appleton's theory *is* too reductive in the direction of biology, to my mind, but Kant, for his part, is also too little conscious of the historical conditions prompting his transcendental account of the nature aesthetic; and neither approach, though for differing reasons, can properly respect the extent to which responses to landscape are shaped by – and the vehicle for – political attitudes).[5] Moreover, one could well quarrel with the implication of the Kant/Adornian line (though it is that of Appleton, too) that a landscape aesthetic is, essentially, a visual affair. Other commentators have, after all, wanted to emphasise the role of the other senses (hearing, smelling, touching) in aesthetic responses to landscape. They have also, relatedly, sought to expose the limits of a contemplative and disinterested view of landscape as passively observed object, and to replace it by a more active and participatory conception.[6] These anti-Kantian moves are of some relevance to the political critique of landscape under review here, and I shall have cause to refer to them again. Suffice it to say in this context, that persuasive as they are in many respects, and surely a needed antidote to the exclusive focus on visual perception, they are not removed from the framework of problems I am noting here. For they, too, will need to make clear how they are defining a specifically 'aesthetic' response to the landscape or environment, and the grounds on which a more multi-perceptual and participatory engagement is to be distinguished as a matter of aesthetic gratification from a more self-preservative concern and involvement. They also need to make clear in what ways, if any, they would want to discriminate between 'environment' and 'landscape' since the argument often appears to rely on a slippage between the two, and many claims made in favour of adopting a more participatory and synaesthetic conception are fully persuasive only if thought of as applying to a habitat-like environment rather than to a landscape conceived as more akin to an artwork. The main point, however, to insist upon here is that any history of the emergence of the nature aesthetic and account of its qualities will necessarily have to address the central issue of what might be termed its logic: the issue of what it means to speak of an 'aesthetic' in contradistinction to any other type of response to the environment; and that the philosophically vexed nature of this will complicate the historical narrative.

Let us also recognise that it is a narrative further complicated by the character of the documentation upon which it is based, since this consists essentially in the commentary, literature and painting produced for and consumed by a privileged social elite. Those who appeal to a history of 'human', or, at any rate, of Western, aesthetic responses to nature and the natural environment, do so on the basis of a very partial body of evidence. This is, of course, a constraint of direct bearing on the aspects of landscape appreciation that have been the target of the cultural studies critique and to which I now want to turn.

We are talking here essentially about a Marxist, or at any rate, leftwing engagement, in the development of which the work of cultural critics such as Raymond Williams, John Berger and John Barrell has been particularly influential, and among historical geographers that of Denis Cosgrove. What has been emphasised, reasonably enough, through this approach is the need to inject a class – and gender – dimension into accounts of landscape appreciation: to recognise the extent to which tastes and fashions in natural scenery or for landscape design and its pictorial and literary representation have been determined by those in positions of socio-economic power in ways that reflect their sense of the world and interests in cultural endorsement. The history of landscape appreciation in Europe is presented from this perspective as a record of the ways of seeing and feeling of the upper and upwardly mobile classes. As Cosgrove has put it, the landscape idea is ideological – it refers to a privileged prospect on nature, the viewpoint of the 'outsider' who enjoyed the leisure requisite to aesthetic contemplation, and is freed from the fixity and immanence within their environment of those who actually work it.[7]

Landscape, then, on this account, is a 'way of seeing' or enframing that requires a certain distance, a standing back, both social and spatial, from that it looks upon, and which is not available to, or at any rate quite different from the experience of, those whose labouring activity and means of livelihood render them 'closer' to the land and more immersed within it. It is a way of seeing, or of representing, that tends always to deny the true harshness of rural existence, and to screen out, or at best, only half-image what John Barrell has referred to as the 'dark side' of the landscape. It is also, we might add, a gaze that abstracts from the changing patterns of land ownership, economic power, and organisation of labour that have gone into the making of the physical territory, and are inscribed within it as an archeological evidence of oppression and inequality traceable in the arrangements of fields systems and country estates, grouse moors and crofters' holdings. Instead, the landscape gaze has typically regarded the rural scene as reflecting not discord and social division, but an organic unity, a harmonious and naturally ordained order of wealth and reproduction, and thus as confirming the privilege and status of the viewer. Typically, too, as Raymond Williams has brought so powerfully to our attention, this naturalisation of a social order goes together with a nostalgic and retrospective yearning for older ways of life (and artistic or literary depictions of them) as being (or capturing) something more authentic in humanity/nature relations, because purportedly closer to nature, and therefore relatively less remote than the present from a mythical pre-cultural point of origin.

Although much of the political commentary on landscape that has been produced from this perspective has had a historical focus, engaging with a past rather than contemporary production and consumption of landscape, one might briefly note here its contemporary relevance for policies on environmental and heritage conservation, where there is still a persistent tendency to abstract from the ways in which the environmental legacy bears witness to a history of power relations, and to present this as if it had always in some sense been commonly owned and enjoyed. In the UK, for example, many of the country houses and estates open to the public are presented as a 'collective' national heritage, thus creating the illusion that those who visit these places (and whose entrance fee often helps to fund the maintenance costs of the landed gentry who continue to own and occupy them) have themselves some stake in properties or landscapes which (without denying their often very powerful aesthetic attractions) it would be more honest to present as monuments to gross inequality and exploitation. On the other hand, public access to lands and monuments, which might more properly be said to be parts of a common heritage, is disputed and often severely restricted.[8]

The focus so far has been on the political critique of the ideological dimensions of *pastoral* landscape and its representation, but similar considerations also apply in the case of the sublime landscape, since this, too, has symbolically endorsed a particular conception of humanity/nature relations, and been invested with normative import for human self-understanding and behaviour. The appreciation and theorisation of the natural sublime in the late eighteenth century has clearly to be regarded in the first instance as a response to Enlightenment de-deification: God, in a sense gets saved by finding his attributes (immensity, infinity) in the vastness of the cosmic space of nature.[9] But there is no doubt, too, that the sublime is to be associated with a lifting of the burden of the past and influx of power over earlier authorities, and hence with the emerging sense of human control over natural forces and release from bigotry and superstitious fear. The frisson induced by the sublime is emblematic in this sense of a new found confidence in human moral autonomy and capacity to contemplate the terrors of nature without quailing: attitudes which find their philosophical confirmation in Kant's analytic of the sublime as reliant on a transcendence over nature rooted in the distinctively human power of reason. By a process of mistaken subreption, according to Kant, we impute the sublime to nature when in reality it is nature that directs us to the sublimity of the human mind, and specifically to the superiority of its powers of reason over those of the faculty of sensibility. But if the sublime aesthetic can be said to be symbolic in a general way of Enlightenment selfhood and responses to nature, it was also confirming the political ascendancy and socio-economic priorities of an entrepreneurial, bourgeois elite blessed by commercial success and the cultural benefits that go with that (and, as such, it was opposed to the beauties of the Arcadian landscape favoured by a decadent – and supposedly effeminate – aristocracy). The impeccably suited gentleman in the Caspar David Friedrich *The Wanderer Above the Sea of Mist,* 1817, famously epitomises this auto-telic and headily Promethean outlook. For the poets, painters and philosophers of the Romantic period, moreover, there is little doubt but that the appreciation of the sublime is the mark of a refined sensibility and virile moral feeling denied to the mass of mortals, or at any rate viewed as achieveable only through culture and education. Wordsworth, for example, argued that although it is "benignly ordained" that all of us should easily find affection for the "ordinary varieties of rural nature", the taste for wilder nature is not a common property, but has, as he puts it, to be "gradually developed both in nations and individuals".[10] Kant also sees the aesthetic appreciation of nature as the mark of a superior moral soul, and although his transcendental analytic is 'democratic' in the sense that it allows that everyone in principle can relish even the sublime, he does acknowledge that a measure of culture is requisite to doing so.[11]

The taste for the Romantic sublime is thus presented as that of the sensitive and solitary nature lover, and it is a definite intimation of much of the commentary on it, that as it is transmitted to the common masses it is passed down only in a banalised and inauthentic form. Thomas Hardy is exceptional in the lack of condescension with which he predicts this eventual transmission in the concluding section of his description of Egdon Heath:

The time seems near, if it has not actually arrived, when the chastened sublimity of a moor,
a sea, or a mountain will be all that is absolutely in keeping with the moods of the more thinking
among mankind. And ultimately, to the commonest tourist, spots like Iceland may become what the
vineyards and myrtle-gardens of South Europe are to him now; and Heidelberg and Baden be passed
unheeded as he hastens from the Alps to the sand-dunes of Schneveningen.[12]

This is far from snooty in tone, yet even Hardy implies that as the sublime becomes the landscape
preference of the "commonest tourist" it must lose something of the rare power it formerly held for the
"more thinking". What is important, it would seem, to the very quality of the experience of the sublime
is that it be an exclusive taste, the appreciation in nature of a vista confirming the subtler instinct and
sensibility of the viewer.

We can still today discern something of this same optic in ecological laments about the popularisation
of wilderness, the tourist quest for sublime experience, the absurdity of the fashion for Arctic holidays,
and so on. Mass tourism does, admittedly, frequently spoil or seriously detract from the beauty of the
environments it popularises. Nor should one overlook the extent to which the tourist industry has
today been responsible for the construction of a certain nature aesthetic. Some of the papers in this
collection highlight various aspects of this construction, particularly in respect of exotic holiday
destinations. One of the problems, too, as Alex Wilson has pointed out in his fine work on *The Culture
of Nature*, is that this construction of taste is tailored to meet modern transport preferences for the
airplane or the motor-car, vehicles which not only tend of their very nature to ruin what they reach,
but also demand an essentially abstracted and one-dimensional perception. In accommodating to this
motorist's aesthetic, the designers of the national parkways, says Wilson, have created an 'automotive
space' such that:

Nature appears to produce itself with no apparent relation to the cultures that inhabit it or use it.
Magnificent vistas now happily present themselves to us without the clutter of human work and
settlement. The seasons begin to be synchronised with the tourist calendar: June is Rhododendron
Time, autumn is Fall Foliage Time, winter is Wonderland.[13]

I am not, then, wanting to dissociate myself from the alarm at the effects of mass invasion into
my favoured beauty spots; nor am I wanting to deny that there is as much evidence for regarding
popular tourist tastes in landscape in our own time as no less a product of cultural construction, than
the landscape gaze of the privileged elites of the past (and as sometimes comparable in instantiating
the gaze of the relatively affluent First World 'outsider'). But I am conscious of a number of tensions in
this area, and particularly that of the paradox of a democratically motivated exposure of the class or
patriarchal dimensions of a landscape 'way of seeing' that veers towards denying that more ordinary
people are possessed of any distinctively aesthetic response to landscape.

Part of the problem here lies in the opposing of a privileged aestheticised landscape way of seeing
to the more authentic, non-ideological, but also *non-aesthetic* response of the worker upon the land.
In expanding on the distinction between the 'outsider' way of seeing of the consumer of landscape
painting/poetry, who may own but does not mix his labour with the environment, and the 'insider'
who lives and works within it, Cosgrove has suggested that for the 'insider' the external world is
unmediated by aesthetic conventions (and, so it is strongly suggested, the experience of it is all
the more authentic).[14] Adorno has claimed somewhat comparably in his section on "Natural Beauty"
in *Aesthetic Theory* that those who have been immersed in working the landscape are incapable

of responding to it aesthetically (although he falls short of suggesting that their response is the more genuine). He writes:

> Times in which nature confronts man overpoweringly allow no room for natural beauty; as is well known, agricultural occupations [the earlier RKP, 1984 translation refers to "peasant populations"], in which nature as it appears is an immediate object of action, allow little appreciation for landscape. Natural beauty, purportedly ahistorical, is at its core historical; this legitimates at the same time as it relativises the concept. Wherever nature was not actually mastered, the image of its untamed condition terrified.[15]

Landscape, then, according to this perspective, only comes into its own (i.e. prospects in nature are only constituted as object of aesthetic appreciation) at the point where nature no longer terrifies, and even then it only figures as a source of pleasure for those who are freed from the necessity of working on the land themselves. Or to put the point even more strongly, if somewhat tendentiously, the appreciation of landscape is here viewed as definitionally elitist, since it was only the economically advantaged echelons, in any historical period, who were in a position, socially and culturally, to experience an aesthetic reaction to their environment. Distinctively aesthetic feelings for the natural environment are presented as confined, of their very nature, to the leisured and culturally educated classes – and are thus also, in Cosgrove's view, if not in Adorno's, something less than authentic, spurious in the aloof and contemplative quality of their gaze.

Now it is quite true, that the evidence for regarding an aesthetic of nature as inherently patrician and elitist is overwhelming – or rather, it is very difficult to gainsay it in the absence of any countervailing tradition. All the same some caution may be called for here. For while it is certainly mistaken to treat the sentiments expressed for nature of a particular group or class as if they had universal application and were those of humanity at large; there is also a presumption in supposing that the feelings which have been given expression are exclusive to the fraction of humanity that gave voice to them, or that the absence of a cultural record bespeaks an absence of sentiment. It may, in other words be as complacent to assume that it has only been the cultural elites that have felt the headiest inspiration for nature, or that their tastes have always cued those of 'peasants' and working people, as it is to overlook their hegemonic role in the creation of a supposedly common aesthetic. There could be some elitism in refusing to credit any universal aesthetic for nature, just as there is in ignoring the favoured positions of those who have done the talking.

Indeed, the most paradoxical aspect of this, as has been noted by a number of commentators, is that the elitist tendency seems most manifest when those who 'do the talking' have discoursed on the inarticulacy of peasants and agricultural labourers as itself as the mark of an enviable closeness to nature: of an immanence within it of an almost animal kind, which is denied to the more self-aware and alienated spectator. I have referred to this elsewhere as the trope of the 'envy of immanence', associating it with Heidegger's presentation of a mute and earthy peasantry as embodying the 'pre-understanding' that is lost to modern technological wisdom, and with ruralism in English poetry. (Some of the most obvious instances are Edward Thomas's celebration of the countryman, 'Lob' for "saying so little compared to what he does", and those poems by Wordsworth (*Michael, Resolution and Independence, Old Man Travelling, Animal Tranquillity and Decay),* which turn on the contrast between the articulate, 'outsider' status of the poet-narrator and the immanent being of the rural worker. For, as Martin Ryle has pointed out, although Wordsworth may present himself in such poems as lacking something that the more immanent figures possess, it is his own difference from them which "endows him with the capacity to meditate on his own responses, in terms shared with his educated readers". Nor can we doubt that "without his learning (with all that this depended on) Wordsworth would hardly have come to formulate his well-known view that 'one impulse from a vernal wood' can be richer in moral instruction than 'books' and 'sages'".[16] In other words, the intellectual (whether Romantic poet or Heideggerian philosopher) who speaks for the feelings for the landscape of the rural worker, has obviously broken with a patrician humanism, and with any explicitly registered appeal to the 'man of culture' as the touchstone of good taste in nature. Yet the romanticisation of rural immanence remains caught nonetheless in the paradox of its own implicit aesthetic transcendence.[17] (In his viciously ironic counterpoint to all such romanticism Kierkergaard, we might note in passing, also hears a voice in the vernal wood, but according to him the trees "whisper all the drivel they have so long been witness to, and ask me in God's name to cut them down so as to be free from all the nonsense of the nature enthusiasts".)[18]

But to revert to the main point: on the one hand we have a perspective on landscape which in recommending, even envying, the 'insider's' freedom from the ideologically inflected aestheticising gaze, can seem too little conscious of the privileges of an aesthetic education denied to the more inarticulate. On the other hand, in focussing on the socially exclusive nature of a distinctively aesthetic response it can also too readily deny any conscious aesthetic sensibility (as opposed to an intuitive and unreflexive 'pre-understanding') to the ordinary worker. And in doing this it also tends to deny the existence of a more universal aesthetic need for nature.

It is in this context that criticism of the overly visual conception of the landscape aesthetic might seem most relevant. If there has been a tendency among critics to deny that those closest to and most immersed within their landscape can be subject to a distinctively aesthetic experience of it, is this not, it might be said, because those doing the denying have been too quick to identify aesthetic response with visual pleasure at the cost of recognising the delights afforded to other senses? If there is some measure of truth in the idea that those more immanently engrossed in their environment are incapable of the self-distancing essential to the adoption of the privileged 'landscape gaze', this in itself does not justify the inference that they are also deprived of any other form of aesthetic response, whether this be to the sounds or smells or tactile qualities or more immediately local and smaller-scale visual aspects.

Given how very few of the non-privileged rural workers have recorded their aesthetic pleasures in the natural environment, whether of a visual or non-visual kind, such claims must remain as relatively unsubstantiated as those they oppose. There is simply no telling how far, and in what ways precisely, nature has delighted those who have never spoken of it. Even where the poet or painter has given us a truly synaesthetic picture of the joys of nature, and is registering a supposedly more popular aesthetic response to its sounds and sights and smells we cannot be sure how universal its actual experience was.[19] Moreover, there can be no move beyond the more Kantian framework of thinking about the landscape aesthetic, with its emphasis on the necessary indifference to the instrumental concerns of self-preservation, that does not come up against the questions noted before about the criteria for imputing a distinctively aesthetic response. If this response has been thought to be essentially a visual and contemplative affair, this no doubt reflects the disposition to view other sensory experiences, especially those of smell and touch, as in some sense less disengaged – as coming with more of the interest that Kant associates with judgements of the 'agreeable' rather than pure aesthetic judgements. To make these points is not to approve the disposition, which is surely contestable: it is not clear, for example, why the pleasure in the scent of the rose or the sea is less disinterested than that in its sight; and, in any case, what of hearing whose pleasures seem entirely on a par with those of vision in respect of their lack of any necessary sensory interest or instrumental objective ? We might object, too, to the overly abstract and schematic division between the senses which this picture encourages, and which is at odds with the interactive and corrective or mutually reinforcing inpact of the differing senses in perceptual experience. So, the point here, to repeat, is not that we have to endorse the Kantian perspective, only to recognise that the proposed alternatives to it are also problematic in certain respects. It is tempting to suppose that one overcomes the elitist and ideological implications of a 'disinterested' aesthetic of nature by moving to one that is less visually fixated and more participatory. Yet critics will still object that such a position rests on a confusion of aesthetic and non-aesthetic criteria. Nor is it obviously any less speculative in its claims to represent a more universal or democratically grounded aesthetic.

We must recognise, in other words, that decisive evidence for imputing distinctively aesthetic feelings for landscape either to rural workers or to the populace at large is not available. But we can agree to this without necessarily sharing in the conclusions of those critics who have moved from the absence of evidence to an unqualified denial of the existence of any such feelings. As I have argued in *What is Nature?*, it is difficult not to feel that myth, religious imagery, popular and folk culture, and the more publicly available forms of art and literature indicate some shared and relatively unmediated appreciation of natural phenomena, including some of the forms of landscape. To suppose otherwise would seem implausible in its denial of any phenomenological response to the beauties of nature; it would be to suppose that cultural forces entirely determine rather than mould or mediate what is or is not an object of aesthetic pleasure. Adorno, to return to him once more, makes the interesting point that:

> Although what is beautiful and what is not cannot be categorically distinguished in nature, the consciousness that immerses itself lovingly in something beautiful is compelled to make this distinction. A qualitiative distinction in natural beauty can be sought, if at all, in the degree to which something not made by human beings is eloquent: in its expression. What is beautiful in nature is what appears to be more than is literally there. Without receptivity there would be no such objective expression, but it is not reducible to the subject; natural beauty points to the primacy of the object in subjective experience.[20]

Sensibility 'discovers' beauty in nature, in a sense imbues it with 'expression', but the object must prompt the response initially. Likewise, the historical mediations will always inflect the subjective response to landscape, but the landscape must also present itself, or figure beforehand as a possible object of the cultural mediation.

Let us add, too, that comparably to the way in which we see the scientific and secular view of nature gaining general acceptance in the Modern period, so we are witness to certain epochal shifts in the aesthetic tastes in landscape whose general form is shared across divisions of class and wealth. The very widespread contemporary preference for wild nature would seem an obvious case in point, for even if this begins as a more purely bourgeois aesthetic, the general preference today can hardly be satisfactorily accounted for without some reference to the more collectively shared experiences of environmental transformation that followed in the wake of the Industrial Revolution. Moreover, if such general social shifts of feeling can be said to have come, at least in part, in reaction to the industrial encroachment upon nature and reflect some commonly shared concern for what has been lost in that process, they are also indicative parodoxically of an underlying trans-epochal communality in human responses. That the new Vale of Tempe, as Hardy puts it, may be a gaunt waste in Thule; that it is now the parts which pre-industrial society reviled as 'nature's pudenda' that are now acclaimed as the most beautiful does not necessarily attest to some profound difference between our affections for nature and those of pre-industrial society. What it suggests, rather, is the extent to which the history of the aesthetic of nature has to be thought in relation to the history of human domination: what we have come to prefer now is itself the effect of human transformations of the landscape and the particular forms of loss and destruction involved in these. But if that is the case, it also in a sense unites us across time with those in the past who, it may be said, did not esteem what we do now precisely because they had yet to experience its demise. What they valued less because of its abundance, we value more because of its progressive erosion. In this sense, one might claim that such shifts in the aesthetic taste in nature speak to something more universal in the patterning of Western responses to it.

My overall argument, then, is that a political approach to landscape needs to recognise both sides of a nature-culture interaction: both the extent to which aesthetic responses to the landscape, and the environment more generally, are, indeed, culturally formed or constructed, and hence relative to particular times, places and constituencies; but also to recognise the limits on this construction, and the extent to which the claims of a democratically motivated green politics to represent the pleasures and solace to be found in the natural landscape presuppose some more commonly grounded aesthetic feeling. T J Clark has suggested in the case of art that to opt for the arbitrariness of the sign and the entirely constructed quality of art's matter, is in practice to exit from the hope of art's inhabiting a public, fully translatable world, and maybe something similar can be said in respect of the aesthetic of nature: that an exclusive emphasis on the plurality and construction of taste leaves too little room for any collective insight into our common ecological predicament.[21] In other words, although we can recognise the political reasons for thinking it illegitimate to lay claim to any universal human feeling for nature or collective aesthetic response to it, we should also recognise that we deny any such common aesthetic only at the cost of undermining that part of the argument for a green politics which appeals to the value we collectively set on nature as a source of pleasure and sensuous gratification.

Some may well object to the underlying presumption in all this that aesthetic sensibility to the natural environment goes together with ecological concern. They may point to the way in which wrecked nature still commands aesthetic attention and has come to figure in certain contexts as the scenario for the experience of a new 'sublime'. Clearly, it would be mistaken to ignore the extent to which contemporary culture, especially some forms of war reportage, cinema, comics and computer games, promotes a dystopian aesthetic which revels in the imagery of wasteland and encourages a heady sense of human power in the evidence of environmental destruction itself. Even if one questions how far these dystopian pleasures are properly those of a nature aesthetic, there is no doubt that they are part of the story of human responses to capitalist economic globalisation and its impacts on the environment, and that we must recognise this countering impulse in any adequately dialectical account of this.

But I would maintain that it is also part of the story that the aesthetic and utilitarian impulses are in many respects inter-dependent, and that what tends to the erosion of nature as a source of aesthetic pleasure also tends to distrain on the interest in a more sustainable use of resources. There is a difference, of course, at the individual level, in the relative status or importance of the aesthetic and the utilitarian requirement, for while an individual can live without the pleasures of a preserved and unpolluted landscape, survival is impossible in the absence of food, warmth, and so on. It is also the case that when we are deprived of food, the need for it nonetheless persists, whereas when deprived of any experience of the pleasures of a flourishing natural environment, the aesthetic need for this will atrophy and no longer figure as in any sense an experienced need. (This may, indeed, have some part to play in the emergence of the contemporary aesthetic of a 'negated' nature.)

But even at the level of the individual, the failure to sense that one is missing this source of aesthetic satisfaction does not mean that some loss has not occurred that will have impact on the general quality of life and interest; and this might be even forcefully argued to be true at a more collective level, in the sense that communities persistently deprived of aesthetic gratification in nature are also in the long run likely to care less for long term human survival and well-being.

1   See *Oxford English Dictionary*, under "Landscape".
2   Cicero, *De Natura Deorum* II, 151-152; see Neil Smith's discussion, *Uneven Development*, Oxford and Cambridge Massachusetts: Blackwell, 1990, pp 45-47. To claim a second nature status for landscape is not to deny that we also speak, on the one hand, of landscapes that are 'wild' or 'sublime', and, on the other, of 'cultural' and, increasingly today, of 'urban' landscapes. But the very fact that we feel the need to append these adjectives indicates that we view these as extensions or departures from a narrower meaning referring us to something conceived as essentially more rural and Arcadian.
3   Appleton, Jay, *The Experience of Landscape*, London: John Wiley and Son, 1986, see especially chapters 1-4 for the exposition of the theory; for some responses to his critics, see "Prospects and refuges revisited", *Environmental Aesthetics:Theory, Research and Applications*, Jack L Nasar, ed., Cambridge: Cambridge University Press: 1988, pp. 27-44.
4   Adorno, T, *Aesthetic Theory*, Robert Hullot-Kentor, trans., London: Athlone, 1997, pp. 65, 70-71.
5   Kant, I, *Critique of Judgement*, Werner S Pluhar, trans., Indianapolis and Cambridge: Hackett, 1987, Book I, "Analytic of the Beautiful". For further discussion of these objections, see Soper, Kate, *What is Nature: Culture, Politics and the Non-Human*, Oxford: Blackwell, 1995, pp. 223-227.
6   This line of argument has been influenced by phenomenology, especially Merleau-Ponty's account of the body and perception. See, for example, Arnold Berleant, "Aesthetic Perception in Environmental Design", in Jack L Nasar, ed., *Environmental Aesthetics*, pp. 84-97; also his *The Aesthetics of the Environment*, Philadelphia: Temple University Press, 1992, chapters 1 and 2.
7   Cosgrove, D, *Social Formation and Symbolic Landscape*, London and Sydney: Croom Helm, 1984, pp. 18-27; Cosgrove refers in these pages to a number of other geographers employing the 'insider/outsider' contrast in their discussion of landscapes. Also, J Barrell's study, *The Dark Side of the Landscape: the Rural Poor in English Painting 1730-1840*, Cambridge: Cambridge University Press, 1980 and Williams, R, *The Country and the City*, London: Palladin, 1973.
8   One might note, too, that the idealised pastoral landscape remains very much in evidence in advertising imagery and copy. See Soper, Kate, *What is Nature?*, p. 194.
9   Tuveson, E L, *The Imagination as a Means of Grace*, Berkeley, CA: California University Press 1960, chapter 3; Weiskel, T, *The Romantic Sublime*, Baltimore: Baltimore University Press, Baltimore, 1970.
10 Wordsworth, William, "Letter on the Projected Windermere Railway", *The Illustrated Wordworth's Guide to the Lakes*, Bicknell, Peter, ed., Exeter: Webbs Bower, 1984. I am indebted here to Martin Ryle's discussion in "After Organic Community: Eco-criticism, Nature and Human Nature", forthcoming in Parham, John, ed., *Literature and the Environmental Tradition*, London: Ashgate, 2001.
11 Kant, *Critique of Judgement*, pp. 124-125.
12 Hardy, Thomas, *The Return of the Native*, London: Macmillan, 1965, pp. 12-13.
13 Wilson, Alex, *The Culture of Nature*, Oxford: Blackwell, 1991, p. 37. In somewhat ironic contrast to Wilson's criticism of the 'motorist's aesthetic' for confining us to a purely visual and one-dimensional experience, we find Arnold Berleant, himself one of the main advocates of a participatory and multi-perceptual aesthetic, calling upon highway engineers to "make highway travel an experience of landscape and not an exercise in endurance". For Berleant the motorcar should be accommodated rather than viewed as hostile to a fully sensual appreciation of nature. See "Aesthetic Perception in environmental design", p. 90; *The Aesthetics of the Environment*, p. 2.
14 Cosgrove, *Social Formation and Symbolic Landscape*, p. 19 and p. 26.
15 Adorno, *Aesthetic Theory*, p. 65.
16 Ryle, Martin H, "After Organic Community: Eco-criticism, Nature and Human Nature", forthcoming in Parham, John, ed., *Literature and the Environmental Tradition*.
17 Soper, *What is Nature?*, p. 238.
18 Kierkegaard, S, *The Concept of Irony*, Capel, Lee M, ed., London: Collins, 1966, p. 23.
19 For some richly evocative examples of such a nature aesthetic in the work of folk or popular poets, see the anonymous Celtic epigrams collected in Jackson, Kenneth H, *A Celtic Miscellany*, London: Routledge and Kegan Paul, 1951, pp. 133-149. (I am grateful to Mark Dorrian for drawing my attention to these). Other, earlier Celtic writing on nature included in Jackson's edition is also very powerful, though it was essentially a courtly production, sponsored by the aristocracy and for its entertainment (see pp. 11 and 63-93).
20 Adorno, *Aesthetic Theory*, pp. 70-71.
21 Clark, T J, *Farewell to an Idea: Episodes from a History of Modernism*, New Haven and London: Yale University Press, 1999, p. 130.

Biographies

Dana Arnold is Professor of Architectural History and Director of the Centre for Studies in Architecture and Urbanism at the University of Southampton. Her recent publications include *Reading Architectural History* (Routledge, 2002), *Re-presenting the Metropolis: Architecture, Urban Experience and Social Life in London 1800- 1840* (Ashgate, 2000) and *The Metropolis and its Image: Constructing Identities for London c. 1750-1950* (Blackwell, 1999). She has held visiting fellowships at Yale University, the Getty Research Institute in Los Angeles and the Centre for Research in Arts, Social Sciences and Humanities at the University of Cambridge.

Jane Avner is a lecturer in English Literature at the University of Paris XIII. She has published on representations of landscape in Renaissance texts and children's literature.

Tim Barringer is an Assistant Professor of the History of Art at Yale University. He has written widely on nineteenth century visual culture and is co-curator of American Sublime (Tate Britain, Philadelphia and Minneapolis, 2002). His books include *Reading the Pre-Raphaelites* (Yale University Press, 1999), *Frederic Leighton: Antiquity, Renaissance, Modernity* (co-edited with Elizabeth Prettejohn, 1998) and *Colonialism and the Object* (co-edited with Tom Flynn, Routledge, 1998).

Jia-Rui Chong completed her M.Phil in 20th-Century English Studies at Oxford University in 2001. She received a BA in American History and Literature from Harvard University in 1999. She is currently a staff writer on the Los Angeles Times.

David Crouch has published in numerous recent papers in geographical and tourism journals and books, including the recent *Visual Culture and Tourism*, (Berg, 2003). His research and writing develop critical perspectives on the bodily consumption of space, particularly conceptualised through performance and practice. This work includes a reflexive consideration of visual art materials as more than the subject of the gaze and its projected semiotics.

Mark Dorrian is a Senior Lecturer in Architecture at the University of Edinburgh. His writing has been published in *Artifice*, *Chora*, *The Journal of Architecture*, *The Journal of Narrative Theory*, and *Word & Image*. He is co-founder, with Adrian Hawker, of the art, architecture and urbanism atelier *Metis*. Their book, *Urban Cartographies*, was published by Black Dog in 2002.

Tim Edensor teaches Cultural Studies at Staffordshire University. He is the author of *Tourists at the Taj* (Routledge, 1998) and *National Identity, Popular Culture and Everyday Life* (Berg, 2002), as well as numerous articles on tourism, walking, Scottish identity and the film *Braveheart*, rurality and car cultures. He is presently writing a book on industrial ruins.

Robert Grant is a PhD student at the University of Kent at Canterbury researching nineteenth century British literature promoting colonisation and emigration. He has contributed essays to a number of historical journals.

Simon Grimble is currently a Research Fellow in English at New Hall, Cambridge. He has recently finished writing a book entitled *Landscape and the 'Condition of England', 1878-1917* (Edwin Mellen Press, forthcoming) and is now working on the representation of urban Britain in recent non-fiction prose, investigative journalism and documentary film.

Kirk Arden Hoppe is an Assistant Professor of African History at the University of Illinois at Chicago. He is currently completing a project on the environmental politics of sleeping sickness control in colonial East Africa.

John Dixon Hunt is Professor of the History and Theory of Landscape in the Graduate School of Fine Arts in the University of Pennsylvania. The author of many books and article on landscape architecture, he is also the editor of *Studies in the History of Gardens and Designed Landscapes* and the series editor for the Penn Press Studies in Landscape Architecture, in which eleven volumes have so far appeared.

Markus Idvall is a researcher and lecturer at the Department of European Ethnology at Lund University in Sweden. His PhD thesis (translated title: *The Power of Maps: the Region as a Societal Vision in the Age of the Öresund Bridge* [2000]) is a cultural analysis of the regionalist movements in southern Sweden in the period after World War II. At present he is examining, from a cultural perspective, questions about transplantation technologies connected to different health issues.

Jenny Iles is a Senior Lecturer in Sociology at the University of Surrey Roehampton. Her research interests include the heritage industry, leisure and tourism. She is currently completing her PhD on contemporary tourism to the First World War battlefields of the Western Front.

Adrian Ivakhiv is an Assistant Professor of Environmental Studies and Humanities at the University of Wisconsin Oshkosh. He is the author of *Claiming Sacred Ground: Pilgrims and Politics at Glastonbury and Sedona* (Indiana University Press, 2001). His writing on environment and culture has appeared in *Topia*, *Organization and Environment*, *Critical Studies*, *Social Compass*, *Musicworks*, and other journals. He is currently researching the politics of public space and urban landscape in post-Soviet Kyiv (Kiev), Ukraine.

Krystallia Kamvasinou is an architect and landscape architect. She is currently undertaking doctoral research at the University of Westminster, London. Her research project, which has been sponsored by IKY, Michelis Foundation and the AHRB, is entitled *Transitional Landscapes: the Relation of Landscape Design to Mobility-travel*

Ewa Kębłowska-Lawniczak is a Lecturer in English Literature at the University of Wroclaw. She has published on inter-art relations in Early Modern drama (J Lyly and W Shakespeare). Since 1999 she has worked mainly on the visual/textual nexus in the avant-garde movements of twentieth century European theatre.

Liam Kelly is Professor of Irish Visual Culture at the School of Art and Design, University of Ulster. Between 1986 and 1992, he was Director of the Orpheus Gallery, Belfast, and between 1996 and 1999 Director of the Orchard Gallery, Derry. He is currently a vice-president of the International Association of Art Critics, Paris (AICA). He curated 'Language, Mapping and Power' in Paris in 1996, as part of *L'imaginaire Irlandais*; and in 1997 organised the AICA international annual congress 'Art and Centres of Conflict: Inner and Outer Realities' in Belfast and Derry. His publications include *Thinking Long: Contemporary Art in the North of Ireland* (1996) and *The City as Art: Interrogating the Polis* (1994).

Andrew Kennedy studied at the Courtauld Institute and was awarded his PhD in 1998. His doctoral thesis was a study of British topographical print series 1720-1840. He has recently written on Samuel and Nathaniel Buck for *Art History* and on Reynolds and Gainsborough monographs for the *Oxford Art Journal*. He currently teaches at Kingston and East London Universities and at the School of Oriental and African Studies, University of London.

Stephen Kite is a Senior Lecturer in Architecture at the School of Architecture Planning and Landscape, University of Newcastle upon Tyne, UK where he is Degree programme Director of the BA in Architectural Studies. His research interests are in the field of the history and theory of architecture and its wider connections to visual culture. He has recently completed doctoral research into the architectonic aspects of the critical writings of Adrian Stokes (1902-1972): *Adrian Stokes – the Critical Writings: An Architectonic Perspective.*

Elizabeth Lebas is a Senior Lecturer in the Art, Philosophy and Visual Culture Academic Group at Middlesex University, north London, where she teaches on issues related to landscape imagery and discourse. Her previous writings on Bermondsey Borough Council in the inter-war period include essays on its filmmaking and gardening activities. She has also written on municipal filmmaking in Britain generally. She is co-editor with Eleonore Kofman of *Henri Lefebvre: Writings on Cities* (1998) and, with Stuart Elden, of *Henri Lefebvre: Selected Writings* (forthcoming). Her present interests centre on religious and secular female landscape discourses and practices in Britain and Quebec.

Patricia Macdonald brings together expertise in biological science, visuality and museology in her writing on environmental representation and interpretation. She is also an internationally celebrated artist-photographer, best known for aerial works made in collaboration with Angus Macdonald, Professor of Architectural Studies, and Head of the School of Arts, Culture and Environment at the University of Edinburgh. Her publications include: *Shadow of Heaven*, (Aurum/Rizzoli, 1989) *Order & Chaos* (Stills, 1990), (with John Berger) *Once in Europa* (Bloomsbury 1999), and *Air works* (Talbot Rice Gallery/BCA, 2001).

Charlotta Malm is pursuing a PhD in Human Geography at Stockholm University. She has previously worked as an assistant archaeologist in the Shetland Islands and has conducted landscape studies for the Swedish National Board of Antiquities. Her current research focuses on contemporary understandings of Shetland landscapes, primarily through the study of everyday life and visual culture.

Frédéric Pousin is a Director of Research at the CNRS (LADYSS UMR 7533) and an associated lecturer at the Ecole d'Architecture de Paris-la-Villette. His current research examines representation in its relationships with architectural and landscape design. His books include *L'Architecture Mise en Scène* (Arguments, 1995) and *Enseigner la Conception Architecturale,* (en coll.) (Ed. de la Villette, réed. 2002). His writing has been published in *Les Annales de la Recherche Urbaine, Les Carnets du Paysage,* and *Cahiers de la Recherche Architecturale et Urbaine.*

Gillian Rose, who has taught social, cultural and feminist geographies at the Universities of London and Edinburgh, now works at The Open University. Her publications include *Feminism and Geography* (Polity Press, 1993) and *Visual Methodologies* (Sage, 2001).

Amy Sargeant qualified as an architect before working as a production designer, and now teaches the history of film and visual media at Birkbeck College, University of London. She has written extensively on Russian and British cinema, especially silent cinema.

Sandra Arnold Scham is an archaeologist who has lived and worked in the Middle East for ten years. She is currently engaged in international research development projects at the University of Maryland including a joint Israeli and Palestinian archeological project on recognising and preserving the common heritage of Israel and the Palestinian National Authority. She is also a contributing editor for *Archaeology Magazine*.

Ursula Seibold-Bultmann is an independent art historian who writes on art and architecture for the Swiss newspaper *Neue Zürcher Zeitung* (Zurich). After some time as a lecturer at the University of Münster and pursuing a freelance career in Germany and the UK, she is now based in Thuringia. Her other publications on art in the landscape include "New Projects for the City of Münster: Ilya Kabakov, Herman de Vries and Dan Graham" in Birksted, J, ed., *Landscapes of Memory and Experience,* (Spon Press, 2001).

Michelle Sipe is a PhD candidate at the University of Florida English Department specialising in Victorian Studies and Feminist Theory. She is currently completing her dissertation, *The Arts of Domesticity, Landscape Aesthetics, and the Cultivation of the Self in Nineteenth Century British Women's Literature.*

Kate Soper is Professor of Philosophy in the Humanities, Arts and Languages department at London Metropolitan University. Her more recent publications include: *What is Nature? Culture, Politics and the Non-Human* (Blackwell, 1995) and (with Martin Ryle) *To Relish the Sublime* (Verso, 2002).

Noa Steimatsky is an Assistant Professor teaching film studies at the Department of the History of Art at Yale University. She has published articles on the cinematic uses of landscape, the intersection of realism and modernism, and Italian cinema, and is completing a book on these topics. She is also engaged in work on rhetorical figuration and allegory in film, and on the human face in the cinema, for which she was a recepient of a Getty fellowship.

Deborah Sutton completed her PhD at Jawaharalal Nerhu University, New Delhi and now teaches history at the University of Lancaster. She is currently preparing the manuscript of her book, *Other Landscapes: Hill communities, Settlers and State on the Colonial Nilgiris,* c. *1820-1900.*

Renata Tyszczuk studied architecture at the University of Cambridge, from where she holds a doctorate in the History and Philosophy of Architecture. She has taught design at the Architectural Association and at the School of Architecture, University of Cambridge, where she is currently First Year Studio Master.